M000310311

Negotiating Commercial Leases

How Owners and Corporate Occupants Can Avoid Costly Errors

Chair

John B. Wood

To order this book, call (800) 260-4PLI or fax us at (800) 321-0093. Ask our Customer Service Department for PLI order number N4-4608, Dept. BAV5.

Practising Law Institute
810 Seventh Avenue
New York, New York 10019

Foreword

This course handbook is one of about 150 published each year by the Practising Law Institute.

Its primary function is to serve as an educational supplement to each program. It may also be used as a reference manual by attorneys and related professionals unable to attend the sessions.

The method of reproduction utilized has been chosen to insure that registrants receive these materials as quickly as possible and in the most usable form practicable.

The Practising Law Institute wishes to acknowledge its debt and extend its sincere appreciation to the authors who have rendered this valuable service. They exemplify the finest tradition of our profession by sharing their expertise with their colleagues.

Prepared for distribution at the
NEGOTIATING COMMERCIAL LEASES:
HOW OWNERS AND CORPORATE OCCUPANTS
CAN AVOID COSTLY ERRORS
Program
New York City, November 3, 1997
San Francisco, November 19, 1997
Chicago, November 20, 1997

CONTENTS:

1

EXCERPTS FROM *NAVIGATING THE DANGEROUS SHOALS OF A COMMERCIAL LEASE*

John B. Wood

CHAPTER 1

WHAT IS A LEASE

It is well to know thine enemy prior to dealing with it. Some people refer to a lease as a contract and others refer to it as a grant, conveyance or a demising. I have even heard of it simply called a document! In truth, a lease is a living hybrid or combination of a contract and a demising of an interest in real estate for a term. This is important to remember throughout a lease review and negotiation since the obligations, actions and remedies for the default in performance of obligations may be treated differently if dealt with in the legal context of a contract or when considered in the realm of the law dealing with landlord and tenant relationships and real estate demisings. Truly, a lease is a written contract which grants an interest for a period of time in a portion of the overall interest known as real estate. Real estate is commonly considered the ownership, in its simplest form, of the land and improvements thereon together with any rights above or below the land itself to build in or to enjoy light, air and rights of passage. A lease grants an interest in or a right to occupy the specified portion of the total real estate interest by an occupant for a period of time and is subject to premature termination in the event that obligations required in order to enjoy the interest are not performed.

The contract portion of the lease duration starts on a date which, in many jurisdictions, is a specific date of contract commencement but in some jurisdictions is referred to "as of" a certain date, which has the added effect of causing the obligations in the contract (liabilities, in many instances) to relate back to a prior period in time before the date it is actually executed. In people language, this is the date on which the contract is actually signed and delivered by both parties. This relating back phenomenon can impact throughout the lease causing obligations of repair for conditions which occurred after the "as of" date but preceding the taking of possession to be the obligation of the tenant or causing certain expenses, rentals, escalations or other payments to retroactively occur when not anticipated by one of the parties (usually always the tenant). It is most important to focus on this contract commencement when you are negotiating a lease because your job may depend on it.

When negotiating and reviewing leases, you will regularly encounter two practices of lease designers. One is a pyramiding, if you will, of defined terms and the other is an intentionally designed interaction of these defined terms throughout the lease (rarely where anticipated) which, because of the definition or operation of a particular concept, causes financial risk or liability along with much political suffering and pain. If the writer has been subtle and crafty, the definitions, when layered one upon the other, will seem and sound quite reasonable and even friendly at times (since they are usually labeled with friendly titles) but will actually mean something considerably different from what was anticipated or expected from the use of the nice words in the definition. Unless the impact of this systematic pyramiding and designed interaction is traced throughout the layering and redefining or adjusting of the definition, the result may be (and usually is) totally unfavorable to the reader-negotiator. It can be like a treasure hunt, with modification of terms showing up in unanticipated portions of the lease, such as exhibits, a work letter or the rules and regulations but having the same force and effect as if appearing in the paragraph originally dealing with the concept. This will leave the lazy or the unfocused reader wandering down what appears to be a very wonderful, friendly path to the reader's and client's ultimate destruction. A fair proof of this recurring result is simply to notice the different answers proffered by different people when asked a simple question, such as that often asked by the executive vice president of the facilities manager, "When does the lease begin?" Difficult answer since the question is not very precise. The contract began on the date specified either at the beginning of the lease or at the end. This may be the date signed, it may be the date delivered or in all likelihood it may be some date in the past that suits the landlord's purposes. That of course, in most instances, will not mean the date that the tenant is allowed to cause work to begin in the premises or the date that tenant or its contractors have the right to take possession or enter into the premises. In most instances, it also is not the date that the obligations to make repairs, provide insurance or other obligations under the lease for the premises began and it certainly will not be the same date that the obligation for payment of rent or other charges will begin. As a matter of fact, if written right, you can make sure that none of the previously mentioned dates for commencement of anything will be the same as the dates for commencement of anything else. If the lease was carefully designed, by the time you are finished listening to answers, no one will have properly answered that question except for the counsel to landlord or a judge, if it becomes an issue. Of course it will become an issue! One might say that it is fairly critical to know <u>when</u> you are getting the space or are obligated to do the things necessary in order to obtain <u>what</u> it is you think you are going to be occupying for however long you might suspect you may be allowed to occupy it for <u>whatever</u> it is you may naively believe it is that you intend to do in <u>whatever</u> it is you may ultimately get. This is what is called layered tenant assumptions at its best! My experience in negotiating thousands of leases has led me to believe that at any point in time a Tenant believes and operates fully believing that they are going to end up with something and pay for it. This is really quite different from what the landlord, who will be giving it, believes he will be giving and what the tenant will be paying him for it. This may also, in most instances, be a different understanding than the broker for the tenant and the broker for the landlord, each having separate ideas, believe is happening in the transaction. It is not uncommon for the lawyers representing the landlord or the tenant also to have a different understanding from all of the other people.

CHAPTER 2

WHO IS THE LANDLORD AND WHO IS THE TENANT

As if it were not enough not to know what you are getting, when you are getting it, and how much and when you are going to pay for it, it is interesting to note that when the parties sign the lease one or more of the transaction participants may not know who is giving it and who might or might not be allowed to utilize it. Having said this, it is important to point out that near the beginning of the lease where there is a date there is usually a recitation of who the landlord and tenant are. But I have seen recitations of who the person who is purported to be the landlord is, but who actually has little or no right to be the lessor or bind the property or the land, and naming a tenant who is actually not going to be the occupant, but which may be a division or an affiliate or a parent of the actual occupant, even though the document defines this entity as actually being the one who must occupy the premises, which of course causes problems right away. In the worst case I have ever seen, the person who was acting as, and believing it was, the agent for the landlord signed the document without authority. It was reflected as agent but defined as the landlord. It actually was an agent of a person who did not even own an interest in the property and was not able to bind or convey the interest it purported to own. But that was alright for the tenant was not the one who was actually going to use the premises although the lease required that the person whose name was reflected as tenant must be the only person to occupy the premises. It wasn't even the entity that was going to write the checks each month to pay the rent. We had a very difficult time after monies were paid sorting out who could sue whom and for what. Granted, these as many practitioners say, were all mere technicalities; but what is leasing without precision. Needless to say, the facilities manager did not last the week.

CHAPTER 3

WHAT IS THE LEASED PREMISES

While it may seem strange that there are actually transactions where the landlord may not even own the building and may have apparently been committed to by an agent who does not even have authority, the tenant is not the one to occupy the premises and that the parties don't know when the lease contract, demising term, obligations, possession or rent commencement occur. It is also curious to know there have also been several examples in life where the demised premises was defined in such a way as to enable no party, including a judge, to agree as to the location, size, measurement and condition of delivery of the space or services to or equipment provided in the space and in some instances even the particular floor of the building where the space was. In one instance we weren't even sure of the building! In that particular instance I was surprised anybody had the courage to bring the signed document to a lawyer. I seem to be in a minority, but I think it is appropriate for job security to focus carefully on each of these aforementioned issues.

CHAPTER 4

TERM OF THE LEASE

It only seems reasonable and practical to have the lease signed prior to the right to occupy the premises. This frequently happens when tenants are required to commit for future space when another tenant is still in occupancy, when landlord has clean up work to do in the premises before giving it to a tenant or when the premises is under construction. The interval between the contract signing and the time of an actual right to possess or occupy the leased premises whether by the tenant or by its contractors or agents is called, not surprisingly or very originally, the contract interval. During this time, the lease is a contract only (and not a demise) in most jurisdictions. After the tenant acquires the right to possess the leased premises (whether exercised or not), the lease becomes a conveyance or a demising. This hybrid document is the lease that most normal people speak of during cocktail conversations. There are different risks and benefits during these differing time periods. One risk is that if due to no fault of the tenant, the contract period goes too much longer than contemplated by the lease so as to frustrate the ability of the tenant to do its work and occupy, with any certainty, the premises in the future, the contract may be treated in most jurisdictions as a contract which may be terminated and with damages given to the tenant. After the tenant acquires the right to take possession of the premises and whether or not the tenant actually does so, the agreement takes on the character of a demising requiring certain procedures to be followed prior to termination which layer over benefits and obligations on a tenant under the Law affectionally known as that of landlord and tenant. In many jurisdictions interpretation and dispute resolution of landlord and tenant laws are regulated by separate divisions of courts which deal only with landlord and tenant matters and summary proceedings.

It is also not unusual for the possession period which commences the demising term, or what is more frequently loosely referred to as the lease term, to occur prior to occupancy which triggers the obligation to pay the fixed rent and in some instances additional rental, escalations and other direct charges for electricity and other uses of building systems. Commonly, the commencement of those obligations is referred to as the rental term commencement. However, it should be noted that there are provisions in leases which cause the rental term commencement to be deemed to have occurred even though there is an abatement of rent and, in certain disputes, that benefit to a tenant of nonpayment of rent can come back to haunt it. As a minimum, I think it would be a good idea for the facilities manager or the project coordinator to be aware of when the contractual obligations, which may have nothing to do with payment of money, begin and to be careful to determine when other penalties and obligations begin to accrue prior to the demising of the premises. It is helpful to differentiate between possession of the premises, right to have possession, actual occupancy and occupancy for conducting normal business operations. Depending on the definitions contained in the lease, any of these could trigger the conversion of this lease from a contract to a demising or from term commencement to rent commencement. This will be discussed further later. There are things that will be covered later on this note such as the obligation to move forward with plans and specifications for the buildout of the premises and provide landlord with other information. Any of these related areas may cause delays in the ability of landlord or tenant to complete the premises and may have very heavy tenant penalties associated therewith camouflaged in the document in an area of the lease which I will refer to as the work agreement. This will be taken up later and dealt with in considerable detail.

The last little tidbit which may become helpful in landlord-tenant guerrilla warfare would be the little known fact that in many jurisdictions a lease once signed by both parties does not need to be delivered. Lawyers use the term execution loosely, but in its proper construction execution means signing and delivering. Deeds and other conveyances (arguably a lease where the contract and demising commence simultaneously) need to be delivered in order to be effective. However, a lease which for a period of time will be in a contract interval, in some jurisdictions, including the writer's, delivery is unnecessary since it is a contract and not a conveyance at that particular time. There have been instances where landlords or tenants have been the last to sign leases and torn them up only to find out through proper and careful pursuit of facts in the courts that they had a binding obligation at the moment of signing. In several instances I remember, these were grave discoveries.

CHAPTER 5

POSSESSION OR CONTROL

The practitioner of facilities management should also be concerned with actions under the lease which may be deemed to cause the demising term to commence prematurely, such as sending an architect into the premises to inspect and to do drawings which, in some jurisdictions, is sufficient for accepting control or possession of the premises and therefore triggering an occupancy or a demising. This particular concept becomes relevant in leases which cause the rent or term commencement to begin when tenant occupies or takes possession or maybe even just has the right to take possession such as being given the keys or sending some architect in to measure. These are not synonyms in most jurisdictions. Occupancy means going into the premises. Occupancy for the purposes of conducting tenant's business means going into the premises and beginning even low-scale or startup business operations. Possession on the other hand can be as simple as accepting the keys without entering or taking control of the premises, sending an agent, contractor or employer into the premises for purposes other then conducting business or actually sending contractors in to begin work. Any of these actions may take the lease out of the contract interval and may trigger liability under the lease and may accelerate obligations for payment of rent and for other direct payments and services.

CHAPTER 6

<u>PREMISES</u>

It is not uncommon to find the leased or demised premises referred to as the leased space, the space, the demised premises, the lease premises, the leased premises, the premises and even in some instances believe it or not the location or area. Just in case you ever wish to find your leased premises, there are certain attributes of a premises that are important to note such as the point on a vertical plane, the floor number, where the premises may be located on a horizontal plane and how much of the plane is occupied by the demised premises. The variations in the resulting obligation to pay rent, repair, tend to or be responsible for such area are significant depending on how a leased premises is described in a lease. Simply stated, people use the measurement definitions in very unusual ways as well as referring to the premises without measurement by sketch or cross-hatching or lining in the area on a floor plan or otherwise etc. etc. etc. There are innumerable problems that come with these non-standardized reflections, including liability that is unthought of and certainly unwelcomed such as being required to pay for, maintain, repair and/or insure areas and equipment therein which one usually would not like to think of as the premises. This may occur when areas are inadvertently (or intentionally) included as leased premises on an exhibit in the lease reflecting a floor plan with the demised area plus other areas marked by cross-hatching. We would do well at this point and for the purposes of the discussion throughout any particular lease to define our terms carefully and fully and remember to check graphic depictions of definitions for corrections or propriety.

CHAPTER 7

AREA

Square footage area is a very illusive term. In every jurisdiction including some small areas within cities, the definition may take on an entirely different aura due to custom of usage than expected by a tenant. Some people actually believe, I am told, that leased area is what they feel that they can walk on and utilize. Either to the landlord's credit or embarrassment, this has never been the case in any jurisdiction in the free world. I like to refer to square footage measurement as rentable (bearing no resemblance to anything in life except your rent payment), carpetable (which obviously is what you can walk on), usable (which is maybe a bit more then you can walk on) and allocable (which is usable plus everything else rationally conceivable). Usable and allocable, when aggregated, may actually equal the rentable area reflected in the lease. It helps for a facilities person to at least understand the concept of area in its simplest and most benign form. I believe this is when zoning regulators got together and envisioned certain horizontal planes stacked vertically to account for space to be occupied for the conducting of business by tenants, for space to be used in common by all for the enjoyment of a building and space to be used only by building facilities and services in order to make the enjoyment of the building possible by way of heating, cooling, telecommunication, etc. This simple concept is commonly referred to as floor area. Of course, this is too simple for any landlord to use because it is an observable, definable, finite and therefore not a very creative or ambiguous measurement upon which to creatively base the rental terms of the lease. In their vision, the regulators would like to see certain density (both building and people traffic) and certain types of utilization mix in urban areas and they do not wish to see conversion of certain areas into rentable, occupiable premises for conducting business. This tends to sidestep their urban planning and overload service and transportation systems. For instance, if a mechanical room is no longer necessary to cool a building because of the miniaturization of the cooling equipment due to advancements in technology, some landlords might convert that to occupiable and rentable area. It does not seem to matter that it was otherwise in some jurisdictions already allocated to be included in rentable area of other tenants. But now, it can be occupied and actually rented as well and maybe counted twice or more. This is called "double dipping" in real estate circles and is considered child's play. I can actually quadra-dip! This of course flies in the face of all the important requirements for zoning, urban occupancy, density and other such niceties. Buildings over the first ten years of their life take on a considerable amount of hidden zoning recharacterization and, therefore, the simple definition is no longer very helpful in leasing. But in the practice it will serve as a bench-mark and as a basis for an understanding of the concept. Assume that a landlord has a floor area of 20,000 square feet. Further assume that 2,000 square feet of that floor area is for building systems and that 1,000 square feet are occupied by columns, riser cabinets and the like. One would believe that you have 17,000 square feet of rentable area. It only seems fair that carpetable areas in the building, if the landlord would like to reflect a lower square footage minimum rent for marketing purposes, should be increased by service and mechanical areas that serve only the demised premises or the demised premises and other premises on an allocable basis. These service areas such as mechanical rooms serving multiple floors, can be allocated on an appropriate square footage basis to the demised premises and would be added to the floor area. One might go further and add lobbies and other common areas by way of allocation to the floor area. In a simpler sense, this would give you the rentable area. Now we have the beginning of the data to discover true area. As we have seen, landlords and zoners do not measure floors necessarily the same way. That is not to say that landlords among themselves measure it the same way either. Contemplate, if you will, a million square foot building where the floors are measured from the center of a convex window at the interior side to the exterior of the interior core area walls. This will give you considerably different measurements for the building than if you measure from the interior of the core interior wall to the exterior of a concave window at center point. Additionally, this would be a different number than measuring the same interior dimensions of the interior wall to the innermost portion of the sill of the window. Add to that the issue of where to measure the interior demising walls demising multi-floor tenancies. Some measure to the interior point, some to the center, some to the illusive "appropriate point". This can be continued for columns, cantilevered space, etc. I have seen the floor area measurements for rentable purposes of a "to-be-built" building grow on a planned building with 927,000 of approved square feet to 1,056,000 of rentable square feet without a great deal of creativity. Later in the life of a building, one can, of course, look to the conversion of no longer necessary storage space, mechanical rooms and abandoned air shafts, slop sinks and telephone switching rooms to make the building grow even further. One might begin to see that the fixed minimum rent may be more a function of profit and debt service underwriting than a true reflection of the cost to occupy traditionally uniform square footage area. Fixing this measurement of the lease, of course, becomes desirable for a tenant. Not only do you have to concern yourselves with it for your floor, you have to concern yourselves with the method and manner for all other floors in the likely event that you will be called upon sometime in life to pay your share of the building expenses or increases therein. It is also good to note that in a large building not everybody has the same basis for measurement or the same numerators and denominators for court allocation in determining the square footage area of the building. That can also partly depend on whether the building area is determined to be occupiable, leased or leasable, floor area for zoning purposes or just some creative other definition. There was actually a case that I was involved with concerning a problem at a midtown law firm which leased a certain number of rentable square feet without checking to see loss factors, as we call it, which is the difference between the usable and the actual rentable numbers. After occupying the premises, the tenant decided that it would sublet a certain portion of excess capacity and decided to sublease 50% of its space. When negotiating the sublease, the square footage of the rentable area prominently appeared in the sublease but the percentage did not. On the later measurement and preparation of the premises for demising to the subtenant it became readily apparent that due to the new measurement of the square footage in the sublease, the tenant would end up with two-thirds of the premises under the master lease instead of 50%. This of course was devastating to the law firm, who called the landlord to ask if there had been some mistake. There had, but it was not the landlord's. It is also remarkable to note that once you may have determined the appropriate measurement of the premises, it becomes increasingly difficult to know what is contained within the premises in the way of fixtures, equipment, wiring, cooling, windows, blinds, ceilings, and floors since the definition does not usually cover three dimensional space. This becomes important for instance if your demised premises is defined by a drawing of crosshatching of an entire floor when read together with other sections of the lease because the tenant may find itself responsible for repairing and replacing all those things within the demised premises drawn by crosshatching including the piping for the floor above because it is in the ceiling on the floor below or within the floor below, part of the elevator systems that pass through the floor, and HVAC equipment. These are traditionally thought of as landlord's responsibility among other things, with the exception, in all jurisdictions, of structural components. Not a nice omission when a tenant is trying to identify and minimize risk and liability.

Another fun area is what does a building sit on? Assuming you have the vertical and horizontal planes defined properly, the other component of real estate which will come back through escalations and other obligations becomes the land. Many leases define it just that way: "the plot of land upon which the building is erected." Depending on how land is measured for zoning, title or facilities operation purposes, it can be 100 acres or it can be only so much of the land as is necessary to support the building, which would be about the same as the floor plate for the ground floor. I have seen obligations and escalations and other charges cover very wide ranges, including land owned by the landlord and by others. The definition frequently is to call the plot of land on which the building or improvements are erected as "hereinafter the land". This is fertile ground (interesting comment) for a great deal of fun and hidden liability which we will cover later, and can include innumerable improvements not being utilized by or benefiting tenant or necessary for its use of the demised premises.

CHAPTER 8

USE

No other section causes more trouble than the use of the leased premises. Uses can be permissive, excluded, exclusive, mandatory, specific or general. Just to name a few more adjectives, they can also be difficult, expensive or impossible depending on how the lease is drafted. Examples of those are of course: "shall be used only for blowing of glass on Thursdays between the hours of 2 and 7" and "drying and painting of glass on Fridays between the hours of 3 and 6" and "by the tenant hereinandabove named only and for no other purpose whatsoever". This really means no other use or no use during any other time or by any other occupant. For a variety of constructions ambiguities we are also not certain of which hours, a.m. or p.m., and whether the stated hours are inclusive or exclusive. There are more restrictive uses than that but it might be hard to imagine. More permissive would be the leased premises may be used for any lawful purpose. It does not say when, how or by actually whom. This of course is the best; however, in the event that there is a particular use that you need and you need to know that the building, zoning and other service needs will be met, including certificates of occupancy, sufficient electricity etc., you must specifically state that as a required use of the tenant. This will serve to obviate the requirement to continue to pay rent if for zoning reasons or certificate of occupancy reasons or even insufficiency of building services or failure of other requirements of the landlord or building, the tenant is unable to utilize the demised premises for the specifically stated purpose. Tenant user groups usually do not like paying rent for premises that they may not occupy for the purposes they explicitly required of their facilities managers. This, of course, has happened before. The logic of this section flows over into who the tenant actually is, how there can be other tenants by assigning, subletting, operating agreements and otherwise. These will all be covered later but the problem rises or falls based on the specific and permissive characterization in the definition of the use.

Uses can be continuous or interruptible, space can be required to be occupied or it can be empty, all or designated areas of spaces can or may be required to be used for specific uses or not; however, all of this must be addressed carefully early on in leases or the pyramiding and reuse of the definitions will later cause all sorts of bad things to befall the tenant. These difficulties have made great cocktail conversation for previously employed facilities directors since damage to tenants usually translates into total destruction of facility directors.

If you are beginning to see a pattern at this point, you may be getting the feeling that all you really need to know in order to become an avid leasing enthusiast you learned by the fourth grade, to wit: who, what, where, when, how, why and how much. I believe if all these questions are carefully answered early on, a lot of the interesting dilemmas which I have observed would have disappeared.

Another area of concern is a use clause in a lease that requires mandatory occupancy of the premises. This kind of requirement is quite appropriate when you are depending on customer traffic, as in a shopping center or in a mixed use project, in order to make all of the occupancies viable or in order to maximize percentage rental income to the landlord. In a commercial office, warehouse, industrial park, or other similar lease situation, however, these are hardly necessary. Similarly, the requirement of the use of the entire premises and a prohibition against vacating the premises should be looked on with disfavor. A landlord has a genuine interest in seeing that the tenant does not <u>abandon</u> the premises. However, the difference between vacating and abandoning is a legal distinction that seems to run uniformly throughout the jurisdictions. Abandonment means vacating the premises with no intention to return to, control, protect, perform in or pay for. Vacating merely means not occupying the premises but otherwise performing under the terms of the lease, such as obligations to insure, to repair, to maintain, and to pay rent.

Additionally, the use may be circumscribed with limitations which prohibit interference with the building's operating systems, such as those for heating and cooling. The character of the use and the manner of use also may be circumscribed to limit interference by way of smell, noise, vibration or debris and supplies maintained in walkway areas throughout the building. These kind of harmony clauses are inserted to enable tenants to get along with one another and to allow landlord to service and operate the building systems in an efficient and cost-effective manner. These kinds of harmonious occupancy clauses, which in their purest sense are benign and important, must be carefully reviewed in order to avoid any impairment of the ability of the tenant to occupy the premises for an intended use which by its very nature may be non-harmonious. The theory is that a tenant with a use that may be different or less harmonious is probably paying a higher rent or has satisfied some other need to get the use it anticipated and should not have other provisions in the lease which impair its ability to benefit from its bargain.

Care and attention must also be given in the use clause to any requirement to obtain licenses and permits for operation within the demised premises. If the clause contemplates specific permits or licenses that deal with a specific use by tenant, such as telecommunications, running a school, running a beauty salon or such other specialized activity like a nuclear reactor, these kinds of permits or licenses should be obtained and maintained by the tenant. In some instances, if such licenses are not maintained the landlord may find itself liable. For example, day care centers or schools operating in office buildings, which have not properly registered nor complied with licensing requirements, may cause a landlord to be liable in the event of a fire, hazard or a death in the demised premises. Landlords, of course, have a valid interest in seeing that tenants do comply. These types of special use requirements should not be confused with general permits or licenses to occupy any demised premises. Many clauses, however, go a little beyond the appropriate boundary and obligate a tenant to obtain and maintain all permits and licenses required in order to "occupy" the demised premises. It seems to me that occupancy permits, certificates of occupancy (permanent or temporary), or any other types of permits which are required for the stated use of the demised premises, including initial alteration permits which were negotiated for in the lease, should be the burden of the landlord. Landlord will have to be specifically required in the lease to obtain them and maintain them as well as take no action which would impair the ability of the tenant to occupy the premises pursuant to them. The absence of a statement to this end can cause endless problems with the tenant in the beginning of the lease and throughout the lease occupancy period, especially if there is a change in law or change in requirements affecting the building or premises and the landlord does not undertake to comply with such changes. Landlord's failure to comply may actually either legally or practically shift the burden to the tenant.

We have also seen situations where a particular use under the zoning resolution for the area appeared not to prohibit the specific use that the tenant intended to employ in the premises, but upon filing of plans and a request for building permits, it was discovered that the building department would not approve the intended alteration for the intended use. This result, although not unusual, was highly disruptive. The matter went to litigation whereupon a lower court ruled that the tenant must continue paying rent. Upon appeal from the lower court ruling the appeals court stated that if the lease and the underlying obligation to pay rent were conditioned upon a specific use of the premises it should have been specified in the lease, along with a representation and warranty of the landlord that the intended use was permitted, and an undertaking by the landlord to deliver the premises in a manner permitting the tenant's special improvements and to obtain a certificate of occupancy allowing for the use. Since no such obligations were contained in its lease, the tenant continued to pay its rent until it went into bankruptcy and ultimately never was able to occupy the premises. How would you like to have a case like that to enhance your career path (or spiral)?

CHAPTER 9

DEMISED PREMISES APPURTENANCES

Appurtenances is just a nice word for what is in the demised premises and who owns it, cares for it and feeds it. As we discussed earlier, sometimes the appurtenances are defined very craftily by reference to a crosshatched schedule buried deep in the heart of the lease or on the very, very last page. Sometimes the very, very last page is omitted from tenant's draft! Sometimes this is an accident! If defined carefully, this can include a lot of landlord's or ownership type properties and equipment, the maintaining, care and feeding of which is expensive and can be by that method thrust upon an unsuspecting tenant. I know of one instance where a crosshatched floor plan picked up a generator that serviced the demised premises plus five other floors. Because of the luck of the draw and the proper level of craftiness on the part of the landlord, that generator was included in the demised premises for care and feeding, and had to be cared for and fed frequently by the tenant. The other tenants got a free ride. Not nice, but an electrifying experience for the facilities manager.

Clauses dealing with appurtenances usually define the improvements and alterations as well as the building systems found within the demised premises and prescribe who owns them, who can depreciate them and who must maintain, repair, restore and refurbish them. Common appurtenances are built-in furniture and fixtures, heating and air conditioning equipment, communication equipment, tile floors, partitioning, panelling and wall treatments. Fixtures have to be watched carefully since those are the things that are installed into real estate and become part of the real property by their attachment. Although commonly occurring in retail and restaurant leases, we have found situations where the trade fixtures of computer, broadcasting and telecommunication companies once installed, even though easily removable, became the property of the landlord. Not only did the landlord get the benefit of depreciation, but at the end of the term of a short term lease the landlord was able to relet the premises to a tenant using just such very expensive equipment. This is a killer not only for the client but also of facilities managers. On the other hand, there once was a case I had where we were careful in the lease to define everything located in the premises at the commencement of occupancy and installed thereafter, no matter who paid for it, as tenant's property able to be removed at the end of the term. Well, wouldn't you know, the landlord put in over $100.00 a square foot of work and the tenant left with the heat, ventilating and air conditioning systems, the security and alarm systems and the fire systems among other things. The same landlord provided water fountains, toilets and sinks which unfortunately were crosshatched as part of the tenant's space even though they were located on a multi-tenanted floor. These were similarly removed by the tenant. It is hard to believe that the facilities manager in that instance didn't become Senior Vice President, but of course, one is never rewarded for what one does right.

The definition of appurtenances and how they are dealt with at the end of the term not only impacts on the financial aspects and reporting of the transaction but also will impact on condemnation and insurance proceeds. So dealing with them appropriately up front will save you time and heartburn later. Of course, I know you may say that just the other day you worked through the trauma of occupying a brand new one hundred story building with its tenant improvements just completed and half of it was condemned! Unlikely to absurd. But once in a while it does make a big difference. It is especially difficult to explain when your client is the one who makes his entire livelihood from these trade fixtures and other appurtenances all of which are required to be left behind at the end of the term or were not paid for after condemnation or replaced by insurance after casualty.

CHAPTER 10

REPAIRS AND VARIOUS OTHER COVENANTS

In many leases, landlords and tenants covenant with respect to repair and maintenance of the building itself, the public portions of the interior and exterior of the building and the demised premises. Some leases contain only covenants of the tenant and the landlord's covenant rests in the law of the jurisdiction or in the common law of implied covenants of repair and maintenance, habitability and quiet enjoyment. One may be rudely surprised at the deficiencies in the common law level of repair if the lease is silent. It therefore seems a good practice to have the landlord covenant as to tenant's expected level of repair. There are, of course, many different levels of repair and varying liabilities and indemnities which run with the particular level of repair. Tenants generally are put in a position of repairing the non-structural portions of the demised premises as well as any other portions of the building, structural or otherwise, which are injured by tenant or its agents, visitors, invitees, etc. Usually landlords will undertake an obligation to perform the level of maintenance and repair consistent with the quality, class or level of the building. For instance, in New York, a lease of space in a first-class building should contain landlord's representation and warranty to provide first-class repair and maintenance. First-class speaks to quality as well as timing.

One must be very careful and clear about who has what obligation for what area of the building with respect to repairs. Landlord may obligate itself to repair public portions of the building and the structural components of the building, but may crosshatch or define the demised premises to include the exterior windows and wall of a curtain wall exterior building. I know of at least two instances where the curtain wall buckled and windows were damaged and the landlord required the tenant to pay for the repair. The tenant, of course, opined that the windows and curtain wall were structural. The courts involved in both cases determined that a curtain wall type of exterior is non-structural and because of the crosshatching it was the obligation of the tenant. A similarly obnoxious result occurred when landlord obligated itself to take care of public area structural portions of the building. However, tenant was to repair everything within the demised premises, structural or otherwise. In this instance, not only did the tenant replace the floor by floor air conditioning system, it also had to replace a portion of the floor that buckled.

In some leases, landlords attempt to shift repair obligations to tenants, including structural obligations, latent defects, remediation of hazardous materials like asbestos and other ownership-type repairs and require tenants to hold the landlord harmless from failure to make those repairs or advise the landlord when such repairs are necessary. Additionally, landlords at times limit their liability or totally exculpate themselves from liability for breakage, and damage or injury resulting from breakage, of steam pipes, water pipes, waste pipes, electrical wiring, etc. These types of clauses and liabilities and responsibilities better suit a net lease such as a ground lease where the tenant controls services and maintains the entire project with minimal or no participation or oversight of the landlord. Where the landlord is running a tower office building, these types of exculpations and indemnities as well as obligations imposed on tenant to make repairs and perform maintenance seem inappropriate to me. These obligations can become exceptionally burdensome and expensive if the tenant is not careful when it receives the premises to make sure that the premises are in a good state of repair allowing the tenant to concern itself only with future routine maintenance. Existing conditions, which upon discovery, would be determined to be violations, hazardous and injurious situations or fire law and insurance underwriting deficiencies, can cause a tenant considerable grief and expense after the lease has been signed. Additionally, changes going forward such as changes in regulations, building ordinances and zoning and fire law requirements can be extremely expensive for a tenant who is required to pay for the cost of putting the premises in compliance. One must watch out for the surprising costs that arise from a cost definition that's expanded in the lease to encompass not only repairs and maintenance, but replacements and improvements.

Running on the same turf with the obligation of landlord to make its repairs is the tenant's right to enforce such obligation if the landlord defaults. Failing all else, the tenant should be allowed to make the repairs that are essential for the enjoyment of the premises and to collect the costs of the repairs from landlord or credit the costs against rent with an interest carry for the unamortized balance until depletion of the credit. You can bet the landlord has that right of self-help and collection in most leases these days by making defaults and cure costs convert to additional rent with interest and enforcement costs. Other areas of concern are how, when, and where repairs are made and how materials and work are staged in order to accomplish the project and minimize the impact to tenant's operations. Timing in many jurisdictions can cause great expense. For instance, repairs required to be made after hours can generate incredible overtime costs and additional charges for security and services in a building. Staging of materials and work can also create havoc and expense if it needs to be accomplished in other premises not controlled by the tenant. A limit of the amount of materials to be maintained in a tenant's premises for a landlord's or other tenant's work should be considered. Any more than a day or two of materials supply may be disruptive. Abatement of rent for the area used by landlord should be considered. Additionally, landlord's right which is reserved to make replacements or improvements which affect the tenant's premises can be awesome in practice. This usually takes the form of erecting additional columns, risers or pipes through the tenant's premises. Replacement of existing columns, risers or pipes is less problematic if put where the old ones were. Just as an example, there was once a building that had an antiques auction floor that was being slabbed over for a new tenancy. The building boasted the benefit of being able to receive ten extra stories of buildable space without depleting its unutilized development rights. The landlord, being the delightful soul he was, decided to lease the existing premises prior to building the extra ten stories which would require support columns, risers, feeders and water columns, all to be projected through the existing premises during construction of the addition. The lease, of course, stated that a minimization of tenant disturbance would be pursued but otherwise also allowed for demised premises space to be taken for new columns, water pipes, risers, etc. all without adjustment of rent for lost area and for disastrous impact on the particular tenant. Also the access to and use of the premises would be affected by staging and by disruption for probably up to two years. Of course the front of the building and lobby would have looked like a disaster area for a very long time, possibly the duration of the lease. During lease negotiation, the landlord refused to remove the rights, but promised faithfully that he would never do such a thing! These are the situations that enrich the soul of any believer. If you are dumb enough to fall for this, then it enriches just the lawyer.

Landlords are infamous for completely exculpating themselves or rather excessively limiting the extent of their liability for negligence for their work or failure to respond to the needs of a tenant or to their obligations under a lease. For instance, buried in many clauses that state that landlords are not responsible for property entrusted to building employees are clauses which limit the landlord's liability or eradicate it entirely for damage to tenant or its property or persons from the negligent effectuating of repairs or replacements in the building or for explosion, falling plaster (of all things!), steam, gas and electricity shorts or leaks, etc., etc. If that wasn't bad enough, the landlord often has the audacity to include those costs and expenses for remediation of such damage to the building in the operating expense escalation clauses. It appears that some landlords have no shame whatsoever. I know of one instance where a landlord sent an unlicensed plumber up to a high floor to work on the plumbing. During his work, the plumber as an afterthought decided to tighten a valve on a high pressure water column without first shutting off the pressure on the lower floor. As could be expected, the valve exploded and flooded several floors before being turned off. The destruction was quite impressive. The landlord of course did not want to pay for the resulting damage. The lease supported his position.

It seems to me only fair in a commercial lease where a tenant is occupying a quality building, that the landlord continue to maintain and repair at that same level throughout the tenancy. Additionally, landlord should maintain insurance for damage, fire and casualty and cover its negligence and damage which may cause business inconvenience or interruption to tenants and to take responsibility for its actions, omissions and their impact on the occupancy of the building. It seems to me that on repairs and negligence, the landlord and tenant can fully insure and look first to their insurance with minimal disruption and impact on the businesses of either. It should be remembered that insurance such as that in most buildings can be obtained and the negligence of landlord and tenant may be properly covered. Insurers will also waive their rights to claim recoupment of losses paid from the negligent party. This is commonly referred to as waiving the insurer's rights of subrogation.

Besides reserving the right to change the public portions or other portions of the building whether voluntarily or as required to effectuate repairs, many landlords in form leases also reserve the right to repair, alter and replace the risers, feeders and columns in the building. They reserve this right while specifically limiting or prohibiting tenant's right to any adjustment of rent for inconvenience, interference with use or expansion of the public portions of the building into the usable area of the demised premises. These clauses may seem innocuous, but during the life of a building because of technological advances risers and feeders for electricity and telecommunications become outmoded. Landlords find themselves packing their buildings with more and more electrical wiring and fiber optics, as well as discovering that the dense packing of wiring from the basement tapering off to the higher floors is now reversed because of telecommunications satellites and send/receive services. Landlords are beginning to find more wires coming from the roof rather than to the basement than ever before. The riser conduits and columns are not sized in most buildings for this inversion of wiring utilization and, therefore, the columns must be expanded into the space of tenants. Since rents in many areas range from $30 to $60 a square foot, an encroachment like this can be expensive to a tenant who must continue to pay for space it no longer is able to use. Adjustments in rent should be required and made in the same ratio as the square footage of the usable area compares to the square footage of the rentable area, which is set forth in the lease. Additionally, the landlord should be required to minimize any interference in the premises caused by the work, the staging of materials and debris and dust. Also the work should be conducted after hours or on weekends even though this may cost the landlord more. To minimize the intrusion of new cabling, the landlord should be required to include the cables, risers and feeders in existing column shafts or adjacent thereto. Only in unusual and necessary circumstances should landlord be allowed to run new shafts or columns through the premises.

Much consideration should be given to the tenant's special use in a building that may be undergoing structural alteration or restoration. For instance, an extremely well-regarded, old line private banking establishment found itself with planks, scaffolding, plywood window protection and other unsightly and noisy accoutrements as new improvements were added to the exterior of its premises. This sort of reconstruction impaired the bank's business considerably, but was allowed in the lease. In the event something as substantial as that might occur, the lease should address the possibility and find a suitable, mutual solution during construction. This may be abatement of rent and a partial and temporary relocation of those parts of the tenant's business on which the construction has the most detrimental impact. Temporary costs, additional rentals and moving expense in and out should also be addressed.

CHAPTER 11

CONDEMNATION

Not a great deal of space will be taken in this handbook for condemnation (nor in many buildings we hope). Condemnation is unlikely to occur, but even if it were a more common occurrence, the issues and concerns to be addressed are beyond the scope of this work. This section will give real estate directors sufficient information to enable them to understand the risks and issues for negotiation. Principally, condemnation is a taking of property by some form of governmental entity with compensation to those whose interest in real estate has been acquired through a condemnation award equal, in theory, to the value of the real property so taken. There is also an award for costs resulting from the condemnation, such as moving expenses and loss of personal property, furniture and removable fixtures, and goodwill if any. Interests in real estate are three-fold. First, there is the fee or true ownership interest in the land and the improvements. Next, is the leasehold interest for a term of years. That is the interest of a tenant who has the right to use the property during the term of its lease. The last is the reversion or remainder interest, which is the value of the real estate after the leasehold interests have expired and the entire interest in the real estate revests in the fee owner of the land. There are other hybrid and modified interests in real estate, but these will suffice to alert the reader to the areas to be addressed for award benefit during negotiation of the lease. The tenant has several concerns in the event of condemnation. The major concern of the tenant is the cost or expense of obtaining comparable space in another building for at least a comparable number of years and at a rental not in excess of the price being paid by the tenant for the premises being condemned. Any increase in the rental for the remainder of the term should be present valued and reimbursed out of the real estate condemnation award. Additionally, a tenant needs to be reimbursed for the residual value of any personal property, furniture and fixtures which are not able to be moved and the fixture footings and other real property improvements that were built by the tenant or for the benefit of the tenant in order to operate in the premises. Moving costs, consulting and brokerage fees, etc. as well as fix-up costs at a new premises should also be considered. Location and goodwill of the business are also of value and should certainly be addressed. The landlord, of course, must replace his property after condemnation and has an interest in seeing that the award justly and completely compensates him for the property so that comparable property can be acquired without expenditure of additional funds beyond the award by the landlord. It should be noted, also, that a mortgagee is equally concerned that the award not be less than the mortgage on the premises. There may be more than one mortgagee, as, for example, leasehold and fee mortgagees. Their concern would be that the award would be equal to or exceed the sum of the outstanding balances of both mortgages. Hence comes the difficulty in assigning or allocating the award to the tenant's interest in the real property vs. the landlord's interest. This difficulty arises out of the fact that mortgagees tend to lend money based on raw land plus improvements as enhanced by tenancy rental flow, expense reimbursements and tenant improvements funded by the landlord. To a mortgagee a creditworthy tenant paying a high rent adds value to the land. However, in real estate theory and condemnation procedure, a tenant's interest is not an addition necessarily to the value of the land, but certainly is a valuable interest and compensable. The greater the disparity between the benefit to the tenant of a below market lease and the market conditions for comparable space plus its tenant improvement residual value, the larger the portion of the award which should go to the tenant. Hence the rub. Since condemning authorities are not known for their generosity and there is usually a battle royal among landlord, tenant and mortgagees for the meager award, this battle is better fought at the beginning during negotiation of the lease, because if not, it will be lost by the tenant in the end. There are endless varieties of methods for dealing with this, but the simplest theory and easiest to negotiate that I have seen has been an allocation of a portion of the award over the term of the lease to tenants with fixtures. That award will usually decline as the fixtures are depreciated and will increase again if they are replaced during the term of the lease. Tax consideration should be given to the value as well as the useful life of the fixtures in reducing the allocation. This also is a helpful, if not mandatory, process when you have leasehold improvements and fixtures of the tenant which are financed. The financing company is interested in having the loan reduced and you can usually time and match the loan payments, the depreciation and tax benefit and the condemnation award allocation.

Attention also has to be given to any loss of abatements of rent during the period of inability to use and restoration of the premises in the event of a partial taking in condemnation. This is most critical during preoccupancy construction and fitup of the premises.

CHAPTER 12

ALTERATIONS

What happens at the building and the demised premises after the lease commences and while the demised premises is being readied for occupancy is usually of considerable interest to both parties since it is a big cost item and is fertile ground for disputes and additional hidden costs. If the tenant was savvy enough to insist upon landlord's representations that the building and the demised premises both complied with all laws, rules, regulations and authorities and that there were no latent defects or imperfections in construction, including undiscovered violations and defects and hazardous materials or conditions, and that the demised premises would be in a condition ready to receive building construction permits and tenant's contemplated alteration work, then going forward in the lease is easier to deal with than if the demised premises were taken "as is" either willingly and knowledgeably, or unwittingly. Assuming this quantum leap in faith (and you should not), then all that has to be worried about is future compliance with existing laws and with new laws.

I have seen better than eighty percent of the time, when tenants have undertaken to prepare the demised premises with initial alterations for occupancy, unanticipated increases in costs and considerable delays in the work resulting from the usual field conditions of the building or demised premises which should have been the landlord's obligation to cure but were not pointed out and provided for in the lease and were not discovered by the tenant's architect. This area has been responsible for the greatest increases in budget, delays in work and increases in the number of transfers, demotions and replacements of facility and leasing directors. One must be on guard for those alterations which a normal tenancy use should expect which trigger the need for otherwise deferred remediation or compliance in the demised premises or building. Handicapped access and asbestos are frequent repeat offenders. The responsibility for these should be sorted out beforehand in the lease.

In addition to discussing appurtenances, it is not unusual for the landlord to prohibit certain alterations and conditions in the premises as well as mandate what has to be removed at the end of the term. I believe the tenant's major concern is to have the ability to utilize the premises for its permitted use throughout its term, including in the event of business changes and technology changes. The landlord, of course, has a very legitimate interest in seeing that the building's floor loads, electrical consumption, heat, noise and order radiation, vibration and other utilization are within safe parameters and within the comfort range for other reasonable tenants. Additionally, a landlord has concerns with the effect on the ability of building systems to deliver heat, ventilation, air conditioning, water and electricity based on modifications or alterations. From this point though, landlords tend to branch out significantly. Some of the additional requirements that may be found would be requirements of advance approval for plans and drawings; insurance for builder's risk together with bonding or security; approval of all contractors; approval of hoisting and delivery times and locations; and supervision and general conditions of the landlord. There are some valid arguments for landlord's pre-review with respect to contractors in the building. Certain contractors have been known to do inferior work and be invasive with respect to other areas, building systems or tenants in the building. Some even seem to attract fires! There is nothing worse than having a sophisticatedly designed building get mucked up (term of art, very sophisticated) by a contractor who produces shoddy work or causes violations and other problems by improper filings of plans or by not following the filed plans and specifications, building department or fire and insurance underwriter recommendations or ordinances. Some landlords, of course, make this a new art form by limiting contractors to those in which landlord has an interest. Some landlords reserve design and content decision rights and basically totally interfere with the ability of a tenant to do its work. It seems to me that a fair stance is that once a tenant has taken possession of the premises it should be allowed to make any non-structural changes that do not detract from the outside appearance and which do not materially and adversely impact on the ability of landlord to efficiently deliver building services or later lease the premises unless the tenant has agreed to remove the alterations and restore the premises. Certain reasonable controls for alterations in excess of $50,000 would seem to include pre-approval of plans for location, floor loads and layout, and a requirement that any liens be removed and appropriate insurance and bonding be obtained. I do not believe that landlords should receive profit, overhead, supervision or general condition fees from tenants for initial alterations to the demised premises. Maybe not even for any alterations. Landlord's attention to the proper alterations in a building would seem to me to be a normal ownership responsibility. Also, it seems fair to me that a tenant should be allowed to remove, provided it restores to its original condition, any installations put into the demised premises at tenant's cost. There are some alterations which landlord would be reasonable in asking to have removed at its election such as unique fixtures and built-ins which are indigenous only to a specific, highly specialized use, as well as floor-through stairwells (big ticket items) which are expensive to install and in all likelihood will need to be restored for a future tenancy. It does not seem unreasonable for a landlord to prescribe that any installations, alterations or repairs be done in accordance with the class and quality of the building. Also, that the materials be new and not subject to financing, liens or UCC filings (under general circumstances). It also is not unusual for major alterations to receive the review of landlord's architect and engineer, the cost of which is usually borne by the party who is successful in negotiation. These clauses can be very subtle and can also be dangerous if not properly addressed or administered over the term of the lease. Two instances that come to mind were that anything put into the premises such as floors, mill work, computer raised floors, ceilings or glass by tenant after its initial occupancy of the building became the responsibility of the tenant for repair, maintenance and cleaning. Additionally, unless approval was obtained for such installations, they were required to be removed. Another clause required all improvements in excess of $25,000 to be logged and recorded for the term of the lease. These installations were required under all circumstances to be removed at the end of the term. Failure to maintain the list and identify the alterations required the entire installation to be removed at the end of the term. These were big costs in both instances. Also, clauses that say that alterations at tenant's expense will be done at such times and in such manner as landlord from time to time shall designate, can be killers. One example I remember was the installation of a very detailed sound studio and broadcasting room for a radio station. The wiring and the partitioning was, of course, extremely intricate as well as the sound deafening and acoustic padding. The landlord exercised its prerogative to require such work to be done after hours and on weekends. The then foreseeable impact on the job was to multiply the entire cost times about three. Although the tenant and almost everybody else determined that this was unreasonable, the clause was entered into in a jurisdiction where any consents and approvals of the landlord, unless required to be reasonable, could be arbitrary. The results, of course, in most instances can and will be quite chilling. Also, imagine the small innocuous clause that says that after landlord has approved the plans and specifications for any alterations, repairs or improvements that any amendments, additions or changes to such plans and specifications shall not be made without the prior written consent of landlord. Additionally, landlord was not required to be reasonable and had no specific time period in which it had to respond. That was not a serious problem here because the tenant's project administrator forgot entirely to ask the landlord after the initial approval and there were some 263 change orders of not inconsequential magnitude. The really unnerving thing was that the alterations and improvements added significant value to the entire installation and otherwise would not have been objectionable from the landlord's viewpoint. However, as it many times happens when landlords and tenants don't get along, the landlord had the right to inspect the completed work and required the tenant to either remove all unapproved work wherever located and restore the premises in accordance with plans originally approved, or obtain landlord's consent to the changes. In this instance, the demand was made not because the landlord truly found the alteration changes and amendments to be objectionable, but because the landlord wished to have relief in the electricity clause where he was losing money. Of course, there was a negotiated settlement. The tenant got its changes and so did the Landlord! In hindsight the budget for construction after considering the addition of the present value of the increased electricity payments to landlord over ten years of the lease, was destroyed and so too was the facilities director's career.

Any mention of redelivery of the premises by the tenant to the landlord at the end of the term that deals with appurtenances should receive careful scrutiny. The jurisdictions differ considerably in their result when construing a clause requiring the tenant to quit and surrender the premises to the landlord "broom clean and in good order and condition at the end of the term." The clause really should require the tenant to quit and surrender the premises broom clean and in good condition subject to reasonable wear and tear and damage by fire or other casualty and condemnation. Even the term "reasonable wear and tear" takes on totally different connotations in various jurisdictions. The best case that comes to mind is an industrial complex where large roller trucks and fork lifts were used regularly up and down the loading bay paths to raise and lower large bundles of paper and metal. The major damage done to the floor over the years, which caused the foundation to actually crumble, was considered reasonable wear and tear for industrial establishments in one jurisdiction because the court determined that the landlord, in the absence of any language to the contrary, understood the particular use and the normal results on concrete floors. In another jurisdiction, the tenant was required to restore the entire floor and grading area based on similar language. It's amazing that people read leases, take the words literally and imply their own understanding without giving consideration to local laws, terms of art or trade usage. The old adage that people hear what they want is still alive and well. It is not surprising also that these unemployed facilities people received differing unemployment benefits in the different jurisdictions.

Landlords have a valid right to be interested in the floor load of their buildings and the positioning and quantity of heavy machinery, safes, vaults, freight or stored matter or equipment and fixtures brought into the demised premises. Reasonable regulation and pre-review can save all parties great difficulty and tenant surprise floor load support costs, but it should be reasonable and there should be a procedure in an expedited manner for the review. This is especially important where the tenant makes its living off of trade fixtures of considerable weight, and it is highly recommended that the engineer of the tenant provide a schedule of specifications as well as relative locations of all equipment to be moved into the premises or to be utilized therein in the foreseeable future. This should be approved prior to lease signing in equipment intensive uses. Usually, along with the lines of the approval and regulation of the location, placement and inclusion of such equipment in the demised premises comes an innocuous little clause that requires tenant to indemnify, insure and hold harmless landlord against any obligations, liability or claims resulting from the presence of any furniture, fixtures or equipment in the demised premises. As you will see in the insurance section, this little sentence can totally undo the insurance nirvana that most landlords and tenants seek to obtain in the equilibrium of commercial insurability. That is, everybody insure, look to their insurance and waive direct actions against each other and subrogation rights of their insurers in the event of any loss.

Along the same lines of tenant's changes and alterations some landlords always get the idea that the landlord may wish to make alterations and changes. I don't believe there is a single jurisdiction which prevents landlord from making reasonable changes or alterations to the building provided there is no negative impact on the tenant with respect to both ingress and egress of the demised premises and the enjoyment of the demised premises. This doesn't seem to satisfy landlords who put in elaborate clauses allowing themselves the right to make improvements, changes and alterations to the building, the common area, the demised premises, the halls, the entrance ways to the building, the entrance ways to the demised premises, the bathrooms and the stairs and to change the address of the building, and even the elevators and the electrical conduits and pipes, just to mention one or two! This is some feat, but can you imagine the impact on the tenant where landlord decides to do something unusual like this? I have, surprisingly, two just such instances to share. The first is a building on Lexington Avenue that had its front entrance on the avenue and two side freight entrances. The landlord figured out that if he moved the front entrance to the building to one of the freight entrances, he could expand the retail Lexington Avenue space by almost 80 percent and make a fortune. Since the clauses in his leases afforded just such a right, he did so. To the chagrin of the tenants one morning they reported to work to find that their entrance was temporarily a grubby loading entrance. Upon inquiry, they were advised that the other side entrance would become the main entrance within six months and that they would have a new address and would have to change all of their stationery and suffer the indignity of having a side street entrance when they had paid for a Lexington Avenue address and entrance rental. As stated earlier, the other such instance was where a building was leased, but had the right to add ten additional floors on the top. The addition of the floors required relocation of the elevator, main water columns, HVAC equipment, front door and bathrooms on all other levels. If you can believe it, I understand that this was done (although I have not confirmed it), including the running of support columns down through the building to support the ten extra floors, with major interference to the tenants, but no substantial interruption of the rent payments! There were some unhappy campers in that building for about two years. One can also argue that there can be a significant impact on the real estate tax and operating cost escalation provisions if the landlord is allowed to improve and add onto the building, even if such addition may not benefit the tenant. The real kicker in New York is the right of the landlord to voluntarily, temporarily or permanently close the windows in the building without interrupting or diminishing the rental flow. This particular clause was born out of the fact that windows sometimes are temporarily boarded up or protected due to construction nearby or because of repair work. Also adjoining property owners would sometimes build a building next to the windows out of which you thought you had a great view. In the old days if this was done without an allowance for such in the lease, rent would abate. Now, of course, it not only does not abate, but if the clause as generally written is taken literally, the courts will uphold the right of the landlord to build a building next door and cut out the light in its entirety. These clauses, of course, should be limited to involuntary closing up of the windows and only on a temporary basis, where view, light and air are important elements of the rental payment. Also they should be carefully drafted to exclude an involuntary boarding up if the landlord is a part owner of the project next door.

44

CHAPTER 13

COMPLIANCE WITH LAWS

Compliance with laws takes on two dimensions, one in time and the other in type. The easiest issue to work with is compliance with laws for the premises and the building occurring prior to the tenant taking occupancy. In most jurisdictions there is no requirement that the demised premises or the building be in any particular condition except as represented through advertising, inspection or representation. Advertising and inspection can be a problem since in a majority of jurisdictions, representations with respect to real estate must be in writing to be valid in a commercial setting. Hence, as you may imagine, most leases don't discuss the issue of the condition of the building or the premises other than to state that landlord makes no representations and tenant takes it "as-is." This is the source of expenditures of more funds than one would ever imagine over the term of a lease. Imagine, if you will, coming into a building with violations of fire laws, hazardous waste laws and handicap access requirements. The tenant does its drawings after signing its lease and begins the process of obtaining permits to demolish the old premises and permits to alter and build the new one. In one of the worst cases I have observed, the tenant's architect discovered, when attempting to obtain the demolition, asbestos and building permits instead of during the feasibility study for candidate premises, that the building was not in compliance with certain fire laws and handicap access laws and the previous installation was not approved by the building department. Architects tend to tell you these things, if left on their own, after you sign the lease! The landlord, of course, did not volunteer to remove any violations in the building or in the premises and many months were lost in the tenant's preparation due to the inability to obtain permits or to settle with the landlord and cause the obstructing violations and conditions to be removed.

In another case with a similar result the landlord represented that there were no violations in the building or the premises which would prohibit the work from being accomplished. In fact, there were not violations of record, but there were conditions present which, if discovered by the building department and the fire department, would have been deemed to be violations. At the time of the request for the permits for demolition and construction, the agencies, of course, found the conditions and issued violations. The tenant, of course, requested the landlord to remove them, but the landlord's argument was really quite good. The landlord maintained it was not responsible since the violations occurred after tenant took occupancy of the premises and there were no violations prior to that time. The judge ruled in the case that had tenant wished a representation from landlord concerning facts or conditions which if discovered or because of passage of time would be deemed to be violations, he should have so written it. Tenant loses, counsel retires! The facilities manager would not have been able to defend against this one, however the facilities manager recommended the deficient attorney. Guilty by association and recommendation. I think a safe road map for facilities people to follow would be to have simple covenants at the beginning of the compliance section requiring landlord to deliver both the building and the demised premises, together with all systems, in such condition as to not be in violation of any laws, ordinances, rules, regulations or authorities whether existing or whether constituting violations upon discovery of the facts. This allows the tenant to commence its building and causes landlord to pay for any discovered conditions which would impede its progress or delay its completion. If one goes the distance to get the representations, one should also obtain an indemnity for damages and costs associated with curing any defects in the building or the premises or any violations or conditions, together with removing any hazardous materials, and also for the reimbursement of costs resulting from the delay in the tenant's work, additional costs of materials and labor and any re-working (affectionately referred to in the trade as "impact costs"), as well as the costs associated with remediation of the condition which was a breach of the warranty. You perhaps noticed that I slipped hazardous materials in in the last sentence. There have been instances in which I have experienced an otherwise sterling delivery of premises by a landlord to a tenant, fully demolished, plans approved and permitted and ready to receive tenant's work, with one exception: the demolition contractors had spilled some chemicals in the premises on the concrete slab floor. The spill was wiped up but not scrubbed out. The spill was fairly toxic, absorbed into the concrete and was properly diagnosed by the tenant's work crew which promptly refused to take control of the job site, lest they be required to remove the materials and incur liability for the spill. Of course, the landlord was not required to deliver the premises spill free, nor was he required to take responsibility for the demolition contractor even though the company was a wholly-owned subsidary of landlord. Ah justice denied! We now, of course, require in essence, representations that the premises will be delivered in all manner and condition susceptible of immediate receipt of tenant's work and obtaining of tenant's permits. Any condition not caused by tenant which occurs that impedes the tenant's progress in commencing its work would be a violation of this representation. Additionally, we require from landlord those permits and certificates of occupancy which are required for tenant to be able to commence its work. Certificates of occupancy are a subject deserving of an entire book and will be left to zoning and construction counsel to sort out. Or give me a call. Suffice it to say that one may do one's work and have a lease to occupy a premises and, nevertheless, be prohibited in so doing by being unable to receive a certificate to occupy the premises and conduct operations. In some jurisdictions the landlord is under no obligation to provide such a certificate. It is always best to require this in a lease. Additionally, in some jurisdictions a certificate of non-applicability is required for asbestos. In some other jurisdictions a removal certificate and an inspection certificate are required. Most tenants and tenant's contractors believe that this should now be a landlord's responsibility and will not take possession of the premises and commence the term of the lease until all of those certificates which are required in order to get building permits have been obtained, are sufficient and are issued.

The second dimension is the type of violation. There are violations that occur because of the particular use of the demised premises and there are violations that occur that are not premises or use related, but real estate and improvement generally related. I think the easy approach for a tenant and the most logical is that landlord, in order to accommodate the specified and permitted uses set forth in the lease, should undertake the necessary alterations and compliance work in order to allow the premises to be so utilized. If there are very special requirements based on tenant's use, many tenants expect to pay for those alterations and accommodations. Irrespective of who pays for the costs associated therewith, it would seem that so long as a tenant uses the premises for the stated permitted use, any alterations or changes which are required because of new violations should not necessarily be the tenant's obligation, unless maybe again they are specific and unusual in scope. In most jurisdictions it is the owner's obligation to continue to cause the building and the premises to comply with all general laws affecting improvements of real estate. Additionally, in most jurisdictions it's the landlord's obligation to continue the building certificate of occupancy in the condition required so as not to interfere with the use contracted for in the lease by the tenant. This also goes for temporary certificates of occupancy being converted into permanent certificates of occupancy at the right time. As with most leases where the tenant has represented that it will take the demised premises in its "as-is" condition together with the building, and which contain statements that landlord makes no representations with respect to the building, premises or tenant's ability to use it for the permitted use. Failure to be able to occupy to conduct business purposes will not relieve the tenant of the obligation to continue to pay rent.

Because of the advent of fire laws and hazardous waste laws, many of the hitherto landlord ownership costs to be absorbed and defrayed by the landlord are being turned into escalation costs or increases to be paid by tenants. Many mortgagees insist that a landlord's profit, which is the source of payment of debt service, not be eroded by unusual changes in laws and compliance costs and requirements. This, of course, raises a new issue for tenants who are otherwise comporting themselves appropriately in the premises under the lease. It is not unusual in some buildings in the Northeast and other major business centers to find that a change of law can require the expenditure of, in some instances, up to $7 to $15 a square foot in a short period of time. In negotiating who is to defray these costs, one should give attention to the benefit period and the remainder of the term of the tenant's lease. This subject is better dispensed with in an escalation and operating expense related section and will be treated there in this book.

The easy subject for compliance with laws is the violation and remediation costs incurred because of tenant's breach of its agreements or covenants under its lease including the conducting of the permitted use. Those, of course, should be paid by the tenant and since failure to correct the condition may subject landlord in certain instances to penalties, liens on the property and criminal liability, the landlord will necessarily require tenant to allow the landlord, after due notice and failure of tenant to remediate, to use self help, remediate the violation and charge the tenant the cost thereof.

Of course, any later performed improvements, alterations or repairs in the building or the premises should, and in all likelihood would, be required to be in compliance with all laws and authorities. The landlord usually reserves the right to inspect tenant's plans for alterations to confirm for itself and its mortgagee that compliance is going to be obtained.

CHAPTER 16

SERVICES

There are very few sections of the lease that cut right to the heart of the ability of the tenant to enjoy their premises. Services such as heating, plumbing, air conditioning, ventilating, elevator and cleaning are the fundamental reason to be in real estate and enjoy the operations of your business. When you get the service, how much service you get, what the quality of the service is, and what is the cost for the service when you don't normally get it, are issues which should be reviewed with great attention and care. It is amazing to me how many leasing specialists sign a lease without determining how much electricity or how much HVAC (heating, ventilating and air conditioning) there is available today and tomorrow or if it is available at all. One story comes to mind where ventilating was not a service provided as a matter of basic cost. It was interesting to find out that the definition didn't include ventilating in the lease and the building was a sealed facade building. So when it was not hot enough to require air conditioning or cold enough to require heating, the building still needed to be ventilated. There was an additional charge for that. The per hour charge wasn't huge, but the total cost was and was out of budget and certainly a windfall to the landlord every day for the entire term of the lease. Additionally, there are instances in older buildings where the air conditioning cools quite a few floors at a time, so that tenants who needed after hours air conditioning for late operations as a matter of routine found out that they had to pay for the cooling of ten floors. The lease did not specify cooling for tenant's floor but did specify a per floor charge with a caveat that in many instances, depending on the floor location of the tenant, more than one floor would have to be cooled. Such floor configurations could run as much as five hundred dollars per hour in some buildings today. I think, as a minimum, tenants should require a certain quality and reasonable quantities of all essential building services to be provided to the demised premises and distributed throughout the demised premises on all business days and during customary business hours; all the foregoing of which should be defined in the lease. Additionally, a tenant should be allowed to have cleaning throughout the demised premises at a standard specified in the lease. There are several buildings in New York City where the specifications for cleaning are subtly, but notoriously, deficient. For one floor in a not too large a floor footprint building, a tenant found out that its additional monthly cleaning was over $25,000 just in order to have the premises cleaned in a manner minimally acceptable to health standards and enjoyment. The really proper level of cleaning would run about $250,000 per year. These things should be discovered and negotiated at the beginning of the relationship rather than after the lease is signed. Another tenant recently had intended to put a quarter floor raised floor environmentally conditioned computer room in its premises only to find out that it could only get sufficient electricity at an incredibly greater cost, but could not put in the supplemental air conditioning packages required to keep the computer room cool. Other instances where tenants have been able to put the systems in, they have found that the cost to put them in and run them was exorbitant. These costs are standard and can be fixed at the beginning of the relationship.

Another concern of tenants is when can the services be interrupted. Normal interruption for repair and maintenance or emergency is understandable, but should be limited where possible so as not to interfere unreasonably with the tenant's operation. Many landlords reserve the right to interrupt the services for alterations or new improvements in the building (building additional building area) or in the event a tenant is even immaterially in default under its lease. These should be scrutinized very carefully and limited to what's appropriate given the operations of the tenant in the premises.

It is of more than passingly of interest to note that in tall buildings in New York City, elevators have become quite a profit center. Many landlords require additional charges for after hours passenger and freight elevator operation. The prices include a components of labor, "supervision" (profit) and electricity. One might note that most of these are paid for elsewhere through escalations or rent inclusion electric. Additionally, landlords are charging freight elevator service charges for move-in, move-out and alterations. These charges may also show up on contractor's invoices as hoisting or temporary services. It is interesting to note that move-in and move-out is generally required to be after hours when the rates are the highest. Tenants should not be required to pay for move-in and move-out freight elevator service, nor should they be required to pay for hoisting of materials to the job site for the initial installation. They should also make sure the landlord isn't charging the tenant's contractors either since the tenant will be later billed for the service by the contractors. The landlord should have some investment in bringing a new tenant into the building. I remember one tenant that was very happy with itself for getting the move-in and the hoisting for initial construction costs removed from the elevator section as well as supervision, profit and general conditions of the landlord usually appearing in the work letter. The small oversight of not having costs removed for the move-out caused the tenant to have to pay a very large cost for the move-out. This helped the landlord make up for its loss on the move-in. Obviously protracted negotiations on leases have their ups and downs (sorry!).

It seems appropriate to me for tenants to require landlord to provide any requested and reasonable amounts of chilled water, condenser water, additional air conditioning, and additional electricity that they may need throughout the term of the lease. Projecting these needs can be difficult but a talented architect aware of technological trends can assist considerably. This savings more than justifies the concerns about costs associated with bringing the architect into the leasing team early on in the process. One should also fix the costs associated with providing the additional or future levels of service at the beginning of the relationship. It costs less than when you later need it.

I think one of the most important concepts when it comes to services arises when other areas of the lease are in dispute. Even if a default has been declared, provided the lease has not been terminated or a court order issued, services should be continued on a regular basis. Services should not be used as leverage or blackmail to extort a tenant's performance where otherwise it would not or should not be required. Also, when additional levels or types of services are needed in buildings, it is incumbent upon tenant to make sure that the lease requires landlord to be reasonable and to accommodate all technological advances and additional needs of tenant where the same are commercially reasonable for the enjoyment of the premises. These days, this of course includes the use of wiring, satellite antenna dishes and considerably more air conditioning and conditioning types of services, equipment and, of course, electricity. Fixing the costs for these accommodations is also extremely important and it seems incumbent upon a tenant to think ahead if it has a ten to twenty year lease to see if these services are available and generally acceptable to tenant as well as landlord and at actual cost to landlord without mark-ups.

CUSTOM OF DEALING AND WAIVERS

It is customary when dealing with services or other obligations under the lease for the landlord and tenant to make accommodations for each other or waive certain requirements or ignore certain defaults. Life under a lease is a very fluid relationship with much interaction, many accommodations and frequent referrals to the original lease document by either party. Oddly enough, once the lease is signed, it's also a recurring phenomena that no one ever looks at the agreement again when they should but operates however they feel is appropriate as, of course, the conduct continues in the relationship. It is also important to take note of who the parties are that are bound after the signing of a lease. The landlords may sell their interest in the building, may do a ground lease for the improvements and/or the land or may reorganize. In those instances, it is important to know who remains bound to perform the obligations of the landlord and receive the rent. In most states these obligations or covenants run with the land or run with the lease. This means that the landlord who is expecting to receive the benefits of the lease, which include rent and other performance by tenants, is also bound and obligated to perform those obligations of the landlord which are to be provided for the rent. Many leases, however, play with this concept and try to sever the obligation of the landlord to perform or grant the benefits required of the landlord to be enjoyed by the tenant from the tenant's obligation to pay its rent and otherwise perform under the lease. In addition to separating the two obligations, they also try to cutoff the obligation of the existing landlord at the time he sells or leases the building and also limit the obligations of the new landlord. A tenant can find itself in an interesting vortex if it finds that its lease severs the obligations of payment and performance by tenant and landlord

54

respectively as well as cuts off the liability of a new successor landlord from pre-existing liabilities of predecessor landlords. In short, a tenant that is paying its rent and performing under its lease may find itself with a new landlord with no liability for obligations under the lease such as tenant work or other concessions or even certain services. The tenant will still be required to pay its rent and will have to look to the prior landlord to satisfy the obligations. If this is also a vortex within the void of a landlord who has limited its liability and any recourse for its obligations to its equity in the project, it's interesting to note that there is no equity in the project because the predecessor landlord will have sold it by then. Although theoretically as interesting as a three dimensional chess board, it can have some very nasty practical results to a tenant who expects to be able to finish its premises and receive certain services for the rent payments that it's making and doesn't like chess. This coupled also with limitations on the covenant of quiet enjoyment which we have discussed earlier can cause a real mess for a tenant. Usually at the time of a substitution of the landlord, the old course of comfortable dealing goes by the way side too. Leases with no waiver clauses limit any impact on the lease of the favorable custom of dealing between the parties which may be at odds with the lease language. The new landlord who probably paid too much for the building will now try to increase costs to the tenants and limit any favorable treatment not expressly required by the lease. Negotiating a lease should be always done with an eye to the "new unfriendly landlord" scenario.

Just as it is important to know thy enemy, it is also important to note which party is the tenant. Tenants, of course, cannot limit (usually) their liability by assignment and subletting since they remain liable under the terms of the lease, but in this context a tenant can find itself in default by changing its entity or by reorganizing or changing its ownership makeup. Partnership tenants can also be made to look like corporate tenants and corporate tenants can be made to have the same liabilities as general partnerships. All these things have been attempted before in leases and unless carefully read can cause great harm. Tenants must pay careful attention these days to these limitations because voluntarily or otherwise they may find themselves in an incurable default situation where they may very well lose their beneficial lease and demised premises improvements. Fear not, much of this subject will be treated in the assignment and subletting topic later.

CHAPTER 17

ELECTRICITY AND WATER

It's amazing how even small children know to ask certain questions on things that are very important to them such as food, water, batteries for their toys and other forms of power. You've heard the questions range among how big, how many, how much, what, where, how, when, why, why again and what if. Now there are very few things in life as important to the enjoyment of a home or an office as the ability to use water and electricity. I can't imagine a premises without heat, ventilation, air conditioning, smoke detectors, power, lights, stereos, refrigerators and toys; all a function of electricity. It seems strange to me that one of the most important areas of a lease is the most taken for granted and least understood by landlords, tenants, architects, engineers and lawyers. There are some landlords that understand the topic very well and many tenants of those landlords help defray the cost and provide the profit for the research and development endeavors of the landlord to creatively maximize their return on such an innocuous area. Once I tested my theory of the almost total absence of knowledge in the field by negotiating for my client, a very sharp landlord, a roof top space lease for a large very sophisticated mobile telephone company. The use of that term dates me a bit, but for those of you who don't remember, that was the predecessor of the cellular phone and was more of a status symbol than business tool. This is because 90% of the time a dial tone was unavailable due to congestion on the few open lines. Nonetheless, it was an extremely profitable area for the telecommunication companies and there were some highly desirable spaces in town on top of strategically located buildings where you could rent gravel for four to five dollars a square foot and buy your electricity from the public utility company at a reasonable price. With respect to electricity, this was not one of such locations. I decided to take the approach of renting the space, which was raw gravel space, but including in the rent a certain factor or amount which we call the rent inclusion electricity factor which represented in its simplest form the price to be paid per square foot for electricity presumably consumed during the year for the transmitters and receivers and other related equipment for this telephone site. Now being adventuresome, I decided to include in that factor not only the probable cost of running the transformers and related equipment as estimated by our electrical engineer, but also a "cost" cushion for administering the billing and a profit factor. Being a good creative soul, I elected to allow the review and adjustment of that figure annually under three scenarios, the first being any change in the rates of the public utility company, the second being any increase in consumption (term of art) of the equipment at the site, and the third being "on occasion", for no particular reason other than if one and two did not catch all changes. The clause worked something like this. The rent was $10.00 a square foot and the rent inclusion factor to be added was $7.00 a square foot. Of course, the actual cost per square foot (for the electricity) was determined to be approximately $4.00 a square foot so the balance was what I refer to as an "extra". Now the impact of the changes in our determination of the consumption per year and the changes in the rates was interesting. The changes in rates by the public utility company servicing the building would cause the rent inclusion factor to be increased in proportion to the percentage increase in the rates. As you know, rates can go up ten to thirty percent a year as they did in some of those years and these would be small pennies per square foot of actual additional costs if you figure the actual kilowatt hours consumed at the actual increase in cost per kilowatt hour. However, there was no real correlation between the actual additional costs of the consumed electricity and my formula which was much more like a porter's wage formula which increased the rent inclusion factor which also contained my extra. It became apparent after five years when the increases in rates percentage-wise were a bit dramatic and the impact on the $7.00 figure was melodramatic. On the consumption front, it might not surprise you that we had what is called the right to conduct an incremental survey. This works in a sort of unusual manner. When the tenant originally installs its equipment and begins its operation, the landlord comes in and does what is called a survey of the inventory of equipment consuming electricity or which could consume electricity if plugged in and operated within the leased area. If done properly, any equipment in or near the leased gravel whether broken, old, boxed, unboxed, plugged in or not, can be captured and included in the survey from time to time. As one might note in the start-up operation at the end of completion of construction, there is very little equipment hanging around the site that is not plugged in and running. But over the years, many pieces of equipment died or wore out and it was cheaper to leave the equipment in place and bolt a new piece next to the old one or on top of it rather than remove the old one. As with most sites this site had several cooling fans, some compressor equipment and a transformer or two together with a transmitter which were no longer operable, but rather than remove them from the site they were just disconnected. Under an incremental survey, any time after the first survey of the premises, the surveyor is instructed, if the clause is written properly and sometimes if not, to inventory all equipment which if plugged in and if operating would consume electricity. Presume it's consuming electricity and presume it consumes it 24 hours a day seven days a week. This is what is called connectable load as opposed to connected and consuming load. Now, the next bit of adjustment comes from assuming all equipment was plugged in and running 24 hours a day, seven days a week, and at its highest electrical needs (or rather demand). Again, if the clause is written creatively enough, one may presume a peak power demand consumption for each piece of equipment. It's good for you to know that there are itty bitty red and blue books floating around for engineers to look at which will tell you the normal consumption, peak consumption and demand characteristics of anything made by mankind that consumes electricity. Our surveyor was very agile in his ability to use his little book and, of course, we priced things that would consume at peak power electricity for only a few seconds in any period of the day, but, of course, we would presume they were consuming at that demand all the time of operation. For instance, think of your air conditioner in your window at home. If you don't have one think of someone else's air conditioner in their window at home. The compressor, when it kicks on, can use 15 amps of power very quickly in order to get running the first time. That will happen for less than two seconds. Thereafter it may run somewhere between four and seven amps in demand. It may run at peak power 40 - 50 seconds a day. The way our surveyor was instructed to price the consumption caused the consumption to be three to four times higher under that scenario, but if you assume that the compressor doesn't run for quite a bit of the time during the day or in winter, the consumption charge for electricity and for units such as that might be 100 times greater than actual consumption, under a properly written aggressive clause. There are many more tricks to this. If you assume the right at each re-survey to do what's called in incremental survey of connectable load, the scenario further plays out by the surveyor keeping the original survey in place and merely adding to the surveyed amount those new pieces of equipment that are being used or that are on the site and sitting around whether or not connected. The old pieces which were obviously no longer working or which were no longer at the site were not deducted from the survey amount. So the survey, of course, is something that incrementally grows and, due to changes in rates and charges of the public utility and the assumptions of the characteristics of consumption, the charge turns into a monster. The logic of this type of electrical consumption bears no resemblance to the actual cost of the electricity consumed by the equipment at the site, you might observe. That is wonderful, but this observation must occur prior to signing the lease. This type of electricity clause is merely a profit vehicle for the landlord if properly drafted and properly administered. I believe this landlord was able to receive the largest price per square foot for gravel anywhere in the upper plane of Manhattan. I do believe it may be a record for many years to come and certainly an embarrassment for the landlord, but more importantly for the telecommunication company whose project director took early retirement about halfway through the initial term after the increases in the electrical expenses began to roll in.

I used the preceding story merely as illustration to cause one not to have their eyes glazed over and rolled back in their head when I do my following discussion on the attributes, requirements and needs of the tenant for electricity, water and other fundamental elements of nature such as sewer service within the demised premises. Defining a few terms at this point will make the discussion easier. Let's have the following terms have the following meanings:

1.   Consumption: The utilization in a particular area, such as the demised premises, of electricity.

2.   Demand: At any particular time, the amount that is being consumed. Therefore, peak demand would be the highest amount of electricity consumed at any point in time within the demised premises. Note that consumption is over a period of time and generally should be measured in 24 hour periods.

3.   Connected Load: What is plugged in.

4.   Connectable Load: What electrical consuming equipment is in the premises which could be connected and which could consume whether or not it is operable.

5.   Power or Load: The amount of watts or kilowatts deliverable to the demised premises.

6.   Watts Per Square Foot: Watts or amps, as converted, to be delivered to a point in the demised premises, hopefully a metered panel, and based on either rentable or usable square feet. This is generally required to be standardized by building codes in most cities except New York City.

7.   Sewer Service: Not the same as water service. Please make sure that you have contracted for a place for the water service to go.

8.   Survey: The review of the things within the demised premises which may consume electricity and what, when and how much they might consume.

9.   Electrical Costs: This, of course, could be anything. Preferably it is the actual cost per kilowatt hour as billed to landlord as evidenced by the bills monthly of the public utility company to the building on average for the entire building consumption for the whole year, taking into account seasonal and time of day surcharges and net of any credits, abatements or incentives, all as divided by twelve months and the total number of rentable square feet in the entire building as well as those spaces which are allocated for escalation purposes to other tenants. This is a heavy statement. If you ask for this from most landlords, they will either not understand you or hate you.

Those who hate you are the guys who otherwise would have stolen from you. Those who don't understand you are probably not making much profit on electricity anyway.

This last statement of cost takes into account something we have not yet discussed, that is, the possibility that the sum of the rent inclusion electric factors of all tenants in the building and for those spaces which should be tenantable and charged accordingly may already equal or exceed the entire building electricity charges. If it doesn't, add it together with the electricity consumed for the common areas such as lobbies, air conditioning systems and mechanical rooms, but excluding other areas which are not to the benefit of all tenants-in-common such as garage and retail space, and this should equal the charge that should be assessed evenly throughout the tenants in the building. Of course, that number minus any work done in the premises by landlords in order to improve, repair or decorate the premises for current or future tenants should also be deducted. Careful attention has to be given to what portions of the electrical, gas, water or other natural resource allocation goes on between tenant's use in its premises and its reimbursement of landlord for operating expense escalations or utility reimbursement or surcharges. One can envision some landlords obtaining reimbursement from between one and a half and three times the entire building electric meter by way of rent inclusion factors, escalations and direct charges for overtime services. One might also understand that after hours heating, ventilating and air conditioning as well as special elevator charges all have a component of labor materials and electricity. If all of those plus after hours lighting and rent inclusion electric factor reimbursements are taken into account, it's a clear picture on what the cost of electricity for public areas, operating expense escalation and demised premises should be. This is not an answer, it is a provocation.

There are other interests of the tenant other than just cost of electricity. With change in electricity and power consumption needs of sophisticated tenants, the big questions, in addition to how much it costs, are how much do I need today, how much will I need tomorrow and will I be able to obtain additional power in the building as my needs and technology change. This is not a simple question, and is rarely voluntarily addressed in the affirmative in a lease. The norm is that electricity is granted by capacity at the time of construction, and that capacity is the minimum that landlord feels it can get away with per usable square foot in the building. Future needs are not guaranteed, and if they are satisfied by a landlord, it is generally with additional sizeable costs and profit factors included. Also if the particular use, which may be unusual and power intensive, is not described in these clauses, it may be prohibited anyway. I cannot tell you the number of tenants that have come to me with problems because the particular use was not allowed, or if they negotiated to have it allowed, there was not enough riser or feeder capacity or power load capability to the demised premises and the cost in order to get the necessary amounts there was extortion by the landlord. In essence, be like a child. Ask what is there, what you can get, how much it costs, where it comes in, when it comes in and will it be available later if you need more. When I say where it comes in, one must be careful to understand that electricity may be delivered to the floor and it may be delivered in 25 different locations. When a tenant takes overall space, one does not necessarily know where the feeders and junction boxes are.

Beware of the premises where you rent a floor and find out that your rent will be increased by an electricity charge that is by way of submetering. Submetering is a wonderful concept and reduces generally the cost to tenants of electricity and levels the playing field more, as if the tenant were purchasing the electricity directly from the public utility at the public utilities rate, except in the event that it is delivered to the floor in seven different locations because the previous tenants all had seven different meters. You must also not assume rates or proper submetering of only consumption in the demised premises. Segregating lines, setting up new junction boxes and redistributing the electricity to the location you need can be a change order exceeding $50,000. Needless to say, electricity can be a shocking financial experience in any move and can severely limit the ability of a tenant to operate in a demised premises that is already leased. Beware up front.

One should also consider what amount should be paid during the construction period. If the landlord is doing a build-to-suit, and is otherwise delivering a turn-key at landlord's cost, electricity and other general conditions should also be at landlord's cost. In many instances it is cheaper during the construction phase than during the occupancy phase for electricity. These should be considered during negotiation, because you can save your legal fees right away just in the intelligent negotiations of the electrical clause or the freight elevator charges.

There are other arguments such as the issues relating to discontinuance of furnishing electricity on a rent inclusion basis. This should not be allowed unless the landlord is compelled by law or public service utility regulation to discontinue. If that is the case, the rent inclusion electric charge should go away, the lines and meters should be installed by landlord at its cost, and service should not be discontinued until direct service is obtained by the tenant. No voluntary discontinuance by a landlord should be allowed. This changes the character of the business terms and also allows for individual retaliation by landlord or extortion. I have seen it all here.

Landlord generally will exculpate itself or limit its liability for loss or damage or inability to use the premises sustained by reason of failure, inadequacy or defect in the character, quantity or supply of electricity or other raw materials to the premises. Many jurisdictions allow this complete exculpation and it is imperative to the practitioner to cause it to be limited to those things not within the control of landlord, or caused by landlord's acts or negligence. I have seen times where landlord has sent unlicensed, inexperienced contractors to the premises to play with power lines and water mains, only to find the premises equipment fried by electrical spikes or shorts or flooded out. I cannot begin to tell you the horror stories which occur because of this. It is important that the landlord understand its liability, act professionally, and have insurance covering these types of losses.

CHAPTER 19

RENTALS

Base Rent

We have already discovered in this work that when you hear the figure of $40.00 per square foot for base rent or fixed rent (used interchangedly here), you should have more questions at that point than answers. I think probably the first question that comes to mind is what is a rentable square foot? What percentage of a rentable square foot can you stand on or can you benefit from? Why aren't there round feet out there just to fool us? Additionally, there are certain components of base rent that we will wish to unbundle. For instance, does the base rent include an inclusion charge for electricity which frequently is affectionately referred to as the rent inclusion electric factor? If yes, then is the base rent increased over the years? If it is increased, is it on a stepped up basis or by application of a consumer price index or other deflator formula? If so, what portion of the base rent should have the deflation application? Clearly, it should not cover those areas already being adjusted or increasing due to cost increases. Therefore the rent inclusion electric factor should be deducted prior to the adjustment. We should now take the time to unbundle the other components of the base rent so that we can have a better understanding of how it and other charges should be dealt with in the many different sections of the lease. Let us assume for the moment that we have a $40.00 per rentable square foot of fixed rent. Let us assume that debit service exclusive of principal amortization is $20.00 a rentable square foot. Let us further assume that the office or other space leases in the building are based on an escalation concept, whereby the landlord will pay the first year's operating expenses and taxes and the tenant will reimburse the landlord over the term of its lease for any increases over the first year costs or frequently referred to as bases. Therefore let us assume that operating expenses for maintaining the building, cleaning and management for the first year will be $5.00 per rentable square foot. Let us assume that real estate taxes and special assessments for the first year will be $7.00 a square foot. Let us further assume that electricity will be $2.00 per rentable square foot and is included in the $40.00 per rentable square foot base rent quote. This of course is generally not the case. Usually the electricity charge gets added on when the lease comes out, but let us assume that all landlords play fair upfront and that is part of the $40.00. Therefore of the $40.00 per rentable square foot, $34.00 represents the costs to feed and clean the building and $6.00 per rentable square foot in year one represents a profit. Let us further assume that as you will see in the subsequent chapters of the book, the maintenance, taxes, operating expenses and electricity will all have their cost increases over the term of the lease which will be reimbursed by the tenant and that the debt service is based on a fixed rate permanent mortgage so that the $20.00 is cost constant over the term of the lease. Therefore the profit portion of the rent is really only 15%, the debt service is approximately 50%, the operating expense is approximately 13%, taxes are approximately 18%, etc. We will also assume (probably improperly) that there is a correlation between the base rent of $40.00 per square foot and the number of rentable square feet in the building which, when multiplied by the base rent, would give you these scenarios. To date we also know that the sum of the demised premises in a building that is fully occupied will be larger than 100% of the carpetable area and may well be 25% greater than what should be the rentable area. But that conversation will be saved and elaborated upon more in the next section. This just helps you see that the 20,000 square foot lease in one building at $40.00 a square foot may be the same as 22,000 square feet in another building at $40.00 a square foot or 18,000 square feet in another building at $40.00 a square foot. That is the easy approach. Now try and compare a $36.00 per square foot base rent to a space quoting for a 20,000 square foot space $40.00 a square foot but is really only 18,000 square feet. Comparing apples to apples becomes considerably more difficult. Next you will add in the variables attributable to the work being performed or the credit given for work by the landlord on the lease, affectionately referred to as the Work Letter, and the assumptions for the components of other rentals, such as escalations for increases over a certain different base amount for taxes, operating expenses, porters wage formula, utility expenses and electricity, which of course you have already discovered. This makes the comparison extremely complicated, but still doable. It must be done of course in the preliminary stages while pricing comparative deals. In truth, it is generally focused on by experienced facilities directors and lawyers, either late in the negotiation or after execution of the lease and this moves us to the next section in the wonderful world of discovery called escalators.

Escalations

It is important to note immediately that the word escalation means exactly what it means. Escalation I believe must be derived from the old Atlantian term escalator, or always going up. Atlantis is where it is because escalations eventually weighted it down. Escalation clauses generally are written in a way that they can never go down and usually cover only increases in costs whether such increases actually occur or not. Given the writer's prejudice on how they work based on the rather crafty ways I have participated in writing them, I will spend a moment to explain some of the issues involved. Some parts of the country have net leases, and some parts have not so net leases. In essence, a net lease is where the tenant pays a smaller base rent per square foot (presumably net of all bases), but then pays a percentage based on its occupancy of the building in relation to all of the leasable areas in the building (we hope) times the actual cost to operate the building plus taxes and any shared common area charges. These are called pass through changes since they are to be paid net of cost markups and discounts to the landlord. The not so net leases are what are generally encountered in office and retail space, and they are those where there is generally a larger base rent figure which presumably is an aggregate of, as we have seen, the profit and other costs bases associated with the building. When these components are bundled in to the base rent, people lose sight of the fact that those should be the numbers used for the base years which landlords expect to cover operating and other expenses of the building including debt service, and over which the tenant is expected to pick up his proportionate cost or expense share. Somehow, there has not always been a coherent direct translation of those numbers into the escalation provisions. Just as certain buildings have different usable to rentable square foot ratios, they also have different competitive advantages or disadvantages in the costs to operate. For instance, there are many buildings in New York City that have real estate taxes in the $6.00 to $8.00 per rentable square foot range. There are also some $12.00 per rentable square foot numbers. Additionally, some buildings have an incredibly disadvantaged position when it comes to utility and electrical efficiency, and their cost per rentable square is much higher than those that are high tech and new. Similar discrepancies occur with respect to operating and cleaning costs for a building that is old versus those one that is new, and versus those that have very sharply negotiated positions in older cleaning contracts, and those which have brand new maintenance and operating contracts which are possibly very advantageous to the unions. Therefore these numbers have to be looked at and unbundled when doing comparisons between to the components of base rent and the actual costs of particular buildings for the base years projecting actual costs of occupancy per building and comparing apples to apples when picking a building out of the candidates. One other note of interest: many of the proposed candidates will have different concepts of base years for each of the different escalations. Some will have the last year as a base year, while some will have split years or half years. Some will have fiscal years covering portions of two calendar years. Some will have the current year of occupancy or the current year of the term (these of course will be considerably different). Some will pick a lease year which actually could be often a year and some months of actual possession by the tenant. In any event, care and attention should be given to these differences in order to have the definitions fully understood. Additionally, the base year may be triggered by the contract portion of the lease term or it may commence on the substantial completion of the premises when delivered by landlord to tenant. This is usually an extremely big difference in economic results and should be observed. Going forward, it should be considered that this principally is a work on commercial office with some retail. There are some very subtle but expensive differences which translate through imperfect parallelisms to all retail, regional malls, mixed use buildings, including residential, office and retail, but with some major costly differences which I usually like to refer to as landlord grabs. Having spent a lot of time designing those leases, I would say that discussions in depth on the differences would be better taken up in other writings of which I am sure there are plenty or soon will be.

Other Considerations

At this point, one might ask, if in any year the market base rent contains a profit portion, or no profit portion if it is a bad year, plus the sum of the other costs representing the bases per square foot being underwritten by landlord, then if the landlord is able, through mirrors, to create a larger than life building because the sum of the demised premises is over 100% of the building size, or is able to apply the bases to the calculation of escalations for the same operating expense taxes, etc. to different tenants or to collect taxes from the tenants in different improvements on the same combined tax lot containing the building which duplicate actual taxes paid or not paid, should the tenant be allowed to have the benefit of landlord collecting more than actual costs by having his base rent reduced to the extent of such over collections or possibly have its expense or tax escalations reduced? If you can even follow this last sentence, you are ready to read leasing speak sentences which are generally longer and just as convoluted! The prior statement though is an interesting concept that has not received a lot of attention by practitioners representing tenants. Quite frankly, I have never heard it raised before, but I think it should be considered as all part of the same linear equation when leasing in a building.

Taxes

In order to understand what a tenant will be paying in the way of tax escalation, one must understand the amount over which it will pay the increases as well as what the definition of taxes really is made up of. The easy one is to figure out what the base year or the base amount or factor for taxes will be, and one might also take the extra time to correlate that to its component in the base rent just to see if it truly pencils out. The more difficult concept is calculating what taxes are. Simplistically, taxes are a payment made by a landlord in most regions to a governmental or quasi-governmental agency resulting from amounts reflecting special or benefit assessments imposed on the property plus tax rates or mill levies applied to the value of the property as determined or assessed by the governmental entity. Special assessments are usually impositions either in dollar amounts per quantity of real estate value, rates or dollars times square foot area, or numbers of people and they are usually paid in installments based on the useful life of the benefit to the benefit district which includes the land and building. These special assessments may be based on land or improvements or both, such as sidewalk, traffic or sewer and water assessments. They also may be benefit related to transportation, landmark displacement or other special governmental related or humanistic related services. One must take the time to make sure that the base taxes, if it is otherwise not a number, includes the concept of that portion of the special assessments, the installments of which fall within the base year period. Also all special assessments should be calculated based on the installment method, whether or not the landlord pays them in installments, so as to smooth out the impact over the term of the lease. Landlords generally fail to include installments of special assessments in the base years. It seems to be a common affliction, and I am not certain how it originated. The other prevailing method among other many types of real estate related taxes is the valuation times a rate approach. Here the taxing authority determines the assessed valuation of the land and the assessed valuation of the improvements upon which a mill or a tax rate levy will be imposed. Land and improvements are generally treated differently. Land may be assessed at a full value and the improvements may be phased in or partially abated. Also, some areas have different rates for the two different components. When determining the taxes, especially for the base year, one must make sure that any reduction or limitation on the full amount of the assessed evaluation of the land or the improvements by way of incentive abatements, or by the timing of when it becomes part of the assessment rules, as fully completed, are not only understood, but that the impact on base taxes is adjusted if appropriate to avoid an artificially low base tax amount above which the tenant will pay future escalations. (This concept is with many thousands of dollars per month and worth the effort to understand this long sentence.) In some jurisdictions, an otherwise completed building with tenants in it may not be on the tax rolls at full value, irrespective of incentive abatements, for up to two years after it is actually physically completed due to technicalities of the assessment rolls. Additionally, even if fully assessed either in dollar amount or assessment, it may reflect additional abatements or what I refer to as a below the line abatement deduction,

70

or an artificially low assessed valuation through an incentive abatement program which erodes or becomes smaller with each year of the program allowing the assessed valuation of the land or the improvements to increase from year to year without regard to the actual increase in the value of the project due to market conditions. If you have noticed, in that last statement, that the assessed value of a project can increase in several different ways simultaneously, then you have not missed the point of this discussion. Just as we have noted that many buildings have different taxes, they also have different base years, as we discussed, base factors, different abatements and different special assessments. They also increase on the tax rolls at different times such as at sales or refinancing. So if one is going to try to calculate the impact of the base amount of taxes that will be paid by landlord, and the amount of increases each year including possibly the first year which will be paid by the tenant, in order to compare these premises with other proposed projects for leasing, one has to dig in to the existing taxable components of real estate taxes, such as land, improvements, air rights or development rights, easements, special assessments, assessed valuations, abatement amounts, free trade zones, payments in lieu of taxes, abatement formulae, etc. before one can come to the appropriate comparable number or calculation. The components of assessable real property rights include the actual land, any improvements on the land, easements benefiting the land, encumbrances on the land, air rights and unutilized development rights (one being a function of real estate and the other being a value conferred or stolen by zoning), income from the property (presumably from advantageous leases such as the ones we are discussing or competitive advantages from lower taxes) and types of use. Once you have determined the property's characterization and assessed valuation after deducting any incentives, abatements and adding any installments or special assessments and determining what is the taxable lot you should be paying for (such as the building plus only so much of the land as should be benefiting the project) under the particular lease, you can go about calculating what the taxes should be for the base year and estimating future escalations. I say include only so much of the land as is necessary to support the building, because there have been some nasty habits recurring over the years in many of the

71

larger cities of including the building that the lease is in with other combined tax lots, which include other excess improvable land and improvements not necessary for, nor even benefiting the enjoyment of the building by the tenant. This I call warehousing at the tenant's expense. Landlords call it involuntary investing by tenants. Once you get through the fluff of understanding that a garage is part of the building, but it services everybody but the tenants, and there are other buildings on the property that may or may not be assessed and may or may not pay their freight on the combined tax lot, one can then start to sort out those payments and those calculations that are relevant in equity or morally to the building wherein lies the possibility of a new facilities manager.

Once you have the hang of how real estate taxes are computed and what the base amount of the taxes will be that the landlord will be funding, it is not as smooth sailing as one might imagine. A facilities manager worth his or her salt will not allow taxes to increase because of additional improvements to the building other than those in the demised premises nor will they allow the base taxes for the base year to be subsequently reduced and have all the subsequent years recalculated. A good example of this is when you are paying that $40.00 a rentable square foot and taxes are $7.00 per square foot for the base year, but there is a little extra word or two inserted in the lease after the base year definition saying "as finally determined". In this instance, these three little words mean that in the second, third or fourth years, depending upon the appeal process for taxes in the particular region, the base year assessments may be redetermined and reduced. So remember now that the tenant is still paying $40.00 per square foot of base rent. However, the landlord at this point after the adjustment is only paying $6.00 per square foot of the base for escalation for taxes. Since he budgeted for $7.00 per square foot and is now paying $6.00, he has $1.00 savings in payments per year for the rest of the term of the lease. However, since the clause allows the landlord to adjust the base year in the lease downward, in subsequent years, that will increase the escalations payable by the tenant per square foot. For instance, if the second year after the assessed valuation adjustment, the taxes per square foot are now $7.00, the tenant will pay an additional $1.00 of escalation per

72

square foot that it had not anticipated. Even though the taxes per square foot are at $7.00, which is the same amount that was anticipated when the $40.00 per square foot rent figure was advertised. Therefore as oddly as it may seem, the landlord has saved $1.00 per square foot per year and the tenant is paying an additional $1.00 per square foot per year, and this will remain so for the remainder of the term of the lease. Of course this is no small amount and has to be defended against. Additionally, some landlords think that if a building is not completely occupied, they should increase the occupying tenant's proportionate share so that it is paying its fair share of taxes based on the percentage of the building actually occupied. Rather than adjust the tenant's proportionate shares for the periods that they are in occupancy during the year, the landlords increase the real estate taxes to an amount.which would reflect a building fully occupied and improved by tenant installations and pass that through to the tenant for application of its tenant's proportionate share. Although there is some argument in favor of this theory with respect to operating expenses, there is no justification whatsoever with respect to real estate taxes. Therefore if a tenant is occupying half the building and its tenant proportionate share is 50%, if it is the sole occupant of the building it should pay presumably under this scenario, 100% of the increases in taxes. That will be a different result than having a tenant pay its tenant proportionate share of 50% times the assessed valuations which presumably in landlord's estimate would occur had the building been fully tenanted and occupied and with all tenant improvements and installations in place. The difference between these two numbers is of course a windfall to the ownership. Side stepping the windfall for the moment, there are certain ownership costs associated with having new or empty buildings. Taxes certainly are one of those ownership costs. Unlike operating expenses which increase by usage of tenants and which may correlate to the usage by one singular tenant in the building, real estate taxes do not.

Two other concepts, which can be elaborated upon during negotiation, are that only taxes paid by landlords should be paid by tenants and only as, if and when paid by the landlords. This is usually quarterly or semi-annually and, provided that tenant's sufficient funds check reaches the landlord within four or five days clearing time prior to landlord having to pay taxes, there is no compelling reason for taxes to be paid monthly or earlier by a tenant. Additionally, these escalations must be based on taxes actually paid as opposed to when assessed. If the taxes are subsequently forgiven before payment, there should be no payment required for that portion by the tenant or, if forgiven after the payment, there should be a refund to the tenant of its share of that excess payment. One also has to allow for subsequent years tax review and reduction proceedings after the base year, both allowing the landlord to recoup a portion of the cost of performing such review procedures and allowing tenant to recoup its fair share of that refund amount which was paid through escalations partly by the tenant. The astute facilities manager should watch out for what is currently in vogue, and that is payment in lieu of taxes. On any taxing lot there may be tax exempt improvements which are assessed, but no taxes are collected. These include governmental entities and charitable and religious entities. Depending on how the clause is written defining taxes, it may be the assessed valuation of all improvements times the tax rate even though the landlord is only paying the amount resulting from that calculation on some rather than on all of the improvements. This also is true in the event of any incentive or other abatement programs. This generates a problem for the base year which is easily overcome by using the assessed valuation times the tax rate for the base year, but in the subsequent years basing it on taxes actually paid or payable, which means that you have an appropriate base year, but you will never pay more taxes on your proportionate share formula than landlord pays for that same share.

Porters Wage or Penny Wage Formulae

Landlords many years ago, in order to avoid disputes and arguments over what constituted a necessary and appropriate operating expense, designed a new way to calculate escalations based on a formula that purported to have a relationship to the cost of running a building, which was the relative increases from year to year of the cost of porters or other comparable union employees as set forth in the union contract for the building or for the industry. In its simplest form, the hourly wage rate of a standard employee would increase from year to year and the number of cents that it increased would then be multiplied by the rentable square footage area of the demised premises and the result would be the escalation for that year. Each subsequent year, the calculation was revisited over the previous years wage hourly rate. The formula in the old days was a small hourly wage and small cents increase applied on what was called a penny for penny escalator. Also square feet were square feet! Early on, landlords discovered that they could make it one and a half, two or even three pennies increase in the tenant's escalation for every one penny increase in the wage rate. As time went on, it became obvious that this was quite a profit center, because as the hourly wage rates got larger, a 10% increase in the wage hourly rate became 300 pennies instead of 10 pennies. Also, one square foot became one and one third square feet. That multiplied by more than a penny for a penny became an incredible increase per square foot for escalations under that formula. It is also good to note that there was no relationship between the increase in hourly salaries and the cost to operate or clean the building. Not being one to be outdone by a small city like Chicago where the penny formula began, New York City decided through certain landlords to add to the computation the hourly rate increase plus the impact on pricing of the hourly rate of fringe benefits which were negotiated on behalf of the union employees rather than hard hour cost increases. As the hourly wage rate became larger, the resistance in union negotiations caused more benefits to occur in the fringe area rather than in the hourly rate so as to make the contract more palatable. It is also interesting to note that if you price fringes based on the hourly impact, you must divide the cost of the fringes or the benefits by the number of hours worked in the fringe period. Well, this generated a great deal of variables and has been a veritable storehouse of creativity for landlords. Not only do many of the landlords use a different denominator for the hours worked for the benefit period, they do not always price the benefit or even the hours in the denominator from year to year consistently and in accordance with any generally accepted standards. One might say that there are so few standards in this field, that of my clients, not a single one of them prices the fringes the same way nor has an hourly wage increase that is even close to the same number from year to year as others. This inconsistency and non-standardized approach to price in the impact of this formula on escalations can make comparison of proposed premises for leasing very difficult. These days if we were to ever agree to a porters wage formula, it would probably be one-half to three-quarters of a penny increase for each penny increased in the actual wage rate without calculation attributable to fringe benefits. However, because of the profit potential, most landlords having significant tenants have moved back to actual net operating expense "pass throughs"; Pass throughs being a thought that the actual cost alone is all that is passed through on a percentage calculation to tenants. I will try ardently to dispel this notion in my next section.

Operating Expense

A more straightforward approach to having a tenant pick up the increase in costs to operate a building is the operating expense pass through. Two concepts are appropriate here, operating expense which means appropriate, reasonable and reasonably necessary expenses incurred in operating the building and not the garage used only by other than tenants. Operating is a pyramid definition on its own which can include management, repair, maintenance, partial replacement, cleaning, decorating, landscaping and possibly altering. There are two ways to define it, the very long way which enumerates everything that can be included in an operating expense and a short way that merely speaks of all costs associated with operating, managing, repairing or replacing portions of the building. Both definitions approach the same reasonable middle ground, but from two different avenues. The smaller clause really allows practically anything that is reasonably appropriate for operating a building to be included, and the other clause only allows those things specifically enumerated to be included. The difference has been bridged by adding at the end of the three page clause, the additional parenthetical or prepositional phrase..."or any other such cost or expense of operating or maintaining the property". So landlords can say it long or short, but whatever is said has to be sorted through carefully and the definition modified to fairly express the parties' intentions on those costs and expenses which are fair game to be included in an operating expense escalation cost. Either way, there should be careful attention given to those exclusions from operating expense which fit the nature of the deal. This varies with a variety of factors including the size of the space being leased and the number of years it is being leased. A large tenant looking for a large block of space for a lot of years is generally making the election to lease in order to avoid those periodic but usually unplanned for capital expenditures associated with ownership. The last thing they would like to do for instance is to come in to a long term lease at a rent which is supposed to even those expenses out over the years only to be charged for large capital improvements or violation curations associated with the ownership position in a building. Therefore one of the first arguments that usually arises is what capital improvements, if any, are allowed to be passed through via operating expense escalations. Those types of capital improvements usually revolve around issues of capital expenditures associated with curing of defects in construction, latent defects or completing construction and original fit-up for operation. Additionally, those capital expenditures associated with curing violations of laws, curing conditions which if discovered would be violations and otherwise putting the premises prior to leasing and other leasable premises and the public portions of the building in compliance and also hazardous substance free. That issue also can be bifurcated and dealt with both during the pre-leasing period and during the term of the lease. Clearly, anything that has occurred up to the time of the commencement of the lease (contract, occupancy or operations as negotiated) should not be passed through via an operating expense clause unless it is for the base year. Ongoing issues are subject to negotiation. Generally large tenants do not allow any capital expenditures benefiting more than one period to be charged as operating expenses. Those that allow it require that the capital expenditure be amortized and included year to year only in the amount representing a straight line basis depreciation and not at all in the last two years of the lease. Many tenants will agree that capital improvement costs can be included for otherwise operating expense saving improvements, but only to the extent of the actual savings or in some instances the estimated potential savings on an annual basis amortized over the useful life of the improvement. There are usually also limitations excluding any reimbursable costs from insurance, condemnation awards, other tenants for direct services and overtime and additional services, as well as levels of service that are greater than the level of service of a particular tenant under the lease. Under duplicative costs would be taxes and electricity payments as opposed to the cost of electricity furnished to non-public areas in the building. Other exclusions include any debt service on mortgages or rental under ground leases, costs of any work in leasable or leased premises (non-public areas), costs associated with professional fees for disputes or litigation with tenants, landlord advertising or promotional expenses, costs for casualty which are or would have been reimbursable by insurance had landlord carried full value insurance, salaries and fringe benefits which are above comparable salaries and benefits for comparable employees, salaries of personnel that are shared among buildings or those above the grade of a building manager, fees or costs in excess of the comparable market value thereof for services rendered by vendors affiliated with landlord, and any type or line item service which landlord is generally providing to the building but not to the tenant under the lease.

In addition to having exclusions, there should also be a general provision requiring all services to be delivered at landlord's actual net cost. Actual at the time of disbursement is an easy concept. Net at any time means that if there are any discounts, volume, credit backs or other payments or benefits received by the landlord related with any service provided to the building, that those find their way back to the benefit of the tenants.

Another area that is quite controversial is those operating expenses resulting from the negligence of the landlord. One example which I gave in this book was that of the landlord who allowed a non-union, non-licensed plumber to come in the building and inspect and work with some of the risers and feeder pipes. The same plumber who affixed his wrench to a high pressure water column in order to tighten a slightly dripping shut-off valve without turning off the pressure in the pipe. The cost associated with repairing the damage from the flood, the impact on the tenants and the damage to the plumbing are things that should be reimbursed by the insurance, but whether or not reimbursed should not find their way to an operating expense escalation clause. The reason I say this is that landlords who operate at least first class buildings are expected to have a certain level of management and operating ability, and they receive a management fee and have a manager specifically paid for that. If there is negligence, then that should come out of the management fee or the ownership pocket.

The grossing up practice we discussed in taxes applies more appropriately to operating expense escalations. For instance, if there is a tenant in the building and it is the only tenant using the elevators, one would expect that if the cost of the elevators went up the next year and still only the one tenant was in the building, it should pay for the entire increase of the operating expense of the elevator over the first year. If for instance the tenant is a 50% occupant of the building, you could either double its tenant proportionate share so that the tenant would pay 100% of the increase for the operating expense attributable to the elevator over the base year, or possibly you could increase the operating expense to a number that would result in approximately the same payment if the building were 100% occupied. Of course it is easier to adjust the finite tenant's proportionate share with accuracy if it is not too complicated with tenants moving in and out of the building, than it is to adjust with accuracy the operating expense that would occur if the building were 100% occupied. In the elevator scenario, if the building were fully occupied I would suspect the expense of the elevator would be more than double what it was in the base year. However, the expense of heating in the winter is significantly less than double the cost if the building was 100% occupied instead of 50% occupied, because the body warmth of human beings in the building in the morning and throughout the day causes the heat requirement from the heating equipment to be considerably less. Tenants should pay careful attention to this aspect of the non-linear relationship of occupancy and resulting operating expense for each type of service. The type of service and the relationship to full occupancy is different in its linear or non-linear reaction to activities resulting from a fully occupied building. The next issue of course is what is a fully occupied building. Most people consider a fully occupied building to be one that at any time has achieved a 90% leased level. Of course you can tell if that is different from occupancy level. Some buildings may never in their lifetime reach a 90% occupancy level. When limitations on the grossing-up or other operating expense concepts are based on an occupancy or a leasing level, careful attention has to be paid to the particular concept to see that it is practically achievable. One instance comes to mind on a rather large space lease where the landlord is not allowed to increase operating expense escalation over a flat rate per square foot with a small increase per annum not to exceed a certain percentage throughout the term of the lease until such time as the building is 90% or greater occupied by tenants. This small increased limitation has significantly hampered the landlord, since the landlord in that instance expected to be about 90% leased within the first two years. The odds are that it may not be 90% occupied for quite some time, if ever.

The vehicle for issuing statements of operating expense escalation, and for the challenge and review thereof, is subject to wide disagreement among practitioners. I will take the risk of saying what I think is fair, and that is that operating expenses should be reflected on a consistent basis from year to year and based upon generally accepted accounting practices as applied by those certified public accountants practicing generally in the first class building market in a particular locale. The expense statements should be in sufficient one line item detail so as to provide a tenant with relevant information and should be in that same detail and prepared the same way from year to year. I do not believe there should be a mini statute of limitations on the right of a tenant to review the expenses or to correct errors, nor should there be a limitation on the landlord's right to correct previously issued statements or issue statements when it has failed to so do. The landlord should have the right to collect operating expense escalations and reasonable estimated installments monthly in arrears and be able to adjust for unanticipated significant increases, but not by more than 3% over the previous year's line item amount. I believe landlords and tenants should reconcile these estimated payments within 30 days after the end of any lease year, and that any underpayments or overpayments should be recouped with interest carried until paid. I also personally believe that disputes evolving out of expense or tax escalations should be decided by arbitrators with 15 years experience in the management of commercial real property and litigation should be avoided. Litigation is an imprecise way of trying to get a lay person through a lot of custom, practice and sophisticated standards and then apply

·

some fairly sophisticated detail in concise contract law thereto. This leaves a lot of room for errors in the administration of the intention of the parties when those who do this all the time are better able to interpret the intent of the contract and apply it to what is custom and practice in the area based on the terms of art used in the lease. It also saves a lot of time and a lot of money.

Consumer Price Index

Landlords typically like to keep the profit portion of their base rent from eroding due to inflation over the years of the lease. If one could believe that all operating and other escalation calculations were merely a pass through of the actual increase in cost to landlord to operate the building and that only 100% of the increases were passed on and reimbursed by the tenant and that, otherwise, the sum of the base years for escalation fit into the base rent number with the appropriate profit portion that the tenant believes is reasonable for a landlord, then I have no problem with the application of the Consumer Price Index to obviate the impact of inflation on the buying power of the profit portion of the base rent dollars to the landlord. Those are a lot of hurdles to jump, and I have not yet met a landlord who could hurdle each one of them with clean hands. Assuming I did, then we could unbundle the particular components of base rent and might find out that somewhere between 15 and 25% of the base rent is profit, and therefore an application of an increase in inflation from year to year on the base rent will be applied only to the extent of the profit portion and in the best case, would not be greater than 25%. I, along with most, disagree as to the type of price index; whether it should be the GNP Deflator Index which has a different bread basket of items than the Consumer Price Index or not is subject to a debate that I will opt out of. One might note that the largest components of the bread basket of items associated with the running and operating of the building would be the increase in the labor rates and the increase in the cost of energy and fuel. Some people tie the escalation to the percentage increase in the rates or costs (two different concepts, you will note) of electricity charges or gas or steam charges, or quite frankly a combination of all three with different rates in the calculation to the portion of the fixed rent. I am sure that you are just as good at modelling numbers and impacts as I am, and I will leave that decision to the economists. The only issues that I feel strongly about are that the deflation mechanism only be applied to the portion of the base rent which is truly otherwise not adjusted for increases in cost, and that is of course the true profit portion, and that the application of whatever formulae is done in such a way that subtle compounding does not occur. An example of compounding, however small, occurs when you take a base rent and add to it the adjustment from one year to the next of the application of the deflator, and the next year take the adjusted base rent and again add to it the next year's adjustment. If you were always to use the original base rent net of any rent inclusion, electric or other type of components and figure the additional rent for that escalation each year, based on a comparison of the current year's deflator index to the first year index, you would have a fair reflection of the intended purpose. Additionally, some landlords, I am sure quite by accident, adjust the base year with the previous year's results of the calculation, except the calculation is based on a comparison of the current year to the base year each time. Believe it or not, I have seen clauses that are read in that way which causes the base rent and even a marginally inflationary period to actually exponentiate. Similarly, such exponentiating equations have found their way to applications on some line items of items in the operating expense clauses, such as the management fee. These are subtly written and rarely understood by lawyers and laymen but must be guarded against.

Escalations in Summary

I guess if you are responsible for the facilities move, and you want to keep your job, you just have to make sure with respect to escalations of the following:

1. Your firm is only paying for its proportionate share of actual taxes paid by the building on the building and not on two football fields attached to some church or city leased, or owned property on the combined tax lot, or on a garage which is built in the building but is used by everybody publicly.

2. If taxes go down on the building that your escalations do not go up by the same amount of the tax saving for the landlord in the base year.

3. If the building is being operated and there is an operating expense escalation that you are only paying for appropriate operations of the building and not buildings in the same tax lot, garage and public parking space, whether or not in the building, to manicure and landscape other parcels which will be built on later, capital improvements for the three-floor cafeteria installed by the landlord in the building to service another tenant, or similar retail space to serve the public, capital or other expenditures paid by the landlord to cure defects, violations or hazardous situations or more than 120% of the overall building escalations.

4. That you only pay for your electricity, heat and moving costs not more than three times.

5. That the deflator index formulation does not allow creeping or galloping profit increase, because it is applied to all of the base rent including the electricity factor, all of which are growing on their own nicely from year to year.

6. That your administrator discovered that you are paying escalations not only for other tenants but prior to occupying the premises and maybe even signing the lease.

7. That there is a miscalculation in your taxes or operating expense and that you are not allowed to cause it to be adjusted.

8. That you are paying taxes even though the landlord is not.

9. That you thought that porters' wages were people who picked up your suitcases at the train station and brought them to the office and you found that those charges were also included in your lease.

CHAPTER 21

SECURITY

This is clearly a misnomer. Security is what the facilities director thought he had when he saw the nice premises in the beautiful building and felt cozy about moving in. This clause also has nothing to do with the fact that you feel you have contracted for certain benefits and services, but what has really happened is you have contracted to pay certain rent on the chance you may occupy your premises and get certain services without any particular guarantees. This is really a section that deals with the security of the landlord at night when he knows that in the event that you may stumble and fall on the several thousand potential default obligations of a tenant under the lease, he will be comfortable because he has some months worth of additional rent prepaid in a deposit called security. Of course the tenant's concern is to minimize security or at least to cause its impact on its balance sheet or at the bank to be felt as little as possible. There are several ways to minimize the impact of security requirements of the landlord. The one that merely shifts the reflection of the security is by an undertaking or a guarantee of an affiliated or unaffiliated company or person for a finite amount of the obligation of payment or performance under the lease. Another way is to deposit securities that have a discounted price, but at maturity equal or exceed the security amount. Another way is to deposit securities equal to the face amount with coupons or interest either going to the landlord or to the tenant as negotiated. Another way which is most popular is the issuance of a sight letter of credit in a form which is generally referred to as clean and evergreen from the tenant's bank to the landlord. The last way of course is to provide cash which should be in a segregated trust account, naming the tenant, benefiting the landlord and insured with interest accounted for and flowing in the agreed manner. Once you have decided the amount and the manner of the security, how it is dealt with by the landlord in the event of default and the timing should be carefully negotiated. For instance, a landlord should not have the right to draw down security unless all of the notice periods and grace periods for cure of the default have occurred. Additionally, if security is allowed to be pulled under the terms of the lease only so much thereof as is required to cure the default should be allowed to be withdrawn, and it should be fully accounted for and only applied in a reasonable manner strictly in accordance with the terms of the lease. A tenant should never deposit security designated as rent payments in advance for some particular portion of the term. This does not carry the same protection as security deposited as security to be held in trust and to be applied as is appropriate. Additionally in the event of the sale of the building, these two types of deposits will be treated differently and only if properly delineated and maintained by the landlord will the tenant be assured of receiving credit for the money deposited. In the event of partial draws of the deposit, the tenant should be notified in advance, have a full accounting and be allowed to replenish the security in the manner provided under the lease. Careful attention should be given to see that there are no liquidated damages where the security is applied and whether or not there are actual costs associated with it. Lastly, any assignment of the security should only go from one landlord to another landlord and only occur provided the preceding landlord assumes the obligations to deal with the security in the manner required under the lease. I see many instances where facility managers have lost their client security as well as their job security by not giving careful scrutiny to security deposit sections of leases.

CHAPTER 22

QUIET ENJOYMENT

This paragraph will have little to do with the hollering that will go on between landlords and tenants and other noise during the term of the lease. This is a legal term of art that has to do with the tenant enjoying its premises, both the benefit of the premises and the ability to operate its intended business in accordance with the terms of the granting without interference from the landlord, and, if written right, from anyone else. Unfortunately these clauses are not written right for a variety of reasons. Assuming by now you know not to care what the reasons are but to get it right, I will take a few moments to try and help the reader through the arcane taverns of the importance of this small clause. Quiet enjoyment means if you perform under your lease and pay your rent that you should be able to do with the premises what you are allowed to do with the premises under the lease for the entire term without anybody else interfering. Anybody else, as we have discovered, means the landlord, people with superior titles such as fee owners, ground lessors or space sublessors and also includes fee and leasehold mortgagees and others who have liens and rights of foreclosure on the building in which the lease should be sacrosanct. There are priorities and timing differences which do not necessarily allow a lease to receive all of this quiet enjoyment protection, and many clauses for those reasons do not give you the full protection you are entitled to. One must make sure that if rent is paid that the obligations of the landlord to perform are unconditional and that if the lease is otherwise subordinate to other superior interest holders, that non-disturbance and recognition agreements are received as necessary from those other interest holders and properly recite the protection expected, and this clause then must provide that the quiet enjoyment will be enjoyed without hindrance from any of those people or anyone else claiming through landlord, under landlord or otherwise. In the event of a breach to this clause, the limitation of the landlord's liability to the interest of the landlord in the building or any exculpation of liability is totally inappropriate since at that particular time there probably will not be any interest in the building and probably something has occurred that should bypass that limitation in any event.

A landlord cannot quibble greatly with this because the clause only gives rise to damages which may be paid only if the landlord has money and/or the building. Beware of consultants, brokers, instant geniuses and experts and other lawyers who may decide that this clause is merely boiler-plate. That term should mean to any facilities manager when he hears it that the facilities manager will be the one boiled on the plate if the clauses are not carefully scrutinized, even though they look beautiful because they are preprinted or highly engraved on a nice piece of parchment paper. They hurt just as much no matter how nicely or formally they are presented.

CHAPTER 23

WORK LETTER

Work Letter is the name given to either a serious exhibit or the last section of a lease that either deals with the work to be performed by landlord and/or tenant in the premises, or sometimes better reviewed from the prospective of the work not to be performed by anybody except at large cost in the demised premises. Work letters are the least understood and the most dangerous of lease components which rank in the level of understanding of the rent inclusion electric clauses, but are guaranteed to cost more money, more time and waste more careers in more fields. This section is probably the single most acclaimed section of a lease for causing the downfall of the largest number of facilities directors over the last ten years. Same with architects. The reason for this, I suspect, is that a work letter usually tells what you can find in your demised premises that already exists, such as the basic core of the building and the shell of the building, together with, in non-layman and generally quite specific terms of art, a description of the electricity or, better stated at this point, the power deliverable to the floor (as opposed to delivered or existing at the floor), heating, ventilating and air conditioning (if provided at all) deliverable to a point outside the demised premises, fire and alarm systems deliverable to a point at the demised premises, sprinklerization if any, lights and other equipment if provided, water columns and hot and cold water, and any waste pipe systems. The way these things are written bear little resemblance to what I just said. Usually, you find the work letter is made up of two concepts. The first concept is what the tenant has to do to provide plans for approval of the landlord and how to deal with the basic work and any unusual work that is going to be included in the premises, as well as penalties, delays and cooperation language. The other section of the work letter deals with what is available or already exists. Usually what exists is in dimensions, numbers, measurements and quality schedules. What will be given, which is usually called building-based standard materials, usually deals with what is available to be provided by landlord and in what quantities in order to be utilized within the demised premises. Two things should be very carefully focused on in the work letter discussion at this point. The first is materials, which does not discuss labor to incorporate the materials in the premises. Materials also do not necessarily represent that all of the materials that are necessary for that particular component are included. For a component for instance which is a door, you need a frame, hardware which includes hinges, doorknobs and doorjambs, together with the door. The cost to incorporate all those materials and actually hang the frame and door is usually not described. This must be ascertained together with unusual field conditions in case you need taller or shorter doors than in most premises. The next issue addressed usually in a backhanded way is that this is the only place in a lease that you will find, without fail, everything being based on a truly carpetable square footage area. As you might notice on some premises, if there is a loss factor approaching 30%, you will only be getting approximately 68 to 70% of the materials and labor you think you are for your premises which you understand to be larger than it is. These three tiny omissions are probably the largest source of problems for tenants. A tenant usually brings its architect and engineer and tenant improvement coordinator consultant in after the lease is either fully negotiated or fully executed. That is a very bad time to find out that what the landlord says he is providing in the way of materials and possibly labor is far short of what is necessary to complete the premises. Additionally, all the grand ideas that the tenant had to have beautiful doors, unusual windows, angular partitions, etc. are usually blown out of the water at that point in time when the architect explains in the budget process that the landlord's charges for these types of work are so astronomical as to make even completing the premises in a standard way a difficulty as opposed to a given. Checking, pricing and evaluating the work letter deficiencies really is something that should be done at the beginning of the lease negotiation. As a matter of fact, savvy tenants have their work coordinators, architects and engineering consultants in place at the time that multiple premises are being evaluated as candidates for the move. At that point, the comparison of what we call apples to apples can be accomplished since the work letter itself can constitute 125 to 150% in the average of the first year's charges for the premises. As you will note, this exceeds all rents, escalations and the entire move cost of furniture, fixtures and equipment. Careful analysis of these deficiencies and negotiation by counsel together with the construction team can save hundreds of thousands of dollars very easily, even on a 15 to 20,000 square foot space. There is no justification whatsoever for not bringing the team together with counsel prior to negotiation of specific leases. This is merely penny wise and the loss of value through negotiation of the work letter is immense.

The other type of work letter content is where you have a very simple work letter that states that the landlord agrees to build the premises to the specifications and drawings, either appended to the lease or as agreed to by landlord and tenant. The only safe way is to do the plans, layouts and specifications prior to signing the lease. This is quite easy since the work can be based on preliminary layout and preliminary architectural plans with specifications for unusual materials, such as doors or lights. The other specifications will be the power load capability, the heating, ventilating, air conditioning, water, etc. to be utilized by the tenant. This is not a substitute for the negotiation of the requirements throughout the term of the lease contained in the body of the lease in the services section; this merely deals with the delivery of the initial construction of the demised premises at initial occupancy. If you have properly written the work letter that we call a turn-key, then there will be no arguments as to the quantities or quality of the materials, any cost with respect to labor, or whether landlord will add supervision, general conditions or profit calculations to the basic building standard costs. There will also be no arguments as to who is responsible to deliver what premises at what time, or the condition of the premises when delivered. Additionally, charges for freight elevators, hoisting or after time work will not be of issue if written properly. In this type of agreement, the time of delivery, penalties or costs associated with delays in work or failure to deliver it in an appropriate time are all issues that have been dispensed with. In a turn-key agreement, not only does the landlord have all those obligations, the fixed rent and escalations (if you were smart enough to require both) will not commence until the period after delivery of the premises which is called the operating abatement. Otherwise it is a construction and operating abatement mixed together which can be eroded by delays in the landlord's work or in the tenant's work. As we have discussed earlier, it is important to delineate abatement periods for construction and for operation in the event that the landlord is not obligating itself to deliver the premises in any particular condition for the initial occupancy.

Assuming the best case scenario, that is, that the landlord is agreeing to provide all materials and all labor for a fixed sum, or is providing it at no cost to tenant without pricing being determined, and is further agreeing to deliver the premises completed in accordance with the tenant's plans and specifications and otherwise the condition required in the lease on a specified date, then the issue of a construction abatement is not important since the landlord will be utilizing the time for construction as it sees fit. What is important is that the landlord's work does not otherwise encroach upon or erode the operating abatement. This can happen due to landlord delays, force majeure or long delivery times or failure to deliver orders for materials. The only other consideration, after you have insured that there is no encroachment of the construction on your operating abatement period, is that the tenant comply with all the requirements of the landlord in order for the landlord to meet the timetables for construction. Those sorts of delays that are caused by the tenant include late or failure of delivery of the working drawings and plans required by landlord from tenant in order to build the premises, the ordering by tenant of unusually unique materials that will have a long time between order and delivery and may also be of the type that cause additional labor and unusually precise work to occur in order to incorporate them into the project, scope changes of the project by tenant which make the character and utilization of the premises significantly different than anticipated in the original drawings, and a large number of change orders of a tenant that do not otherwise change the scope of the design or the utilization of the premises, but rather result from tenant changing its mind on where it wants its wall socket, switches and partitioning. These changes and delays are usually referred to as tenant delays, and will cause the operating abatement period to erode and may also impact both on penalties and additional costs for the job which will be required to be paid by the tenant. Facilities managers have learned to isolate the user groups of their corporations from the landlord and contractors during the design and build phase, because user groups usually form committees that have fine tuning and additional requirements and requests that occur throughout the construction period. It is mentally interesting to see how a committee involved at the user level can cause a project to change in scope dramatically and run the bill up sometimes as high as 250% of the planned construction cost and cause the abatement period to erode at an alarming rate. There are even some examples where these changes and their impact on the building process have caused penalties to occur which are staggering in proportion to the otherwise significant construction cost. These penalties and costs have been responsible for quite a few tenants being unable to occupy their premises due to their inability to fund the impact cost on their work.

No matter what type of work letter you encounter, attention should be given to compliance with those time requirements and specific working requirements of a tenant set forth in the work letter and also requiring specific time periods for the landlord to comply with. Usually landlords do not undertake to review the tenant's plans within 10 business days and to review resubmitted plans that had been partially rejected within 3 business days. Unless you take the time to require landlord to have time periods and quality performance standards, it will be difficult, if not impossible, when the tenant is charging up tenant delays to be able to adjust them or reduce them, because of landlord's contribution to the delays or additional costs. All these things must be focused upon in order to have an orderly reconciliation at the end of the work for who caused what to whom, and what was the cost associated therewith.

One will also encounter from time to time a landlord that takes a very aggressive hands-on interest in the plan and specification process and may cause the plans to be rewritten and amended for debatable items. Landlords traditionally will attempt to cause the plans to conform with local fire laws and building codes, but there are times when landlords will have special requests. Landlords generally do not take responsibility for the design and specifications of the premises, leaving that to the tenant's architect. However, if a landlord elects to partially reject plans or specifications in order to modify a specific item, the landlord should then take responsibility for the plans and specifications and the impact on the construction job and the ability to obtain certificates of occupancy resulting from this intervention. Most work letters do not cause landlord to have any responsibility whatsoever or even be deemed to be representing that the plans and specifications, when approved, will work in the building or comply with any building type regulations. These responsibilities should be reviewed critically with assignment of responsibility, whether it is a turn-key operation or the tenant is building the premises to suit, to see that those who intervene and cause changes have responsibility for such changes.

Another issue which occurred in a modified turn-key was where the landlord agreed to do whatever work was required by the tenant, had certain building standard materials, and fixed the price of labor at the request of the tenant, but then gave a credit, not representing that the credit would fully defray all the costs of tenant for its build out. If the tenant has been savvy by having its counsel and construction team work out the pricing of the building standard materials and labor, seeing that sufficient materials will be provided for the idea behind the structuring of the premises and a bidding process, or an ability to fairly price out in a non-profit way the work other than building standard, which is usually called tenant's extra work, is imperative. Approval of tenant's extras also should be carefully reviewed so that the long lead time or other cost increasing and abatement period eroding concepts do not surface later in the construction.

If you have taken the time during negotiation to carefully negotiate and prescribe how the premises is to be delivered for receiving construction in the body of the lease, both in compliance, hazardous materials, conditions which would be violations and violations of building, zoning and fire law requirements, then discussing what gets put into the premises by whom, and at what cost and during what period, leaves you 90% complete in your process. The thing that is missing is when all else fails and the premises has been under construction for three times as long as you expected, and it appears for whatever reason, including landlord's intervening bankruptcy, that the premises will not be completed, the tenant then should have what we call a blow-out date, or a date after which the tenant can terminate the lease for failure of landlord to complete the premises. If this is the case, you also have to account for any rentals that may have occurred, and any work payments and materials incorporated into the premises of tenant. Some tenants also wish to take over under a self-help rule and complete the premises and have credits for the costs plus interest carry against the rentals. This is particularly helpful when the landlord finds itself in a bankruptcy situation, but the building is otherwise viable.

This is the conclusion of what I consider the compartmentalization approach to getting your hands around building out and moving into the newly demised premises. If you have properly caused the premises to be delivered for the construction process, and carefully delineated who builds, with what materials, at what cost and in what time period, then you only have to deal with the impacts that occur during the construction process which cause non-compliance with building or zoning or inability to use. Then the process will be which of the architect, the engineer, the construction entity, tenant or landlord has caused the premises to fail to be able to meet the standard of performance required by tenant or to obtain the necessary certification of completion such as a certificate of occupancy. At that point, all of those parties will be pointing fingers at each other, but it will be reasonably able to be determined if you have criteria and benchmarks for the beginning of the process and standards at the end to see who has stepped out of those. Unless you have carefully dealt with the delivery of the premises or the condition at the end and described who has what responsibility for what work in the middle portion, called the construction phase, it will be totally impossible to assign responsibility and therefore liability for increased costs, delays and penalties. Additionally, if there is simultaneous access to the premises for work by tenant during the time that the landlord is doing a turn key construction operation, you will find yourself in a very difficult position trying to sort out the responsibility for impacts possibly caused by tenant's contractors working simultaneously in the construction critical path with landlord's contractors, absent these standards and attention at the beginning and end of the process.

Unless you have a great deal of experience in the construction phase, and that does not mean doing it once or twice over a ten year period, I would suggest that you have in addition to your architect and your general contractor or construction manager, a project management and construction consulting

94

coordinator who in essence is a very experienced facilities manager that does not work on a full time basis as permanently employed by any particular company, but is hired by a company that is anticipating a move to come in-house on a project fee basis and consult on the areas such as reviewing architects, use of the premises, reviewing the lease with the lawyer, supervising and coordinating with the contractor, designing and purchasing telecommunication systems, telephonics and other in-house facility requirements and actually coordinating and retaining the moving company to move and set up the new premises. At this writing there are very few people like that. Most are what are referred to as tenant move coordinators. Tenant move coordinators only coordinate the actual moving of the furniture, furnishings and equipment from one premises to the next. Architects generally coordinate the design and construction phase and sometimes the selection and installation of the telephonics and otherwise, but do not do this in-house. They of course have their own bias and would lose their independence if they did it in-house and they would not be very good watch dogs of themselves anyway. A consultant such as this, whose primary responsibility is to work with the client both for the use of the user group and the people who are responsible for the overall facilities move cost, usually runs about $20,000 to $45,000 or translated to space between $1.00 and $3.00 per rentable square footage of space leased per job. It has been my experience that the few of them that are employed from job to job and move from client to client have saved four and five times their actual costs per project. Now that some of those are joining forces and are actually turning into companies to provide this service without having to move from employer to employer, the state of the art is becoming considerably better, and the breadth of their services considerably more consumer friendly. These people and these companies are considered reasonable expenses both to save money and to increase job security for facilities managers.

NOTES

2

MATERIALS REFLECTING FUNDAMENTAL BUSINESS TERMS FOR OFFICE AND MIXED USE / RETAIL PROJECTS

submitted by John B. Wood

STANDARD FORM OF OFFICE LEASE
The Real Estate Board of New York, Inc.

Agreement of Lease, made as of this ▮▮▮▮ day of September 1997 ▮▮▮▮, between

▮▮▮▮▮▮▮▮▮▮▮▮▮▮ party of the first part, hereinafter referred to as OWNER, ~~and~~ or sometimes LANDLORD, and the ▮▮▮▮▮▮▮▮▮▮.

party of the second part, hereinafter referred to as TENANT,

Witnesseth: Owner hereby leases to Tenant and Tenant hereby hires from Owner certain premises (the "Initial Delivery Premises") as set forth in Schedule A, attached hereto (the "Demised Premises" or sometimes "Premises" or "demised premises") in the building known as ▮▮▮▮▮▮▮ in the Borough of ▮▮▮▮▮ , City of New York, for the term of as set forth in Article 40

~~(or until such term shall sooner cease and expire as hereinafter provided) to commence on the day of nineteen hundred and , and to end on the day of and both dates inclusive,~~ at an annual rental rate ~~of~~ as set forth in Article 40.

~~which Tenant agrees to pay in lawful money of the United States which shall be legal tender in payment of all debts and dues,~~ public and private, at the time of payment, in equal monthly installments in advance on the first day of each month during said term, at the office of Owner or such other place as Owner may designate, without any set off or deduction whatsoever, except ~~that Tenant shall pay the first monthly installment(s) on the execution hereof (unless this lease be a renewal).~~

In the event that, at the commencement of the term of this lease, or thereafter, Tenant shall be in default in the payment of rent to Owner pursuant to the terms of another lease with Owner or with Owner's predecessor in interest, Owner may at Owner's option and without notice to Tenant add the amount of such arrears to any monthly installment of rent payable hereunder and the same shall be payable to Owner as additional rent.

The parties hereto, for themselves, their heirs, distributees, executors, administrators, legal representatives, successors and assigns, hereby covenant as follows:

Rent: 1. Tenant shall pay the rent as above and as hereinafter provided

Occupancy: 2. Tenant shall use and occupy demised premises for any lawful purpose and as executive, operational and general operations offices and for no other purpose.

Tenant Alterations: 3. Tenant shall make no changes in or to the demised premises of any nature without Owner's prior written consent. Subject to the prior written consent of Owner, and to the provisions of this article, Tenant, at Tenant's expense, may make alterations, installations, additions or improvements which are non-structural and which do not affect utility services or plumbing and electrical lines, in or to the interior of the demised premises by using contractors or mechanics first approved in each instance by Owner. Tenant shall, before making any alterations, additions, installations or improvements, at its expense, obtain all permits, approvals and certificates required by any governmental or quasi-governmental bodies and (upon completion) certificates of final approval thereof and shall deliver promptly duplicates of all such permits, approvals and certificates to Owner and Tenant agrees to carry and will cause Tenant's contractors and sub-contractors to carry such workman's compensation, general liability, personal and property damage insurance as Owner may require. If any mechanic's lien is filed against the demised premises, or the building of which the same forms a part, for work claimed to have been done for, or materials furnished to, Tenant, whether or not done pursuant to this article, the same shall be discharged by Tenant within thirty days thereafter, at Tenant's expense, by payment or filing the bond required by law. All fixtures and all panelling, partitions, railings and like installations, installed in the premises at any time, either by Tenant or by Owner on Tenant's behalf, shall, upon installation, become the property of Owner and shall remain upon and be surrendered with the demised premises unless Owner, by notice to Tenant no later than twenty days prior to the date fixed as the termination of this lease, elects to relinquish Owner's right thereto and to have them removed by Tenant, in which event the same shall be removed from the premises by Tenant prior to the expiration of the term, at Tenant's expense. Nothing in this Article shall be construed to give Owner title to or to prevent Tenant's removal of trade fixtures, moveable office furniture and equipment, but upon removal of any such from the premises or upon removal of other installations as may be required by Owner, Tenant shall immediately and at its expense, repair and restore the premises to the condition existing prior to installation and repair any damage to the demised premises or the building due to such removal. All property permitted or required to be removed, by Tenant at the end of the term remaining in the premises after Tenant's removal shall be deemed abandoned and may, at the election of Owner, either be retained as Owner's property or may be removed from the premises by Owner, at Tenant's expense.

Maintenance and Repairs: 4. Tenant shall, throughout the term of this lease, take good care of the demised premises and the fixtures and appurtenances therein. Tenant shall be responsible for all damage or injury to the demised premises or any other part of the building and the systems and equipment thereof, whether requiring structural or nonstructural repairs caused by or resulting from carelessness, omission, neglect or improper conduct of Tenant, Tenant's subtenants, agents, employees, invitees or licensees, or which arise out of any work, labor, service or equipment done for or supplied to Tenant or any subtenant or arising out of the installation, use or operation of the property or equipment of Tenant or any subtenant. Tenant

shall also repair all damage to the building and the demised premises caused by the moving of Tenant's fixtures, furniture and equipment. Tenant shall promptly make, at Tenant's expense, all repairs in and to the demised premises for which Tenant is responsible, using only the contractor for the trade or trades in question, selected from a list of at least two contractors per trade submitted by Owner. Any other repairs in or to the building or the facilities and systems thereof for which Tenant is responsible shall be performed by Owner at the Tenant's expense. Owner shall maintain in good working order and repair the exterior and the structural portions of the building, including the structural portions of its demised premises, and the public portions of the building interior and the building plumbing, electrical, heating and ventilating systems (to the extent such systems presently exist) serving the demised premises. Tenant agrees to give prompt notice of any defective condition in the premises for which Owner may be responsible hereunder. There shall be no allowance to Tenant for diminution of rental value and no liability on the part of Owner by reason of inconvenience, annoyance or injury to business arising from Owner or others making repairs, alterations, additions or improvements in or to any portion of the building or the demised premises or in and to the fixtures, appurtenances or equipment thereof. It is specifically agreed that Tenant shall not be entitled to any setoff or reduction of rent by reason of any failure of Owner to comply with the covenants of this or any other article of this Lease. Tenant agrees that Tenant's sole remedy at law in such instance will be by way of an action for damages for breach of contract. The provisions of this Article 4 shall not apply in the case of fire or other casualty which are dealt with in Article 9 hereof.

Window Cleaning: 5. Tenant will not clean nor require, permit, suffer or allow any window in the demised premises to be cleaned from the outside in violation of Section 202 of the Labor Law or any other applicable law or of the Rules of the Board of Standards and Appeals, or of any other Board or body having or asserting jurisdiction.

Requirements of Law, Fire Insurance, Floor Loads: 6. Prior to the commencement of the lease term, if Tenant is then in possession, and at all times thereafter, Tenant, at Tenant's sole cost and expense, shall promptly comply with all present and future laws, orders and regulations of all state, federal, municipal and local governments, departments, commissions and boards and any direction of any public officer pursuant to law, and all orders, rules and regulations of the New York Board of Fire Underwriters, Insurance Services Office, or any similar body which shall impose any violation, order or duty upon Owner or Tenant with respect to the demised premises, whether or not arising out of Tenant's use or manner of use thereof, (including Tenant's permitted use) or, with respect to the building if arising out of Tenant's use or manner of use of the premises or the building (including the use permitted under the lease). Nothing herein shall require Tenant to make structural repairs or alterations unless Tenant has, by its manner of use of the demised premises or method of operation therein, violated any such laws, ordinances, orders, rules, regulations or requirements with respect thereto. Tenant may, after securing Owner to

10 Owner's satisfaction against all damages, interest, penalties and expenses, including, but not limited to, reasonable attorney's fees, by cash deposit or by surety bond in an amount and in a company satisfactory to Owner, contest and appeal any such laws, ordinances, orders, rules, regulations or requirements provided same is done with all reasonable promptness and provided such appeal shall not subject Owner to prosecution for a criminal offense or constitute a default under any lease or mortgage under which Owner may be obligated, or cause the demised premises or any part thereof to be condemned or vacated. Tenant shall not do or permit any act or thing to be done in or to the demised premises which is contrary to law, or which will invalidate or be in conflict with public liability, fire or other policies of insurance at any time carried by or for the benefit of Owner with respect to the demised premises or the building of which the demised premises form a part, or which shall or might subject Owner to any liability or responsibility to any person or for property damage. Tenant shall not keep anything in the demised premises except as now or hereafter permitted by the Fire Department, Board of Fire Underwriters, Fire Insurance Rating Organization or other authority having jurisdiction, and then only in such manner and such quantity so as not to increase the rate for fire insurance applicable to the building, nor use the premises in a manner which will increase the insurance rate for the building or any property located therein over that in effect prior to the commencement of Tenant's occupancy. Tenant shall pay all costs, expenses, fines, penalties, or damages, which may be imposed upon Owner by reason of Tenant's failure to comply with the provisions of this article and if by reason of such failure the fire insurance rate shall, at the beginning of this lease or at any time thereafter, be higher than it otherwise would be, then Tenant shall reimburse Owner, as additional rent hereunder, for that portion of all fire insurance premiums thereafter paid by Owner which shall have been charged because of such failure by Tenant. In any action or proceeding wherein Owner and Tenant are parties, a schedule or "make-up" of rate for the building or demised premises issued by the New York Fire Insurance Exchange, or other body making fire insurance rates applicable to said premises shall be conclusive evidence of
11 the ~~facts~~ therein stated and of the several items and charges in the fire insurance rates then applicable to said premises. Tenant shall not place a load upon any floor of the demised premises exceeding the floor load per square foot area which it was designed to carry and which is allowed by law. Owner reserves the right to prescribe the weight and position of all safes, business machines and mechanical equipment. Such installations shall be placed and maintained by Tenant, at Tenant's expense, in settings sufficient, in Owner's judgement, to absorb and prevent vibration, noise and annoy-
12 ance.

Subordination: 7. This lease is subject and subordinate to all ground or underlying leases and to all mortgages which may now or hereafter affect such leases or the real property of which demised premises are a part and to all renewals, modifications, consolidations, replacements and extensions of any such underlying leases and mortgages. This clause shall be self-operative and no further instrument of subordination shall be required by any ground or underlying lessor or by any mortgagee, affecting any lease or the real property of which the demised premises are a part. In confirmation of such subordination, Tenant shall from time to time execute promptly any certificate that Owner may request. 13

Property Loss, Damage Reimbursement Indemnity: 8. Owner or its agents shall not be liable for any damage to property of Tenant or of others entrusted to employees of the building, nor for loss of or damage to any property of Tenant by theft or otherwise, nor for any injury or damage to persons or property resulting from any cause of whatsoever nature, unless caused by or due to the negligence of Owner, its agents, servants or employees. Owner or its agents will not be liable for any such damage caused by other tenants or persons in, upon or about said building or caused by operations in construction of any private, public or quasi public work. If at any time any windows of the demised premises are temporarily closed, darkened or bricked up (or permanently closed, darkened or bricked up, if required by law) for any reason whatsoever including, but not limited to Owner's own acts, Owner shall not be liable for any damage Tenant may sustain thereby and Tenant shall not be entitled to any compensation therefor nor abatement or diminution of rent nor shall the same release Tenant from its obligations hereunder nor constitute an eviction. Tenant shall indemnify and save harmless Owner against and from all liabilities, obligations, damages,
14 penalties, claims, costs and expenses for which Owner shall not be reimbursed by insurance, including reasonable attorneys fees, paid, suffered or incurred as a result of any breach by Tenant, Tenant's agents, contractors, employees, invitees, or licensees, of any covenant or condition of this lease, or the carelessness, negligence or improper conduct of the Tenant, Tenant's agents, contractors, employees, invitees or licensees. Tenant's liability under this lease extends to the acts and omissions of any sub-tenant, and any agent, contractor, employee, invitee or licensee of any
15 sub-tenant. In case any action or proceeding is brought against Owner by reason of any such claim, Tenant, ~~upon written~~ notice from Owner, will, at Tenant's expense, resist or defend such action or proceeding by counsel approved by Owner in writing, such approval not to be unreasonably withheld.
16

Destruction, Fire and Other Casualty: 9. (a) If the demised premises or any part thereof shall be damaged by fire or other casualty, Tenant shall give immediate notice thereof to Owner and this lease shall continue in full force and effect except
as hereinafter set forth. (b) If the demised premises are partially damaged 17
or rendered partially unusable by fire or other casualty, the damages thereto shall be repaired by and at the expense of Owner and the rent and other items of additional rent, until such repair shall be substantially completed, shall be apportioned from the day following the casualty according to the part of the premises which is usable. (c) If the demised premises are totally
damaged or rendered wholly unusable by fire or other casualty, then the 17
rent and other items of additional rent as hereinafter expressly provided shall be proportionately paid up to the time of the casualty and thenceforth shall cease until the date when the premises shall have been repaired and restored by Owner (or sooner reoccupied in part by Tenant then rent shall be apportioned as provided in subsection (b) above), subject to Owner's right to elect not to restore the same as hereinafter provided. (d) If the
demised premises are rendered wholly unusable for (whether or not the 17
demised premises are damaged in whole or in part) if the building shall be so damaged that Owner shall decide to demolish it or to rebuild it, then, in any of such events, Owner may elect to terminate this lease by written notice to Tenant, given within 90 days after such fire or casualty, or 30 days after adjustment of the insurance claim for such fire or casualty, whichever is sooner, specifying a date for the expiration of the lease, which date shall not be more than 60 days after the giving of such notice, and upon the date specified in such notice the term of this lease shall expire as fully and completely as if such date were the date set forth above for the termination of this lease and Tenant shall forthwith quit, surrender and vacate the premises without prejudice however, to Landlord's rights and remedies against Tenant under the lease provisions in effect prior to such termination, and any rent owing shall be paid up to such date and any payments of rent made by Tenant which were on account of any period subsequent to such date shall be returned to Tenant. ~~Unless Owner shall serve a termination notice as provided for herein, Owner shall make the repairs and restorations under the conditions of (b) and (c) hereof, with all reasonable expedition, subject to delays due to adjustment of insurance claims, labor~~ 18
~~troubles and causes beyond Owner's control~~. After any such casualty, Tenant shall cooperate with Owner's restoration by removing from the premises as promptly as reasonably possible, all of Tenant's salvageable inventory and moveable equipment, furniture, and other property. Tenant's
liability for rent shall resume five (5) days after written notice from Owner 19
that the premises are substantially ready for Tenant's occupancy. (e) Nothing contained hereinabove shall relieve Tenant from liability that may
exist as a result of damage from fire or other casualty. Notwithstanding 20
the foregoing, including Owner's obligation to restore under subparagraph (b) above, each party shall look first to any insurance in its favor before making any claim against the other party for recovery for loss or damage resulting from fire or other casualty, and to the extent that such insurance is in force and collectible and to the extent permitted by law, Owner and Tenant each hereby releases and waives all right of recovery with respect to subparagraphs (b), (d), and (e) above, against the other or any one claiming through or under each of them by way of subrogation or otherwise. The release and waiver herein referred to shall be deemed to include any loss or damage to the demised premises and/or to any personal property, equipment, trade fixtures, goods and merchandise located therein. The foregoing release and waiver shall be in force only if both releasors' insurance policies contain a clause providing that such a release or waiver shall not invalidate the insurance. If, and to the extent, that such waiver can be obtained only by the payment of additional premiums, then the party benefiting from the waiver shall pay such premium within ten days after written demand or shall be deemed to have agreed that the party obtaining insurance coverage shall be free of any further obligation under the provisions hereof with respect to waiver of subrogation. Tenant acknowledges that Owner will not carry insurance on Tenant's furniture and/or furnishings or any fixtures or equipment, improvements, or appurtenances removable by Tenant and agrees that Owner will not be obligated to repair any damage thereto or replace the same. (f) Tenant hereby waives the provisions of Section 227 of the Real Property Law and agrees that the provisions of this article shall govern and control in lieu thereof.

Eminent Domain: 10. If the whole or any part of the demised premises shall be acquired or condemned by Eminent Domain for any public or quasi public use or purpose, then and in that event, the term of this lease shall cease and terminate from the date of title vesting in such proceeding and Tenant shall
have no claim for the value of any unexpired term of said lease and assigns 21
to Owner, Tenant's entire interest in any such award. Tenant shall have the
right to make an independent claim to the condemning authority for the 22
value of Tenant's moving expenses and personal property, trade fixtures and equipment, provided Tenant is entitled pursuant to the terms of the lease to remove such property, trade fixture and equipment at the end of the term and provided further such claim does not reduce Owner's award.

Assignment, Mortgage, Etc.: 11. Tenant, for itself, its heirs, distributees, executors, administrators, legal representative, successor and assigns, expressly covenants that it shall not assign, mortgage or encumber this agreement, nor underlet, or suffer or permit the demised premises or any part thereof to be used by others, without the prior written consent of Owner in each instance. Transfer of the majority of the stock of a corporate Tenant or the majority partnership interest of a partnership Tenant shall be deemed an assignment. If this lease be assigned, or if the demised premises or any part thereof be underlet or occupied by anybody other than Tenant, Owner may, after default by Tenant, collect rent from the assignee, under-tenant or occupant, and apply the net amount collected to the rent herein reserved, but no such assignment, underletting, occupancy or collection shall be deemed a waiver of this covenant, or the acceptance of the assignee, under-tenant or occupant as tenant, or a release of Tenant from the further performance by Tenant of covenants on the part of Tenant herein contained. The consent by Owner to an assignment or underletting shall not in any wise be construed to relieve Tenant from obtaining the express consent in writing of Owner to any further assignment or underletting. 23

Electric Current: 12. Rates and conditions in respect to submetering or rent inclusion, as the case may be, to be added in RIDER attached hereto. Tenant covenants and agrees that at all times its use of electric current shall not exceed the capacity of existing feeders to the building or the risers or wiring installation and Tenant may not use any electrical equipment which, in Owner's opinion, reasonably exercised, will overload such installations or interfere with the use thereof by other tenants of the building. The change at any time of the character of electric service shall in no wise make Owner liable or responsible to Tenant, for any loss, damages or expenses which Tenant may sustain.

Access to Premises: 13. Owner or Owner's agents shall have the right (but shall not be obligated) to enter the demised premises in any emergency at any time, and, at other reasonable times, to examine the same and to make such repairs, replacements and improvements as Owner may deem necessary and reasonably desirable to the demised premises or to any other portion of the building or
which Owner may elect to perform. Tenant shall permit Owner to use and 24
maintain and replace pipes and conduits in and through the demised premises and to erect new pipes and conduits therein provided they are concealed within the walls, floor, or ceiling. Owner may, during the progress of any work in the demised premises, take all necessary materials and equipment into said premises without the same constituting an eviction nor shall the Tenant be entitled to any abatement of rent while such work is in progress nor to any damages by reason of loss or interruption of business or otherwise. Throughout the term hereof Owner shall have the right to enter the demised premises at reasonable hours for the purpose of showing the same to prospective purchasers or mortgagees of the building, and during the last six months of the term for the purpose of showing the

Rider to be added if necessary.

5 same to prospective tenants. If Tenant is not present to open and permit an entry into the demised premises, Owner or Owner's agents may enter the same whenever such entry may be necessary or permissible by master key or forcibly and provided reasonable care is exercised to safeguard Tenant's property, such entry shall not render Owner or its agents liable therefor, nor in any event shall the obligations of Tenant hereunder be
26 affected. If during the last month of the term Tenant shall have removed all or substantially all of Tenant's property therefrom Owner may
immediately enter, alter, renovate or redecorate the demised premises 27
~~without limitation or abatement of rent, or incurring liability to Tenant for any compensation and such act shall have no effect on this lease or Tenant's~~
28 ~~obligations hereunder.~~

Vault, Vault Space, Area: 14. No Vaults, vault space or area, whether or not enclosed or covered, not within the property line of the building is leased hereunder, anything contained in or indicated on any sketch, blue print or plan, or anything contained elsewhere in this lease to the contrary notwithstanding. Owner makes no representation as to the location of the property line of the building. All vaults and vault space and all such areas not within the property line of the building, which Tenant may be permitted to use and/or occupy, is to be used and/or occupied under a revocable license, and if any such license be revoked, or if the amount of such space or area be diminished or required by any federal, state or municipal authority or public utility, Owner shall not be subject to any liability nor shall Tenant be entitled to any compensation or diminution or abatement of rent, nor shall such revocation, diminution or requisition be deemed constructive or actual eviction. Any tax, fee or charge of municipal authorities for such vault or area shall be paid by Tenant.

Occupancy: 15. Tenant will not at any time use or occupy the demised premises in violation of the certificate of occupancy issued for the building of which the demised premises are a part. Tenant has inspected the premises and accepts them as is, subject to the riders annexed hereto, ~~with respect to Owner's work, if any. In any event,~~
29 Owner makes no representation as to ~~the condition of~~ the premises and Tenant agrees to ~~accept the same~~ subject to violations, whether or not of ~~record~~.

Bankruptcy: 16. (a) Anything elsewhere in this lease to the contrary notwithstanding, this lease may be cancelled by Owner by the sending of a written notice to Tenant within a reasonable time after the happening of any one or more of the following events: (1) the commencement of a case in bankruptcy or under the laws of
30 any state naming Tenant as the debtor; or (2) the making by Tenant of an assignment or any other arrangement for the benefit of creditors under any state statute. Neither Tenant nor any person claiming through or under Tenant, or by reason of any statute or order of court, shall thereafter be entitled to possession of the premises demised but shall forthwith quit and surrender the premises. If this lease shall be assigned in accordance with its terms, the provisions of this Article 16 shall be applicable only to the
party then owning Tenant's interest in this lease. 31

(b) it is stipulated and agreed that in the event of the termination of this lease pursuant to (a) hereof, Owner shall forthwith, notwithstanding any other provisions of this lease to the contrary, be entitled to recover from Tenant as and for liquidated damages an amount equal to the difference between the rent reserved hereunder for the unexpired portion of the term demised and the fair and reasonable rental value of the demised premises for the same period. In the computation of such damages the difference between any installment of rent becoming due hereunder after the date of termination and the fair and reasonable rental value of the demised premises for the period for which such installment was payable shall be discounted to the date of termination at the rate of four percent (4%) per annum. If such premises or any part thereof be re-let by the Owner for the unexpired term of said lease, or any part thereof, before presentation of proof of such liquidated damages to any court, commission or tribunal, the amount of rent reserved upon such re-letting shall be deemed to be the fair and reasonable rental value for the part or the whole of the premises so re-let during the term of the re-letting. Nothing herein contained shall limit or prejudice the right of the Owner to prove for and obtain as liquidated damages by reason of such termination, an amount equal to the maximum allowed by any statute or rule of law in effect at the time when, and governing the proceedings in which, such damages are to be proved, whether or not such amount be greater, equal to, or less than the amount of the difference referred to above.

Default: 17. (1) If Tenant defaults in fulfilling any of the covenants of this lease ~~other than the covenants for the payment of rent or additional rent~~; or if the demised premises become ~~vacant or~~ deserted; or if any execution or attachment shall be issued against Tenant or any of Tenant's property whereupon the demised premises shall be taken or occupied by someone other than Tenant; or if this lease be rejected under §235 of Title 11 of the U.S. Code (bankruptcy code); ~~or if Tenant shall fail to move into or take possession of the premises within thirty (30) days after the commencement of the term of this lease~~, then, in any one or more of such events, upon Owner serving a written fifteen (15) days notice upon Tenant specifying the nature of said default and upon the expiration of said fifteen (15) days, if Tenant shall have failed to comply with or remedy such default, or if the said default or omission complained of shall be of a nature that the same cannot be completely cured or remedied within said fifteen (15) day period, and if Tenant shall not have diligently commenced curing such default within such fifteen (15) day period, and shall not thereafter with reasonable diligence and in good faith, proceed to
remedy or cure such default, then Owner may serve a written ~~five (5)~~ days' 32
notice of cancellation of this lease upon Tenant, and upon the expiration of 32
said ~~five (5)~~ days this lease and the term thereunder shall end and expire as
fully and completely as if the expiration of such ~~five (5)~~ day period were the 32
day herein definitely fixed for the end and expiration of this lease and the term thereof and Tenant shall then quit and surrender the demised premises to Owner but Tenant shall remain liable as hereinafter provided.

(2) If the notice provided for in (1) hereof shall have been given, and the term shall expire as aforesaid; or if Tenant shall make default in the payment of the rent reserved herein or any item of additional rent herein mentioned or any part of either or in making any other payment
herein required; then and in any of such events Owner may ~~without~~ notice, 33
re-enter the demised premises either by force or otherwise, and dispossess Tenant by summary proceedings or otherwise, and the legal representative of Tenant or other occupant of demised premises and remove their effects and hold the premises as if this lease had not been made, and Tenant hereby waives the service of notice of intention to re-enter or to institute legal proceedings to that end. If Tenant shall make default hereunder prior to the date fixed as the commencement of any renewal or extension of this lease, Owner may cancel and terminate such renewal or extension agreement by written notice.

Remedies of Owner and Waiver of Redemption: 18. In case of any such default, re-entry, expiration and/or dispossess by summary proceedings or otherwise, (a) the rent shall become due thereupon and be paid up to the time of such re-entry, dispossess and/or expiration, (b) Owner may re-let the premises or any part or parts thereof, either in the name of Owner or otherwise, for a term or terms, which may at Owner's option be less than or exceed the period which would otherwise have constituted the balance of the term of this lease and may grant concessions or free rent or charge a higher rental than that in this lease, and/or (c) Tenant or the legal representatives of Tenant shall also pay Owner as liquidated damages for the failure of Tenant to observe and perform said Tenant's covenants herein contained, any deficiency between the rent hereby reserved and/or covenanted to be paid and the net amount, if any, of the rents collected on account of the lease or leases of the demised premises for each month of the period which would otherwise have constituted the balance of the term of this lease. The failure of Owner to re-let the premises or any part or parts thereof shall not release
or affect Tenant's liability for damages. In computing such liquidated 34
damages there shall be added to the said deficiency such expenses as Owner may incur in connection with re-letting, such as legal expenses, reasonable
attorneys' fees, brokerage, advertising and for keeping the demised 35
premises in good order or for preparing the same for re-letting. Any such liquidated damages shall be paid in monthly installments by Tenant on the rent day specified in this lease and any suit brought to collect the amount of the deficiency for any month shall not prejudice in any way the rights of Owner to collect the deficiency for any subsequent month by a similar proceeding. Owner, in putting the demised premises in good order or preparing the same for re-rental may, at Owner's option, make such alterations, repairs, replacements, and/or decorations in the demised premises as Owner, in Owner's sole judgement, considers advisable and necessary for the purpose of re-letting the demised premises, and the making of such alterations, repairs, replacements, and/or decorations shall not operate or be construed to release Tenant from liability hereunder as aforesaid. Owner shall in no event be liable in any way whatsoever for
failure to re-let the demised premises, or in the event that the demised 36
premises are re-let, for failure to collect the rent thereof under such re-letting, and in no event shall Tenant be entitled to receive any excess, if any, of such net rents collected over the sums payable by Tenant to Owner hereunder. In the event of a breach or threatened breach by Tenant of any of the covenants or provisions hereof, Owner shall have the right of injunction and the right to invoke any remedy allowed at law or in equity as if re-entry, summary proceedings and other remedies were not herein provided for. Mention in this lease of any particular remedy, shall not preclude Owner from any other remedy, in law or in equity. Tenant hereby expressly waives any and all rights of redemption granted by or under any present or future laws in the event of Tenant being evicted or dispossessed for any cause, or in the event of Owner obtaining possession of demised premises, by reason of the violation by Tenant of any of the covenants and conditions of this lease, or otherwise.

Fees and Expenses: 19. If Tenant shall default in the observance or performance of any term or covenant on Tenant's part to be observed or performed under or by virtue of any of the terms or provisions in any article of this lease, after notice if required and upon expiration of any applicable grace period if any, (except in an emergency), then, unless otherwise provided elsewhere in this lease, Owner may immediately or at any time thereafter and without notice perform the obligation of Tenant thereunder. If Owner, in connection with the foregoing or in connection with any default by Tenant in the covenant to pay rent hereunder, makes any expenditures or incurs any obligations for the payment of money, including but not limited to reasonable attorneys' fees, in instituting, prosecuting or defending any action or proceeding, and prevails in any such action or proceeding then Tenant will reimburse Owner for such sums so paid or obligations incurred with interest and costs. The foregoing expenses incurred by reason of Tenant's default shall be deemed to be additional rent hereunder and shall be paid by Tenant to Owner within ten (10) days of rendition of any bill or statement to Tenant therefor. If Tenant's lease term shall have expired at the time of making of such expenditures or incurring of such obligations, such sums shall be recoverable by Owner, as damages.

Building Alterations and Management: 20. Owner shall have the right at any time without the same constituting an eviction and without incurring liability to Tenant therefor to change the arrangement and/or location of public entrances, passageways, doors, doorways, corridors, elevators, stairs, toilets or other public parts of the building and to change the name, number or designation by which the building may be known. There shall be no allowance to Tenant for diminution of rental value and no liability on the part of Owner by reason of inconvenience, annoyance or injury to business arising from Owner or other Tenants making any repairs in the building or any such alterations, additions and improvements. Furthermore, Tenant shall not have any claim against Owner by reason of Owner's imposition of such controls of the manner of access to the building by Tenant's social or business visitors as the Owner may deem necessary for the security of the building and its occupants.

37

No Representations by Owner: 21. ~~Neither~~ Owner nor Owner's agents have made any representations or promises with respect to the physical condition of the building, the land upon which it is erected or the demised premises, the rents, leases, expenses of operation or any other matter or thing affecting or related to the premises except as herein expressly set forth and no rights, easements or licenses are acquired by Tenant by implication or otherwise except as expressly set forth in the provisions of this lease. Tenant has inspected the building and the demised premises and is thoroughly acquainted with their condition and agrees to take the same "as is" and acknowledges that the taking of possession of the demised premises by Tenant shall be conclusive evidence that the said premises and the building of which the same form a part were in good and satisfactory condition at the
time such possession was so taken, except as to latent defects. All 38
understandings and agreements heretofore made between the parties hereto are merged in this contract, which alone fully and completely expresses the agreement between Owner and Tenant and any executory agreement

hereafter made shall be ineffective to change, modify, discharge or effect an abandonment of it in whole or in part, unless such executory agreement is in writing and signed by the party against whom enforcement of the change, modification, discharge or abandonment is sought.

End of Term: 22. Upon the expiration or other termination of the term of this lease, Tenant shall quit and surrender to Owner the demised premises, broom clean, in good order and condition, ordinary wear and damages which Tenant is not required to repair as provided elsewhere in this lease excepted, and Tenant shall remove all its property. Tenant's obligation to observe or perform this covenant shall survive the expiration or other termination of this lease. If the last day of the term of this Lease or any renewal thereof, falls on Sunday, this lease shall expire at noon on the preceding Saturday unless it be a legal holiday in which case it shall expire at noon on the preceding business day.

Quiet Enjoyment: 23. Owner covenants and agrees with Tenant that upon Tenant paying the rent and additional rent and observing and performing all the terms, covenants and conditions, on Tenant's part to be observed and performed, Tenant may peaceably and quietly enjoy the premises hereby demised, subject, nevertheless, to the terms and conditions of this lease including, but not limited to, Article 31 hereof. ~~and to the ground leases, underlying leases and mortgages hereinbefore mentioned.~~

~~Failure to Give Possession:~~ 24. If Owner is unable to give possession of the demised premises on the date of the commencement of the term hereof, because of the holding-over or retention of possession of any tenant, undertenant or occupants or if the demised premises are located in a building being constructed, because such building has not been sufficiently completed to make the premises ready for occupancy or because of the fact that a certificate of occupancy has not been procured or for any other reason, Owner shall not be subject to any liability for failure to give possession on said date and the validity of the lease shall not be impaired under such circumstances, nor shall the same be construed in any wise to extend the term of this lease, but the rent payable hereunder shall be abated (provided Tenant is not responsible for Owner's inability to obtain possession or complete construction) until after Owner shall have given Tenant written notice that the Owner is able to deliver possession in condition required by this lease. If permission is given to Tenant to enter into the possession of the demises premises or to occupy premises other than the demised premises prior to the date specified at the commencement of the term of this lease, Tenant covenants and agrees that such possession and/or occupancy shall be deemed to be under all the terms, covenants, conditions and provisions of this lease except the obligation to pay the fixed annual rent set forth in the preamble to this lease. The provisions of this article are intended to constitute "an express provision to the contrary" within the meaning of Section 223-a of the New York Real Property Law. ——39

No Waiver: 25. The failure of ~~Owner~~ to seek redress for violation of, or to insist upon the strict performance of any covenant or condition of this lease or of any of the Rules or Regulations, set forth or hereafter adopted by Owner, shall not prevent a subsequent act which would have originally constituted a violation from having all the force and effect of an original violation. The receipt by Owner of rent and/or additional rent with knowledge of the breach of any covenant of this lease shall not be deemed a waiver of such breach and no provision of this lease shall be deemed to have been waived by Owner unless such waiver be in writing signed by Owner. No payment by Tenant or receipt by Owner of a lesser amount than the monthly rent herein stipulated shall be deemed to be other than on account of the earliest stipulated rent, nor shall any endorsement or statement of any check or any letter accompanying any check or payment as rent be deemed an accord and satisfaction, and Owner may accept such check or payment without prejudice to Owner's right to recover the balance of such rent or pursue any other remedy in this lease provided. No act or thing done by Owner or Owner's agents during the term hereby demised shall be deemed an acceptance of a surrender of said premises, and no agreement to accept such surrender shall be valid unless in writing signed by Owner. No employee of Owner or Owner's agent shall have any power to accept the keys of said premises prior to the termination of the lease and the delivery of keys to any such agent or employee shall not operate as a termination of the lease or a surrender of the premises.

Waiver of Trial by Jury: 26. It is mutually agreed by and between Owner and Tenant that the respective parties hereto shall and they hereby do waive trial by jury in any action proceeding or counterclaim brought by either of the parties hereto against the other (except for personal injury or property damage) on any matters whatsoever arising out of or in any way connected with this lease, the relationship of Owner and Tenant, Tenant's use of or occupancy of said premises, and any emergency statutory or any other statutory remedy. It is further mutually agreed that in the event Owner commences any possession or action for possession including a summary proceeding for possession of the premises, Tenant will not interpose any counterclaim of whatever nature or description in any such proceeding including a counterclaim under Article 4 except for statutory mandatory counterclaims.

~~Inability to Perform:~~ ~~27. This Lease and the obligation of Tenant to pay~~ rent hereunder and perform all of the other covenants and agreements hereunder on part of Tenant to be performed shall in no wise be affected, impaired or excused because Owner is unable to fulfill any of its obligations under this lease or to supply or is delayed in supplying any service expressly or impliedly to be supplied or is unable to make, or is delayed in making any repair, additions, alterations or decorations or is unable to supply or is delayed in supplying any equipment, fixtures, or other materials if Owner is prevented or delayed from so doing by reason of strike or labor troubles or any cause whatsoever including, but not limited to, government preemption or restrictions or by reason of any rule, order or regulation of any department or subdivision thereof of any government agency or by reason of the conditions which have been of are affected, either directly or indirectly, by war or other emergency.

Bills and Notices: 28. Except as otherwise in this lease provided, a bill, statement, notice or communication which Owner may desire or be required to give to Tenant, shall be deemed sufficiently given or rendered if, in writing, delivered to Tenant 40 personally or sent by registered or certified mail addressed to Tenant at the

[3 ☞] **Rider to be added if necessary.**

building of which the demised premises form a part or at the last known residence address or business address of Tenant or left at any of the aforesaid premises addressed to Tenant, and the time of the rendition of such bill or statement and of the giving of such notice or communication shall be deemed to be the time when the same is delivered to Tenant, mailed, or left at the premises as herein provided. Any notice by Tenant to Owner must be served by registered or certified mail addressed to Owner at the address first hereinabove given or at such other address as Owner shall designate by written notice.

Services Provided by Owners: 29. As long as Tenant is not in default under any of the covenants of this lease beyond the applicable grace period provided in this lease for the curing of such defaults, Owner shall provide: (a) necessary elevator facilities on business days from 8 a.m. to 6 p.m. and have one elevator subject to call at all other times; (b) heat to the demised premises when and as required by law, on business days from 8 a.m. to 6 p.m.; (c) water for ordinary lavatory purposes, but if Tenant uses or consumes water for any other purposes or in unusual quantities (of which fact Owner shall be the sole judge), Owner may install a water meter at Tenant's expense which Tenant shall thereafter maintain at Tenant's expense in good working order and repair to register such water consumption and Tenant shall pay for water consumed as shown on said meter as additional rent as and when bills are rendered; (d) cleaning service for the demised premises on business days at Owner's expense provided that the same are kept in order by Tenant. ~~If, however, said premises are to be kept clean by Tenant, it shall be done at Tenant's sole expense, in a manner reasonably satisfactory to Owner and no one other than persons approved by Owner shall be permitted to enter said premises or the building of which they are a part for such purpose.~~ Tenant shall pay Owner the cost of removal of any of Tenant's refuse and rubbish from the building. (e) If the demised premises are serviced by Owner's air conditioning/cooling and ventilating system, air conditioning/cooling will be furnished to tenant from May 15th through September 30th on business days (Mondays through Fridays, holidays excepted) from 8:00 a.m. to 6:00 p.m., and ventilation will be furnished on business days during the aforesaid hours except when air conditioning/cooling is being furnished as aforesaid. If Tenant requires air conditioning/cooling or ventilation for more extended hours or on Saturdays, Sundays or on holidays, as defined under Owner's contract with Operating Engineers Local 94-94A, Owner will furnish the same ~~at Tenant's expense~~ [3 ☞] **RIDER to be added in respect to rates and conditions** —42 for such additional service; (f) Owner reserves the right to stop services of the heating, elevators, plumbing, air-conditioning, electric, power systems or cleaning or other services, if any, when necessary by reason of accident or for repairs, alterations, replacements or improvements necessary or desirable in the judgment of Owner for as long as may be reasonably required by reason thereof. ~~If the building of which the demised premises~~ —43 ~~are a part supplies manually operated elevator service, Owner at any time may substitute automatic control elevator service and proceed diligently with alterations necessary therefor without in any wise affecting this lease or the obligation of Tenant hereunder.~~

Captions: 30. The Captions are inserted only as a matter of convenience and for reference and in no way define, limit or describe the scope of this lease nor the intent of any provisions thereof.

Definitions: 31. The term "office", or "offices", wherever used in this lease, shall not be construed to mean premises used as a store or stores, for the sale or display, at any time, of goods, wares or merchandise, of any kind, or as a restaurant, shop, booth, bootblack or other stand, barber shop, or for other similar purposes or for manufacturing. The term "Owner" means a landlord or lessor, and as used in this lease means only the owner, or the mortgagee in possession, for the time being of the land and building (or the owner of a lease of the building or of the land and building) of which the demised premises form a part, so that in the event of any sale or sales of said land and building or of said lease, or in the event of a lease of said building, or of the land and building, the said Owner shall be and hereby is entirely freed and relieved of all covenants and obligations of Owner hereunder, and it shall be deemed and construed —44 without further agreement between the parties or their successors in interest, or between the parties and the purchaser, at any such sale, or the said lessee of the building, or of the land and building, that the purchaser or the lessee of the building has assumed and agreed to carry out any and all covenants and obligations of Owner, hereunder. The words "re enter" and "re-entry" as used in this lease are not restricted to their technical legal meaning. The term "business days" as used in this lease shall exclude Saturdays, Sundays and all days as observed by the State or Federal Government as legal holidays and those designated as holidays by the applicable building service union employees service contract or by the applicable Operating Engineers contract with respect to HVAC service. Wherever it is expressly provided in this lease that consent shall not be unreasonably withheld, such consent shall not be unreasonably delayed.

Adjacent Excavation-Shoring: 32. If an excavation shall be made upon land adjacent to the demised premises, or shall be authorized to be made, Tenant shall afford to the person causing or authorized to cause such excavation, license to enter upon the demised premises for the purpose of doing such work as said person shall deem necessary to preserve the wall or the building of which demised premises form a part from injury or damage and to support the same by proper foundations without any claim for damages or indemnity against Owner, or diminution or abatement of rent.

Rules and Regulations: 33. Tenant and Tenant's servants, employees, agents, visitors, and licensees shall observe faithfully, and comply strictly with, the Rules and Regulations and such other and further reasonable Rules and Regulations as Owner or Owner's agents may from time to time adopt. ~~Notice of any~~ —45 ~~additional rules or regulations shall be given in such manner as Owner may elect.~~ In case Tenant disputes the reasonableness of any additional Rule or Regulation hereafter made or adopted by Owner or Owner's agents, the parties hereto agree to submit the question of the reasonableness of such Rule or Regulation for decision to the New York office of the American Arbitration Association, whose determination shall be final and conclusive upon the parties hereto. The right to dispute the reasonableness of any additional Rule or Regulation upon Tenant's part shall be deemed waived unless the same shall be asserted by service of a notice, in writing upon Owner within ~~fifteen (15)~~ days after the giving of notice thereof. Nothing —46 in this lease contained shall be construed to impose upon Owner any duty or obligation to enforce the Rules and Regulations or terms, covenants or conditions in any other lease, as against any other tenant and Owner shall not be liable to Tenant for violation of the same by any other tenant, its servants, employees, agents, visitors or licensees.

Security: 34. Tenant has deposited with Owner the sum of
$ as security for the faithful
[B☞] performance and observance by Tenant of the terms,
provisions and conditions of this lease; it is agreed that in the event Tenant defaults in respect of any of the terms, provisions and conditions of this lease, including, but not limited to, the payment of rent and additional rent, Owner may use, apply or retain the whole or any part of the security so deposited to the extent required for the payment of any rent and additional rent or any other sum as to which Tenant is in default or for any sum which Owner may expend or may be required to expend by reason of Tenant's default in respect of any of the terms, covenants and conditions of this lease, including but not limited to, any damages or deficiency in the re-letting of the premises, whether such damages or deficiency accrued before or after summary proceedings or other re-entry by Owner. In the event that Tenant shall fully and faithfully comply with all of the terms, provisions, covenants and conditions of this lease, the security shall be returned to Tenant after the date fixed as the end of the Lease and after delivery of entire possession of the demised premises to Owner. In the event of a sale of the land and building or leasing of the building, of which the demised premises form a part, Owner shall have the right to transfer the security to the vendee or lessee and Owner shall thereupon be released by Tenant from all liability for the return of such security; and Tenant agrees to look to the new Owner solely for the return of said security, and it is agreed that the provisions hereof shall apply to every transfer or assignment made of the security to

[B☞] Space to be filled in or deleted.

a new Owner. Tenant further covenants that it will not assign or encumber or attempt to assign or encumber the monies deposited herein as security and that neither Owner nor its successors or assigns shall be bound by any such assignment, encumbrance, attempted assignment or attempted encumbrance.

—— 47

Estoppel 35. Tenant, at any time, and from time to time, upon
Certificate: at least 10 days' prior notice by Owner, shall
execute, acknowledge and deliver to Owner, and/or to any other person, firm or corporation specified by Owner, a statement certifying that this Lease is unmodified and in full force and effect (or, if there have been modifications, that the same is in full force and effect as modified and stating the modifications), stating the dates to which the rent and additional rent have been paid, and stating whether or not there exists any default by Owner under this Lease, and, if so, specifying each such default.

Successors 36. The covenants, conditions and agreements con-
and Assigns: tained in this lease shall bind and inure to the benefit
of Owner and Tenant and their respective heirs, distributees, executors, administrators, successors, and except as otherwise provided in this lease, their assigns. Tenant shall look only to Owner's estate and interest in the land and building, for the satisfaction of Tenant's remedies for the collection of a judgment (or other judicial process) against Owner in the event of any default by Owner hereunder, and no other property or assets of such Owner (or any partner, member, officer or director thereof, disclosed or undisclosed), shall be subject to levy, execution or other enforcement procedure for the satisfaction of Tenant's remedies under or with respect to this lease, the relationship of Owner and Tenant hereunder, or Tenant's use and occupancy of the demised premises.

In Witness Whereof, Owner and Tenant have respectively signed and sealed this lease as of the day and year first above written.

LANDLORD: ███████████████

Witness for Owner:

....

By : ....

....

TENANT: ███████████████

Witness for Tenant:

By : ....

....

ACKNOWLEDGEMENTS

CORPORATE OWNER
STATE OF NEW YORK, ss.:
County of

On this day of , 19
before me personally came
to me known, who being by me duly sworn, did depose and say that he resides in
that he is the of
the corporation described in and which executed the foregoing instrument, as OWNER; that he knows the seal of said corporation; the seal affixed to said instrument is such corporate seal; that it was so affixed by order of the Board of Directors of said corporation, and that he signed his name thereto by like order.

....

CORPORATE TENANT
STATE OF NEW YORK, ss.:
County of

On this day of , 19
before me personally came
to me known, who being by me duly sworn, did depose and say that he resides in
that he is the of
the corporation described in and which executed the foregoing instrument, as TENANT; that he knows the seal of said corporation; the seal affixed to said instrument is such corporate seal; that it was so affixed by order of the Board of Directors of said corporation, and that he signed his name thereto by like order.

....

INDIVIDUAL OWNER
STATE OF NEW YORK, ss.:
County of

On this day of , 19
before me personally came
to be known and known to me to be the individual described in and who, as OWNER, executed the foregoing instrument and acknowledged to me that he executed the same.

....

INDIVIDUAL TENANT
STATE OF NEW YORK, ss.:
County of

On this day of , 19
before me personally came
to be known and known to me to be the individual described in and who, as TENANT, executed the foregoing instrument and acknowledged to me that he executed the same.

....

GUARANTY

FOR VALUE RECEIVED, and in consideration for, and as an inducement to Owner making the within lease with Tenant, the undersigned guarantees to Owner, Owner's successors and assigns, the full performance and observance of all the covenants, conditions and agreements, therein provided to be performed and observed by Tenant, including the "Rules and Regulations" as therein provided, without requiring any notice of non-payment, non-performance, or non-observance, or proof, or notice, or demand, whereby to charge the undersigned therefor, all of which the undersigned hereby expressly waives and expressly agrees that the validity of this agreement and the obligations of the guarantor hereunder shall in no wise be terminated, affected or impaired by reason of the assertion by Owner against Tenant of any of the rights or remedies reserved to Owner pursuant to the provisions of the within lease. The undersigned further covenants and agrees that this guaranty shall remain and continue in full force and effect as to any renewal, modification or extension of this lease and during any period when Tenant is occupying the premises as a "statutory tenant." As a further inducement to Owner to make this lease and in consideration thereof, Owner and the undersigned covenant and agree that in any action or proceeding brought by either Owner or the undersigned against the other on any matters whatsoever arising out of, under, or by virtue of the terms of this lease or of this guarantee that Owner and the undersigned shall and do hereby waive trial by jury.

Dated: .... 19 ....

....
Guarantor

....
Witness

....
Guarantor's Residence

....
Business Address

....
Firm Name

STATE OF NEW YORK) ss.:

COUNTY OF)

On this day of , 19 , before me personally came ....
to me known and known to me to be the individual described in, and who executed the foregoing Guaranty and acknowledged to me that he executed the same.

....
Notary

IMPORTANT - PLEASE READ

RULES AND REGULATIONS ATTACHED TO AND MADE A PART OF THIS LEASE IN ACCORDANCE WITH ARTICLE 33.

1. The sidewalks, entrances, driveways, passages, courts, elevators, vestibules, stairways, corridors or halls shall not be obstructed or encumbered by any Tenant or used for any purpose other than for ingress or egress from the demised premises and for delivery of merchandise and equipment in a prompt and efficient manner using elevators and passageways designated for such delivery by Owner. There shall not be used in any space, or in the public hall of the building, either by any Tenant or by jobbers or others in the delivery or receipt of merchandise, any hand trucks, except those equipped with rubber tires and sideguards. If said premises are situated on the ground floor of the building, Tenant thereof shall further, at Tenant's expense, keep the sidewalk and curb in front of said premises clean and free from ice, snow, dirt and rubbish.

2. The water and wash closets and plumbing fixtures shall not be used for any purposes other than those for which they were designed or constructed and no sweepings, rubbish, rags, acids or other substances shall be deposited therein, and the expense of any breakage, stoppage, or damage resulting from the violation of this rule shall be borne by the Tenant who, or whose clerks, agents, employees or visitors, shall have caused it.

3. No carpet, rug or other article shall be hung or shaken out of any window of the building and no Tenant shall sweep or throw or permit to be swept or thrown from the demised premises any dirt or other substances into any of the corridors or halls, elevators, or out of the doors or windows or stairways of the building and Tenant shall not use, keep or permit to be used or kept any foul or noxious gas or substance in the demised premises, or permit or suffer the demised premises to be occupied or used in a manner offensive or objectionable to Owner or other occupants of the building by reason of noise, odors, and/or vibrations, or interfere in any way with other Tenants or those having business therein, nor shall any bicycles, vehicles, animals, fish, or birds be kept in or about the building. Smoking or carrying lighted cigars or cigarettes in the elevators of the building is prohibited.

4. No awnings or other projections shall be attached to the outside walls of the building without the prior written consent of Owner.

5. No sign, advertisement, notice or other lettering shall be exhibited, inscribed, painted or affixed by any Tenant on any part of the outside of the demised premises or the building or on the inside of the demised premise if the same is visible from the outside of the premises without the prior written consent of Owner, except that the name of Tenant may appear on the entrance door of the premises. In the event of the violation of the foregoing by any Tenant, Owner may remove same without any liability, and may charge the expense incurred by such removal to Tenant or Tenants violating this rule. Interior signs on doors and directory tablet shall be inscribed, painted or affixed for each Tenant by Owner at the expense of such Tenant, and shall be of a size, color and style acceptable to Owner.

6. No Tenant shall mark, paint, drill into, or in any way deface any part of the demised premises or the building of which they form a part. No boring, cutting or stringing of wires shall be permitted, except with the prior written consent of Owner, and as Owner may direct. No Tenant shall lay linoleum, or other similar floor covering, so that the same shall come in direct contact with the floor of the demised premises, and, if linoleum or other similar floor covering is desired to be used an interlining of builder's deadening felt shall be first affixed to the floor, by a paste or other material, soluble in water, the use of cement or other similar adhesive material being expressly prohibited.

7. No additional locks or bolts of any kind shall be placed upon any of the doors or windows by any Tenant, nor shall any changes be made in existing locks or mechanism thereof. Each Tenant must, upon the termination of his Tenancy, restore to Owner all keys of stores, offices and toilet rooms, either furnished to, or otherwise procured by, such Tenant, and in the event of the loss of any keys, so furnished, such Tenant shall pay to Owner the cost thereof.

8. Freight, furniture, business equipment, merchandise and bulky matter of any description shall be delivered to and removed from the premises only on the freight elevators and through the service entrances and corridors, and only during hours and in a manner approved by Owner. Owner reserves the right to inspect all freight to be brought into the building and to exclude from the building all freight which violates any of these Rules and Regulations of the lease or which these Rules and Regulations are a part.

9. Canvassing, soliciting and peddling in the building is prohibited and each Tenant shall cooperate to prevent the same.

10. Owner reserves the right to exclude from the building all persons who do not present a pass to the building signed by Owner. Owner will furnish passes to persons for whom any Tenant requests same in writing. Each Tenant shall be responsible for all persons for whom he requests such pass and shall be liable to Owner for all acts of such persons. Tenant shall not have a claim against Owner by reason of Owner excluding from the building any person who does not present such pass.

11. Owner shall have the right to prohibit any advertising by any Tenant which in Owner's opinion, tends to impair the reputation of the building or its desirability as a building for offices, and upon written notice from Owner, Tenant shall refrain from or discontinue such advertising.

12. Tenant shall not bring or permit to be brought or kept in or on the demised premises, any inflammable, combustible, explosive, or hazardous fluid, material, chemical or substance, or cause or permit any odors of cooking or other processes, or any unusual or other objectionable odors to permeate in or emanate from the demised premises.

13. If the building contains central air conditioning and ventilation, Tenant agrees to keep all windows closed at all times and to abide by all rules and regulations issued by Owner with respect to such services. If Tenant requires air conditioning or ventilation after the usual hours, Tenant shall give notice in writing to the building superintendent prior to 3:00 p.m. in the case of services required on week days, and prior to 3:00 p.m. on the day prior in case of after hours service required on weekends or on holidays. Tenant shall cooperate with Owner in obtaining maximum effectiveness of the cooling system by lowering and closing venetian blinds and/or drapes and curtains when the sun's rays fall directly on the windows of the demised premises.

14. Tenant shall not move any safe, heavy machinery, heavy equipment, bulky matter, or fixtures into or out of the building without Owner's prior written consent. If such safe, machinery, equipment, bulky matter or fixtures requires special handling, all work in connection therewith shall comply with the Administrative Code of the City of New York and all other laws and regulations applicable thereto and shall be done during such hours as Owner may designate.

15. Refuse and Trash. (1) Compliance by Tenant. Tenant covenants and agrees, at its sole cost and expense, to comply with all present and future laws, orders, and regulations of all state, federal, municipal, and local governments, departments, commissions and boards regarding the collection, sorting, separation and recycling of waste products, garbage, refuse and trash. Tenant shall sort and separate such waste products, garbage, refuse and trash into such categories as provided by law. Each separately sorted category of waste products, garbage, refuse and trash shall be placed in separate receptacles reasonably approved by Owner. Such separate receptacles may, at Owner's option, be removed from the demised premises in accordance with a collection schedule prescribed by law. Tenant shall remove, or cause to be removed by a contractor acceptable to Owner, at Owner's sole discretion, such items as Owner may expressly designate. (2) Owner's Rights in Event of Noncompliance. Owner has the option to refuse to collect or accept from Tenant waste products, garbage, refuse or trash (a) that is not separated and sorted as required by law or (b) which consists of such items as Owner may expressly designate for Tenant's removal, and to require Tenant to arrange for such collection at Tenant's sole cost and expense, utilizing a contractor satisfactory to Owner. Tenant shall pay all costs, expenses, fines, penalties, or damages that may be imposed on Owner or Tenant by reason of Tenant's failure to comply with the provisions of this Building Rule 15, and, at Tenant's sole cost and expense, shall indemnity, defend and hold Owner harmless (including reasonable legal fees and expenses) from and against any actions, claims and suits arising from such noncompliance, utilizing counsel reasonably satisfactory to Owner.

Address

Premises

TO

STANDARD FORM OF

Office Lease

The Real Estate Board of New York, Inc.

© Copyright 1994. All rights Reserved. Reproduction in whole or in part prohibited.

Dated 19

Rent Per Year

Rent Per Month

Term
From
To

Drawn by ....

Checked by ....

Entered by ....

Approved by ....

Rider ("Rider I") of Numbered Insertions 1 to 47 to preprinted portion of Lease to supplement Lease between ██████████████████████ ("Owner") and ████████ ████████████████████ ("Tenant") covering the rentable area designated as in Schedule A (the "Demised Premises") in the building commonly known and referred to at ████████ ██████████████████████ (the "Building")

Article 3

Insert 1:   "which consent shall not be (a) required, with respect to painting and decorations or to such other non structural changes not affecting the Certificate of Occupancy of the Building costing below $150,000.00 or (b) unreasonably withheld or delayed, with respect to such changes in excess of $150,000.00, so long as, in both instances, such changes do not affect the structure of the building, or interfere with building services or the use of the building by other tenants except to the extent such can be accommodated by offsetting work approved by Owner and paid for by Tenant."

Insert 2:   "which consent shall be given as aforesaid"

Insert 3:   "which approval shall not be unreasonably withheld";

Insert 4:   "reasonably"

Article 4

Insert 5:   "reasonably"

Insert 6:   "air conditioning, elevator, toilet,"

Insert 7:   "unless due to Owner's or such contractor's negligence."

Insert 8:   ", except as expressly set forth in this Lease."

Article 6

Insert 9:   "Tenant (unless Tenant shall have been the previous owner of the Building) shall have no obligation to cure violations of conditions which existed at the Building prior to the occupancy of Tenant and the commencement of the Term of this Lease for such relevant space."

Insert 10:   "reasonable"

Insert 11:   "rates"

Insert 12:   "Owner shall, at its own cost and expense, comply with all other laws, rules, orders, regulations, ordinances, building, fire or health codes and other similar requirements affecting real estate generally and the Building specifically (the "Requirements") which require structural repairs to or structural alteration of the Building or the Demised Premises, unless such repairs or alterations are necessitated by the particular use of the Demised Premises by Tenant for other than general office use or if such non-compliance preexisted Tenant's becoming Tenant hereunder and occurred during a period when Tenant owned the Building, but may contest, appeal and defer compliance with such Requirements provided that the use or occupancy of the Demised Premises by Tenant shall not be interfered with and Tenant is not subject to prosecution for a criminal offense by reason of such noncompliance by Owner. Without limiting the generality of the foregoing, except as hereinafter otherwise provided, Owner shall be required, at its own expense, to make all alterations and installations in and to the Building and the Demised Premises and to take any other action and incur any other expenses in order to comply with New York City Local Law #5, or any amendment thereof or any law or ordinance similar or as successor thereto, including, without limitation, the installation of sprinkler and/or smoke or fire detection systems, or any other similar systems unless such alterations or installations are necessitated by the particular use of the Demised Premises by Tenant other than for general office purposes; provided, however, that if such law requires any alterations or installations with respect to partitioning or any other installations made by Tenant, such work shall be done by Tenant at its sole cost and expense." Owner shall also cause the Building to comply with the Americans With Disabilities Act ("ADA") or any Amendment thereof or law or ordinance similar or as successor thereto. Provided however if any space be occupied by ███████████████████████████ as Tenant and any such non-compliance of the Building with the Requirements existed while ███████████████ ████████ was the Owner of the Building, ███████████████████ ██████ shall be required to cause such compliance irrespective of whether it is an owner or tenant at the Building at ███████████████████████ cost and expense."

Article 7

Insert 13:   "Notwithstanding the foregoing, this Lease shall not be subject and subordinate to any future ground or underlying leases or to any future

106

mortgages which may hereafter affect the real property or the building of which the Demised Premises form a part, or to any renewals, modifications, consolidations, replacements or extensions thereof, unless the holder of each such mortgage and/or the Owner under each such lease shall agree in writing for the benefit of Tenant, that as long as Tenant shall not be in default under any of the covenants, terms or conditions of this Lease on the part of Tenant to be performed and observed beyond the applicable periods of notice and grace, if any, such holder or Owner shall not join Tenant as a defendant in any action brought to foreclose any such mortgage or terminate any such ground or underlying lease due to a default by the tenant thereunder, and shall recognize Tenant's right to possession under this Lease for the term demised hereunder notwithstanding the foreclosure of any such mortgage or the termination of any such ground or underlying lease, provided the Tenant shall agree to attorn to the holder of any such mortgage or the purchaser at a foreclosure sale or the Owner under any such ground or underlying lease, if any such party shall become the Owner under this Lease. Owner represents that to the best of its knowledge there are no existing mortgages on the real property or the Building of which the Demised Premises form a part, and that there are no ground or underlying leases on all or any portion of such real property or Building."

Article 8

Insert 14:   "or for which insurance coverage is not available under existing policies or which would not have been available had Owner maintained the insurance required by the terms of the Lease,"

Insert 15:   "after reasonable advance written notice to Tenant"

Insert 16:   "or Tenant's insurance carrier."

Article 9

Insert 17:   "or inaccessible"

Insert 18:   "If as a result of fire or other casualty, the Demised Premises shall be damaged in whole or in part and if Owner fails to commence the repair thereof within three (3) months followed such destruction and thereafter fails to diligently complete such repair, Tenant may terminate this Lease by giving Owner written notice which shall state the termination date of this Lease, which date shall be not less than five (5) nor more than sixty (60) days after the giving of such notice, whereupon the terms hereof shall end on the date specified in such notice as if such date were the original date set forth herein for the expiration of the Term. If Owner has commenced the repair thereof within said three (3) months following such destruction,"

Insert 19:   "and the Demised Premises are so ready"

Insert 20:   "Owner shall maintain broad form commercial general liability insurance on a per occurrence basis with liability coverage of not less than $ 20,000,000.00 and shall maintain broad form 'all risk' insurance coverage against loss or damage by fire and other risks and hazards as shall be customary for first class buildings similar to that of the Building of not less than the full replacement value thereof.   In the event that Owner fails to maintain such insurance or elects to self insure certain coverage, losses or certain values, for the purposes of this Lease, Owner shall be deemed to be fully insured and shall look to its insurance for any damages, claims or losses not covered or coverable by the insurance required to be obtained by Tenant hereunder. Provided Tenant maintains the prescribed insurance coverage, as set forth in this Lease, Owner hereby does waive all rights of direct claim against Tenant for any loss, damage or injury to the Building or contents thereof caused by or resulting from or related with Tenant or its uses of the Demised Premises and whether or not such Tenant's prescribed insurance is maintained, provided such loss is covered by Owner's insurance as hereinabove provided or would have been covered had Owner maintained the policy of insurance as hereinabove provided Owner shall be deemed to and does hereby waive any rights of direct action or claims against Tenant for such loss, injury or casualty. Owner shall also obtain and maintain waivers of its insuror's rights of subrogation against Tenant for any claims, losses or injuries and shall obtain and maintain such endorsement or clauses in its insurance policies as shall be required to effectuate such waivers provided such waivers are available and do not invalidate Owner's insurance coverage."

Article 10

Insert 21:   "Notwithstanding the aforesaid provisions, Owner shall not have the right to terminate this Lease in the event of a condemnation of 25% or less of the Demised Premises and such shall result in a proportionate reduction of the rent. For purposes of this Article 10, a condemnation shall be defined to include action which results in the termination of this Lease or blocks access to the Demised Premises."

Insert 22:   "a reduction of rent in the event of a condemnation which affects access to the Demised Premises and"

108

Article 11

Insert 23: "Notwithstanding the foregoing, Tenant shall have the right, without the consent of Owner, to assign this Lease or to sublet all or a portion of the Demised Premises to (i) any corporation or agency which controls, is controlled by, or is under the common control with, Tenant; (ii) any corporation or agency into which or with which Tenant, merges or consolidates; (iii) any other governmental corporation or agency of the State of New York or any political subdivision thereof; (iv) any corporation or agency which acquires all or substantially all of the business and assets of Tenant, provided that in any of the foregoing events, (i) such assignee shall expressly agree in writing for the benefit of owner to assume all of Tenant's obligations hereunder accruing after the effective date of assignment and (ii) Tenant, shall remain liable for the performance of all of Tenant's obligations hereunder. In addition, Tenant shall have the right to allow any of the corporations described in the preceding sentence (hereinafter referred to as the "Affiliates") to occupy portions of the Demised Premises in accordance with the provisions of this Lease."

Article 13

Insert 24: "Except in the event of an emergency or where such entry is required by law, Owner's right of entry shall be exercised following reasonable advance notice to Tenant. Owner agrees that while exercising such right of entry or making such repairs, replacements or improvements, Owner shall use best efforts to avoid interfering with Tenant's business or disrupting the same."

Insert 25: ", provided that no 'to let' or 'for sale' signs shall be posted on the Demised Premises during the term of this Lease."

Insert 26: "Owner shall not forcibly enter the Demised Premises except in the event of an emergency or where required by law."

Insert 27: "whereupon this Lease shall terminate."

Insert 28: "Subject to its reasonable security regulations, Owner agrees that the Premises will be accessible twenty-four hours a day, seven days a week."

Article 15

Insert 29: "Owner represents that the certificate of occupancy for the Building permits the occupancy of the Demised Premises for the Article 2 permitted purposes and that the certificate of occupancy shall not be modified in any way which curtails such uses."

Article 16

Insert 30:   "which is not dismissed within sixty (60) days"

Insert 31:   "Notwithstanding the foregoing, if following an assignment by Tenant, Tenant remains liable for the performance of Tenant's obligations under this Lease, neither the bankruptcy, insolvency, reorganization, or arrangement of the party then owning Tenant's interest in the Lease, nor the occurrence of any of the other events described in this Article 16 shall constitute a default by the then tenant in its obligations hereunder and if the named Tenant as assignor hereunder is performing and paying rent, in that event, such named Tenant shall have the right in Owner's name to regain possession of the Demised Premises."

Article 17

Insert 32:   "ten (10)"

Insert 33:   ", upon five (5) days' written"

Article 18

Insert 34:   "but Owner shall use reasonable efforts to re-let the Demised Premises."

Insert 35:   "reasonable"

Insert 36:   "but Owner shall use reasonable efforts to re-let the Demised Premises,"

Article 21

Insert 37:   "Except as expressly provided herein, neither"

Insert 38:   "and other matters set forth in the Lease";

Article 25

Insert 39:   "either party"

Article 28

Insert 40:   "an executive officer of"

Article 29

Insert 41:   "its direct cost, at Tenant's expense, pro-rated among all tenants in the building requesting the same. Owner shall remove normal amount of trash, rubbish and waste from the Demised Premises at Owners expense."

Insert 42:   "At Owner's net out of pocket expense for Tenant's reimbursement. Owner, at Owner's cost and expense, shall supply a sufficient electrical supply for Tenant's normal business operations, but in no event less than 8 watts per rentable square foot."

Insert 43:   "Subject to its reasonable security regulations, Owner agrees that the Demised Premises will be accessible twenty-four (24) hours a day, seven (7) days a week."

Article 31

Insert 44:   "arising from and after the date thereof"

Article 33

Insert 45:   "Any additional rules or regulations shall be adopted only after written notice to Tenant."

Insert 46:   "thirty (30)"

Insert 47:   "Owner agrees that it shall not enforce the rules and regulations more stringently against Tenant than against any other tenant of the building. Additionally, no rules and regulations shall increase Tenant's monetary obligations or materially reduce Tenant's rights under this Lease nor shall Tenant be required to comply with any rules and regulations which prevent Tenant's permitted uses of the Demised Premises."

RIDER II OF ADDITIONAL PROVISIONS (the "Rider II") to Lease dated [199], between [   ] ("Owner") and [   ] ("Tenant") conveying certain premises (the "Demised Premises") in the building known as [   ] (the "Building")

40. TERM, BASE RENT AND USE AND OCCUPANCY:

Section I: Term and Use:

A. The term of this Lease (the "Term") shall commence on the later to occur of (i) March 31, 1998 or (ii) the date all of the Initial Delivery Space shall have been delivered to Tenant in the "Delivery Condition" (as hereinafter defined) (the "Commencement Date") and shall expire and end three (3) years after the Commencement Date (the "Expiration Date") unless such Term shall sooner terminate. Subject to and in accordance with the other terms and conditions of this Lease, Tenant shall use the Demised Premises solely for the purpose of conducting general operations and executive offices (the "Permitted Use"). Tenant agrees not to use or permit or suffer the use of the Demised Premises for any other business or purpose. Owner covenants, warrants and represents to deliver the Initial Delivery Space on or before March 31, 1998 and Owner's obligations so to do shall be deemed to survive the sale and closing thereof of the Property to Tenant or any other purchaser.

B. Tenant shall (1) keep and maintain the Demised Premises and Tenant's personal property and signs therein or thereon and the interior portions of all windows, doors and all glass or plate glass in a neat, clean, sanitary and safe condition; (2) apply for, secure, maintain and comply with

1

all licenses or permits which may be required for the conduct by Tenant of the Permitted Use and to pay, if, as and when due all license and permit fees and charges of a similar nature in connection therewith and provide Owner with copies thereof upon request; (3) not operate its business under this Lease so as to breach or violate any restrictive covenant contained in any other lease entered into by Tenant or violate any restrictive agreement contained in any contract entered into by Tenant, or violate any restrictive agreement contained in any judgment or decree imposed upon Tenant.

Section II: RENT:

A. Commencing the Commencement Date, Tenant covenants and agrees to pay to Owner fixed minimum rent (the "Base Rent") during the Term at the rate of Twelve ($12.00) Dollars per square foot of the Demised Premises per annum. The Base Rent shall be paid in equal monthly installments, in advance, on the first day of each and every calendar month during the Term, subject to adjustments as hereinafter provided in this Lease.

B. The Base Rent shall be paid at Owner's election by wire transfer or check drawn on a local New York City Clearing House Association member bank by Tenant to Owner in lawful money of the United States at the office of Owner or such other place as Owner may designate, without any demand therefor and without any set-off or deduction whatsoever.

C. Provided Tenant shall not be in default pursuant to the terms of this Lease, Base Rent for the month of _____, 19__ shall be abated.

41. AS-IS POSSESSION; OWNER'S AND/OR TENANT'S INITIAL WORK:

Tenant acknowledges that neither Owner, nor Owner's agents, have made any representations or promises in regard to the Demised Premises except with respect to its obligation to deliver the Initial Delivery Space and any other future additional space to be delivered hereunder in the

2

"Delivery Condition." The taking of possession of the Demised Premises by Tenant shall be conclusive evidence as against Tenant that Tenant accepts the same "as-is" and that the Demised Premises (except for the need for any Tenant's work or work to render the space in the "Delivery Condition", as such term is hereinafter defined) and the Building and general area in the Demised Premises proximity were in good and satisfactory condition at the time such possession was taken.

The "Delivery Condition" shall mean that the space comprising the Demised Premises shall be violation condition free with respect to Requirements and free of any hazardous materials or contamination and containing such furniture, fixtures, decorations and equipment as set forth in Schedule "B" hereto.

42. ADDITIONAL RENT TAXES:

A. For the purposes of this Lease, the following definitions shall apply:

1. "Taxes" shall mean the taxes and assessments and special assessments levied, assessed or imposed upon the buildings comprising and/or the land and interests in the land under, including any land(s) dedicated to the use of, the property known as [   ] (hereinafter the"Property"), by any governmental bodies or authorities. If at any time after the date hereof the methods of taxation prevailing on the date hereof shall be altered so that in lieu of, or as an addition to or as a substitute for the whole or any part of the taxes, assessments, levies, impositions or charges now levied, assessed or imposed on real estate and the improvements thereof, there shall be levied, assessed or imposed (i) a tax, assessment, levy, imposition or charge on the rents received therefrom, or (ii) a license fee measured by the rent payable by Tenant to Owner, or (iii) any other additional or substitute tax, assessment, levy, imposition or charge, then all such taxes, assessments, levies, impositions or charges or the part thereof so measured or based shall be deemed to be included

3

within the term "Taxes" for the purposes hereof. Taxes shall be calculated by aggregating all assessments, levies, and impositions and multiplying the sum (or sums if different categories) obtained thereby by the applicable "tax rate(s)" of the taxing authorities and adding to the product obtained thereby, the aggregate of the products of the special assessments as multiplied by the applicable "tax rates". In the event more than one measurement of assessed valuation is utilized by an applicable taxing authority, the measurement upon which the applicable tax rate is applied by the taxing authority as a basis to calculate and collect taxes shall be deemed to be the measurement of assessments, charges or impositions in determining Taxes for the purposes of this Article.

2. Taxes payable on the Property shall mean all Taxes required to be paid to the assessing authority to the extent of and resulting solely and only from, the leasing of the Demised Premises by Tenant or those claiming thru Tenant as sublessee or assignee.

3. If and so long as Tenant shall be a governmental agency or an entity which is tax exempt under the applicable Tax assessment laws affecting the Property no Taxes shall be deemed payable under this Article.

4. "Tax Year" shall mean the fiscal year for which Taxes are levied by the governmental authority.

B. Tenant shall pay as additional rent for such Tax Year an amount equal to the Taxes for such Tax Year payable by Owner for the Project which are solely attributable to the Demised Premises. The amount payable by Tenant is hereinafter called the "Tax Payment." The Tax Payment shall be prorated, if necessary, to correspond with that portion of a Tax Year occurring within the Term and portions of any Tax Year during which Tenant shall be or become a type of entity causing Taxes to become payable as set forth hereinabove. The Tax Payment shall be payable by Tenant

4

semi-annually in advance within ten (10) days after receipt of a demand from Owner therefor, which demand shall be accompanied by Owner's computations of the Tax Payment and relevant Tax bills. Owner may estimate such Tax Payment and shall adjust such estimate annually to correspond to actual Taxes paid.

C. If Owner shall receive a refund for any Tax Year in respect of which a Tax Payment shall have been made by Tenant, Owner shall repay to Tenant, Tenant's applicable share of such refund after deducting therefrom the costs and expenses of obtaining such refund. If Owner should effect a reduction in assessed valuation, thus reducing the amount of Taxes which would otherwise be payable by Tenant hereunder, Tenant shall pay, upon demand, to Owner, Tenant's applicable share of the costs and expenses of obtaining such reduction of assessed value.

D. With respect to any period at the commencement or expiration of the Term when Tenant's entity status may have changed as above stated, which shall constitute a partial Tax Year, Owner's statement shall apportion the amount of the additional rent due hereunder. The obligation of Tenant in respect of such additional rent applicable to (i) the last year of the Term or part thereof or (ii) the last year of this Lease, if this Lease shall terminate prior to its Term, shall survive the expiration of the Term of this Lease or the earlier termination of this Lease, as the case may be.

43. BROKER:

Tenant covenants, warrants and represents to Owner that it dealt with no broker, finder or similar person except [   ] ("Broker") with respect to consummating this Lease, that no conversations or prior negotiations were had by Tenant or anyone acting on behalf of Tenant with any broker, finder or similar person other than Broker concerning the renting of the Demised Premises. Tenant agrees to indemnify and hold Owner harmless against and from all costs,

5

expenses, damages and liabilities, including reasonable attorney's fees and court costs, arising from any claims for brokerage commissions, finder's fees or other compensation resulting from or arising out of any conversations, negotiations or actions had by Tenant or anyone acting on behalf of Tenant with any broker, finder or similar person other than Broker. Tenant shall defend against any such claim by attorneys reasonably satisfactory to Owner and shall not enter into any settlement agreement with respect thereto without either (i) depositing the amount of such claim together with all costs of Owner associated with defense of such claim, in trust, with Owner for payment of such settlement or (ii) first receiving written authorization therefor, specific in scope and authority, from Owner.

44. TENANT'S CERTIFICATE:

Tenant shall, without charge at any time and from time to time, within thirty (30) days after request by Owner, certify (by written instrument, duly executed, acknowledged and delivered) to Owner and/or any mortgagee, assignee of any mortgagee or purchaser, or any proposed mortgagee, assignee of any mortgagee or purchaser, or any other person, firm or corporation specified by Owner:

A. that this Lease is unmodified and in full force and effect (or if there has (have) been any modification(s), that the same is in full force and effect as modified and stating the modification(s));

B. whether or not there are then existing any setoffs or defenses against the enforcement of any of the agreements, terms, covenants or conditions hereof upon the part of Tenant to be performed or complied with (and, if so, specifying the same);

C. whether or not Tenant is aware of any default by Owner of any of the agreements, terms, covenants or conditions hereof upon the part of Owner to be performed or complied with (and, if so,

6

118

specifying the same); and

D. the date, if any, to which Base Rent, additional rent and other charges hereunder have been paid in advance.

45. INDEMNITY:

A. Tenant hereby agrees to defend, pay, indemnify and save free and harmless Owner, and any fee owner or ground or underlying lessors of the Property, to the full extent permitted by law, from and against any and all claims, demands, liabilities, fines, suits, actions, proceedings, orders, decrees, and judgments of any kind or nature by or in favor of anyone whomsoever and from and against any and all costs and expenses, including reasonable attorney's fees and court costs, arising from and in connection with loss of life, bodily or personal injury or damage to property arising, directly or indirectly, out of or from or on account of any occurrence in, upon, at or from the Demised Premises occasioned wholly or in part by Tenant through the use and occupancy of the Demised Premises or any improvements therein or appurtenances thereto, or by any act or omission or negligence of Tenant or any subtenant, concessionaire or licensee of Tenant, or the respective employees, agents, invitees, customers or contractors in, upon, at or from the Demised Premises or its appurtenances or any common areas of the Property, together with the property adjoining the Property.

B. Tenant and all those claiming by, through, or under Tenant shall store their property in and shall occupy and use the Demised Premises and any improvements therein and appurtenances thereto and all portions of the Property solely at their risk and Tenant and all those claiming by, through or under Tenant hereby release Owner and any fee owner or ground or underlying lessors of the Property, to the full extent permitted by law, from all claims, of every kind, including loss of

7

life, bodily or personal injury, damage to merchandise, equipment, fixtures or other property, or damage to business or for business interruption, arising directly or indirectly out of or from or on account of such occupancy and use.

C. Owner shall not be responsible or liable for damages at any time to Tenant, or to those claiming by, through or under Tenant, for any loss of life, bodily or personal injury, or damage to property or business, or for business interruption, that may be occasioned by or through the acts, omissions or negligence of any other persons, or any other tenants or occupants of any portion of the Property or the stores adjoining the Property.

D. Neither Owner nor fee owner or ground or underlying lessors of the Property shall be responsible or liable for damages at any time, for any defects, latent or otherwise, in any buildings or improvements in the Property or any of the equipment, machinery, utilities, appliances or apparatus therein, nor shall Owner be responsible or liable for damages at any time for loss of life, or bodily or personal injury or damage to property, or for business interruption, to any person or any property or business of Tenant or those claiming by, through or under Tenant, caused by or resulting from bursting, breaking, leaking, running, seeping, overflowing or backing up of water, steam, gas or sewage, in any part of the Demised Premises or caused by or resulting from acts of God or the elements, or resulting from any defect or negligence on the occupancy, construction, operation or use of any buildings or improvements in the Property, including the Demised Premises, and the stores adjoining the Property or any of the equipment, fixtures, machinery, appliances or apparatus therein.

E. After any litigation or proceeding between the parties hereto, the successful party shall be entitled to all costs, expenses and reasonable attorney's fees that it may actually incur in enforcing

8

120

the terms of this Lease against the other party. The successful party shall be deemed to be the one who shall have obtained a final unappealable order or judgment with respect to the such litigation or proceeding. Tenant shall pay to Owner, as additional rent, within ten (10) days after being billed therefore, all costs, expenses and reasonable attorney's fees incurred by Owner in enforcing any of the terms or covenants of this Lease against Tenant or in defending any action or proceeding brought by Tenant against Owner in which Tenant fails to secure a final unappealable judgment against Owner.

F. Tenant expressly acknowledges that all the foregoing provisions of this Paragraph shall apply and become effective from and after the date Owner shall deliver possession of the Demised Premises to Tenant in accordance with the terms of this Lease.

46. WAIVER OF LIABILITY:

Anything contained in this Lease to the contrary notwithstanding, Tenant shall look solely to the estate and property of Owner in the land and buildings comprising the Property of which the Demised Premises forms a part and the rentals therefrom for the collection of any judgment (or other judicial process) requiring the payment of money by Owner in the event of any default or breach by Owner with respect to any of the terms, covenants and conditions of this Lease to be observed and performed by Owner, subject, however, to the prior rights of any ground or underlying lessor or the holder of any mortgage covering the Property; and no other assets of Owner shall be subject to levy, execution or other judicial process for the satisfaction of Tenant's claims. In the event Owner conveys or transfers its interest in the Property or in this Lease, except as a collateral security for a loan, upon such conveyance or transfer, Owner(and in the case of any subsequent conveyances or transfers, the then grantor or transferor) shall be entirely released and relieved from all liability with

9

respect to the performance of any terms, covenants and conditions on the part of Owner to be performed hereunder from and after the date of such conveyance or transfer, provided that any amounts then due and payable to Tenant by Owner(or by the then grantor or transferor) or any other obligations then to be performed by Owner(or by the then grantor or transferor) for Tenant under any provisions of this Lease, shall either be paid or performed by Owner(or by the then grantor or transferor) or such payment or performance assumed by the grantee or transferee; it being intended hereby that the covenants and obligations on the part of Owner to be performed hereunder shall be binding on Owner, its successors and assigns only during and in respect of their respective periods of ownership of an interest in the Property or in this Lease. This provision shall not be deemed, construed or interpreted to be or constitute an agreement, express or implied, between Owner and Tenant that Owner's interest hereunder and in the Property shall be subject to impressment of any equitable lien or otherwise.

47. OWNER'S CONSENTS:

With respect to any provision of this Lease which provides, in effect, that Owner shall not unreasonably withhold or unreasonably delay any consent or any approval, Tenant shall, in no event, be entitled to make, nor shall Tenant make, any claim, and Tenant hereby waives any claim, for money damages; nor shall Tenant claim any money damages by way of setoff, counterclaim or defense, based upon any claim or assertion by Tenant that Owner has unreasonably withheld or unreasonably delayed any consent or approval; but Tenant's sole remedy shall be an action or proceeding to enforce any such provision, or for specific performance, injunction or declaratory judgment and recovery of legal fees should it prevail as expressly set forth in this Lease.

48. FURTHER PROVISIONS AS TO DEFAULT:

10

A. Additional rent shall consist of all such sums of money beyond the Base Rent as shall become due and payable by Tenant hereunder. Owner shall have the same remedies for default in the payment of additional rent as for a default in payment of Base Rent.

B. If Tenant shall fail to pay any installment of Base Rent or any amount of additional rent for more than ten (10) days after the same becomes due and payable, Tenant shall pay Owner late charge of ten ($.10) cents for each dollar of such Base Rent or additional rent as shall not have been paid to Owner within said ten (10) day period. Such late charge shall be without prejudice to any of Owner's rights and remedies hereunder or at law for non-payment of rent and shall be in addition thereto and be deemed to be additional rent.

C. If Tenant shall fail to pay (i) any installment of Base Rent or any amount of additional rent or (ii) any other sum of money which shall become due and payable by Tenant to Owner pursuant to the terms of this Lease or by reason of Tenant's occupancy of the Demised Premises for a period of ten (10) days after the date on which such installment or payment is due, Tenant shall pay interest thereon at a rate equal to the lesser of the per annum rate of three (3%) percent in excess of the prime rate from time to time announced by [   ] as its prime lending rate, calculated on the basis of the actual days elapsed, based on a 360-day year, or the maximum rate of interest allowed by applicable law(s), if any, then prevailing, from the date on which such installment or payment is due to the date of payment thereof, and such interest shall be deemed to be additional rent.

D. Nothing contained in Article 17 shall be deemed to require Owner to give the notices therein or herein provided for prior to the commencement of a summary proceeding for nonpayment of rent or a plenary action for the recovery of rent on account of any default in the payment of the

11

same, it being intended that such notices are for the sole purpose of creating a conditional limitation hereunder pursuant to which this Lease shall terminate and if Tenant thereafter remains in possession or occupancy, it shall become a holdover tenant.

E. Any default in the performance of the obligations of Tenant, its successors, affiliates or assigns, under any other lease between Owner and Tenant, its successors, affiliates or assigns, shall at the election of Owner be deemed a default under this Lease and compliance with the notice provisions under such other lease shall be deemed compliance with the notice provisions under this Lease. Any default under this Lease shall at the election of Owner be deemed a default under any other lease between Owner and Tenant or its successors, affiliates or assigns and compliance with the notice provisions under such other lease. The security held under this Lease may be applied to satisfy the obligations of Tenant or its successors, affiliates or assigns under any other such lease and any security under any other such lease may be applied to satisfy the obligations of Tenant or its successors, affiliates or assigns under this Lease.

49. ADDENDA TO ARTICLE 21 (END OF TERM):

A. Tenant hereby indemnifies Owner against any liability resulting from delay by Tenant in surrendering the Demised Premises upon the termination of this Lease as provided therein, including any claims made by any succeeding tenant or prospective tenant founded upon such delay. Owner hereby indemnifies Tenant against any loss or damage resulting from Owner's delay or failure to deliver the Initial Delivery Premises or portions thereof as required in the Lease to be delivered March 31, 1998 and such indemnity and liability shall survive the sale and closing thereof of the Property to Tenant or any other purchaser.

B. In the event Tenant remains in possession of the Demised Premises after the expiration

12

124

of the Term or earlier termination of this Lease without the execution of a new lease, (i) Owner shall be entitled to all of the rights and remedies which are available to a Owner against a tenant holding over after the expiration of a term and to such other rights and remedies as may be provided for in this Lease, at law or in equity, and (ii) Tenant, at the option of Owner, shall be deemed to be occupying the Demised Premises as a tenant from month to month, at a monthly rental equal to the product of 125% times the Base Rent, plus additional rent payable during the last month of the Term of this Lease, subject to all of the other terms of this Lease insofar as the same are applicable to a month-to-month tenancy.

50. INSURANCE:

Tenant agrees to secure and keep in force from and after the date Owner shall deliver possession of the Demised Premises to Tenant and throughout the Term of this Lease, at Tenant's own cost and expense (A) Commercial General Liability Insurance with a minimum limit of liability of Ten Million Dollars ($10,000,000) combined single limit; and which insurance shall contain (1) contractual liability covering all written contracts including this Lease, (2) personal injury liability including libel and slander, false arrest, defamation of character, wrongful eviction, invasion of privacy and deletion of the employee/agent/contractor exclusion, (3) fire damage legal liability on real property in the minimum amount of Five Million Dollars ($5,000,000), (4) water damage legal liability in the minimum amount of One Million Dollars ($1,000,000), and (5) additional interest of Owners respects Tenant's occupancy of, and operation at, the Demised Premises; (B) Non-Owned and Hired Car Automobile Liability insurance in the minimum amount of Three Hundred Thousand Dollars ($300,000) combined single limit; and (C) Worker's Compensation Insurance, as required by law.

13

125

51. INSURANCE CARRIERS; EVIDENCE OF INSURANCE; MUTUAL WAIVERS:

A. All policies of insurance procured by Tenant shall be issued on New York State Department of Insurance approved forms and by insurance carriers licensed to offer insurance in New York.

B. Before Owner shall deliver possession of the Demised Premises to Tenant, Tenant shall provide Owner with certificates of insurance evidencing the insurance coverages set forth in this Article. Such certificates shall provide that, in the event of cancellation or material change, thirty (30) days prior written notice shall be given to Owner and all such other named insureds.

C. Each policy of insurance shall contain a waiver of the insurance carrier's right of subrogation against the Owner, superior mortgagee and superior owners respects loss, damage or destruction by fire or other insured casualty occurring while this Lease is in effect.

D. All insurance procured by Owner and/or Tenant under this Article shall be issued in the names and for the benefit of Owner, Tenant and, unless Owner otherwise requests, any superior Owner and any superior mortgagee, as their respective interests may appear, and shall contain an endorsement that each Owner, superior owner and superior mortgagee, although named as an insured, nevertheless shall be entitled to recover under said policies for any loss or damage occasioned to it, its agents, employees, contractors, directors, shareholders, partners and principals (disclosed and undisclosed) by reason of the negligence of Owner or Tenant, its servants, agents, employees and contractors. In the case of insurance against damage by fire or other casualty, to the Property the policy or policies shall provide that loss shall be adjusted jointly with Owner and Tenant, and, at Owner's election, shall be payable to Owner, to be held and disbursed as provided in this Lease, or to any superior mortgagee under a standard mortgagee clause, or to any superior

14

126

landlord.

52. ADDENDUM TO ARTICLE 11 (ASSIGNMENT, MORTGAGE, ETC.):

If Tenant is a corporation or partnership, and if at any time during the Term there shall occur either (i) the issuance of interests in Tenant (whether stock, partnership interest or otherwise) to any person or group of related persons, whether in a single transaction or a series of related or unrelated transactions, in such quantities that after such issuance such person or group shall have control of Tenant, or (ii) a transfer of more than 50% in interest of Tenant (whether stock, partnership interest or otherwise) by any party or parties in interest whether in a single transaction or a series of related or unrelated transactions or by operation of law, the same shall be deemed an assignment of this Lease, except that the transfer of the outstanding capital stock of any corporate Tenant, by persons or parties (other than persons or parties owning 5% or more of the voting stock of such corporation) through the "over-the-counter" market or any recognized national securities exchange, shall not be included in the calculation of such 50%. In the event an issuance or transfer referred to in clause (i) or (ii) of the first sentence of this Article shall occur, Tenant shall so notify Owner and Owner shall have the right, at its option, to terminate this Lease by notice to Tenant given within thirty (30) days thereafter or within ninety (90) days after Owner shall have received other notice thereof. For the purposes of this Article, stock ownership shall be determined in accordance with the principles set forth in Section 544 of the Internal Revenue Code of 1954, as the same existed on August 16, 1954.

53. FURTHER PROVISIONS AS TO PAYMENT OF RENT:

A. If the date of commencement of the Term shall not occur on the first day of a calendar month, the annual rent installment for such calendar month shall be prorated on a per diem basis and Owner shall credit the excess amount paid on the execution of this Lease for the payment of Base

Rent for the next succeeding calendar month.

B. . If the Base Rent or any additional rent shall be or become uncollectible, reduced or required to be refunded by virtue of any law, governmental order or regulation, or direction of any public officer or body pursuant to law, Tenant shall enter into such agreement or agreements and take such other action (without additional expense to Tenant) as Owner may request, as may be legally permissible, to permit Owner to collect the maximum annual rent and additional rent which may from time to time during the continuance of such rent restriction be legally permissible, but not in excess of the amounts of Base Rent or additional rent payable under this Lease. Upon the termination of such rent restriction prior to the termination of the Term of this Lease, (a) the annual rent and additional rent, after such termination, shall become payable under this Lease in the amount of the Base Rent and additional rent set forth in this Lease for the period following such termination, and (b) Tenant shall pay to Owner, to the maximum extent legally permissible, an amount equal to (i) the additional annual rent and additional rent which would have been paid pursuant to this Lease, but for such rent restriction, less (ii) the annual rent and additional rent paid by Tenant to Owner during the period that such rent restriction was in effect.

54. ADDENDUM TO ARTICLE 27 (BILLS AND NOTICES):

Notwithstanding the provisions of Article 28, if there occurs any temporary or permanent interruption of any mail service, lasting more than five (5) consecutive business days, notices may be given by telegram or personal delivery, but shall not be effective until personally received by an executive officer of a party which is a corporation, or a partner of a party which is a partnership, or principal of any other entity.

55. PERMITS:

16

Tenant shall not use or suffer or permit any person to use the Demised Premises for any unlawful purposes and shall obtain and maintain at Tenant's sole cost and expense all licenses and permits from any and all governmental authorities having jurisdiction of the Demised Premises which may be necessary for the conduct of Tenant's business therein. Tenant shall comply with all applicable laws, resolutions, codes, rules and regulations of any department, bureau, agency or any governmental authority having jurisdiction over the operation, occupancy, maintenance and use of the Demised Premises for the purposes set forth herein. Tenant agrees to indemnify and save Owner harmless from and against any claim, penalty, loss, damage or expense (including reasonable attorneys' fees and disbursements) imposed by reason of a violation of any applicable law or the rules and regulations of governmental authorities having jurisdiction related to Tenant's use and occupancy of the Demised Premises.

56. SIDEWALKS:

Tenant agrees not to encumber or obstruct or permit the encumbrance or obstruction, whether by the parking of vehicles or otherwise, of the sidewalks or curbs adjacent or leading to the Demised Premises.

57. EASEMENT FOR PIPES:

Tenant shall permit Owner to erect, use, maintain and repair pipes, ducts, cables, conduits, plumbing, vents and wires in, to and through the Demised Premises as and to the extent that Owner may now or hereafter deem to be necessary or appropriate for the proper operation and maintenance of the building or to the extent necessary to accommodate the requirements of adjoining or other tenants. All such work shall be done, so far as practicable, in such manner as to avoid unreasonable interference with Tenant's use of the premises.

17

129

58. SIGNS:

A. Tenant shall have the right to install and maintain, at its own expense, various elevator, lobby and directory signs subject to the written approval of Owner as to dimensions, material, content, location and design, which approval Owner agrees not to unreasonably withhold. Tenant shall comply with all of the laws, orders, rules and regulations of the governmental authorities having jurisdiction thereover, including zoning laws, building codes and all requirements of insurance underwriters and boards. Tenant shall obtain and pay for all permits required therefor. No sign shall be manufactured and/or installed on the building until all approvals and permits are first obtained and copies thereof delivered to Owner with evidence of payment for any fees pertaining thereto. Tenant agrees to pay all annual renewal fees pertaining to Tenant's signs. Tenant shall maintain any such signs or other installation in good condition and repair. Other than such permitted signs, Tenant shall not place or install or suffer to be placed or installed or maintain any sign upon or outside the Demised Premises or in the Property. Tenant shall not place or install or suffer to be placed or installed or maintain on the exterior of the Demised Premises any awning, canopy, banner, flag, pennant, aerial, antenna or the like; nor shall Tenant place or maintain on the glass of any window or door of the Demised Premises any sign, decoration, lettering, advertising matter, shade or blind or other thing of any kind. Owner shall have the right, with or without notice to Tenant, to remove any signs installed by Tenant in violation of this Paragraph and to charge Tenant for the cost of such removal and any repairs necessitated thereby, without liability to Tenant for such removal.

B. In the event Owner or Owner's representatives shall deem it necessary to remove any such sign in order to paint or to make any other repairs, alterations or improvements in or upon the

18

130

Building or the Demised Premises or any part thereof, Owner shall have the right to do so, provided the same be removed and replaced at Tenant's expense, whenever the said repairs, alterations or improvements shall have been completed.

59. ADDENDUM TO ARTICLE IV (REPAIRS):

If any damage to the plumbing system used in the Property (whether such damage is within or outside the Demised Premises) occurs on account of any action, omission to act or negligence of Tenant or Tenant's employees, agents or contractors, Owner shall make such repairs and Tenant, upon demand by Owner, shall pay to Owners additional rent, an amount equal to the cost of such repairs plus fifteen (15%) percent thereof as compensation for the cost of supervising such repairs.

60. COVENANT AGAINST LIENS:

Tenant shall do all things necessary to prevent the filing of any mechanic's or other lien against the Demised Premises or any other portion of the Property or the interest of Owner or any ground or underlying lessors therein or the interest of any mortgagees or holders of any deeds of trust covering any portion of the Property by reason of any work, labor, services or materials performed or supplied or claimed to have been performed for or supplied to Tenant, or anyone holding the Demised Premises, or any part thereof, through or under Tenant. If any such lien shall at any time be filed, Tenant shall either cause the same to be vacated and canceled of record within thirty (30) days after the date of the filing thereof or, if Tenant in good faith determines that such lien should be contested, Tenant shall furnish such security, by surety bond or otherwise, as may be necessary or be prescribed by law to release the same as a lien against the real property and to prevent any foreclosure of such lien during the pendency of such contest. If Tenant shall fail to vacate or release such lien in the manner and within the time period aforesaid, then, in addition to any other right or

19

remedy of Owner resulting from Tenant's said default, Owner may, but shall not be obligated to, vacate or release the same either by paying the amount claimed to be due or by procuring the release of such lien by giving security or in such other manner as may be prescribed by law. Tenant shall repay to Owner on demand, all sums disbursed or deposited by Owner pursuant to the foregoing provisions of this Paragraph, including Owner's cost and expenses and reasonable attorneys' fees incurred in connection therewith. However, nothing contained herein shall imply any consent or agreement on the part of Owner or any ground or underlying lessors or mortgagees or holders of deeds of trust covering any portion of the Property to subject their respective estates or interests to liability under any mechanic's or other lien law, whether or not the performance or the furnishing of such work, labor, services or materials to Tenant or anyone holding the Demised Premises, or any part thereof, through or under Tenant, shall have been consented to by Owner or any such parties.

61. RELATIONSHIP OF PARTIES:

Nothing contained in this Lease shall be deemed to constitute or be construed or implied to create the relationship of principal and agent, partnership, joint venture or any other relationship between the parties hereto, other than the relationship of Owner and tenant.

62. CONSTRUCTION; GOVERNING LAW:

A. If any of the provisions of this Lease or the application thereof to any person or circumstances, shall, to any extent, be invalid or unenforceable, the remainder of this Lease, or the application of such provision or provisions to persons or circumstances other than those as to whom or which it is held invalid or unenforceable, shall not be affected thereby, and every provision of this Lease shall be valid and enforceable to the fullest extent permitted by law. In the event of any conflict between provisions contained in the printed form of this Lease and any Rider provision in

20

Rider I or Rider II, the terms of the applicable Rider provision will govern and control, however, Rider II shall control any conflicts among Riders. The terms (i) "Owner" and "Landlord", (ii) "Demised Premises and "Premises" (whether or not capitalized) and (iii) "rent", "Fixed Rent" and "Base Rent" as appearing in this Lease shall be as logical and applicable for each conceptual category (i), (ii) and (iii), afforded the same meaning and be deemed interchangeable. The term "Rental(s)" or "rental(s)") shall mean Base Rent and additional rentals. The word "Term" shall mean the period commencing with date of this Lease unless such other date is set forth as the "Commencement Date" of the Term and shall end on the stated expiration date unless sooner terminated.

B. This Lease shall be governed in all respects by the laws of the State of New York applicable to contracts made and to be performed wholly within New York.

63. LEASE NOT BINDING UNLESS EXECUTED:

Submission by Owner of this Lease for execution by Tenant shall confer no rights nor impose any obligations on either party unless and until both Owner and Tenant shall have executed this Lease and duplicate originals thereof shall have been delivered to the respective parties.

64. ENTIRE AGREEMENT:

This Lease constitutes the entire Agreement between the parties and no earlier statements or prior written matter shall have any force or effect. Tenant agrees that it is not relying on any representations or agreements other than those contained in this Lease.

65. RECORDING:

Tenant may record this Lease or a memorandum thereof reflecting the terms hereof.

66. ADDITIONAL RULES AND REGULATIONS:

21

A. The sidewalks, entrances, driveways, passages, courts, vestibules, stairways, corridors and halls shall not be obstructed or encumbered by any tenant or used for any purpose other than for ingress to and egress from the Demised Premises and for delivery of merchandise and equipment in a prompt and efficient manner using areas designated for such delivery by Owner.

B. The water and plumbing fixtures shall not be used for any purposes other than those for which they were designed or constructed and no sweepings, rubbish, rags, acids or other substances shall be deposited therein, and the expense of any breakage, stoppage, or damage resulting from the violation of this rule shall be borne by the tenant who, or whose clerks, agents, employees or visitors, shall have caused it.

C. No tenant shall sweep or throw or permit to be swept or thrown from the Demised Premises any dirt or other substances into any of the streets, or out of the doors or windows or stairways of the building, and no tenant shall use, keep or permit to be used or kept any foul or noxious gas or substance in the Demised Premises, or permit or suffer the Demised Premises to be occupied or used in a manner offensive or objectionable to Owner or other occupants of the Property by reason of noise, odors and/or vibrations, or interfere in any way with other tenants or those having business therein, nor shall any animals (except seeing eye dogs) or birds be kept in or about the Property.

D. No tenant shall mark, paint, drill into, or in any way deface any part of the Demised Premises or the building. No boring, cutting or stringing of wires shall be permitted, except with the prior written consent of Owner, and as Owner may direct.

67. COMPLIANCE-ENVIRONMENTAL LAWS:

A. Tenant agrees to fully comply with, and to take no action or fail to take any action which

22

shall or may result in a violation of any federal, state or local law, statute, code, ordinance, regulation, rule or other requirement (including, but not limited to, consent decrees and judicial or administrative orders), relating to health or safety or the environment, all as amended or modified from time to time (collectively, "Environmental Laws"). Tenant shall not engage in operations at the Demised Premises or in the Building which involves the generation, manufacture, refining, transportation, treatment, storage, handling or disposal of "hazardous substances" or "hazardous wastes," as such terms are defined under any Environmental Laws. Tenant further covenants that it will not cause or permit to exist as a result of an intentional or unintentional action or omission on its part, the releasing, spilling, leaking, pumping, pouring, emitting, emptying or dumping from, on or about the Building or the land on which it is located of any hazardous substances or hazardous wastes. In the event that any lien shall be asserted against Owner, any property of Owner, the Demised Premises, the Building, the land or the Property in connection with any Environmental Laws as a result of any act or failure to act by Tenant, Tenant covenants and agrees to immediately discharge such lien, or cause the same to be discharged, by bonding or as otherwise allowed by law is discharged within three (3) days after the filing thereof.

B. Notwithstanding the foregoing, Tenant shall, at Tenant's own expense, make all submissions to, provide all information to, and comply with all requirements of all Environmental Laws and each and every federal, state or local agency, authority, bureau, division and board (collectively, the "Authorities"). Should the Authorities deem that a cleanup plan be prepared and that a cleanup be undertaken because of any spills or discharges of hazardous substances or hazardous wastes at the Demised Premises caused by Tenant which occur during the Term of this Lease and are caused by Tenant, then Tenant shall, at Tenant's own expense, prepare and submit the

23

required plans and financial assurances, and carry out the approved plans. Tenant's obligations under this Article shall also arise if there is any closing, terminating or transferring of or changes in operations of an establishment at the Demised Premises pursuant to Environmental Laws. At no expense to Owner, Tenant shall promptly provide all information required by Owner for preparation of non-applicability affidavits and shall promptly sign such affidavits when requested by Owner. Tenant shall indemnify, defend and save harmless Owner from all costs, penalties, fines, suits, procedures, claims and actions of any kind, including reasonable attorneys' fees, arising out of or in any way connected with any spills or discharges of hazardous substances or hazardous wastes at the Demised Premises which occur during the Term of this Lease; and from all costs, penalties, fines, suits, procedures, claims and actions of any kind, including reasonable attorneys' fees, arising out of Tenant's failure to provide all information, make all submissions and take all actions required by any and all Environmental Laws and/or the Authorities. Tenant's obligations and liabilities under this paragraph shall continue so long as the Authorities retain jurisdiction over Owner, the Building or the Demised Premises. Tenant's failure to abide by the terms of this paragraph shall be subject to equitable relief.

C. With respect to Tenant's occupancy of the Demised Premises, Tenant shall promptly provide Owner with any notices, correspondence and submissions made by Tenant to or received by Tenant from the Authorities.

D. In the event of Tenant's failure to comply in full with this Article, Owner may, at its option, perform any and all of Tenant's obligations as aforesaid and all costs and expenses incurred by Owner in the exercise of this right shall be deemed to be additional rent payable in accordance with this Article.

24

136

E. Tenant's obligations under this Article shall only extend to actions or conditions caused by Tenant occurring on and after the Commencement Date and shall survive the expiration or sooner termination of this Lease.

68. PLANS AND SPECIFICATIONS:

Tenant hereby agrees to prepare detailed plans and specifications for any alterations, additions or improvements to be made in the Demised Premises by Tenant pursuant to the terms of this Lease. Upon completion of such plans, Tenant shall deliver copies of plans to Owner for approval. Within a reasonable time after delivery of the plans, such time not to exceed fifteen (15) days, Owner shall either approve (if acceptable to Owner) the drawings or advise Tenant specifically wherein the plans and specifications are not approved and propose specifically the changes recommended. Within ten (10) days after receipt of Owner's specified objections and recommendations, Tenant shall resubmit the plans and specifications to Owner for approval and the above procedure shall be repeated. In the event Owner gives timely notice of continued objections, the changes shall be made by Tenant's architect in such manner as to conform with Owner's requirements. Tenant shall reimburse Owner for all costs and expenses incurred in Owner's review of Tenant's plans.

It is understood that Tenant shall be solely responsible for the plans and specifications or other construction documents used by Tenant in connection therewith and for any liabilities or obligations based upon or in connection with the construction contracts and for any loss or damage resulting from the use of any of the foregoing and Tenant hereby releases, discharges, indemnifies, defends and holds Owner harmless from and against any and all liabilities or claims for damages of losses of any kind, whether legal or equitable, or from any action, and the expenses of defending any

25

action, arising or alleged to arise out of or in connection with the performance of any work pursuant thereto. Tenant at Owner's request shall defend, at Tenant's cost and expense, any claim, action or proceeding in connection with or based upon any of the foregoing or the work done in performance thereof.

After the approval of plans and specifications by Owner and the award of contracts to contractors reasonably acceptable to Owner, Tenant shall promptly proceed to make the alteration, addition or improvement in accordance with the drawings, plans and specifications and other documents used in connection therewith.

Tenant covenants that it will use its best efforts to have the alteration, addition or improvement made with a minimum of delay and in a good and workmanlike manner and will pay promptly all amounts due in connection with the construction. Upon completion of the addition, alteration or improvement, Tenant shall provide Owner with two (2) copies of "as built" plans certified by the general contractor and architect as correct.

69. WAIVER OF TRIAL BY JURY:

It is mutually agreed by and between Owner and Tenant that the respective parties hereto shall and they hereby do waive trial by jury to the extent allowed by law in any action, proceeding or counterclaim brought by either party hereto against the other on any matters whatsoever arising out of or in any way connected with this Lease, the Demised Demised Premises, the relationship of Owner and Tenant, and any emergency statutory or any other statutory remedy. It is further mutually agreed that in the event Owner commences any summary proceeding for possession of the Premises, Tenant will not interpose any non-compulsory counterclaim of whatever nature or description in any such proceeding.

70. CANCELLATION OPTION:

A. For the purposes of this Article, the following definitions shall apply:

The term "Cancellation Date" shall mean the day set forth in each of Tenant's notices for the Term to end with respect to the applicable space consisting of the full floors from time to time so identified.

B. Subject to the provisions hereof, Tenant shall from time to time have the right to cancel this Lease with respect to all or portions of the Demised Premises consisting of full floors as of the Cancellation Date, which right to cancel shall be exercisable by Tenant giving written notice thereof to Owner on or before each Cancellation Date. Provided that Tenant shall have complied with the foregoing requirements, then, the Lease Term shall with respect to such identified space terminate upon the Cancellation Date as if such date were the Expiration Date and all applicable terms affected thereby such as the Demised Premises and all Rentals shall be adjusted accordingly.

71. SATELLITE ANTENNA:

A. Subject to the provisions of this Article, Tenant may install, operate and maintain in a location on the roof of the Building microwave, satellite or other antenna communications systems (herein called the "Satellite Antenna") that transmits and receives signals to or from other communications installations located off-site. Owner consents to such installation, operation and maintenance of the Satellite Antenna at locations to be mutually agreed upon by Owner and Tenant on the roof. Tenant is permitted, subject to the provisions of this Lease and solely at Tenant's cost and expense, to install, operate and maintain the Satellite Antenna, as well as the conduits and cables necessary for the construction and operation of the Satellite Antenna from the roof to the Demised Premises through then available sleeves located in the Building communications

27

closets, provided that: (i) the installation thereof (including all structural reinforcement, framing and waterproofing) shall be performed subject to the provisions, (ii) Tenant shall obtain and maintain all operating permits and approvals to effectuate compliance with all applicable legal requirements (including any requirements of the Federal Communications Commission), (iii) Tenant shall comply with all applicable legal requirements, in connection with such installation, (iv) Tenant shall promptly repair any damage to Property, including the Building caused by such installation, operation or maintenance, and (v) Tenant shall remove the Satellite Antenna and any related conduits and cables and repair any resulting damage (whether caused by installation or removal) to such Property at or prior to the Expiration Date. Tenant shall have the right, in common with others, of reasonable access to the roof and Building communications closets for the installation, operation, maintenance and removal of the Satellite Antenna and related conduits and cables, and for the partial or complete replacement of the foregoing, subject to the provisions of this Lease and to such other reasonable conditions imposed by Owner.

B. Notwithstanding the foregoing provisions of this Article, Tenant shall not have the right to install at a location, or, if initially installed, to thereafter operate or maintain at the conflicting location, the Satellite Antenna to the extent that Owner shall reasonably determine that the same will interfere with the use or operation (including the reception and transmission of signals to and from the same) of other existing satellite antennae, microwave dishes or other communications equipment on the roof.

C. Owner, at Owner's expense, shall have the right, on not less than five (5) days prior written notice (except in the event of emergency, in which event no notice shall be required), to relocate the Satellite Antenna, which expense shall include the removal of the Satellite Antenna

28

140

and the related conduits and cables, the purchasing of materials and equipment necessary for the relocation thereof and the reinstallation of the Satellite Antenna and such conduits and cables at such other location on the roof as shall be designated by Owner. In connection with the foregoing: (i) Owner shall select an alternative location for the Satellite Antenna that shall be no less favorable for the reception and transmission of signals to and from the Satellite Antenna as the previous location, (ii) except in cases of emergency, Owner shall perform the relocation so as to minimize interference with the reception of and/or transmission of signals to and from the Satellite Antenna during any period that Tenant shall be using the Satellite Antenna for the reception or transmission of signals, and (iii) Tenant shall cooperate with Owner in all reasonable respects relating to any such relocation.

D. The rights granted in this Article are granted in connection with, and as part of the rights created under, this Lease, and are not separately transferable or assignable other than in connection with an assignment of Tenant's rights under this Lease as permitted by this Lease.

E. Nothing contained in this Article shall be deemed to be a lease by Owner to Tenant of any portion of the Roof.

72. EXPANSION OPTIONS:

A. Provided that this Lease shall be in full force and effect and that Tenant shall not then be in default (after notice and the expiration of the applicable cure period) with respect to any of the obligations of Tenant under this Lease, Tenant shall have the option from time to time ("Expansion Option"), to lease each floor (or portion thereof) of space (as the same becomes available due to vacating by an existing occupant) from Owner up to a total of Five Hundred (500,000) Thousand square feet of Demised Premises. Each Expansion Option shall be exercisable only by Tenant having given written notice thereof to Owner (the "Expansion Notice"), not later than thirty (30) days after Owner gives Tenant written notice of the availability of each such full floor or portion thereof. The amount of rent to be paid by Tenant to Owner with respect to each Expansion Space shall be the same Basic Rent per square foot and on the same measurement basis as the Initial Delivery Space. If Tenant shall timely exercise each Expansion Option, Owner shall deliver possession of the relevant Expansion Space to Tenant on or about the day set forth in Owner's notice as the date of availability of such Expansion Space, subject to delays beyond Owner's reasonable control.

B. Each Expansion Space, shall be delivered to Tenant in its then "as is" condition with the furniture, fixtures, equipment and decorations as set forth in Schedule B and in the Delivery Condition. Owner shall not lease any space in the Building nor consent to any subleasing or assignment (unless required under the relevant existing lease) without first offering such space to Tenant. Owner shall have no obligation to perform any work or alterations in order to prepare the relevant Expansion Space for Tenant's initial occupancy thereof other than repairs thereto as required to comply with the Delivery Conditions or as required for all space under the Lease.

C. From and after each relevant Expansion Space Commencement Date, the provisions of this Lease shall apply to the relevant Expansion Space, except that:

(i) The term "Demised Premises"shall be deemed to include the relevant Expansion Space;

(ii) Basic Rent shall be increased by the relevant Expansion Space rental per square foot;

(iii) Tenant's Tax Payment if applicable shall be recalculated in the manner set forth in this Lease; and

142

(iv)   The Lease Term with respect to each relevant Expansion Space shall be co-terminus with the Lease Term and/or any Renewal Term for the Demised Premises.

73. OPTION TO RENEW:

A. Provided that Tenant is not in default beyond any applicable cure period under any of the terms, obligation or covenants of this Lease at the time of the exercise of this option and at the time of the commencement of the First Renewal Term (as hereinafter defined), Tenant shall have the right, at its option, to extend the original Lease Term ("Original Term"), for one renewal term ("Renewal Term") of three (3) years, to commence immediately following the expiration of the Original Term, by giving written notice ("Tenant's Notice") to Owner not less than nine (9) months prior to the stated expiration date of this Lease and, upon the giving of Tenant's Notice, this Lease, subject to the provisions hereof, shall be automatically extended for the Renewal Term with the same force and effect as if the Renewal Term had been originally included in the Lease Term. All of the terms, obligations, covenants and conditions of this Lease shall continue in full force and effect during the Renewal Term except that the terms of this Lease relating to the performance of any Tenant's or Owner's work shall not be applicable to the Renewal Term, and there shall be no further privilege of extension of this Lease beyond the Renewal Term. The Base Rent payable by Tenant during the Renewal Term shall be the sum of Fifteen ($15.00) Dollars per square foot contained in the Demised Premises per annum, payable in equal monthly installments in advance on the first day of each and every calendar month during the Renewal Term.

B. The termination, expiration, cancellation, assignment or surrender of this Lease as to the entire Demised Premises shall terminate any rights of Tenant pursuant to this paragraph.

74. JOINT AND SEVERAL LIABILITY:

31

If Tenant is comprised of one or more parties or entities then the liability of all such parties or entities shall be joint and several.

75. OPTION TO PURCHASE:

Landlord and Tenant acknowledge that Landlord by agreement dated February 27, 1997 entered into an option to sell the Building to ("   ") pursuant to the terms and under the conditions contained in such Agreement (the "Option"). Landlord warrants, covenants and represents to Tenant that in the event the [   ]Option is not properly and completely exercised or, if exercised, goes into default, Landlord will sell, transfer and convey the Building, land thereunder and all appurtenances thereto on the same terms and conditions as set forth in a "Contract of Sale" entered into between Landlord and Tenant or their affiliates which may become executed at a time subsequent to the date of this Lease or if no Contract of Sale is executed, then on the same terms and conditions as set forth in the [   ] Option or as presented to [   ] by Landlord. Landlord warrants, covenants and represents that it will take all action and use best efforts to effectuate such sale, conveyance or transfer to Tenant and defend title against claims of [   ] and indemnify, defend and hold Tenant harmless from claims of [   ] relating with or arising out of the Option or this Lease or this option of Tenant to purchase. In the event Landlord is prevented from effectuating the intent of this Article, as soon thereafter as such prohibition is lifted, Landlord will promptly perform pursuant to the terms hereof. The right of Tenant to purchase pursuant to this Article shall survive the termination of this Lease or expiration of the Term of this Lease. Landlord covenants, warrants and represents that it will otherwise comply with all the terms, covenants and conditions as set forth in the Contract of Sale or herein contained in order to effectuate the transaction contemplated hereby.

32

144

LANDLORD:

By_____

TENANT:

By_____

33

Schedule A
[Demised Premises Stacking and Layout]

Section I:

Initial Delivery Premises

Section II:

Temporary Space

Section III:

Expansion Space

Schedule B
[Furniture, Fixtures and Equipment]

Inventory of all Furniture, Fixtures, Equipment, Partitions and Decorations Floor by Floor

Schedule C
[Cleaning Specifications]

NOTES

3

ADDITIONAL FINANCIAL TERMS FOR MIXED USE BUILDINGS OR RETAIL PROPERTIES

submitted by John B. Wood

Section II: CONSUMER PRICE INDEX:

The annual rental rate currently specified to be paid by Tenant at the time, from time to time, of each calculation hereunder (the "Base Rent"), shall be used as a basis to calculate additional rent as of the times and in the manner set forth in this Section II and as a result thereof, Tenant shall pay the additional rent as hereinafter provided:

A. For the purposes of this Section II, the following definitions shall apply:

(1) "Price Index" shall mean the "Consumer Price Index for all Urban Consumers, New York - Northeastern New Jersey, (1982-1984=100), issued and published by the Bureau of Labor Statistics of the United States Department of Labor.

(2) "Base Price Index" shall mean the Price Index as it exists on the date hereof.

B. Effective as of each January and July subsequent to the date hereof, the Base Rent shall be utilized as a basis for calculation of the additional rent under this Section, as follows:

(1) The July calculation shall be based on eighty (80%) percent of the percentage difference between the Price Index for the preceding month of June and the Base Price Index. In the event that the Price Index for June in any calendar year during the Term reflects an increase over the Base Price Index, then the Base Rent hereunder as of the July 1st following such month of June shall be multiplied by eighty (80%) percent of the percentage difference between the

1

Price Index for June and the Base Price Index, and the resulting amount shall be additional rent effective as of such July 1st. Such additional rent shall thereafter be payable hereunder, in equal monthly installments, until it is readjusted pursuant to the terms of this Section II.

(2) The January calculation shall be based on eighty (80%) percent of the percentage difference between the Price Index for the preceding month of December and the Base Price Index. In the event that the Price Index for December in any calendar year during the Term reflects an increase over the Base Price Index, then the Base Rent hereunder as of the January 1st following such month of December shall be multiplied by eighty (80%) percent of the percentage difference between the Price Index for December and the Base Price Index, and the resulting amount shall be additional rent effective as of such January 1st. Such additional rent shall thereafter be payable hereunder, in equal monthly installments, until it is readjusted pursuant to the terms of this Section II.

The following illustrates the intention of the parties hereto as to the computation of the additional rent resulting from this Consumer Price Index adjustment as applied from time to time to the Base Rent:

Assuming that (i) the Base Rent is $100,000, (ii) the Base Price Index is 255.4 and (iii) the Price Index for the particular June or December, is 280.9, then the percentage of increase is 10.0%. The sum of $100,000 would be multiplied by 80% of 10%, or 8%, resulting in an annual additional rental of

2

$8,000 effective as of the immediately following July 1 or January 1, as the case may be. Such $8,000 would be payable by Tenant in equal monthly installments in advance thereafter until the next such calculation and adjustment.

C. In the event that the Price Index ceases to use the 1982-1984 average of 100" as the basis of calculation, or if a substantial change is made in the terms or number of items or composition thereof contained in or utilized by the Price Index, then the Price Index shall be adjusted to the figure that would have been arrived at had the manner of computing the Price Index in effect on the date hereof not been altered. In the event such Price Index (or a successor or substitute index) is not available, a reliable governmental or other non-partisan publication, selected by Landlord, evaluating the information used in determining the Price Index, shall be used.

D. Landlord shall cause statements of the additional rent provided for in this Section II to be prepared in reasonable detail and delivered to Tenant. In no event shall the additional rent payments being paid immediately prior to each such adjustment be reduced by virtue of any succeeding adjustment occurring under this Section II. Any delay or failure of Landlord, beyond July or January of any calendar year, in computing or billing for such additional rent hereinabove provided, shall not constitute a waiver of or in any way impair the continuing obligation of Tenant to pay such additional rent.

Section III: PERCENTAGE RENT:

A. For the purposes of this Lease, the following definitions shall apply:

(1)   "Annual Sales Base" shall mean $(_____) (or average over a specified

3

157

term; i.e. 3rd through 12th months of 1st year).

(2)   "Gross Sales" shall mean the dollar aggregate of (a) the entire amount of the price charged for all goods, wares and merchandise sold, leased, licensed or delivered and all charges for all services sold or performed by Tenant from all business conducted at, upon or from the Demised Premises by Tenant, whether made for cash, by check, on credit, charge accounts or otherwise, without reserve or deduction for inability or failure to collect the same, including, but not limited to, transactions (i) where the orders therefor originate from or are accepted by Tenant at the Demised Premises, but delivery or performance thereof is made from or at any other place; all sales made and orders received in or at the Demised Premises shall be deemed made and completed therein, even though the payment or account may be transferred to another office for collection, and all orders which result from solicitation outside the Demised Premises where such solicitation is conducted by personnel operating from or reporting to or under the control or supervision of Tenant shall be deemed part of Gross Sales; (ii) pursuant to mail, telephone, telegraph or other similar device whereby orders are received or billed from the Demised Premises; (iii) by means of mechanical or other vending devices; (iv) originating from whatever source, and which Tenant in the normal and customary course of Tenant's operations would credit or attribute to Tenant's business conducted in the Demised Premises, and (b) all monies or other things of value received by Tenant from Tenant's operations at, upon or from the Demised Premises which are neither included in nor excluded from Gross Sales by other provisions of this definition, but without any duplication,

4

including, without limitation, finance charges, cost of gift or merchandise certificates and all deposits not refunded to customers. Each charge or sale upon installment or credit shall be treated as a sale for the full price in the month during which such charge or sale is made, irrespective of the time when Tenant shall receive payment (whether full or partial) therefor. No deduction shall be allowed from Gross Sales for uncollectible credit accounts. Each lease or rental of merchandise shall be treated as a sale in the month during which such lease or rental is made, for a price equal to the total rent payable. For the purpose of ascertaining the amount of Gross Sales upon which the payment of Percentage Rent is to be computed hereunder, the following may be deducted from Gross Sales: (1) the exchange or merchandise between stores of Tenant or its subsidiaries where such exchanges are made solely for the convenient operation of Tenant's business and not for the purpose of consummating a sale which has been made at, upon or from the Demised Premises; (2) returns to shippers or manufacturers; (3) sales of trade fixtures after use thereof, which are not part of Tenant's stock in trade and not sold in the regular course of Tenant's business; (4) cash or credit refunds made upon transactions included within Gross Sales but not exceeding the selling price of the merchandise returned by the purchaser and accepted by Tenant; and (5) the amount of any local, County, State or Federal sales, luxury or excise tax on such sales provided such tax is both added to the selling price and paid to the taxing authority by Tenant (but not any vendor of Tenant); provided, however, no franchise or capital stock tax and income or similar tax based upon income, profits or gross sales as such, shall be deducted from Gross

5

Sales in any event whatsoever. For the purposes of this Paragraph, the term "Tenant" shall be deemed to include any of Tenant's subtenants, concessionaires and licensees, or any other occupant of the Demised Premises.

(3)   "Lease Year" shall mean a period of twelve (12) full, consecutive calendar months during the Term, with the first such period commencing on (_____) 199_, and each succeeding Lease Year commencing on of such succeeding year; provided that the last Lease Year (referred to as a "partial Lease Year") shall be deemed to mean the eight (8) months period from 199_ through 19__.

(4)   "Percentage Rent Period" shall mean monthly.

(5)   "Percentage Rent Rate" shall mean twenty-five (25%) percent.

(6)   "Periodic Sales Base" shall mean $ (Annual Sales Base/12).

B. In addition to the Base Rent and as part of the total rentals to be paid for each Lease Year or partial Lease Year, Tenant shall pay to Landlord, as additional rent (hereinafter referred to as "Percentage Rent"), a sum equal to the amount, if any, by which Tenant's Gross Sales exceed the Annual Sales Base multiplied by the Percentage Rent Rate.

C. Percentage Rent shall be determined and paid, without any prior demand therefor, within thirty (30) days after the last day of each Percentage Rent Period during the Term, except that if the commencement date of the Lease is other than the first day of a calendar month, the Gross Sales during the period of the first partial month shall be added to the Gross Sales during the next succeeding full Percentage Rent Period. The amount of each payment of Percentage Rent shall be equal to the amount, if any, by which Tenant's Gross Sales for the immediately preceding Percentage

6

160

Rent Period exceed the Periodic Sales Base multiplied by the Percentage Rent Rate. The Annual Sales Base and the Periodic Sales Base, whichever the case may be, shall be prorated for any partial Lease Year upon the basis of one-twelfth (1/12th) for each full month of such partial Lease Year, plus an amount equal to one-three hundred sixtieths (1/360ths) for each day if the commencement date of this Lease is other than the first day of the month. At the end of each Lease Year, the Percentage Rent shall be adjusted to a Lease Year basis and the balance of the Percentage Rent due, if any, shall be paid within sixty (60) days after the end of such Lease Year, including the last Lease Year hereof, as to which Tenant's obligation shall survive the expiration or sooner termination of the Lease Term. if at the end of any Lease Year, the total amount of the Percentage Rent reserved hereunder and paid by Tenant exceeds the total amount of such rent required to be paid by Tenant during or from such Lease Year, Tenant shall receive a credit equivalent to such excess which may be deducted by Tenant from the next accruing payment of Percentage Rent or, during the last Lease Year, and provided Tenant is not then in default of any of its obligations under this Lease, Landlord will refund such excess to Tenant within thirty (30) days following Landlord's receipt of Tenant's statement of Gross Sales covering the preceding Lease Year. Each Lease Year shall be considered as an independent accounting period for the purpose of computing the amount of Percentage Rent due, if any. The amount of Gross Sales in any Lease Year shall not be carried over into any other Lease Year.

D. If the Base Rent shall abate or be reduced as a result of any event mentioned under Paragraph 9, hereof, then the amount of the Annual Sales Base and Periodic Sales Base, respectively, shall be reduced in proportion to the decrease in the Base Rent.

E. BOOKS AND RECORDS:

7

161

Tenant shall prepare and keep for a period of not less than thirty-six (36) months following the end of each Lease Year, neat, true and accurate books of account and records, conforming to sound and accepted accounting principles and practices, consistently applied, including, but not limited to, sales tax and other reports filed with governmental agencies, all purchases and receipts of merchandise, inventories and all sales and other transactions by Tenant from which Gross Sales at, upon or from the Demised Premises can be determined. Tenant agrees to record all sales, at the time each sale is made, whether for cash or credit, in a cash register or registers containing locked-in cumulative tapes with cumulation capacity, and such other control features as may be reasonably required by Landlord.

F. REPORTS:

Tenant agrees to submit to Landlord on or before the thirtieth (30th) day following the end of each calendar month during the Term (including the thirtieth (30th) day following the end of the Term, as to which Tenant's obligation shall survive the expiration of the Term) a written statement, signed and certified to be true and correct by Tenant (or by an authorized officer, if Tenant is a corporation), showing the amount of Gross Sales derived from the business conducted at, upon or from the Demised Premises by Tenant (and all subtenants, concessionaires, licensees or any other occupant of the Demised Premises) during the preceding calendar month, and an itemization of all permissible deductions therefrom. Tenant further agrees to submit to Landlord on or before the sixtieth (60th) day following the end of each Lease Year or partial Lease Year (including the last Lease Year hereof, as to which Tenant's obligation shall survive the expiration of the Term) a written statement, signed and certified by Tenant (or by an authorized officer, if Tenant is a corporation) to be true and correct, showing the amount of such Gross Sales during the preceding Lease Year or

8

partial Lease Year and an itemization of all permissible deductions therefrom. Said annual statement shall also be duly certified to be true and correct and in compliance with the definition of Gross Sales contained in this Paragraph by an independent certified public accountant in accordance with sound and accepted accounting principles and practices consistently applied. The statements referred to in this Paragraph shall be in such form and style and shall contain such details and information as Landlord may reasonably require. The acceptance by Landlord of payments of Percentage Rent or reports thereof shall be without prejudice and shall in no event constitute a waiver of Landlord's right to claim a deficiency in the payment of Percentage Rent or to audit Tenant's books and records, as hereafter set forth. The Gross Sales for any portion of the calendar month prior to the commencement of the first full calendar month, shall be included in the monthly report for said first full month. If Tenant's Gross Sales are required to be reported on any Federal, State or local sales tax or similar tax return and Gross Sales as so reported on any of said returns (as herein defined and provided) shall exceed the Gross Sales as reported by Tenant (as herein defined and provided), then the Gross Sales shall be taken at the highest figure so reported. If any governmental authority shall increase the Gross Sales (as herein defined and provided) reported by Tenant on any such tax return, after audit, for any Lease Year for which such sales have been reported, then Tenant shall notify Landlord promptly of such increase, supply to Landlord a true copy of such audit and pay at that time any additional Percentage Rent due.

G. AUDIT: Landlord shall have the right, at any reasonable time and from time to time, to cause a complete audit of all statements of Gross Sales and in connection with such audit, to examine Tenant's books of account and records (including all supporting data and any other records from which Gross Sales may be tested or determined) of Gross Sales disclosed in any statement given to

9

163

Landlord by Tenant, and Tenant shall make all such books of accounts and records available for such examination at the office where same are regularly maintained. Landlord shall have the right to copy and duplicate such information as Landlord may require. If any such audit discloses that the actual amount of Gross Sales exceeds the amount reported, then Tenant shall pay Landlord all additional Percentage Rent due Landlord and if the excess of Gross Sales so disclosed shall be more than one (1%) percent, Tenant shall also then pay the cost of such audit and examination. The furnishing by Tenant of any fraudulent statement shall constitute a breach of this Lease. If any audit shall be commenced by Landlord or if there shall arise a difference or dispute concerning Gross Sales, then and in any such event, Tenant's books of account and records, (including all supporting data and any other records from which Gross Sales may be tested or determined) shall be preserved and retained by Tenant until such audit has been completed or a final resolution or final determination of such difference or dispute or any related litigation. Any information obtained by Landlord as a result of such audit shall be treated as confidential, except in any litigation or proceeding between the parties and, except further, that Landlord may disclose such information to prospective purchasers, to prospective or existing lenders, to prospective or existing ground lessors and in any statement filed with the Securities and Exchange Commission, Internal Revenue Service, or other governmental agency or pursuant to any subpoena or judicial process. If Landlord shall fail to audit any such statement within thirty-six (36) months after the same has been received by Landlord, then any such report shall be deemed conclusively true and correct, except as to any fraudulent statement; in addition, Landlord and Landlord's authorized representative shall have the right to examine Tenant's books of accounts and records and procedures for keeping same during regular business hours and shall have the right to have a representative on the Demised Premises to check, verify and tabulate

Gross Sales, and to examine books of accounts and records and procedures for keeping same including control features affecting the determination of Gross Sales.

Section IV: COMMON AREA CHARGES:

Tenant shall pay Landlord as additional rent hereunder Tenant's Proportionate Share of the (a) costs of maintaining, managing, insuring, lighting, operating, securing, repairing, replacing and providing services to the Shopping Center and cleaning and removing snow and ice from the parking lot and sidewalks (whether included within, or adjoining the Shopping Center) and (b) costs of any security guards used to police or patrol the Shopping Center (the costs in (a) and (b) described, are hereinafter referred to as "common area charges"). Landlord shall send a statement to Tenant from time to time setting forth the amount of Tenant's Proportionate Share of the aforesaid common area charges.

Section V: MISCELLANEOUS:

A. Tenant's obligation to pay the additional rents as provided for in this Article 42 shall survive the expiration or earlier termination of this Lease.

B. Every notice, demand or statement given by Landlord pursuant to this Article 42 shall be conclusive and binding upon Tenant, unless (1) within thirty (30) days after the receipt of such notice Tenant shall notify Landlord that it disputes the correctness of the notice, specifying the particular respects in which the notice is claimed to be incorrect, and (2) if such dispute shall not have been settled by agreement, Tenant shall submit the dispute to arbitration within ninety (90) days after the date of said notice, the absence of which shall be deemed a waiver of such dispute by Tenant. Pending the determination of such dispute, Tenant shall continue to pay Base Rent and additional rent in accordance with Landlord's notice without prejudice to Tenant's position. If such

11

dispute is determined in Tenant's favor, Landlord shall, on demand, pay Tenant (without interest) the amount so overpaid by Tenant.

C. Landlord's failure to render any statements, however designated or named, for any period pursuant to which additional rent is calculated and/or billed, shall not prejudice Landlord's right to thereafter render any such statement with respect to any such period or with respect to any subsequent period, nor shall the rendering of any such statement prejudice Landlord's right to render a corrected statement for any period. Nothing herein contained shall restrict Landlord from issuing a statement at any time there is an adjustment in Base Rent or additional rent pursuant to this Article 42 or any other Article of this Lease, during any year or at any time thereafter.

67. COMMON AREAS:

All common areas and other common facilities (hereinafter collectively called "common areas") made available by Landlord in or about the Shopping Center shall be subject to the exclusive control and management of Landlord, expressly reserving to Landlord, without limitation, the right to erect, install, replace and remove kiosks, planters, pools, sculpture and free-standing buildings. Commons areas (as initially constructed or as the same may at any time thereafter be enlarged, reduced, altered, replaced or removed) shall mean all areas, spaces, facilities, improvements, buildings, equipment, signs and special services from time to time made available by Landlord for the common and joint use and benefit of Landlord, Tenant and other tenants and occupants of the Shopping Center and their respective employees, agents, subtenants, concessionaires, licensees, customers and invitees, which may include, without limitation (but shall not be deemed a representation as to their availability), the sidewalks, parking areas, access roads, driveways, landscaped areas, truck serviceways, tunnels, loading docks, pedestrian shopping areas (enclosed or

12

166

open), courts, stairs, ramps, elevators, escalators, comfort and first aid stations, public washrooms, community hall or auditorium and parcel pick-up stations. Landlord hereby expressly reserves the right, from time to time, to construct, maintain, replace, remove and operate lighting and other facilities, equipment and signs on all of said common areas; to police the same; to change the area, level, remove and operate lighting and other facilities, equipment and signs on all of said commons areas; to build multi-story parking facilities; to restrict parking by Tenant and other tenants and occupants of the Shopping Center and their respective employees, agents, subtenants, concessionaires, licensees, customers and invitees; to enforce parking charges (by operation of meters or otherwise) mandated by governmental authorities; to close temporarily all or any portion of the common areas for the purpose of making repairs or changes thereto or to effect construction, repairs or changes within the Shopping Center; and to discourage non- customer parking; and to establish, modify, revoke and enforce reasonable rules and regulations with respect to the common areas and the use to be made thereof, including, without limitation, the designation of the days and hours the common areas shall be open. Tenant shall make no claim against Landlord by reason of Landlord's failure to uniformly enforce such rules and regulations against all tenants and occupants of the Shopping Center. Tenant shall upon request promptly furnish to Landlord the license numbers of the vehicles operated by Tenant, its concessionaires and licensees, and their respective officers, agents and employees. In the event Landlord promulgates rules and regulations designating specific areas in which vehicles owned or operated by Tenant, its concessionaires and licensees, or any of their respective officers, employees and agents, must be parked and prohibiting the parking of any such vehicles in any other part of the common areas, Landlord may cause to be towed away any such vehicles which are parked in common areas in violation of such rules and regulations, at the expense

13

of Tenant, and Tenant (i) waives liability of Landlord to Tenant and (ii) agrees to indemnify and save free and harmless Landlord, from and against any and all claims, demands, fines, suits, actions, proceedings, orders, decrees and judgments by or in favor of Tenant's concessionaires and licensees, or any of their respective officers, employees and agents, in the event that such towing is done. Tenant further agrees, after notice thereof, to abide by such rules and regulations and to use its best efforts to cause its concessionaires, licensees, officers, employees, agents, customers and invitees to abide thereby. If any vehicle of Tenant, its concessionaires and licensees, or of any of their respective officers, agents or employees, is parked in any part of the Shopping Center other than the employee parking area(s) designated by Landlord, Tenant shall pay to Landlord, upon demand, an amount equal to the daily rate therefor so established by Landlord from time to time. The net income derived by Landlord in any Lease Year from any such charges shall be credited against common areas charges. Tenant is hereby given a non-exclusive and non-transferable license (in common with all others to whom Landlord has or may hereafter grant rights) to use, during the Term, the common areas of the Shopping Center as they may now or at any time during the Term exist, provided, however, that if the size, location or arrangement of such common areas or the type of facilities at any time forming a part thereof be changed or diminished, Landlord shall not be subject to any liability therefor, nor shall Tenant be entitled to any compensation or diminution or abatement of rent therefor, nor shall such change or diminution of such areas be deemed a constructive or actual eviction. Tenant agrees that Landlord may, at any time and from time to time, increase, reduce or change the number type, size, location, elevation, nature and use of any of the common areas, make installations therein, move and remove the same, erect and lease or sell advertising space and erect buildings anywhere in the Shopping Center. In order to establish that

14

all or any portion of the Shopping Center is and will continue to remain private property and to prevent a dedication thereof or the accrual of any rights to any person or to the public therein, Landlord hereby reserves the unrestricted right to close to the general public all or any portion of the Shopping Center owned, leased or controlled by Landlord to the extent and for the period necessary to prevent such dedication to accrue, and, in connection therewith, to seal off all entrances to the Shopping Center, or any portion thereof. Tenant hereby acknowledges, consents and agrees that any and all services, facilities and access by the public to the Demised Premises or to the Shopping Center may be suspended in whole or in part during such temporary times as all of the department stores adjoining the Shopping Center are not open for business, on legal holidays, on such other days as may be declared by local, State or Federal authorities or employees' unions, if any, as days of observance, and during any periods of actual or threatened civil commotion, insurrection or other circumstances beyond Landlord's control when Landlord, in Landlord's reasonable judgment, shall deem the suspension of such services, facilities and access necessary for the protection or preservation of persons or property or otherwise as required by law. Common areas shall not be used for solicitations, distributions of handbills or other advertising matter, demonstrating or any other activities that would in Landlord's judgment interfere with the use of the common areas or with the conduct of business or the rights of other tenants. Landlord shall operate, manage, equip, light, repair, replace and maintain the common areas and keep order and security therein all in such manner as Landlord in its reasonable discretion, may from time to time determine, and Landlord shall have the right and exclusive authority to employ and discharge all personnel connected therewith.

15

169

NOTES

4

OPERATING EXPENSES AND CAM / HIDDEN AGENDAS AND CORPORATE GUERRILLA WARFARE TACTICS

Michael E. Meyer

I.   AUDIT RIGHT PROVISIONS.

A.   <u>BACKGROUND AND PURPOSE</u>.

Any responsible tenant will always insist upon the right to audit, review and copy the landlord's books and records pertaining to operating expenses. There are literally thousands of entries that are made during the course of a Lease Year by a landlord in computing operating expenses and it would take a near miracle for someone not to make an unintentional error in connection with the computation and allocation of each component of operating expenses. Apart from the inevitable human errors, there are many items of expenses which are "borderline" and where it is difficult to decide whether such expense item should properly be included or excluded as an operating expense. Even if the correct decision is made to include such item as an operating expense, frequently a secondary decision has to be made as to whether or not such items should be capitalized and amortized, and if so for how long. Accordingly, any tenant and landlord who sign a lease should acknowledge, without guilt, shame or embarrassment, the simple fact that the operating expenses are unlikely ever to be set forth with 100% accuracy in any operating expense statement prepared by a Landlord or even a group of saints (not that the two are necessarily mutually exclusive).

Most landlords today pay a great deal of attention to operating expenses in an effort to have them compiled in a accurate and fair manner consistent with the provisions of the lease. They are willing to cooperate with the legitimate goals of its tenants to review and confirm the accuracy of the compilation of operating expenses and to obtain refunds or credits if operating expenses were overcharged. However, many landlords are scared of the hidden agenda tactics used by some tenants through the audit provision. A hidden agenda for some tenants is to create an audit provision which will not only simply allow a tenant to confirm whether or not the operating expenses have been accurately kept, but rather to give a tenant a right to "extort" a landlord or to terminate its lease merely because the tenant has been overcharged.

In most instances, separate and apart from any demand by a tenant for a provision to review operating expenses, landlords have frequently included in their standard form an audit provision. In many cases, these landlords simply recognize the inevitability of a tenant asking for an audit right and preferred to insert a provision that was favorable to the landlord. However, sophisticated landlords now realize that even if an audit right was not included in a lease, there are obvious ways that a tenant could challenge a bill and a statement for operating expenses. Where the tenant wants to contest whether an expense item was properly included as an operating expense, the tenant could do so under the laws of

-2-

174

almost every state and would be subject to the applicable statute of limitations for a written contract as to the "cutoff" time period before such a challenge would be barred. In many states, the statute of limitations for a written contract is four years and hence landlords wanted to include an audit right provision, if for no other reason than to create a contractual statute of limitations which would have a shorter time period than the one provided by statute.

B.   TIME PERIOD CUTOFFS.

In the back and forth negotiations as to the appropriate time periods by which an audit must be undertaken and a challenge presented, many tenants did not want to have any time period cutoff other than the applicable statute of limitation. Landlords would frequently argue that they "needed to close their books" and would argue for a short time period of anywhere from thirty days to six months, arguing that the landlord simply could not allow any uncertainty with respect to operating expenses to last for a period in excess of a few months, because it needed to close its books. Sophisticated tenants advise landlords that they might agree to the shortened time period and simply audit within that shortened time period provided that the landlord would agree that the landlord would not submit any item to be subsequently included in operating expenses if such item was not submitted within the negotiated few month time period. However, landlords and tenants would quickly acknowledge that

-3-

there were many bills and expenses that might be overlooked during a short time period or not even submitted to the landlord within a short time period (this is very typical with respect to items pertaining to taxes) and the typical time period agreed to by a landlord and a tenant as an absolute cutoff as to both sides ranges from two years to three years.

C. WHO PERFORMS THE AUDIT.

The question is to who performs an audit used to be one of great controversy. Typically, landlords used to argue that the audit could only be performed by (in times past) a big eight accounting firm. The landlords would make this argument for the unarticulated reason and their belief that the big eight accounting firms were almost always "naive" and "unsophisticated" when it came to operating expense audits and, in fact, this was frequently true. Landlords feared audits performed by the so-called "contingent fee auditors" who they believe were ruthless, uncouth, and, even worse, excellent and sophisticated in reviewing and auditing records pertaining to operating expenses. Many of these so-called contingent fee auditors consisted of bright accountants and former property managers who knew exactly what landlords did, why they did it, and where to look. This issue has become largely moot because over the last five years the level of expertise, with respect to audits of operating expenses, by the major national accounting

-4-

firms has reached the same level as the expertise formerly possessed solely by the contingent fee auditors.

D.   CONTRACTUAL NEGOTIATED RESTRICTIONS ON TENANT.

Most landlords have now "crossed the bridge" and agree to an extended time period to audit and to allow almost anyone to audit their books and records. In exchange these landlords want to contractually constrict the use of certain "tactics" by tenants with hidden agendas.

In order to eliminate one of the "extortion" tactics used by tenants with a hidden agenda, landlords are willing to grant a tenant an extended period of time to review the operating expense statements and to use almost anyone the tenant desires to perform the audit, provided that the tenant's real purpose is simply to make sure that it was not overcharged and, if the audit determines that the tenant was overcharged, then to only let the tenant recover the amount of the overcharge.

(1)   CONFIDENTIALITY AGREEMENT.

Sophisticated landlords will insist upon a confidentiality provision as a condition of the Tenant's exercise of an audit right. Confidentiality provisions simply require the tenant, and any auditor that it uses, to agree that it will not disclose the results of the audit to anyone. In some cases, landlords

-5-

even seek to restrict a particular auditor from using those audits results to canvas the other tenants of the building if an error was made. The landlords have done this in response to tactics used by many tenants who have discovered an error, and regardless of whether the error was intentional, threaten to disclose the fact of the error to everyone in an effort to force the landlord into a settlement which may be in fact higher than the tenant would otherwise be entitled to receive simply based on the merits of the issue.

(2) <u>CURE OF DEFAULT AS A CONDITION TO PROCEED WITH AUDIT</u>.

Landlords have also realized that frequently an audit right is not used until the tenant has clearly defaulted with respect to some other provision of the lease (frequently the failure to pay Base Rent) and the Tenant is seeking to create leverage. Therefore landlords frequently insist that no audit may take place if the tenant is then in default under any of the provisions of the lease or if the tenant has refused to make payments that have been billed for under the Base Rent provision or the operating expense provision. Landlords will frequently agree that the payments can be made under protest pending the outcome of the arbitration, but they do not want a tenant to be able to withhold the payment of rent or operating expenses pending the completion of an audit.

-6-

(3) <u>LIMITATION ON TERMINATION RIGHT</u>.

Sophisticated landlords have occasionally been burned by tenants who will assert a claim that they have been overcharged for operating expenses and then seek to terminate the lease as a result of the breach, in addition to seeking the normal recovery of the amount of the overcharge, plus interest, plus in some cases audit fees. These tenants will assert that because the landlord overcharged for operating expenses, and did so intentionally (and this is almost always the case because a landlord has made a conscious decision to treat an item as an operating expense and if that decision turns out, with hindsight, to be incorrect, then the decision would have been intentional but not necessarily culpable). These tenants assert that because the landlord has breached its obligations under the lease (by overcharging), then the tenant should have the right to terminate its lease. Some tenants have asserted the right to terminate from time to time because they understand the effect this tactic has on a landlord, especially if the tenant could reach its goal in having an unsophisticated or an inexperienced trier of fact decide the issue. Accordingly, landlords have sought to simply include a provision that limits the defendant's remedy to a right to recover the amount of the overcharge plus interest, and, in some cases, where the overcharge exceeds a certain percentage, its audit fees while specifically requiring the tenant to give up its right to terminate.

-7-

179

(4) ARBITRATION RATHER THAN LITIGATION.

Tenants who make claims that are "suspect" (such as
asserting a termination right") need to find an inexperienced
(from a real estate leasing standpoint) trier of fact since
anyone who actively practices real estate leasing law
understands that, by the very nature of the process, it is
virtually impossible to calculate operating expenses with
precise accuracy. Inevitably, from time to time operating
expenses will be overcharged and sophisticated landlords and
tenants would have anticipated that under those circumstances,
the tenant should be able to recover the amount of the
overcharge plus interest (and in some cases audit fees and
attorneys' fees). However, it is unrealistic to believe that
any landlord or tenant entering into a lease, would ever believe
that a remedy available to a tenant for an overcharge of
operating expenses by a landlord would be the right of
termination for a tenant. This theory, besides creating heart
murmurs for all lenders, simply is unrealistic and the
inequities are glaring, especially in situations where the
landlord has paid a significant brokers' commission, tenant
improvement allowance, free rent and the like. Most lawyers
believe that tenants asserting a claim for termination of the
lease because of an overcharge are not seeking "justice," but
rather are engaging in gamesmanship to get out of a lease under
circumstances where the tenant has too much space at above
market rents.

-8-

E.   WHEN TO AUDIT.

Tenants, in negotiating and asserting its rights under an audit provision, need to be careful to make sure that they vigorously pursues their rights. A landlord, with a hidden agenda, certainly would like to delay any audit of its books, in part because landlords go into "denial" because they do not really believe that the tenant is making a legitimate claim or that the landlord has in fact made errors. Apart from these reasons, landlords realize that if an error was made, the longer it takes a particular tenant to discover that error the better it may be for the landlord with respect to any other tenants in the building who have shorter contractual time periods to audit and hence will have their claims for audits barred by the contractual statute of limitations. Most experienced leasing lawyers recommend that a tenant audit the first full year of operating expenses for two reasons. First, if the lease involves a Base Year, the tenant wants to make sure that it causes the landlord to preserve those records and the tenant will be able to establish what items were and were not included during the Base Year. Second, by auditing during the first year, the tenant sends a message to the landlord that it will always be diligent in asserting its rights and hence a landlord will be much more careful in making sure that the operating expenses are carefully and correctly computed and compiled. In many instances, when errors are made in connection with operating expenses, the errors were primarily caused by the

-9-

individuals who compiled the operating expenses simply following the landlord's standard form lease and not even looking at any of the inclusions or exclusions or restrictions in any particular tenant's lease.

F.   REMEDIES.

Careful tenants bargain for the right not only to recover the amount of any overcharge, plus interest at the Interest Rate, but if an overcharge exceeds a certain percentage or amount, to recover the costs of the audit and their attorney fees.

G.   SURVIVABILITY.

In order to make sure that the right to recover for overcharge or underpayment of Operating Expense proceeds smoothly, landlord and tenants are including "survivability provisions" in their leases.

H.   SELECTING THE TRIER OF FACT.

Landlords and tenants without a hidden agenda should hopefully want to have any dispute pertaining to operating expenses resolved by an arbitrator who is experienced in real estate leasing matters. Most experienced lawyers recommend that the arbitrator be a lawyer who has had 10 or more years of

-10-

182

experience representing landlords and tenants in real estate leasing matters as the arbitrator. This will eliminate or minimize the need for "expert testimony" and should minimize the chance for a ridiculous result because an experienced arbitrator will quickly understand what should and should not be included as an operating expense because of his or her knowledge of the custom or practice and a close reading of the bargain for provisions in the lease.

I.   CHECKLIST.

When landlords and tenants eliminate any gamesmanship from the process they do not seek to outsmart each other or to pursue hidden agenda goals, then agreeing upon a fair audit provision should result in the following agreements being incorporated into the audit provision.

(1)   tenant should have a right to audit, review and copy landlord's books and records;

(2)   A tenant may not conduct an audit if it's default under the lease;

(3)   a tenant may not conduct an audit if it is withholding base rent or operating expenses until the audit is completed;

-11-

(4) a tenant may not conduct an audit unless it agrees to a confidentiality restriction;

(5) an overcharge of operating expenses by landlord shall not entitle tenant to terminate a lease;

(6) tenant and landlord shall be barred from asserting any right to charge additional operating expenses or to claim a refund for operating expenses if such right is not asserted and an arbitration or litigation commenced within three years from the date that landlord furnished tenant with an operating expenses statement or, when appropriate, a supplemental operating expense statement;

(7) the tenant may conduct the audit itself or by utilizing an accounting firm or a firm that simply specializes in auditing operating expenses;

(8) in the event that the audit reveals an overcharge, the amount of the overcharge with interest at the Interest Rate shall be refunded by the landlord to the tenant unless the tenant elects to have such amount credited against the rents next due and owing under the lease;

(9) tenants should be allowed to offset against Base Rent a final award or judgment as to the overpayment of Operating Expenses, if not paid within thirty days;

-12-

(10) if the amount of the error by the landlord exceeds a certain percentage (typically 3-5%), then the landlord shall pay for the cost of the audit; and

(11) the procedure for determining any dispute pertaining to operating expense should involve an arbitration where the arbitrator is defined as someone who has had 10 or more years of experience as a lawyer handling real estate leasing matters.

II.   OPERATING EXPENSE PROVISIONS.

   A.   BACKGROUND AND PURPOSE.

The purpose of operating expense provisions is to allow the landlord to recover from its tenants the insurance, taxes and operating expenses incurred by the landlord as to the premises leased by each tenant, and the tenant's pro rata share of the insurance, taxes and operating expenses applicable to the common areas.

Most landlords when drafting leases go to great pains to have a provision for the inclusion of operating expenses which includes anything that is imaginable and occasionally, certain things which are almost unimaginable (reserves and debt service). Tenants and their lawyers fall into the same trap and one of the contests that is entered into year after year by lawyers representing tenants is which lawyer can come up with

-13-

the largest number of operating expense exclusions. The issues of controversy pertaining to operating expenses are normally very few. Most landlords and tenants would agree, even if there was no provision in the lease providing for the exclusion, that no landlord could include leasing commissions, tenant improvement allowances, litigation costs with other tenants who don't pay rent, etc. as part of Operating Expenses.

B.   CONTROVERSIAL EXCLUSIONS.

Currently, the areas where disputes almost always arise that need to be recognized up front and negotiated are as follows:

(1) Items pertaining to the Building Structure and the Building Systems and Capital Expenditures. A tenant leasing a full floor might be "surprised" as to the economic consequences which might result when a new law is enacted, such as the laws in the not so distant past pertaining to the installation of sprinklers and/or ADA work with respect to washrooms. If the lease is not clearly focused, a dispute could arise as to who should perform and pay for such work. Typically, most people would agree that if a tenant was leasing a full floor, and was in the last year of a three-year lease, and a law was enacted during the last year of the lease term requiring sprinklers to be installed within the premises during such year, and/or requiring ADA modifications to be made to the washrooms during

-14-

the last year of the lease term, that it would be unfair to have the tenant make what would typically be considered capital expenditures, or pay for the entire cost of installing sprinklers in that floor or bringing the washrooms up to ADA compliance. Sprinklers would have a life span of approximately 50 years and modifications to the washroom to comply with ADA would have a long life span. Typically, tenants bargaining over that issue would believe that such items should not be the tenant's responsibility but should be the landlord's responsibility. Similarly, the landlord should have a right to capitalize those expenditures, amortize them over the useful life, and include the amortized portion as the operating expenses.

The provision for operating expense exclusions typically contain a provision which allows landlords to pass through to tenants the cost of capital expenditures made to comply with newly enacted laws and for cost saving purposes provided that with respect to newly enacted laws, the expenditures are amortized over the useful life and provided with respect to cost saving capital expenditures, that the amount of the expenditure does not exceed the amount saved and that such amounts are amortized over the useful life.

-15-

C.   <u>GROSS-UP PROVISION</u>.

There are many disputes over the gross-up provision. However, parties who are not involved with hidden agendas or gamesmanship, readily agree that it would be fair, in every lease (except where a tenant is leasing the entire building) for a gross-up provision to be included in the lease for the protection of both the landlord and the tenant. Once the parties agree that a gross-up provision should be allowed and should be included, then it is important to have the correct gross-up provision. In order to fully gross up operating expenses, the variable portion of operating expenses should be grossed up to what they would had been had the building been 100% leased with all tenants in occupancy of the premises and paying full rent (as contrasted with free rent, half rent, and the like). In many instances, older leases have a gross-up provision for 95% which makes little sense. The 95% number was initially utilized by landlords when granting base years since under a 95% gross-up definition, it would be possible for a landlord to only have to gross up the operating expenses to 95% during the base year and if during subsequent lease years the building was 100% occupied, then an unfair (but beneficial to the landlord) comparison would be created. When some landlords converted over to net leases, they forgot why they utilized a 95% gross-up provision and utilized a 95% gross-up provision in net leases which would have the effect of short changing the landlord. Simply grossing up leases for what the variable

-16-

188

operating expenses would have been had the building been 100%
occupied during a particular lease year will create the correct
result.

We have added the phrase "with all tenants paying full
rent . . ." to the old gross up provision to clarify an issue
which should need no clarification and probably is implied in
the standard gross-up provision. In situations where tenants
receive free rent, then a landlord should have the right (and
the obligation) to gross up operating expenses to what they
would have been had such tenants not been receiving free rent.
This would make sure that a proper management fee was allocated
to the year (in situations where management fees are, as they
typically are, calculated as a percentage of gross revenues) and
will properly gross up the gross receipts where the gross
receipts tax is passed through as an operating expense (as it
typically is). Where this is not done, a landlord in certain
years would not get the intended benefits that it should have
anticipated. In situations where a tenant has a base year, if
that tenant and other tenants are receiving free rent, the base
year could be grossly understated and significantly harm the
tenant for all years during the lease term if there was not
imputed into the base year the gross receipts tax and management
fee that would have been incurred had all tenants been paying
full rent.

-17-

III. <u>SAMPLE NEGOTIATED OPERATING EXPENSE AND RELATED PROVISIONS</u>.

    A.   <u>LANDLORD'S BOOK AND RECORDS</u>.

    (1) **In General**. In the event that Tenant disputes the amount of Additional Rent set forth in any annual Statement or Supplemental Statement delivered by Landlord, then subject to the terms and conditions of Section 4.7.2, below, Tenant shall have the right to provide Notice to Landlord that it intends to inspect and copy, or cause the "Tenant Parties," as that term is defined in Section 10.1 of this Lease, to inspect and copy Landlord's accounting records for the Expense Year covered by such Statement or Supplemental Statement during normal business hours ("Tenant Review"), provided, however, that in the event that Tenant shall employ or retain a third party to inspect Landlord's accounting records (a "Third Party Auditor"), then as a condition precedent to any such inspection, Tenant shall deliver to Landlord a copy of Tenant's written agreement with such Third Party Auditor, which agreement shall include provisions which stated that (i) Landlord is an intended third-party beneficiary of such agreement, (ii) such Third Party Auditor will not in any manner solicit or agree to represent any other tenant of the Project with respect to an audit or other review of Landlord's accounting records at the Project, and (iii) such Third Party Auditor shall maintain in strict confidence any and all information obtained in connection with the Tenant Review and shall not disclose such information to any

-18-

person or entity other than to the management personnel of Tenant. Any Tenant Review shall take place in Landlord's office at the Project or at such other location in Los Angeles County as Landlord may reasonably designate, and Landlord will provide Tenant with reasonable accommodations for such Tenant Review and reasonable use of such available office equipment, but may charge Tenant for telephone calls and photocopies at Landlord's Actual Cost. Tenant shall provide Landlord with not less than two (2) weeks' prior written notice of its desire to conduct such Tenant Review. In connection with the foregoing review, Landlord shall furnish Tenant with such reasonable supporting documentation relating to the subject Statement as Tenant may reasonably request, including any previous audit conducted by Landlord with respect to the Expense Year in question. In no event shall Tenant have the right to conduct such Tenant Review if Tenant is then in "Default," as that term is defined in Article 19 under the Lease with respect to any of Tenant's monetary obligations, including, without limitation, the payment by Tenant of all Additional Rent amounts described in the Statement which is the subject of Tenant's Review, which payment, at Tenant's election, may be made under dispute. In the event that following Tenant's Review, Tenant and Landlord continue to dispute the amounts of Additional Rent shown on Landlord's Statement or Supplemental Statement and Landlord and Tenant are unable to resolve such dispute, then either Landlord or Tenant may submit the matter to arbitration pursuant to Section 29.17 of this Lease and the proper amount of the

-19-

disputed items and/or categories of Direct Expenses to be shown on such Statement shall be determined by such proceeding producing an "Arbitration Award" as that term is defined in Section 29.17.3.2 of this Lease. The Arbitration Award shall be conclusive and binding upon both Landlord and Tenant. If the resolution of the parties' dispute with regard to the Additional Rent shown on the Statement, pursuant to the Arbitration Award reveals an error in the calculation of Tenant's Share of Direct Expenses to be paid for such Expense Year, the parties' sole remedy shall be for the parties to make appropriate payments or reimbursements, as the case may be, to each other as are determined to be owing. Any such payments shall be made within thirty (30) days following the resolution of such dispute. At Tenant's election, Tenant may treat any overpayments resulting from the foregoing resolution of such parties' dispute as a credit against Rent until such amounts are otherwise paid by Landlord. Tenant shall be responsible for all costs and expenses associated with Tenant's Review, and Tenant shall be responsible for all reasonable audit fees, attorney's fees and related costs of Tenant relating to an Arbitration Award (collectively, the "Costs"), provided that if the parties' final resolution of the dispute involves the overstatement by Landlord of Direct Expenses for such Expense Year in excess of five percent (5%), then Landlord shall be responsible for all Costs. An overcharge of Operating Expenses by Landlord shall not entitle Tenant to terminate this Lease. Subject to the terms of Section 4.7.2, below, this provision shall survive the termination of this

-20-

192

Lease to allow the parties to enforce their respective rights hereunder.

(2) _Termination of Rights_. In the event that, within two (2) years following receipt of any particular Statement or Supplemental Statement, as applicable, Tenant or Landlord shall fail to either (i) fully and finally settle any dispute with respect to such Statement or Supplemental Statement, as applicable, or (ii) submit the dispute to arbitration in accordance with the terms of Section 4.7.1, above, then Tenant shall have no further right to conduct a Tenant Review or to dispute the amount of Additional Rent set forth in the applicable Statement or Supplemental Statement, as applicable.

B.   ARBITRATION.

(1) _Arbitration_. With the exception of the arbitration provisions which shall specifically apply to the determination of the Fair Market Rental Rate, as set forth in Exhibit "J" attached hereto, the provisions of this General Condition G contain the sole and exclusive method, means and procedure to resolve any and all disputes or disagreements, including whether any particular matter constitutes, or with the passage of time would constitute, an event of default ("Event of Default"). The parties hereby irrevocably waive any and all rights to the contrary and shall at all times conduct themselves in strict, full, complete and timely accordance with the provisions of this

-21-

General Condition G. Any and all attempts to circumvent the
provisions of this General Condition G shall be absolutely null
and void and of no force or effect whatsoever. As to any matter
submitted to arbitration to determine whether it would, with or
without the passage of time, constitute an Event of Default,
such matter shall not constitute an Event of Default and such
passage of time shall not commence to run until any such
affirmative determination, so long as it is simultaneously
determined that the challenge of such matter as a potential
Event of Default was made in good faith, except with respect to
the payment of money. With respect to the payment of money,
such passage of time shall not commence to run only if the party
which is obligated to make the payment does in fact make the
payment to the other party. Such payment can be made "under
protest," which shall occur when such payment is accompanied by
a good-faith notice stating why the party has elected to make a
payment under protest. Such protest will be deemed waived
unless the subject matter identified in the protest is submitted
to arbitration as set forth in the following:

       (a)   <u>Arbitration Panel</u>. Within ninety (90) days
after delivery of written notice ("Notice of Dispute") of
the existence and nature of any dispute given by any party
to the other party, and unless otherwise provided herein in
any specific instance, the parties shall each:
((1) appoint one (1) lawyer actively engaged in the
licensed and full-time practice of law, specializing in

-22-

194

real estate, in the County of San Diego for a continuous period immediately preceding the date of delivery ("Dispute Date") of the Notice of Dispute of not less than ten (10) years, but who has at no time ever represented or acted on behalf of any of the parties, and ((2) deliver written notice of the identity of such lawyer and a copy of his or her written acceptance of such appointment and acknowledgment of and agreement to be bound by the time constraints and other provisions of this General Condition G ("Acceptance") to the other parties hereto. The party who selects the lawyer may not consult with such lawyer, directly or indirectly, to determine the lawyer's position on the issue which is the subject of the dispute. In the event that any party fails to so act, such arbitrator shall be appointed pursuant to the same procedure that is followed when agreement cannot be reached as to the third arbitrator. Within ten (10) days after such appointment and notice, such lawyers shall appoint a third lawyer (together with the first two (2) lawyers, "Arbitration Panel") of the same qualification and background and shall deliver written notice of the identity of such lawyer and a copy of his or her written Acceptance of such appointment to each of the parties. In the event that agreement cannot be reached on the appointment of a third lawyer within such period, such appointment and notification shall be made as quickly as possible by any court of competent jurisdiction, by any licensing authority, agency or organization having

-23-

jurisdiction over such lawyers, by any professional association of lawyers in existence for not less than ten (10) years at the time of such dispute or disagreement and the geographical membership boundaries of which extend to the County of San Diego or by any arbitration association or organization in existence for not less than ten (10) years at the time of such dispute or disagreement and the geographical boundaries of which extend to the County of San Diego, as determined by the party giving such Notice of Dispute and simultaneously confirmed in writing delivered by such party to the other party. Any such court, authority, agency, association or organization shall be entitled either to directly select such third lawyer or to designate in writing, delivered to each of the parties, an individual who shall do so. In the event of any subsequent vacancies or inabilities to perform among the Arbitration Panel, the lawyer or lawyers involved shall be replaced in accordance with the provisions of this General Condition G as if such replacement was an initial appointment to be made under this General Condition G within the time constraints set forth in this General Condition G, measured from the date of notice of such vacancy or inability, to the person or persons required to make such appointment, with all the attendant consequences of failure to act timely if such appointed person is a party hereto.

-24-

196

(b) <u>Duty</u>. Consistent with the provisions of
this General Condition G, the members of the Arbitration
Panel shall utilize their utmost skill and shall apply
themselves diligently so as to hear and decide, by majority
vote, the outcome and resolution of any dispute or
disagreement submitted to the Arbitration Panel as promptly
as possible, but in any event on or before the expiration
of thirty (30) days after the appointment of the members of
the Arbitration Panel. None of the members of the
Arbitration Panel shall have any liability whatsoever for
any acts or omissions performed or omitted in good faith
pursuant to the provisions of this General Condition G.

(c) <u>Authority</u>. The Arbitration Panel shall
((1) enforce and interpret the rights and obligations set
forth in the Lease to the extent not prohibited by law,
((2) fix and establish any and all rules as it shall
consider appropriate in its sole and absolute discretion to
govern the proceedings before it, including any and all
rules of discovery, procedure and/or evidence, and
((3) make and issue any and all orders, final or otherwise,
and any and all awards, as a court of competent
jurisdiction sitting at law or in equity could make and
issue, and as it shall consider appropriate in its sole and
absolute discretion, including the awarding of monetary
damages (but shall not award consequential damages to
either party and shall not award punitive damages except in

-25-

197

situations involving knowing fraud or egregious conduct
condoned by, or performed by, the person who, in essence,
occupies the position which is the equivalent of the chief
executive officer of the party against whom damages are to
be awarded), the awarding of reasonable attorneys' fees and
costs to the prevailing party as determined by the
Arbitration Panel and the issuance of injunctive relief.
If the party against whom the award is issued complies with
the award, within the time period established by the Arbitration Panel, then no Event of Default will be deemed to
have occurred, unless the Event of Default pertained to the
non-payment of money by Tenant or Landlord, and Tenant or
Landlord failed to make such payment under protest.

(d) Appeal. The decision of the Arbitration
Panel shall be final and binding, may be confirmed and
entered by any court of competent jurisdiction at the
request of any party and may not be appealed to any court
of competent jurisdiction or otherwise except upon a claim
of fraud on the part of the Arbitration Panel. The
Arbitration Panel shall retain jurisdiction over any
dispute until its award has been implemented, and judgment
on any such award may be entered in any court having
appropriate jurisdiction.

(e) Compensation. Each member of the
Arbitration Panel ((1) shall be compensated for any and all

-26-

198

services rendered under this General Condition G at a rate of compensation equal to the sum of (1. Two Hundred Fifty Dollars ($250.00) per hour and (2. the sum of Ten Dollars ($10.00) per hour multiplied by the number of full years of the expired Term under the Lease, plus reimbursement for any and all expenses incurred in connection with the rendering of such services, payable in full promptly upon conclusion of the proceedings before the Arbitration Panel. Such compensation and reimbursement shall be borne by the nonprevailing party as determined by the Arbitration Panel in its sole and absolute discretion.

C.   SURVIVAL OF PROVISIONS UPON TERMINATION OF LEASE.

This Lease shall survive the expiration of the Term to the extent necessary that any term, covenant or condition of this Lease which requires the performance of obligations or forbearance of an act by either party hereto after the termination of this Lease. Such survival shall be to the extent reasonably necessary to fulfill the intent thereof, or if specified, to the extent of such specification, as same is reasonably necessary to perform the obligations and/or forbearance of an act set forth in such term, covenant or condition. Notwithstanding the foregoing, in the event a specific term, covenant or condition is expressly provided for in such a clear fashion as to indicate that such performance of an obligation or forbearance of an act is no longer required,

-27-

then the specific shall govern over this general provisions of this Lease.

D. BUILDING STRUCTURE AND BUILDING SYSTEMS.

Landlord agrees that at all times it will maintain the structural portions of the Building, including the foundation, floor/ceiling slabs, roof, curtain wall, exterior glass and mullions, columns, beams, shafts (including elevator shafts), stairs, parking areas, stairwells, escalators, elevator cabs, plazas, pavement, sidewalks, curbs, entrances, landscaping, art work, sculptures, washrooms, mechanical, electrical and telephone closets, and all Common Areas and public areas (collectively, "Building Structure") and the mechanical, electrical, life safety, plumbing, sprinkler systems (connected to the core) and HVAC systems (including primary and secondary loops connected to the core) ("Building Systems") in first class condition and repair and shall operate the Building as a first class office building. Notwithstanding anything in this Lease to the contrary, Tenant shall not be required to make any repair to, modification of, or addition to the Building Structure and/or the Building Systems and/or the Site except and to the extent required because of Tenant's use of all or a portion of the Premises for other than normal and customary business office operations.

-28-

E.   INTEREST RATE.

The "Interest Rate" is defined as the lesser of ((1) the
rate publicly announced from time to time, by the largest (as
measured by deposits) state chartered bank operating in
[*California*], as its Prime Rate or its Reference Rate or other
similar benchmark, plus two percent (2%), or ((2) the maximum
rate permitted by law.

F.   OPERATING EXPENSE ADJUSTMENTS.

[Commencing with the first (1st) day after the Base Year
described in provision (n) of the Fundamental Lease Provisions,]
Tenant shall pay, in addition to the Base Rent computed and due
pursuant to Section 3.1, an additional sum as an operating
expense adjustment ("Operating Expense Adjustment") equal to
Tenant's Pro Rata Share (as defined in Section 4.3) of [any
excess] Operating Expenses (as defined in Section 4.3) [over the
Allowance as defined in Section 4.3 hereof]. Base Rent and the
sums paid pursuant to Sections 4.1, 4.2, and 4.3 are sometimes
collectively referred to as "Gross Rent."

A.   Procedure for Payment of Operating Expense
Adjustments. Tenant shall pay for Tenant's Pro Rata Share of
[any excess] Operating Expenses [over the Allowance] as follows:

-29-

201

1. Landlord may, from time to time by providing at least thirty (30) days advance written notice to Tenant, reasonably estimate in advance the amounts Tenant shall owe on a monthly basis for Operating Expenses **[over the Allowance]** for any full or partial calendar year of the Term. Such estimate shall not exceed 105% of the previous year's Actual Operating Expenses unless evidenced by increases in existing rates or fees with evidence of such increases provided to Tenant ("specifically justified"). In such event, Tenant shall pay such estimated amounts, on a monthly basis, on or before the first day of each calendar month, together with Tenant's payment of Base Rent. Such estimate may be reasonably adjusted from time to time (but not more than once in any twelve (12) month period) by Landlord by written notice to Tenant. **[NOTE: Delete bracketed words for Net Lease in Sections 4.1, 4.2(a), (b), (c), (d) and (f) and 4.3 and 4.4(d).]**

2. Within one hundred twenty (120) days after the end of each calendar year [after the Base Year], or as soon thereafter as practicable, Landlord shall provide a statement itemized on a line item by line item basis (the "Statement") to Tenant showing: a. the amount of actual Operating Expenses for such calendar year and for the preceding calendar year, b. any amount paid on an estimated basis by Tenant toward [excess] Operating Expenses [over the Allowance] during such calendar year and c. any revised

-30-

estimate of Tenant's obligations for [excess] Operating Expenses [over the Allowance] for the current calendar year, not to exceed 105% of the Actual Operating Expenses for the prior year unless specifically justified.

3.   If the Statement shows that Tenant's estimated payments were less than Tenant's actual obligations for [excess] Operating Expenses [over the Allowance] for such year, Tenant shall pay the difference. If the Statement shows an increase in Tenant's estimated payments for the current calendar year, Tenant shall pay the difference between the new and former estimates, for the period from January 1 of the current calendar year through the month in which the Statement is sent.   Tenant shall make such payments within thirty (30) days after Tenant receives the Statement.

4.   If the Statement shows that Tenant's estimated payments exceeded Tenant's actual obligations for [excess] Operating Expenses [over the Allowance], Tenant shall receive a credit of such difference against payments of Rent next due.   If the Term shall have expired and no further Rent shall be due, Tenant shall receive a refund of such difference within thirty (30) days after Landlord sends the Statement.   [If the Statement shows the Actual Operating Expenses have fallen below the Allowance, Tenant shall receive a credit for such differential against rents

-31-

next due and owing or if the Lease has terminated, Tenant shall receive, and Landlord shall pay to Tenant a refund of such differential within thirty (30) days of the date the statement was issued.]

5.   So long as Tenant's obligations hereunder are not materially adversely affected, Landlord reserves the right to change, from time to time, but not more frequently than once in any twelve (12) month period, the manner or timing of the foregoing payments. No delay by Landlord in providing the Statement (or separate statements) shall be deemed a default by Landlord but any delay by Landlord (or any successor to Landlord in the event the Building is conveyed to a new owner during the Lease Term) in billing Tenant for any Operating Expenses of more than three (3) years, or two (2) years if this Lease has terminated, from the date Landlord incurred such Operating Expenses shall be deemed a waiver of Landlord's right to require payment of Tenant's obligations for any such Operating Expenses.

6.   If Tenant's obligation to pay Operating Expense Adjustments commences other than on January 1, or ends other than on December 31, Tenant's obligation to pay estimated and actual amounts toward [excess] Operating Expenses [over the Allowance] for such first or final calendar years shall be prorated to reflect the portion of

-32-

such years included within the period for which Tenant is obligated to pay Operating Expense Adjustments. Such proration shall be made by multiplying the total estimated or actual (as the case may be) [excess] Operating Expenses [over the Allowance] for such calendar years by a fraction, the numerator which shall be the number of days within the period for which Tenant is obligated to pay Operating Expenses Adjustments during such calendar year, and the denominator of which shall be the total number of days in such year.

       7.   If in any year after the Base Year, Operating Expenses are lower than the Operating Expenses in the Base Year, Tenant shall receive a credit against Base Rent equal to the difference between the Operating Expenses during the Base Year and the Operating Expenses during the subsequent year.

       B.   <u>Certain Defined Terms</u>.   "Tenant's Pro Rata Share" means the ratio, as determined from time to time, of the rentable square feet of the Premises to the rentable square feet in the Building. Subject to <u>Section 1.3</u> of the Lease, Tenant's Pro Rata Share as of the Commencement Date is stipulated to be the percentage set forth in provision (o) of the Fundamental Lease Provisions. ["Allowance" shall be the total dollar amount of Operating Expenses incurred by Landlord (grossed up as provided below) during the Base Year for the Building, which

-33-

Base Year is set forth in provision (n) of the Fundamental Lease Provisions.] "Operating Expenses" are defined to be the sum of all costs, expenses, and disbursements, of every kind and nature whatsoever, and the Taxes, incurred by Landlord in connection with the management, maintenance, operation, administration and repair of all or any portion of the Building including, but not limited to, the following, but subject to the exclusions from Operating Expenses listed in Section 4.4 below:

    1.   *****All costs for materials, utilities, goods and services (but excluding all costs for materials, utilities, goods and services furnished by Landlord which are not required to be furnished by Landlord, and which have been directly paid for by Tenant or other tenants to Landlord and to the extent Tenant directly and separately pays Landlord or the provider of such electric power, and also excluding all costs for electrical power other than the cost of the electrical power required to operate the common areas of the Building)***;**

    2.   All wages and benefits and costs of employees or independent contractors or employees of independent contractors, but only to the extent they are engaged in the operation, maintenance and security of the Building;

-34-

206

3. All expenses for janitorial, maintenance, security and safety services;

4. All repairs to, replacement of, and physical maintenance of the Building, including the cost of all supplies, uniforms, equipment, tools and materials;

5. Any license, permit and inspection fees required in connection with the operation of the Building;

6. Any auditor's fees for accounting provided for the operation and maintenance of the Building;

7. Any legal fees, costs and disbursements as would normally be incurred in connection with the operation, maintenance and repair of the Building;

8. All reasonable fees for management services provided by a management company or by Landlord or an agent of Landlord not to exceed the lower of _____ percent (____%) of office space rental income or the amount that would have been charged by a first class management company unaffiliated with Landlord;

9. The annual amortization (amortized over the useful life but in no event less than five (5) years) of costs, including financing costs, if any, incurred by

-35-

Landlord after the Commencement Date for any capital improvements installed or paid for by Landlord and required by any new (or change in) laws, rules or regulations of any governmental or quasi-governmental authority (collectively "Laws") which are enacted after the Commencement Date;

10. The annual amortization (amortized over the useful life) of costs, including financing costs, if any, of any equipment, device or capital improvement purchased or incurred as a labor-saving measure or to affect other economies in the operation or maintenance of the Building (provided the annual amortized cost does not exceed the actual cost savings realized *****and such savings do not redound primarily to the benefit of any particular tenant*****);

11. All insurance premiums and other charges (including the amount of any deductible payable by Landlord with respect to damage or destruction to all or any portion of the Building but in no event more than $25,000 per year) incurred by Landlord with respect to insuring the Building including, without limitation, the following to the extent carried by Landlord: a. fire and extended coverage insurance, windstorm, hail, and explosion; b. riot attending a strike, civil commotion, aircraft, vehicle and smoke insurance; c. public liability, bodily injury and property damage insurance; d. elevator insurance; e.

-36-

workers' compensation insurance for the employees specified in Section 4.3(b) above; f. boiler and machinery insurance, sprinkler leakage, water damage, property, burglary, fidelity and pilferage insurance on equipment and materials; g. loss of rent, rent abatement, rent continuation, business interruption insurance, and similar types of insurance (but only to the extent of increases in the cost of such coverage over the cost that would have been incurred for the same coverage in the Base Year); h. earthquake, floor, tornado, and hurricane insurance to the extent available on a commercially reasonable basis; and i. such other insurance as is customarily carried by operators of Comparable Buildings;

12. All actual taxes, assessments, levies, charges, water and sewer charges, rapid transit and other similar or comparable governmental charges (collectively "Taxes") levied or assessed on, imposed upon or attributable to the calendar year in question a. to the Building, and/or b. to the operation of the Building, including but not limited to Taxes against the Building, personal property taxes or assessments levied or assessed against the Building, together with any costs incurred by Landlord, including attorneys' fees, in contesting any such Taxes but excluding any tax measured by gross rentals received from the Building, any net income, franchise, capital stock, succession, transfer, gift, estate or

-37-

inheritance taxes imposed by the State of [*California*] or
the United States or by their respective agencies, branches
or departments;

13.   Minor capital improvements, tools or
expenditures to the extent each such improvement or
acquisition costs less than Three Thousand Dollars
($3,000.00) and the total cost of same are not in excess of
Ten Thousand Dollars ($10,000) in any twelve (12) month
period; and

14.   Such other usual costs and expenses which
are commonly incurred by other landlords for the purpose of
providing for the .on-site operation, servicing, maintenance
and repair of Comparable Buildings.

***If the Building does not have at least one hundred
percent (100%) of the rentable area of the Building occupied
during any calendar year period (including any calendar year(s)
falling within the Base Year), then the variable portion of
Operating Expenses for such period shall be deemed to be equal
to the total of the variable portion of Operating Expenses which
would have been incurred by Landlord if one hundred percent
(100%) of the rentable area of the Building had been occupied
for the entirety of such calendar year with all tenants paying
full rent, as contrasted with free rent, half rent or the like
("Gross-Up Provision")***. [NOTE: For leases where Tenant is

-38-

leasing the entire Building, delete all words, wherever occurring, between triple asterisks (***). NOTE: In this paragraph only, if Tenant is leasing the entire Building and if this Lease is a net lease, substitute the following: *Because this is a net lease and because Tenant is leasing one hundred percent (100%) of the Building, the variable portion of Operating Expenses shall not be grossed up.*] Notwithstanding the foregoing, Landlord shall not recover as Operating Expenses more than 100% of the Operating Expenses actually paid by Landlord. The annual amortization of costs shall be determined by dividing the original cost of such capital expenditure by the number of years of useful life of the capital item acquired. Operating Expenses shall be computed according to the cash or accrual basis of accounting, as Landlord may elect in accordance with standard and reasonable accounting principles employed by Landlord.

If Landlord receives a refund or credit of Operating Expenses subsequent to the year in which such expense was paid and charged to Operating Expenses, Landlord shall pay to Tenant the amount of such refund or credit to the extent Tenant directly or indirectly was charged for such Operating Expenses during a prior year.

C.   Exclusion from Operating Expenses.

1.   Notwithstanding anything in the definition
of Operating Expenses in the Lease to the contrary,
Operating Expenses shall not include the following, except
to the extent specifically permitted by a specific
exception to the following:

a.   Any ground lease rental;

b.   Costs of items considered capital
repairs, replacements, improvements and equipment
under generally accepted accounting principles
consistently applied or otherwise ("Capital Items");
except for those Capital Items specifically permitted
in subitems (i), (j) and (m) in the definition of
Operating Expenses set forth in Section 4.3;

c.   Rentals for items (except when needed
in connection with normal repairs and maintenance of
permanent systems) which if purchased, rather than
rented, would constitute a Capital Item which is
specifically excluded in (ii) above (excluding,
however, equipment not affixed to the Building which
is used in providing janitorial or similar services);

-40-

d.　　Costs incurred by Landlord for the
repair of damage to the Building, to the extent that
Landlord is or should be reimbursed by insurance
proceeds, and costs of all capital repairs, regardless
of whether such repairs are covered by insurance and
costs due to repairs resulting from an earthquake or
flood to the extent such costs exceed $25,000;

e.　　*****Costs, including permit, license and
inspection costs, incurred with respect to the
installation of tenant or other occupants' improvements in the Building or incurred in renovating or
otherwise improving, decorating, painting or
redecorating vacant space for tenants or other
occupants of the Building*****;

f.　　Depreciation, amortization and interest
payments, except as provided herein and except on
materials, tools, supplies and vendor-type equipment
purchased by Landlord to enable Landlord to supply
services Landlord might otherwise contract for with a
third party where such depreciation, amortization and
interest payments would otherwise have been included
in the charge for such third party's services, all as
determined in accordance with generally accepted
accounting principles, consistently applied, and when
depreciation or amortization is permitted or required,

-41-

the item shall be amortized over its reasonably anticipated useful life;

g.   Marketing costs, including without limitation, leasing commissions, attorneys' fees in connection with the negotiation and preparation of letters, deal memos, letters of intent, leases, subleases and/or assignments, space planning costs, and other costs and expenses incurred in connection with lease, sublease and/or assignment negotiations and transactions with Tenant or present or prospective tenants or other occupants of the Building;

h. *****Expenses in connection with services or other benefits which are not offered to Tenant or for which Tenant is charged for directly but which are provided to another tenant or occupant of the Building*****;

i.   Costs incurred by Landlord due to the violation by Landlord *****or any tenant***** of the terms and conditions of any lease of space in the Building;

j.   Overhead and profit increment paid to Landlord or to subsidiaries or affiliates of Landlord for goods and/or services in or to the Building to the extent the same exceeds the costs of such goods and/or

-42-

services rendered by unaffiliated third parties on a competitive basis;

k.   Interest, principal, points and fees on debts or amortization on any mortgage or mortgages or any other debt instrument encumbering the Building or the Site (except as permitted in (ii) above);

l.   Landlord's general corporate overhead and general and administrative expenses;

m. Any compensation paid to clerks, attendants or other persons in commercial concessions operated by Landlord or in the parking garage of the Building or wherever Tenant is granted its parking privileges and/or all fees paid to any parking facility operator (on or off Site) [*(provided, however, that if **Landlord provides such parking to Tenant free of charge or at a reduced rate, to the extent that Tenant's Pro Rata Share of such expenses exceeds any amount paid by Tenant for such parking, these expenses may be included as a part of Operating Expenses)*];

n.   Rentals and other related expenses incurred in leasing HVAC systems, elevators or other equipment ordinarily considered to be Capital Items, except for (1) expenses in connection with making

-43-

minor repairs on or keeping Building Systems in operation while minor repairs are being made and (2) costs of equipment not affixed to the Building which is used in providing janitorial or similar services;

o.   Advertising and promotional expenditures, and costs of signs in or on the Building identifying the owner of the Building ***or other tenants' signs***;

p.   ***The cost of any electric power used by any tenant in the Building in excess of the Building-standard amount, or electric power costs for which any tenant directly contracts with the local public service company or of which any tenant is separately metered or submetered and pays Landlord directly; provided, however, that if any tenant in the Building contracts directly for electric power service or is separately metered or submetered during any portion of the relevant period, the total electric power costs for the Building shall be "grossed up" to reflect what those costs would have been had each tenant in the Building used the Building-standard amount of electric power***;

q. ***Services and utilities provided, taxes attributable to, and costs incurred in connection with

-44-

216

the operation of the retail and restaurant operations in the Building, except to the extent the square footage of such operations are included in the rentable square feet of the Building and do not exceed the services, utility and tax costs that would have been incurred had the retail and/or restaurant space been used for general office purposes***;

r. Costs incurred in connection with upgrading the Building to comply with life, fire and safety codes, ordinances, statutes or other laws [in effect prior to the Commencement Date], including, without limitation, the ADA, including penalties or damages incurred due to such non-compliance;

s. Tax penalties incurred as a result of Landlord's failure to make payments and/or to file any tax or informational returns when due;

t. Costs for which Landlord has been compensated by a management fee, and any management fees in excess of those management fees which are normally and customarily charged by landlords of Comparable Buildings;

u. Costs arising from the negligence or fault of ***other tenants or*** Landlord or its

-45-

agents, or any vendors, contractors, or providers of materials or services selected, hired or engaged by Landlord or its agents including, without limitation, the selection of Building materials;

v. Notwithstanding any contrary provision of the Lease, including, without limitation, any provision relating to capital expenditures, any and all costs arising from the presence of hazardous materials or substances (as defined by Applicable Laws in effect on the date this Lease is executed) in or about the Premises, the Building or the Site including, without limitation, hazardous substances in the ground water or soil, not placed in the Premises, the Building or the Site by Tenant;

w. Costs arising from Landlord's charitable or political contributions;

x. Costs arising from defects in the base, shell or core of the Building or improvements installed by Landlord or repair thereof;

y. Costs arising from any mandatory or voluntary special assessment on the Building or the Site by any transit district authority or any other

-46-

governmental entity having the authority to impose
such assessment;

z. Costs for the acquisition of (as contrasted
with the maintenance of) sculpture, paintings or other
objects of art;

aa. Costs (including in connection therewith all
attorneys' fees and costs of settlement judgments and
payments in lieu thereof) arising from claims,
disputes or potential disputes in connection with
potential or actual claims litigation or arbitrations
pertaining to Landlord and/or the Building and/or the
Site;

ab. Costs associated with the operation of the
business of the partnership or entity which
constitutes Landlord as the same are distinguished
from the costs of operation of the Building, including
partnership accounting and legal matters, costs of
defending any lawsuits with or claims by any mortgagee
(except as the actions of Tenant may be in issue),
costs of selling, syndicating, financing, mortgaging
or hypothecating any of Landlord's interest in the
Building, costs of any disputes between Landlord and
its employees (if any) not engaged in Building
operation, disputes of Landlord with Building

-47-

management, or outside fees paid in connection with
disputes with other tenants;

**[*ac.   Any increase of, or reassessment in,
real property taxes and assessments in excess of two
percent (2%) of the taxes for the previous year,
resulting from either (1) any sale, transfer, or other
change in ownership of the Building or the Site during
the Lease Term or from major alterations,
improvements, modifications or renovations to the
Building or the Site (collectively, "Transfers"), or
(2) any action, including, without limitation,
judicial action or action by initiative, which serves
to repeal, modify and/or limit the application of
Article XIIIA of the California Constitution
(otherwise known as Proposition 13);*];**

ad.   Costs of any "tap fees" or any sewer or
water connection fees for the benefit of any
particular tenant in the Building;

ae. Costs incurred in connection with any
environmental clean-up, response action, or
remediation on, in, under or about the Premises or the
Building, including but not limited to, costs and
expenses associated with the defense, administration,
settlement, monitoring or management thereof;

-48-

220

af.   Any expenses incurred by Landlord for use of
any portions of the Building to accommodate events
including, but not limited to shows, promotions,
kiosks, displays, filming, photography, private events
or parties, ceremonies, and advertising beyond the
normal expenses otherwise attributable to providing
Building services, such as lighting and HVAC to such
public portions of the Building in normal Building
operations during standard Building hours of
operation;

ag.   Any entertainment, dining or travel expenses
for any purpose;

ah.   Any flowers, gifts, balloons, etc. provided
to any entity whatsoever, to include, but not limited
to, Tenant, *****other tenants*****, employees, vendors,
contractors, prospective tenants and agents;

ai.   Any "validated" parking for any entity;

aj.   Any "finders fees", brokerage commissions,
job placement costs or job advertising cost;

ak.   Any "above-standard" cleaning, including,
but not limited to construction cleanup or special
cleanings associated with parties/events and specific
tenant requirements in excess of service provided to

-49-

Tenant, including related trash collection, removal,
hauling and dumping;

al.   The cost of any magazine, newspaper, trade
or other subscriptions;

am.   The cost of any training or incentive
programs, other than for tenant life safety
information services;

an.   The cost of any "tenant relations" parties,
events or promotion not consented to by an authorized
representative of Tenant in writing;

ao.   "In-house" legal and/or accounting fees;

ap.   Reserves for bad debts or for future
improvements, repairs, additions, etc.; and

(xliii)   Any other expenses which, in accordance
with generally accepted accounting principles, consistently
applied, would not normally be treated as Operating Expenses by
landlords of Comparable Buildings.

2.   It is understood that Operating Expenses
shall be reduced by all cash discounts, trade discounts,
quantity discounts, rebates or other amounts received by

-50-

222

Landlord or Landlord's managing agent in the purchase of any goods, utilities, or services in connection with the operation of the Building. Landlord shall make payments for goods, utilities, or services in a timely manner to obtain the maximum possible discount. If Capital Items which are customarily purchased by landlords of Comparable Buildings are leased by Landlord, rather than purchased, the decision by Landlord to lease the item in question shall not serve to increase Tenant's Pro Rata Share of Operating Expenses beyond that which would have applied had the item in question been purchased. Any repair or maintenance costs which are covered by a warranty or service contract in the Base Year shall be imputed into the Allowance.

3.   In the event any facilities, services or utilities used in connection with the Building are provided from another building owned or operated by Landlord or vice versa, the costs incurred by Landlord in connection therewith shall be allocated to Operating Expenses by Landlord on a reasonably equitable basis.

4.   For the purpose of payment of Operating Expenses, to the extent Landlord pays Taxes and/or insurance premiums less frequently than monthly, the cost of same shall not be included in Operating Expenses but shall be separately calculated, with Tenant being obligated

-51-

to pay Tenant's Pro Rata Share of same on the later of five (5) business days after receipt of an invoice from Landlord or ten (10) days prior to the date Landlord is obligated to pay same to the taxing authority or insurance company.

5.   In the event Tenant ceases to occupy (but still lease) the entire Premises or one or more floors of the Premises or elects to provide services and utilities to its Premises that Landlord previous provided, Tenant shall receive a credit against Rent equal to the cost of electricity, janitorial service, water, HVAC and any other variable expenses not incurred as a result of such vacancy or because of Tenant's election to provide such services or utilities.

6.   In the event that Landlord receives a Proposition 8 reduction in Taxes attributable to the Base Year, then Taxes for the Base Year and any subsequent year shall be computed as if no Proposition 8 tax reduction was obtained during the Base Year and any subsequent year ("Proposition 8 Protection").

G.   <u>ACTUAL COSTS</u>.

Landlord shall charge Tenants, and Tenant shall pay Landlord, for all additional services and utilities provided by

Landlord to Tenant pursuant to Tenant's request, an amount equal to the incremental extra out of pocket costs incurred by Landlord in providing same, without markup for administrative costs (except the extent not duplicative of operating expenses), profit overhead, or depreciation.

H.   CONSENT/DUTY TO ACT REASONABLY.

Regardless of any references to the terms "sole" or "absolute" (but except for matters which ((1) could have an adverse effect on the structural integrity of the Building Structure, as defined in General Condition N, ((2) could have an adverse effect on the Building Systems, as defined in General Condition N, or ((3) could have an effect on the exterior appearance of the Building, whereupon in each such case Landlord's duty is to act in good faith and in compliance with the Lease), any time the consent of Landlord or Tenant is required, such consent shall not be unreasonably withheld, conditioned or delayed. Whenever this Lease grants Landlord or Tenant the right to take action, exercise discretion, establish rules and regulations or make allocations or other determinations (other than decisions to exercise renewal options), Landlord and Tenant shall act reasonably and in good faith and take no action which might result in the frustration of the reasonable expectations of a sophisticated tenant or landlord concerning the benefits to be enjoyed under this Lease.

-53-

NOTES

NOTES

5

LONG RANGE PLANNING - EXIT STRATEGY

Linda D. White

I. Introduction

In negotiating the lease a tenant's desire is to maintain flexibility. The lease should follow (not dictate) the business needs of the tenant. The tenant realizes that during the term of the lease the tenant's business may grow, thus requiring more space in the existing facility or in a different facility. The tenant may merge or sell its assets.

The landlord on the other hand, while trying to accommodate the tenant, wants to maximize the profit from the leased space and to maintain control over the identity of its tenants.

The lease clauses which affect the tenant's ability to grow and contract and to control its business needs are the assignment and subletting clause, the expansion clauses (expansion rights, rights of first refusal, rights of first offer), the renewal clause, clauses dealing with options to reduce space and early termination rights, clauses allowing the landlord to substitute premises and the yield-up (costs to vacate) clause.

II. Assignment/Subletting

A. From the Landlord's Perspective

1. To consent or not to consent

a. Does state law require a reasonableness standard?

b. Specific standards and prohibitions which may appear in the lease:

(1) Financial condition and character of subtenant

(2) Nature of proposed use by subtenant (subtenant must not breach another tenant's exclusive use clause)

(3) No subleasing to other tenants in the building

(4) No subleasing to governmental entities

(5) Limits on multiple subtenants (issues involved in converting a single-tenant floor to a multi-tenant floor)

(6) Tenant must not be in default

(7) Loss of expansion/extension rights by tenant

(8) Limits on certain benefits, i.e., caps on taxes/operating expenses (items personal to tenant)

2. The consent letter:

a. Is for landlord's protection

b. Is not a non-disturbance agreement (doesn't agree to honor subrent on tenant default)

c. Restricts sub-subleasing or amendment without landlord consent

d. Specifies no release of prime tenant's liability

e. Permits landlord to collect subrent and building charges directly

f. Adds subtenant to indemnity and insurance obligations

g. Gives landlord option to keep subtenant if prime tenant defaults

h. Specifies that certain rights are personal to the prime tenant

3. Recapture and profit-sharing

a. Should landlord have the right to recapture?

(1) Under the office lease

(2) Under the retail lease

(3) Non-compete/exclusive use considerations

b. When should the right of recapture be triggered -- upon prime tenant's decision to sublease or presentation of an actual subtenant?

   (1) If landlord initially passes on the recapture right but the tenant fails to find a subtenant or assignee within a given time frame, should the landlord's rights kick in again?

c. Sharing profits

   (1) What is the right percentage?

   (2) Should prime tenant recover its costs of subletting before any sharing with landlord or pro rate over sublease term?

   (3) What costs are included?

   (4) Should prime tenant's cost of carrying the space while it is seeking a subtenant be deemed a recoverable cost?

4. Controlling "in substance" assignments

   a. Sale of stock or partnership interests to avoid assignment restrictions

b. Use of net worth test

c. Reaffirmation of guaranties

d. Tenant mix issues (i.e., again question of exclusives)

e. Avoid release of liability on transfers to affiliates

f. Avoid prime tenant's ability to mortgage or assign its leasehold interest

g. Provide that certain rights (i.e., expansion, extension, name rights) are personal to prime tenant and do not run for the benefit of prime tenant's assignee or subtenant

B. From the Prime Tenant's Perspective

1. Limiting prime tenant's liability

a. Best case - obtain release of liability from landlord

b. Avoid responsibility to subtenant for landlord's failure to perform

c. Obtain security deposit and indemnities from subtenant

d. Require subtenant to carry insurance naming both landlord and prime tenant

2. Determine subtenant's ability to comply with use clause and prime lease restrictions

3. Interrelationship of fire and casualty provisions in the sublease and prime lease

4. Interrelationship of holdover provisions in the sublease and prime lease

5. Would an assignment or subletting later restrict the prime tenant from restructuring the lease with the landlord upon a further downsizing of prime tenant?

6. Once the prime tenant assigns the prime lease, it no longer has any possessory rights to the leased space (even though it still has the obligation to pay rent). What is the prime tenant to do upon the assignee's bankruptcy so as to mitigate its loss?

7. Would the restrictions on subleasing and assignment preclude the prime tenant from selling its business?

   a. Avoid restrictions on subleasing and assignment which would affect mergers, acquisitions and restructures

b. Must landlord consent be obtained

c. Impact if consent is necessary and not given

8. What is the impact of the death, disability or withdrawal of one or more partners in a partnership tenant?

a. Will this be deemed an impermissible assignment of the prime lease?

b. Will such assignment constitute a default under the prime lease?

C. From the Subtenant's Perspective

1. Risks of subleasing

a. From a prime tenant in financial trouble

b. In the event the landlord goes bankrupt·

2. Ability to obtain a non-disturbance agreement from the landlord

a. Will the rent remain the same if sublease becomes a prime lease

3. Ability to cure prime tenant defaults

4. Ability of subtenant to obtain services from landlord

5. Maximize flexibility

    a. Maintain expansion and extension rights contained in the prime lease

        (1) Will the landlord limit the prime tenant's rights to expand or extend the term upon a subletting?

        (2) Ability of subtenant or assignee to exercise rights if prime tenant fails to exercise

    b. Are there any other rights which are personal to prime tenant which will not be available to subtenant or assignee?

III.   Expansion Rights

    A. Specific rights to expand

       1. When must the tenant deliver notice of its exercise

       2. Defining the window in which landlord must deliver the space

    B. Right of First Refusal

1. Continuing right v. one time right

2. How much time does the tenant have to decide to take the space?

3. Impact on landlord's ability to market the space

C. Right of First Offer

    1. Continuing right v. one time right

    2. When must landlord again give tenant notice if no third party has been obtained to date?

D. Terms of the Expansion

    1. What is the rental?

        a. Current rental rate v.

        b. Market rental rate - how define

            (1) Market rent in comparison with market rent in other buildings v.

            (2) Market rent for tenants in the Building who are expanding

        c. Impact of concessions

        d. Use of arbitration

    2. Amount and location of the space

      a. Contiguous to the existing Premises

      b. Must the tenant take all of the space offered?

  3. Improvement of the expansion space

      a. Tenant takes space "as-is"

      b. Landlord provides a prorated or market tenant improvement allowance

  4. Coterminous with existing term

  5. Should tenant's failure to exercise the first option preclude it from exercising the second option?

  6. Inability of landlord to deliver (i.e., failure of existing tenant to vacate)

IV. Renewal Rights

  A. Number of options

  B. Timing of exercise

  C. Determination of rental rate - same concerns as in the expansion arena

  D. Partial renewal

V. Termination Rights

A. Tenant's right to give back all or a portion of the space

    1. Who pays to construct demising walls if only a portion of the space is given back?

    2. Who decides what space to give back - space given back must be leasable by landlord

    3. Impact on tenant's other options (i.e., future rights to expand)

B. Termination Fee

    1. Amount

        a. Unamortized costs of tenant improvements and brokerage commissions

        b. Payment of a portion of rent going forward

    2. Timing of payment

C. Timing of Notice by tenant

VI. Substitution of Premises by Landlord

A. Criteria of new space

    1. Location in building

    2. Comparable space

  B. Costs of move

    1. Moving costs, cabling, stationery, etc.

    2. Borne by landlord

VII. Yield-Up

  A. In what condition must the tenant surrender the premises?

    1. "As-is" but broom clean

    2. In the condition tenant received the premises

      a. Before or after tenant improvements are constructed

  B. Obtain landlord's consent to remove/leave improvements at time plans for such improvements are submitted to landlord for approval.

  C. Timing of removal of improvements

    1. If all such improvements are not removed by the Termination Date under the lease is tenant in a hold-over situation?

Selected Lease Provisions -

EXHIBIT 1

RESTRICTIONS ON
"IN-SUBSTANCE" ASSIGNMENTS

Example 1:

For the purposes of this subsection (A), (i) the sale, transfer or issuance of a majority of the issued and outstanding capital stock of any corporate tenant, or of a corporate subtenant, or the sale, transfer or issuance of a majority of the total interest in any partnership tenant or subtenant, however accomplished, whether in a single transaction or in a series of related or unrelated transactions, shall be deemed an assignment of this Lease, or of such sublease, as the case may be or (ii) a takeover agreement or similar agreement whereby the obligations of Tenant under this Lease are assumed by another party shall be deemed a transfer of this Lease.

Notwithstanding anything to the contrary contained herein, Tenant may assign this Lease to or permit any corporation or other business entity which is and continues at all times to control, be controlled by, or be under common control with Tenant (each a "related corporation") to sublet the Premises for any of the purposes permitted to Tenant under this Lease (subject however to compliance with Tenant's obligations under this Lease) provided that (i) Tenant shall not then be in default (after any applicable grace and/or cure periods set forth in subsection ___ in the performance of any of its obligations under this

Lease), (ii) prior to such assignment or subletting, Tenant furnishes Landlord with the name of any such related corporation, together with evidence reasonably satisfactory to Landlord that the proposed assignee or subtenant, as the case may be, is a related corporation of Tenant, (iii) in the reasonable judgment of Landlord, the proposed assignee or subtenant is in keeping with the standards of Landlord for the Building and (iv) in the event of an assignment or a sublease of all or substantially all of the Premises, the assignee or sublessee shall have a net worth computed in accordance with generally accepted accounting principles at least equal to the net worth of Tenant named herein on the date of this Lease, and proof satisfactory to Landlord of such net worth shall have been delivered to Landlord at least ten (10) days prior to the effective date of any such transaction. Any subletting to a related corporation shall not be deemed to vest in such related corporation any right or interest in this Lease or the Premises nor shall it relieve, release, impair or discharge any of Tenant's obligations hereunder. For the purposes hereof, "control" shall be deemed to mean ownership of not less than fifty-one percent (51%) of all of the voting stock of such corporation or not less than fifty-one percent (51%) of all of the legal and equitable interest in any other business entities.

The provisions of this Section shall not apply to transactions with a corporation into or with which Tenant is merged or consolidated or to which substantially all of Tenant's assets are transferred, provided that in any of such events (i) the successor to Tenant has a net worth computed in accordance with generally accepted accounting principles at least equal to the net worth of Tenant named herein on the date of this Lease and (ii) proof satisfactory to Landlord of such net worth shall have been delivered to Landlord at least ten (10) days prior to the effective date of any such transaction.

Example 2:

Tenant shall not, without the prior written consent of Landlord: (a) assign, mortgage, pledge, encumber or otherwise transfer this Lease, the term or estate hereby granted, or any interest hereunder; (b) permit the Premises or any part thereof to be utilized by anyone other than Tenant (whether as concessionaire, franchisee, licensee, permittee or otherwise); or (c) except as hereinafter provided, sublet or offer or advertise for subletting the Premises or any portion thereof. Any assignment, mortgage, pledge, encumbrance, transfer or sublease without Landlord's consent shall be voidable at Landlord's election. Landlord has entered into this Lease with Tenant in order to obtain the unique attraction to Tenant's Trade Name and the unique merchandising mix and product line associated with Tenant's business as described in Section _____ hereof, and Landlord has specifically relied on the identity and special skill of Tenant in its ability to conduct the specific business identified in Section _____ hereof, and the foregoing prohibition against assignment or subletting or the like is expressly agreed to by Tenant as an inducement to Landlord to lease the Premises to Tenant. For the purposes of this Section _____, (i) the transfer of this

Lease from Tenant by merger, consolidation or dissolution or any change in ownership or power to vote a majority of the voting stock in Tenant outstanding at the time of execution of this instrument shall constitute an assignment for the purpose of this Lease, provided, however, that: 1) acquisition of a majority of the stock of a corporate tenant by any corporation, the stock of which is listed on either the New York or American Stock Exchange or the merger of a corporate tenant into such a corporation, the stock of which is so listed, shall not itself be deemed to be a violation hereof; or 2) transfer of stock to members of the _____ family (meaning the spouse, lineal descendants and their spouses of _____ and to trusts created for the benefit of such persons) shall not itself be deemed to be a violation hereof, (ii) other than as permitted in clause (i) above, a takeover agreement or similar agreement whereby the obligations of Tenant under this Lease are assumed by another party shall be deemed a transfer of this Lease, (iii) any person or legal representative of Tenant, to whom Tenant's interest under this Lease passes by operation of law, or otherwise, shall be bound by the provisions of this Section 11.01, (iv) if Tenant consists of more than one person, a purported assignment, voluntary, involuntary, or by operation of law by any of the persons executing this Lease shall be deemed a voluntary assignment of this Lease by Tenant and (v) a modification, amendment or extension of a sublease shall be deemed a sublease. Notwithstanding anything to the contrary contained herein, any rights and/or options of first offer, refusal or extension granted to Tenant shall be personal to the Tenant named herein and shall be deemed null and void in the event of any assignment of this Lease or sublease of all or substantially all of the Premises.

Example 3:

Notwithstanding any provision herein to the contrary or reference herein to concessionaires or subtenants or otherwise, except as hereinafter provided, Tenant agrees not to assign or in any manner transfer this Lease or any estate or interest therein, and not to lease or sublet the leased premises or any part or parts thereof or any right or privilege appurtenant thereto, and not to allow anyone to conduct business at, upon or from the leased premises (whether as concessionaire, franchisee, licensee, permittee, subtenant, department operator or otherwise), either by voluntary or involuntary act of Tenant or by operation of law or otherwise; provided, however, the foregoing shall not be applicable to an assignment of this Lease by operation of law unless and until there shall also be a default in the Tenant's obligations under this Lease. The taking of the estate of Tenant created by this Lease under writ of execution shall not be considered an assignment of this Lease by operation of law. Landlord has entered into this Lease with Tenant in order to obtain for the benefit of Center the unique attraction of Tenant's trade name set forth in Section 1.01(1) hereof and the unique merchandising mix and product line associated with Tenant's business as described in Section 8.01, and Landlord has specifically relied on the identity and special skill of Tenant in its ability to conduct the specific business identified in Section 8.01, and the foregoing prohibition on assignment or subletting or the like is expressly agreed to by Tenant as an inducement to Landlord to lease to Tenant.

Notwithstanding the foregoing, if Tenant is not in default under this Lease, Tenant shall have the right, subject to obtaining Landlord's prior written consent thereto, which shall not be withheld or delayed unreasonably, to transfer or assign this Lease or sublet the whole of the leased premises to any entity, provided that the following conditions are met:

(i) such transferee, assignee or subtenant ("Transferee") has a current net worth of not less than Five Million Dollars ($5,000,000.00), determined according to generally accepted accounting principles, consistently applied;

(ii) the Transferee shall own and operate at least three (3) other stores which carry on the type of business for which the Transferee intends to use the leased premises;

(iii) the proposed use to be made of the leased premises by the proposed Transferee shall be a lawful retail use which is typically or normally found in comparable shopping centers, and which (a) shall not violate any exclusive use provisions or use restriction contained in any other lease or other agreement pertaining to Center, (b) shall not be the same as or substantially similar to the primary use of any other store in Center, and (c) shall not be any of the following uses:

_____

EXHIBIT 2

RESTRICTIONS ON
PARTNERSHIP TRANSFERS

Example 1:

Notwithstanding anything to the contrary contained herein, (i) a withdrawal or change, whether voluntary, involuntary or by operation of law or in one or more transactions, of partners (other than Messrs. Smith, Jones, Green and Black) owning directly or indirectly a controlling interest in Tenant shall not be deemed an assignment of this Lease so long as Messrs. Smith, Jones, Green and Black are shareholders in the resulting entity; (ii) if Tenant is a corporation, any merger, consolidation or other reorganization of Tenant, or the sale, transfer or redemption of a direct or indirect controlling interest in the capital stock of Tenant (other than by Messrs. Smith, Jones, Green or Black), in one or more transactions, shall not be deemed a voluntary assignment of this Lease so long as Messrs. Smith, Jones, Green and Black are shareholders in the resulting entity; and (iii) a restructuring of Tenant from a partnership to a professional corporation or limited liability company shall not be deemed an assignment of this Lease and subject to the provisions of this <u>Section</u> so long as Messrs. Smith, Jones, Green and Black are shareholders in the resulting entity. Neither this Lease nor any interest therein nor any estate created thereby shall pass by operation of law or otherwise to any trustee, custodian or receiver in bankruptcy of Tenant or any assignee for the assignment of the benefit of creditors of Tenant. Notwithstanding anything herein to the contrary, the death of (x) either Messrs. Smith or Jones or (y) any two of Messrs. Smith, Jones, Green and Black (other than both Messrs. Smith and Jones) during the Term shall not constitute an assignment in violation of this Lease. Tenant has informed Landlord that Tenant carries and Tenant agrees to continue to carry during the Term "Key Man" insurance in an amount not less than $6 million on Messrs. Smith and Jones.

Example 2:

A. If Tenant is a corporation (other than a corporation whose stock is traded through a national or regional exchange or over-the-counter), any transaction or series of transactions (including, without limitation, any dissolution, merger, consolidation or other reorganization of Tenant, or any issuance, sale, gift, transfer or redemption of any capital stock of Tenant, whether voluntary, involuntary or by operation of law, or any combination of any of the foregoing transactions) resulting in the transfer of control of Tenant, other than by reason of death, shall be deemed to be transfer of Tenant's interest under this lease for the purpose of Sections __ and __. If Tenant is a partnership, any transaction or series of transactions resulting in the transfer of control of Tenant, other than by reason of death, shall be deemed to be a transfer of Tenant's interest under this lease for the purposes of Sections __ and __. The term "control" as used in this Section __ means (i) if Tenant is a corporation, a change or series of changes in ownership of stock which would result in direct or indirect change in ownership by the stockholders or an affiliated group of stockholders of fifty percent (50%) or more of the outstanding stock as of the date such corporation became "Tenant" under this lease and (ii) if Tenant is a partnership, a change or series of changes in the ownership of general partnership interests which would result in direct or indirect change in ownership by the general partners of more than fifty percent (50%) of the general partnership interests as of the date the partnership became "Tenant" under the lease; provided that as to the Original Tenant Partnership or any Successor Partnership or Successor Company (as such terms are hereinafter defined), a change of control shall mean the withdrawal as general partners, shareholders or members (as the case may be) (other than withdrawal due to death or disability) from such Original Tenant Partnership or Successor Partnership or Successor Company of at least four (4) of the original seven (7) partners executing this lease on behalf of the Tenant within any one twelve (12) month period ("Substantial Change of Control"). In the case of a Substantial Change of Control, the general partners, shareholders or members (as the case may be) then remaining shall, within a reasonable period of time (not to exceed thirty (30) days) seek to obtain Landlord's consent to such Substantial Change of Control as if the resulting partnership or company were an assignee (which consent shall not be unreasonably withheld, as provided above), and may, at its election, propose that liability of the remaining partners, shareholders or members (as the case may be) be limited to assets of the partnership or company in the same manner as is set forth in Section __ hereinbelow (it being understood, however, that no such limitation shall affect any then existing guaranty of lease executed by the original seven (7) partners executing this lease on behalf of the original Tenant). Provided that all required information has been provided as required for an assignment, Landlord agrees to respond to the request for consent within thirty (30) days. If Landlord's consent is not obtained, the prior Tenant partnership or company shall remain Tenant, such new resulting partnership or company shall not be permitted to retain possession as Tenant, and an unpermitted assignment shall be deemed to have occurred.

B. The Original Tenant Partnership shall also have the right to assign this lease or sublet all or a majority of the Rentable Area of the Premises to a Successor Partnership or a Successor Company without Landlord's consent, so long as (A) Tenant notifies Landlord in writing not less than ten (10) days in advance of the intended assignment or subletting, (B) in Landlord's reasonable determination the assignee or sublessee has the financial strength (financial strength, in the case of a law firm to include, without limitation, adequate cash flow and diversity of clients assuring diverse sources of revenue) to perform its obligations under the assignment or sublease as the case may be, and (C) the intended use of the Premises by the assignee or sublessee will not violate the provisions of Section __ of this lease. For purposes of this lease, "Successor Partnership" means any partnership, the majority of whose general partners were general partners of the Original Tenant Partnership, which succeeds to the business and assets of Original Tenant Partnership, and which assumes the obligations of Original Tenant Partnership. For purposes of this lease, "Successor Company" means a corporation or limited liability company, the majority of whose shareholders or members, as the case may be, were general partners of Original Tenant Partnership, which succeeds to the business and assets of Original Tenant Partnership, and which assumes the obligations of Original Tenant Partnership. For purposes of this lease, "Original Tenant Partnership" shall mean the original named Tenant and any successor thereto from time to time resulting from changes in the ownership of general partnership interests of said original named Tenant, which changes do not result in a Substantial Change in Control.

EXHIBIT 3

STANDARD LANDLORD PROVISION

ASSIGNMENT AND SUBLETTING

A. Subject to any provisions of this <u>Section</u> to the contrary, Tenant shall not, without the prior written consent of Landlord, (i) assign, convey or mortgage this Lease or any interest hereunder; (ii) permit to occur or permit to exist any assignment of this Lease, or any lien upon Tenant's interest, voluntarily or by operation of law; (iii) sublet the Premises or any part thereof; (iv) advertise as available for sublet or assignment all or any portion of the Premises; or (v) permit the use of the Premises by any parties other than Tenant and its employees. Any such action on the part of Tenant shall be void and of no effect. There shall be no partial assignment of Tenant's interest in this Lease. The term "sublease" and all words derived therefrom, as used in this <u>Section</u>, shall include any subsequent sublease or assignment of such sublease and any other interest arising under such sublease. Landlord's consent to any assignment, subletting or transfer or Landlord's election to accept any assignee, subtenant or transferee as the tenant hereunder and to collect rent from such assignee, subtenant or transferee shall not release Tenant or any subsequent tenant from any covenant or obligation under this Lease. Landlord's consent to any assignment, subletting or transfer shall not constitute a waiver of Landlord's right to withhold its consent to any future assignment, subletting, or transfer. Landlord may condition its consent upon execution by the subtenant or assignee of an instrument confirming such restrictions on further subleasing or assignment and joining in the waivers and indemnities made by Tenant hereunder insofar as such waivers and indemnities relate to the affected space. Without limitation of the foregoing, Tenant agrees to indemnify, defend and hold Landlord and its employees, agents, their officers and partners harmless from and against any claims made by any broker or finder for a commission or fee in connection with any subleasing or assignment by Tenant or any subtenant or assignee of Tenant.

B. If Tenant desires the consent of Landlord to an assignment or subletting, Tenant shall submit to Landlord at least thirty (30) days prior to the proposed effective date of the assignment or sublease a written notice which includes:

(1) all documentation then available related to the proposed sublease or assignment (copies of final executed documentation to be supplied on or before the effective date); and

(2) sufficient information to permit Landlord to determine the identity and character of the proposed subtenant or assignee and the financial condition of the proposed assignee.

C. In addition to withholding its consent Landlord shall have the right to terminate this Lease as to that portion of the Premises which Tenant seeks to assign or sublet, whether by requesting

Landlord's consent thereto or otherwise. Landlord may exercise such right to terminate by giving written notice to Tenant at any time prior to Landlord's written consent to such assignment or sublease. In the event that Landlord exercises such right to terminate, Landlord shall be entitled to recover possession of and Tenant shall surrender such portion of the Premises on the later of (i) the proposed date for possession by such assignee or subtenant, or (ii) ninety (90) days after the date of Landlord's notice of termination to Tenant.

D. In the event that Landlord consents to any assignment or sublease of any portion of the Premises, as a condition of Landlord's consent, if Landlord consents, Tenant shall pay to Landlord any reasonable attorneys' fees and expenses incurred by Landlord in connection with such assignment or sublease plus one hundred percent (100%) of all Sublease Profits (as defined below) derived by Tenant from such assignment or sublease. "Sublease Profits" shall mean the entire excess, after deduction of all reasonable costs of subletting, of revenues generated by the subleasing or assignment of the Premises or portions thereof over the Rent applicable thereto. All such revenues shall be applied first to reimbursement of such costs of subletting until they are paid in full. Tenant shall furnish Landlord with a sworn statement, certified by an officer of Tenant, setting forth in detail the computation of Sublease Profits, and Landlord, or its representatives, shall have access to the books, records and papers of Tenant in relation thereto, and to make copies thereof. If a part of the consideration for such assignment shall be payable other than in cash, the payment to Landlord shall be payable in accordance with the foregoing percentage of the cash and other non-cash considerations in such form as is reasonably satisfactory to Landlord. Such percentage of Sublease Profits shall be paid to Landlord promptly by Tenant upon Tenant's receipt from time to time of periodic payments from such assignee or subtenant or at such other time as Tenant shall realize Sublease Profits from such assignment or sublease. If such sublease or assignment is part of a larger transaction in which other assets of Tenant are being transferred, the consideration for the assignment or sublease shall be a reasonable allocation of the total value received minus a reasonable allocation of the total expenses incurred in connection with such transaction.

E. If Tenant is a partnership, a withdrawal or change, whether voluntary, involuntary or by operation of law or in one or more transactions, of partners owning directly or indirectly a controlling interest in Tenant shall be deemed an assignment of this Lease and subject to the provisions of this Section __. If Tenant is a corporation, any dissolution, merger, consolidation or other reorganization of Tenant, or the sale, transfer or redemption of a direct or indirect controlling interest in the capital stock of Tenant, in one or more transactions, shall be deemed a voluntary assignment of this Lease and subject to the provisions of this Section __. Neither this Lease nor any interest therein nor any estate created thereby shall pass by operation of law or otherwise to any trustee, custodian or receiver in bankruptcy of Tenant or any assignee for the assignment of the benefit of creditors of Tenant.

ASSIGNMENT AND SUBLETTING

A. Subject to any provisions of this <u>Section</u> to the contrary, Tenant shall not, without the prior written consent of Landlord <u>(which consent shall not be unreasonably withheld or delayed beyond ten (10) days)</u>, (i) assign, convey or mortgage this Lease or any interest hereunder; (ii) permit to occur or permit to exist any assignment of this Lease, or any lien upon Tenant's interest, voluntarily or by operation of law; (iii) sublet the Premises or any part thereof; (iv) advertise as available for sublet or assignment all or any portion of the Premises; or (v) permit the use of the Premises by any parties other than Tenant and its employees. Any such action on the part of Tenant shall be void and of no effect. There shall be no partial assignment of Tenant's interest in this Lease. The term "sublease" and all words derived therefrom, as used in this <u>Section</u> , shall include any subsequent sublease or assignment of such sublease and any other interest arising under such sublease. Landlord's consent to any assignment, subletting or transfer or Landlord's election to accept any assignee, subtenant or transferee as the tenant hereunder and to collect rent from such assignee, subtenant or transferee shall not release Tenant or any subsequent tenant from any covenant or obligation under this Lease. Landlord's consent to any assignment, subletting or transfer shall not constitute a waiver of Landlord's right to withhold its consent to any future assignment, subletting, or transfer. Landlord may condition its consent upon execution by the subtenant or assignee of an instrument confirming such restrictions on further subleasing or assignment and joining in the waivers and indemnities made by Tenant hereunder insofar as such waivers and indemnities relate to the affected space. Without limitation of the foregoing, Tenant agrees to indemnify, defend and hold Landlord and its employees, agents, their officers and partners harmless from and against any claims made by any broker or finder for a commission or fee in connection with any subleasing or assignment by Tenant or any subtenant or assignee of Tenant.

Landlord's consent to any sublease and/or assignment shall not be unreasonably withheld or delayed beyond ten (10) days; however, Tenant agrees that Landlord shall be acting reasonably when such consent is not granted if: (I) in the reasonable judgment of Landlord, the subtenant or assignee is of a character or engaged in a business which is not in keeping with the standards of Landlord for the Building; (2) in the reasonable judgment of Landlord, the purposes for which the subtenant intends to use the Premises are not in keeping with the standards of Landlord for the Building, or are in violation of the terms of any other leases in the Building, it being understood that the purpose for which subtenant intends to use the Premises may not be in violation of this Lease; (3) the portion of the Premises to be sublet does not have appropriate means of ingress and egress and suitable for normal renting purposes; (4) the subtenant is a government (or a subdivision or agency thereof), except as specifically provided below; (5) the sublessee is not, in the judgment of Landlord, solvent; or (6) Tenant is in Default under this Lease. Landlord's consent to any subletting or Landlord's election to accept any subtenant as the tenant hereunder and to collect rent from such subtenant shall not release Tenant or any subsequent tenant from any covenant or obligation under this Lease. Notwithstanding anything in this Lease to the contrary, Tenant shall have the right to sublease or assign all or a portion of this Lease to any government agency, provided that (x) such sublease or assignment does not impose any obligations, restrictions or duties on Landlord not contained in this Lease and expressly prohibits such agency from any subsequent sublease or assignment of such space, and (y) the aggregate amount of square footage for all such subleases and/or assignments to government agencies does not exceed _____ square feet of Rentable Area.

B. If Tenant desires the consent of Landlord to an assignment or subletting, Tenant shall submit to Landlord at least thirty (30) days prior to the proposed effective date of the assignment or sublease a written notice which includes:

(1) all documentation then available related to the proposed sublease or assignment (copies of final executed documentation to be supplied on or before the effective date); and

(2) sufficient information to permit Landlord to determine the identity and character of the proposed subtenant or assignee and the financial condition of the proposed assignee.

C. In addition to withholding its consent Landlord shall have the right to terminate this Lease as to that portion of the Premises which Tenant seeks to assign or sublet, to any entity other than an entity described in Section ____ hereof (whether by requesting Landlord's consent thereto or otherwise) in the last two (2) years of the initial twenty (20) year Lease Term. Landlord may exercise such right to terminate by giving written notice to Tenant at any time prior to Landlord's written consent to such assignment or sublease. In the event that Landlord exercises such right to terminate, Landlord shall be entitled to recover possession of and Tenant shall surrender such portion of the Premises on the later of (i) the proposed date for possession by such assignee or subtenant, or (ii) ninety (90) days after the date of Landlord's notice of termination to Tenant.

D. In the event ~~that Landlord consents to any assignment or sublease of any portion of the Premises, as a condition of Landlord's consent, if Landlord consents, Tenant shall pay to Landlord any reasonable attorneys' fees and expenses incurred by Landlord in connection with~~ of any assignment of Tenant's interest in the Lease or subletting of all or any part of the Premises pursuant to this Section ____, Tenant shall retain all profits from such assignment or ~~sublease plus one hundred percent (100%) of all Sublease Profits (as defined below) derived by Tenant from such assignment or sublease. "Sublease Profits" shall mean the entire excess, after deduction of all reasonable costs of subletting, of revenues generated by the subleasing or assignment of the Premises or portions thereof over the Rent applicable~~

263

~~thereto. All such revenues shall be applied first to reimbursement of such costs of subletting until they are paid in full. Tenant shall furnish Landlord with a sworn statement, certified by an officer of Tenant, setting forth in detail the computation of Sublease Profits, and Landlord, or its representatives, shall have access to the books, records and papers of Tenant in relation thereto, and to make copies thereof. If a part of the consideration for such assignment shall be payable other than in cash, the payment to Landlord shall be payable in accordance with the foregoing percentage of the cash and other non-cash considerations in such form as is~~ subletting and shall not be obligated to reimburse Landlord for Landlord's costs of document review in connection therewith. Notwithstanding anything in this Lease to the contrary,   shall have the right to exercise the renewal option contained in Section   for the benefit of any assignee or sublessee provided that (x)   remains liable on the Lease to the extent herein provided and (y) the space occupied by the assignee(s)/sublessee(s) is located within the space for which Tenant is otherwise renewing the Lease in accordance with Section   hereof or the assignee(s)/sublessee(s) seeking to benefit from the extension of the Term occupies space located on either the top or bottom floor of the space then comprising the Premises.

    E. Notwithstanding anything herein to the contrary, Tenant shall have the right to assign this Lease or to sublet the Premises or any part thereof to any of the following organizations without obtaining Landlord's prior consent:

(i) any organization resulting from a merger or consolidation with Tenant; or

(ii) any organization succeeding to the business and assets of Tenant or the Chicago office of Tenant; or

(iii) any firm, corporation, partnership, association, subsidiary or other entity which is directly owned and/or controlled by Tenant or in which Tenant has a substantial economic interest;

provided that any transfer pursuant to clauses (i), (ii) or (iii) above shall be subject to the condition that any such assignment, sublease or transfer shall be subject to all of the terms, covenants and conditions of this Lease and such assignee, sublessee or transferee shall expressly assume the obligations of Tenant under this Lease by a document reasonably satisfactory to Landlord. ~~Such percentage of Sublease Profits shall be paid to Landlord promptly by Tenant upon Tenant's receipt from time to time of periodic payments from such assignee or subtenant or at such other time as Tenant shall realize Sublease Profits from such assignment or sublease. If such sublease or assignment is part of a larger transaction in which other assets of Tenant are being transferred, the consideration for the assignment or sublease shall be a reasonable allocation of the total value received minus a reasonable allocation of the total expenses incurred in connection with such transaction.~~

E. If Tenant is a partnership, a withdrawal or change, whether voluntary, involuntary or by operation of law or in one or more transactions, of partners owning directly or indirectly a controlling interest in Tenant shall be deemed an assignment of this Lease and subject to the provisions of this Section __. If Tenant is a corporation, any dissolution, merger, consolidation or other reorganization of Tenant, or the sale, transfer or redemption of a direct or indirect controlling interest in the capital stock of Tenant, in one or more transactions, shall be deemed a voluntary assignment of this Lease and subject to the provisions of this Section __ and Tenant. Nothing herein shall be deemed to relieve from liability hereunder. Neither this Lease nor any interest therein nor any estate created thereby shall pass by operation of law or otherwise to any trustee, custodian or receiver in bankruptcy of Tenant or any assignee for the assignment of the benefit of creditors of Tenant.

NEGOTIATED PROVISION 2
(Marked to show changes from Standard Form)

ASSIGNMENT AND SUBLETTING

A. Subject to any provisions of this <u>Section</u> to the contrary, Tenant shall not, without the prior written consent of Landlord, (i) assign, convey or mortgage this Lease or any interest hereunder; (ii) permit to occur or permit to exist any assignment of this Lease, or any lien upon Tenant's interest, voluntarily or by operation of law; (iii) sublet the Premises or any part thereof; (iv) advertise as available for sublet or assignment all or any portion of the Premises <u>(provided, however, that Landlord agrees not to unreasonably withhold or delay its consent to any request by Tenant to so advertise)</u>; or (v) permit the use of the Premises by any parties other than Tenant and its employees. Any such action on the part of Tenant shall be void and of no effect. There shall be no partial assignment of Tenant's interest in this Lease. The term "<u>sublease</u>" and all words derived therefrom, as used in this <u>Section</u>, shall include any subsequent sublease or assignment of such sublease and any other interest arising under such sublease. Landlord's consent to any assignment, subletting or transfer or Landlord's election to accept any assignee, subtenant or transferee as the tenant hereunder and to collect rent from such assignee, subtenant or transferee shall not release Tenant or any subsequent tenant from any covenant or obligation under this Lease. Landlord's consent to any assignment, subletting or transfer shall not constitute a waiver of Landlord's right to withhold its consent to any future assignment, subletting, or transfer. Landlord may condition its consent upon execution by the subtenant or assignee of an instrument confirming such restrictions on further subleasing or assignment and joining in the waivers and indemnities made by Tenant hereunder insofar as such waivers and indemnities relate to the affected space. Without limitation of the foregoing, Tenant agrees to indemnify, defend and hold Landlord and its employees, agents, their officers and partners harmless from and against any claims made by any broker or finder for a commission or fee in connection with any subleasing or assignment by Tenant or any subtenant or assignee of Tenant.

Landlord's consent to any sublease and/or assignment shall not be unreasonably withheld, conditioned or delayed beyond ten (10) business days; however, Tenant agrees that Landlord shall be acting reasonably when such consent is not granted if: (I) in the reasonable judgment of Landlord, the subtenant or assignee is of a character or engaged in a business which is not in keeping with the standards of Landlord for the Building; (2) in the reasonable judgment of Landlord, the purposes for which the subtenant intends to use the Premises are not in keeping with the standards of Landlord for the Building, or are in violation of the terms of any other leases in the Building, it being understood that the purpose for which subtenant intends to use the Premises may not be in violation of this Lease; (3) the portion of the Premises to be sublet does not have appropriate means of ingress and egress and suitable for normal renting purposes; (4) the subtenant is a government (or a subdivision or agency thereof), except as specifically provided below; (5) the sublessee is not, in the judgment of Landlord, solvent; or (6) Tenant is in Default under this Lease. Landlord's consent to any subletting or Landlord's election to accept any subtenant as the tenant hereunder and to collect rent from such subtenant shall not release Tenant or any subsequent tenant from any covenant or obligation under this Lease.

B. If Tenant desires the consent of Landlord to an assignment or subletting, Tenant shall submit to Landlord at least ~~thirty (30)~~ twenty-five (25) days prior to the proposed effective date of the assignment or sublease a written notice which includes:

~~(1)~~(i) all documentation then available related to the proposed sublease or assignment (copies of final executed documentation to be supplied on or before the effective date); and

~~(2)~~(ii) sufficient information to permit Landlord to determine the identity and character of the proposed subtenant or assignee and the financial condition of the proposed assignee.

C. ~~In addition to withholding its consent Landlord shall have the right to terminate this Lease as to~~ If, at any time, Tenant intends to assign or sublet any portion of the Premises, Tenant shall, before marketing the same, so notify Landlord in writing, which notice shall specifically indicate that portion of the Premises Tenant intends to assign or sublet. Thereafter, Landlord shall have the right to terminate this Lease as to that portion of the Premises which Tenant seeks to assign or sublet, ~~whether by requesting Landlord's consent thereto or otherwise.~~ Landlord may exercise such right to terminate by giving written notice to Tenant ~~at any time prior to Landlord's written consent to such assignment or sublease~~ within ten (10) business days from Tenant's written notice. If Landlord elects to exercise its recapture right, Tenant may rescind its request to assign or sublease the Premises by notice to Landlord within ten (10) days after receipt of Landlord's notice. In such event all notices shall be deemed withdrawn. In the event that Landlord exercises such right to terminate, Landlord shall be entitled to recover possession of and Tenant shall surrender such portion of the Premises ~~on the later of (i) the proposed date for possession by such assignee or subtenant, or (ii)~~ ninety (90) days after the date of Landlord's notice of termination to Tenant. If Landlord does not exercise its right to recapture, Landlord shall be deemed to have waived its right to recapture that portion of the Premises designated in Tenant's notice for the period of one hundred eighty (180) days after the date of such notice. Notwithstanding the provisions of the foregoing sentence to the contrary, (A) if, after expiration of such one hundred eighty day (180) period, Tenant still desires to assign or sublet any portion of the Premises designated in Tenant's notice, Tenant shall be required to resubmit to Landlord a notice of such intent and Landlord shall then have the right to recapture the same, (B) if, within such one hundred eighty (180) day period,

Tenant enters into an agreement to sublease or assign any space in addition to or less than the space identified in Tenant's notice, Tenant shall be required to submit to Landlord a notice of such proposed transaction and Landlord shall then have the right to recapture the same, and (C) the provisions of this Section shall not be deemed to affect Landlord's rights to withhold consent to any sublease or assignment in accordance with the terms of this Section or Tenant's obligations under this Section .

D.   In the event that Landlord consents to any assignment or sublease of all or any portion of the Premises, as a condition of Landlord's consent, if Landlord consents, Tenant shall pay to Landlord ~~any reasonable attorneys' fees and expenses~~ all out-of-pocket costs incurred by Landlord in connection with such assignment or sublease plus ~~one hundred~~ fifty percent ~~(100%)~~(50%) of all Sublease Profits (as defined below) derived by Tenant from such assignment or sublease within ten (10) days after the same are received by Tenant. "Sublease Profits" shall mean the entire excess, after deduction of all reasonable costs (including, without limitation, customary brokerage commissions, rental concessions, marketing costs, lease assumption payments, tenant improvement allowances and legal costs) of assignment or subletting actually incurred by Tenant, of revenues actually received and generated by the subleasing or assignment of the Premises or portions thereof over the Rent applicable thereto. All such revenues shall be applied first to reimbursement of such costs of subletting until they are paid in full. Tenant shall furnish Landlord with a sworn statement, certified by an officer of Tenant, setting forth in detail the computation of Sublease Profits, and Landlord, or its representatives, shall have access to the books, records and papers of Tenant in relation thereto, and to make copies thereof. If a part of the consideration for such assignment shall be payable other than in cash, the payment to Landlord shall be payable in accordance with the foregoing percentage of the cash and other non-cash considerations in such form as is reasonably satisfactory to Landlord. Such percentage of Sublease Profits shall be paid to Landlord promptly by Tenant upon Tenant's receipt from time to time of periodic payments from such assignee or subtenant or at such other time as Tenant shall realize Sublease Profits from such assignment or sublease. If such sublease or assignment is part of a larger transaction in which other assets of Tenant are being transferred, the consideration for the assignment or sublease shall be a reasonable allocation of the total value received minus a reasonable allocation of the total expenses incurred in connection with such transaction.

E. ~~If Tenant is a partnership, a withdrawal or change, whether voluntary, involuntary or by operation of law or in one or more transactions, of partners owning directly or indirectly a controlling interest in Tenant shall be deemed an assignment of this Lease and subject to the provisions of this Section __. If Tenant is a corporation, any dissolution, merger, consolidation or other reorganization of Tenant, or the sale, transfer or redemption of a direct or indirect controlling interest in the capital stock of Tenant, in one or more~~

~~transactions, shall be deemed a voluntary assignment of this Lease and subject to the provisions of this Section~~ Notwithstanding anything herein to the contrary, Tenant shall have the right to assign this Lease or to sublet the Premises or any part thereof to any of the following organizations without obtaining Landlord's prior consent:

(i)   any organization resulting from a merger or consolidation with Tenant; or

(ii)   any organization succeeding to the business and assets of Tenant; or

(iii) any firm, corporation, partnership, association, subsidiary or other entity which is directly owned and/or controlled by Tenant or in which Tenant has a substantial economic interest;

provided that any transfer pursuant to clauses (i), (ii) or (iii) above shall be subject to the condition that any such assignment, sublease or transfer shall be subject to all of the terms, covenants and conditions of this Lease and such assignee, sublessee (to the extent appropriate, which in the case of a sublessee shall be limited to its sublease obligations) or transferee shall expressly assume the obligations of Tenant under this Lease by a document reasonably satisfactory to Landlord and Tenant. Nothing herein shall be deemed to relieve   from liability hereunder; provided, that   shall have no further liability under this Lease if the proposed sublessee or assignee shall have a net

273

worth of $100,000,000 as determined at the time of such sublease or assignment. Neither this Lease nor any interest therein nor any estate created thereby shall pass by operation of law or otherwise to any trustee, custodian or receiver in bankruptcy of Tenant or any assignee for the assignment of the benefit of creditors of Tenant._____ shall provide Landlord with written notice of any such assignment or subletting made pursuant to this Section ____ within ten (10) business days after the occurrence of the same.

F. Notwithstanding anything herein to the contrary, in the event Tenant has sublet more than twenty-five percent (25%) of the Premises, Tenant may not extend the Term of the Lease as provided in Section ____ hereof or exercise the expansion options provided in Section ____ hereof.

EXHIBIT 4

RIGHTS PERSONAL TO TENANT

For purposes of this lease, an "Affiliate" shall mean any corporation, partnership, joint venture or other entity (i) which controls _____, either directly or indirectly through other wholly-owned subsidiaries; (ii) which is under the control of _____, either directly or indirectly; (iii) which is under common control with _____, either directly or indirectly; or (iv) which results from a merger or consolidation with or reorganization of _____.

Wherever there is a reference in this lease to rights being personal to _____ or personal to _____ and its Affiliates, such reference shall mean that those rights may not be assigned, granted or transferred by Tenant to any person, corporation, partnership or entity (especially an assignee of this lease, any subtenant or any entity to whom Landlord will be directly leasing space upon release of Tenant under Section __) other than an Affiliate where specifically stated herein.

EXHIBIT 5

EXPANSION RIGHTS

Example 1:

EXPANSION OF THE PREMISES

a.   **Expansion Spaces**. Tenant shall have the right hereinafter described in this Section 30 to expand the Premises by leasing (i) approximately _____ square feet of Rentable Area on the _____ (___) floor of the Building (the "First Expansion Space") on or about the _____ (___) Lease Year (the "First Expansion Option") and (ii) approximately _____ square feet of Rentable Area on the _____ (___) floor of the Building (the "Second Expansion Space") on or about the _____ (___) Lease Year (the "Second Expansion Option").   The First Expansion Space and the Second Expansion Space are sometimes referred to herein collectively as the "Expansion Spaces" and individually as an "Expansion Space".   Tenant shall exercise its right to add such Expansion Space by written notice to Landlord given no later than (a)_____ (___) months prior to the _____ (___) anniversary of the Commencement Date as to the First Expansion Space and (b)_____ (___) months prior to the _____ (___) anniversary of the Commencement Date as to the Second Expansion Space.   The exact location of each Expansion Space is to be contiguous to the Premises at a location determined by Landlord in its sole discretion. If Tenant fails to give the advance notice required herein to Landlord by the specified date with respect to an Expansion Space, Tenant will be deemed to have declined to exercise its right to lease such Expansion Space. If Tenant fails to exercise its option under this Section 30(a) as to the First Expansion Space, Tenant shall lose its rights hereunder as to the Second Expansion Space.

b.   **Expansion Window.** To permit Landlord flexibility in leasing the Expansion Spaces prior to Tenant's need for such space, Landlord may deliver the First Expansion Space to Tenant between the _____ (___) anniversary of the Commencement Date and a date _____ (___) months after the _____ (___) anniversary of the Commencement Date (the "First Expansion Window") and the Second Expansion Space to Tenant between the _____ (___) anniversary of the Commencement Date and a date _____ (___) months after the _____ (___) anniversary of the Commencement Date (the "Second Expansion Window"). Landlord will specify the dates on which it intends to deliver the Expansion Spaces to Tenant (the "First Expansion Date" and "Second Expansion Date" respectively) by written notice given to Tenant not less than _____ (___) months prior to the date that Landlord intends to deliver the Expansion Space to Tenant.

c. **Mechanics of Expansion**. Upon the exercise by Tenant of its right to expand as provided in this Section 30, Landlord and Tenant shall promptly proceed to enter into a written agreement modifying this Lease to include such Expansion Space in the Premises. The Expansion Space so included will be considered to be a part of the Premises as of the First Expansion Date or Second Expansion Date, respectively, subject to the provisions of Section 30(e) hereof. The Expansion Spaces shall be governed by all the terms of this Lease, except that (i) Tenant's Proportionate Share shall be increased accordingly, (ii) the Base Rent for each Expansion Space will be at the annual per square foot rate of $_____, and (iii) possession of an Expansion Space shall be delivered to Tenant in an "as is" condition, provided, however, Landlord shall pay Tenant a construction Allowance in the amount of _____ per square foot of Rentable Area in the Expansion Space in accordance with Landlord's then standard Work Letter.

d. **Delays**. Landlord will use reasonable diligence to make each Expansion Space available to Tenant on the applicable Expansion Date. If Landlord is unable to do so for reasons beyond Landlord's reasonable control (however, Landlord's leasing of Expansion Space to other tenants shall be deemed to be within Landlord's control), Landlord will not be liable for such failure or inability, nor shall this failure or inability impair the validity of this Lease, nor extend the Term, but the Expansion Space will not become a part of the Premises, and therefore the commencement of Tenant's obligation to pay Rent on such space shall be deferred, until possession is delivered to Tenant.

e.   **Conditions to Exercise.** If on the date when Tenant notifies Landlord of its election to exercise an Expansion Option, Tenant shall be in Default hereunder or otherwise in default in the performance of any of the terms, covenants or conditions contained in this Lease, or if at any time following the exercise of an Expansion Option and prior to the applicable date that Tenant is to take possession of an Expansion Space Tenant shall be in Default hereunder or otherwise in default in the performance of any of the terms, covenants or conditions contained in this Lease, Landlord shall have the option, on written notice to Tenant, to declare Tenant's election to expand to be void and of no effect.

f.   **Early Addition of Expansion Space.**

If at any time within _____ (__) months after the Commencement Date, Tenant desires to add either the First Expansion Space or both Expansion Spaces to the Premises, and Tenant gives Landlord written notice of its intent within such

_____ (__) month period, then Landlord shall build out the Expansion Space(s) as provided in the Tenant Work Letter attached hereto as Exhibit B and the Expansion Space(s) shall be deemed part of the Premises as of the date of substantial completion of the Work as to such Expansion Space(s). Tenant's Proportionate Share shall increase accordingly and the Base Rent for such Expansion Space shall be the Base Rent per square foot of Rentable Area then applicable to the Premises. If Tenant adds the First Expansion Space only to the Premises pursuant to this Section 30(f), then the Second Expansion Option shall become the First Expansion Option and the Second Expansion Option shall be terminated.

Example 2:

OPTIONS TO EXPAND.

D. Expansion Options. In addition to the expansion options contained in Sections 28 and 31 hereof, Tenant shall have the following two (2) options (individually, an "Expansion Option", and collectively, the "Expansion Options") each to add at Tenant's option between 10,000 and 15,000 square feet of Rentable Area to the Premises (subject to Landlord's right to increase or decrease such number by 2,000 square feet of Rentable Area) for the then remaining Term of this Lease upon the same terms, covenants and conditions contained in this Lease except as otherwise specifically provided in this Section 29. Each such area is sometimes referred to herein as an "Expansion Space", with the numerical reference preceding such term (e.g., "First Expansion Space") referring to Expansion Space described in the Expansion Plan (as defined in Section 29.B. below). Landlord shall, within ten (10) Business Days following Tenant's election to obtain Expansion Space (which election(s) shall be made by Tenant not later than the dates set forth in the following chart), give Tenant written notice (the "Specification Notice") of the specific size and location of the contiguous space that will comprise each particular Expansion Space and, subject to Section 29C hereof, the dates on which such spaces shall be delivered to Tenant. The timing of Tenant's exercise of its Expansion Options hereunder shall be as follows:

Expansion Option/ Space Called	Date on Which Tenant Must Provide Exercise Expansion Option ("Expansion Option Exercise Date")*	Rent Abatement for Expansion Space**	Delivery Window*	Allowance (Per Square Foot) of Rentable Area)**
First/First Expansion Space	Not later than February 1, 2000	5 months	Between February 1, 2001 and July 1, 2001	$50.00
Second/Second Expansion Space	Not later than February 1, 2003	1 month	Between February 1, 2004 and July 1, 2004	$25.00

*   Each Expansion Option may be accelerated and will be available to Tenant upon thirty (30) day written notice by Tenant and with no additional delivery window if the applicable Expansion Space is not under lease on the date such written notice from Tenant is given.

** Rent abatement and Allowance will apply to the Base Rent set forth on Exhibit D to this Lease and the Additional Rent which is applicable at the time of delivery of a particular Expansion Space in the event that the Base Rent payable with respect to such Expansion Space is equal to the then current Base Rent.

Notwithstanding anything in this Lease to the contrary, Tenant's election not to exercise the First Expansion Option provided for herein shall not affect Tenant's right to exercise the Second Expansion Option granted hereunder.

E. <u>Expansion Space.</u> Landlord shall, subject to the provisions of this <u>Section 29B</u>, make Expansion Space available to Tenant on the 25th floor of the Building; provided, however, that if Tenant has returned any Contraction Space to Landlord pursuant to <u>Section 28C</u> hereof, such Contraction Space shall constitute the First Expansion Space and, to the extent that any of the Contraction Space remains following Tenant's exercise of the First Expansion Option, such remaining Contraction Space shall constitute the Second Expansion Space (or a portion thereof). Each Expansion Space shall contain between 10,000 and 15,000 square feet of Rentable Area as designated by Tenant, subject to Landlord's right to increase or decrease the amount specified by Tenant by 2,000 square feet of Rentable Area, and the location of the first portion of the applicable Expansion Space made available to Tenant shall be positioned to allow Tenant to extend its internal staircase and to have direct access to the applicable elevator lobby. Tenant shall notify Landlord in writing of Tenant's election to exercise or not exercise each Expansion Option not later than the Expansion Option Exercise Date applicable to such Expansion Option. Notwithstanding anything herein to the contrary, upon completion of Tenant's current space analysis (but not later than the Commencement Date), Tenant and Landlord together shall, in a detailed written instrument (the "Expansion Plan"), specify in detail the amount, location and timing of each Expansion Space; however, those modifications must take into account sizes and timing which allow the Landlord to manage and lease those Expansion Spaces prior to the exercise of an Expansion Option pursuant to this Section.

Should Tenant elect not to exercise the First Expansion Option hereunder to acquire the First Expansion Space associated with such option ("Unobtained Expansion Space"), the parties agree that the location of the Second Expansion Space subject to the Expansion Option which remains to be exercised by Tenant shall be the Unobtained Expansion Space, and Landlord shall be free to lease the Second Expansion Space hereunder to third party tenants without restriction.

In the event that Tenant exercises its right of first offer contained in Section 30 hereof with respect to any Expansion Space for a term coterminous with the Term of this Lease, such exercise shall be deemed an early exercise of the Expansion Option relating to such space and Tenant shall not be entitled to exercise any rights for space in the Building on the date set forth in the chart in Section 29A for exercise of such Expansion Option.

Notwithstanding anything contained herein to the contrary, Tenant shall have the right to exercise the Expansion Options granted pursuant to this Section 29 at any time prior to the applicable Expansion Option Exercise Date if at the time of Tenant's early exercise of an Expansion Option the

Expansion Space applicable to such Expansion Option shall be unleased.

F.   Delivery Window. To permit Landlord flexibility in leasing the Expansion Spaces prior to Tenant's need for such Expansion Spaces, Landlord may deliver each Expansion Space within the applicable Delivery Window therefor as set forth in Section 29A hereof.

G.   Expansion Conditions. Tenant's notice of exercise of an option for Expansion Space shall be effective only if at the time of service of such notice of exercise the following conditions shall be satisfied:

(i) No Default shall exist at the time of such notice; and

(ii)   This Lease shall not have been terminated and shall be in full force and effect.

H.   Mechanics of Expansion. Upon the exercise by Tenant of its right to expand as provided in this Section, Landlord and Tenant shall promptly proceed to enter into a written agreement modifying this Lease to include such Expansion Space in the Premises and providing that the Term of the Lease shall be coterminous with respect to the initial Premises and such Expansion Space. Each Expansion Space (or part thereof) shall become part of the Premises upon its delivery to Tenant vacant and ready for commencement of construction of Tenant's improvements. Tenant's obligation to pay

Rent on such Expansion Space (and the Rent abatement for such space as set forth in Section 29A hereof) shall not commence for a period of three (3) months following Landlord's delivery to Tenant of possession of such space vacant and ready for commencement of Tenant Work; provided, however, that if no Monetary Default by Tenant exists hereunder on the date that any such installment is due, Rent for such Expansion Space shall be abated in full for such Expansion Space for the number of calendar months set forth in the table in Section 29A hereof. The Rent payable by Tenant with respect to any Expansion Space shall be the lesser of (x) the then current Rent in effect under this Lease (in the event that this clause (x) is applicable) in which event Tenant shall receive, among other things, the rent abatements and tenant allowances described in this Section and in Section 29.G below), and (y) ninety percent (90%) of the then current Market Rent (as in Section 31 defined below), which Market Rent shall include any rent abatements and tenant allowances which are then taken into account in determining such Market Rent. Landlord's determination of the applicable Rent for an Expansion Space shall be set forth in the Specification Notice for such space. If the parties are unable to agree on a Market Rent for the Expansion Space after sixty (60) days following Tenant's receipt of Landlord's estimate of Market Rent then Tenant may elect in writing to (i) promptly enter into binding arbitration in accordance with the provisions of Section 32 hereof or (ii) revoke its election to lease such Expansion Space, in which case Tenant shall have no further rights under this Section and Landlord may lease the Premises to a third party tenant free of the provisions of Section 29 hereof. The Expansion Spaces shall be governed by all the terms of this Lease, except that Tenant's Proportionate Share shall be increased accordingly.

I. Tenant Allowance for Expansion Space. In the event that the Base Rent payable by Tenant with respect to an Expansion Space shall be equal to the then current Base Rent payable by Tenant hereunder, then Landlord shall make available to Tenant an allowance to defray part or all of the costs of improving the Expansion Space, acquiring or installing furniture, fixtures and equipment therein and paying the space planning (including design cost and cost of the construction plans), relocation and other so-called "soft-costs" related thereto equal to (i) $50.00 per square foot of Rentable Area for any portion of the First Expansion Space, and (ii) $25.00 per square foot of Rentable Area of the Second Expansion Space. The procedure for the payment of the allowance for the Expansion Space will be in accordance with Section 5 of the Tenant Work Letter.

J. Tenant Work for Additional Space. Tenant shall have the right to select a general contractor and subcontractors to perform work on any Expansion Space, space obtained pursuant to Section 30 hereof ("Right of First Offer Space") or Renewal Expansion Space (as defined in Section 31 below), provided that such general contractor and subcontractors are on the Landlord's approved list at the time the selection is made. Notwithstanding anything in the preceding sentence to the contrary, Tenant shall be required to use Landlord's then current Building engineering firms to do the mechanical/electrical/plumbing engineering work, respectively. Tenant shall take possession of any Expansion Space for purposes of construction in its then "as-is" condition, subject to the obligations of Landlord, if any, contained in the following sentence. Landlord shall, at its sole cost, provide the "Base Building Work" described in Section 1 of the Tenant Work Letter for all Expansion Spaces, Right of First Offer Spaces and Renewal Expansion Space (all or a portion of which Base Building Work may have already been performed by Landlord with respect to such Expansion Spaces, as more particularly set forth on Attachment A attached to the Work Letter), and Tenant acknowledges and agrees that, to the extent Landlord has not completed all of the Base Building Work for such Expansion Spaces, Landlord shall have the right to perform such work concurrently with the completion of Tenant's work on such Expansion Spaces, Right of First Offer Spaces or Renewal Expansion Space. Tenant shall pay, within thirty (30) days after being billed therefor, all actual out-of-pocket expenses incurred by Landlord in connection with Landlord's review of any such Tenant's work and the plans and specifications therefor; provided that Landlord shall not charge any supervision fees in connection with any Tenant work on any Expansion Space, Right of First Offer Space or Renewal Expansion Space. Landlord and Tenant shall cooperate in performing any work to be completed concurrently by the parties so that any preconditions to the other's installations are satisfied when required under normal construction scheduling and sequencing. The parties agree that, except for the "Base Building Work" described above, Landlord has not agreed to perform any additional work with respect to any Expansion Space, Right of First Offer Space or Renewal Expansion Space leased by Tenant hereunder. In the event that Tenant desires for Landlord to perform any such additional work, Landlord and Tenant shall enter into a written agreement in form and substance mutually satisfactory to such parties.

Example 3:

RIGHT OF FIRST OFFER

If at any time after _____ and prior to the first day of the _____ (___) Lease Year, any space becomes available for leasing on the _____ (___) Floor of the Building, and if Tenant is not then in Default hereunder, then Landlord shall not lease such space to any party without first giving Tenant (i) notice of the availability of such space which shall include a description of the space, the proposed term and rental rate (including escalations, if any), abatements and allowances, if any, and other economic concessions that Landlord believes that it would agree to with respect to such space (the "Offered Terms") and (ii) five (5) days after the date of such notice in which to commit in writing to lease such space on the Offered Terms for the remainder of Term, taking into account any modifications in such Offered Terms required by the fact that the remaining Term may be longer or shorter than that proposed by Landlord, and otherwise on the terms, covenants and conditions contained in this Lease. If Tenant fails, refuses or is otherwise unable to commit to such a lease within the 5-day period, Landlord shall have the right to lease the space to any third party or parties on such terms as are acceptable to Landlord, subject to Tenant's Expansion Option(s) hereunder, if any.

EXHIBIT 6

RENEWAL RIGHTS

Example 1:

TENANT'S OPTION TO RENEW

The Tenant is hereby granted _____ (___) _____ (___) year option(s) to renew the Lease ("Renewal Option"). If the Tenant desires to exercise the Renewal Option, it shall so notify the Landlord, in writing, not later than the first day of the twenty-fourth (24th) month prior to the then current expiration date of the Term. Such notice shall only be effective if delivered at a time when the Tenant is not in Default hereunder or otherwise in default in the performance of any of its obligations under the terms and provisions of this Lease. Within thirty (30) days following its receipt of Tenant's notice of its desire to exercise the Renewal Option, given at the time and in the manner provided above, Landlord shall prepare and transmit to Tenant an appropriate amendment to this Lease extending the Term for _____ (___) years ("Extended Term") and specifying (i) the Base Rent for such extension, which shall be the base rental rate then being offered and accepted by Landlord to other tenants of comparable size and location renewing leases in the Building, as reasonably determined by Landlord and evidenced by recent transactions which shall be disclosed to Tenant ("Market Rent") and (ii) that all other terms and conditions during the Extended Term are the same as those during the Term, except for any expansion rights, reduction rights or limitations on taxes and operating expenses. In the event the Tenant shall fail for any reason to execute and deliver the lease amendment within twenty (20) business days of Tenant's receipt of the same, or if Tenant shall be in Default hereunder or otherwise in default in the performance of any of its obligations under the terms and provisions of this Lease at the commencement date of any Extended Term, then in either such event, at Landlord's option, Tenant's purported exercise of its Renewal Option shall be of no force or effect and the Renewal Option and any subsequent Renewal Options shall become null and void.

Example 2:

OPTION TO EXTEND TERM.

The Tenant is hereby granted two (2) options to extend the Term for a period of five (5) years for each such option (and a total of ten (10) years if both such options are exercised) with respect to all or any portion of the Premises (each, a "Renewal Option"). Notwithstanding anything contained in this Lease to the contrary, Tenant agrees that there shall be a single Termination Date for those portions of the Premises leased by Tenant pursuant to the Renewal Option. If the Tenant desires to exercise a Renewal Option, it shall so notify the Landlord, in writing, not later than the first day of the twelfth (12th) month prior to the then applicable Termination Date of the Lease. Such notice shall designate which portion of the Premises Tenant desires to occupy during the renewal period (which portion shall be not less than _____ square feet of Rentable Area including the ____ floor of the Building, subject to Tenant's right to increase such number (provided that with respect to any space designated by Tenant which does not constitute an entire floor of the Building, such space shall constitute not less than one-quarter (1/4) of a floor)) and shall only be effective if delivered at a time when the Tenant is not in Default of its obligations under the terms and provisions of the Lease. Within thirty (30) days following its receipt of Tenant's notice of its desire to exercise the Renewal Option, given at the time and in the manner provided above, the Landlord shall prepare and transmit to the Tenant an appropriate lease amendment to the Lease extending the Term a period of five (5) years (each, an "Extended Term") and specifying (i) the Base Rent for such Extended Term, which rent shall, (1) for the first Extended Term, be the lesser of (a) 90% of the then current Market Rent, and (b) $22.00 per square foot of Rentable Area, and (2) for the second Extended Term, be 95% of the then current Market Rent, and (ii) that all other terms and conditions during the Extended Term are the same as those during the Term, except for any expansion rights, reduction rights and limitations on Taxes and Operating Expenses. As used herein, the term "Market Rent" shall mean the base rental rate then being offered by Landlord and accepted by other tenants for comparable leases in the Building (including size and location and including all applicable market escalations, rental and other concessions, abatements, limitations on taxes and operating expenses, allowances, commissions and tenant improvements), as reasonably determined by Landlord and evidenced by recent leases (dated within nine (9) months preceding Tenant's notice to Landlord) which have been executed and approved by all necessary parties and which shall be disclosed to Tenant (subject, however, to the terms of any confidentiality provisions contained within any such leases, and in any event Tenant agrees that it shall keep confidential all such information furnished to Tenant). If Tenant disagrees with Landlord's estimation of the Market Rent, it must so notify Landlord in writing within thirty (30) days after Tenant's receipt thereof and specify Tenant's estimation of the Market Rent. In the event that there have been no recent leasing transactions in the Building at the time of the determination of Market Rent, then Landlord shall estimate Market Rent based on transactions in down-town Chicago office buildings comparable to the Building occurring within nine (9) months preceding Tenant's notice to Landlord) involving tenants of comparable size to Tenant, the terms of which (to the extent available to Landlord) shall be disclosed to Tenant. If the parties are unable to agree on a Market Rent for the Extended Term after sixty (60) days following Landlord's receipt of Tenant's estimation of Market Rent Tenant may elect in writing to (i) promptly enter into binding arbitration in accordance with the provisions of Section 32 hereof or (ii) revoke its election to exercise the Renewal Option, in which case Tenant shall have no further rights under this Section and Landlord may lease the Premises to a third party tenant free of the provisions of Section 29 hereof. As used in this Lease the defined term "Term" shall be deemed to include each Extended Term if Tenant exercises its option with respect thereto under this Section 31.

EXHIBIT 7

TERMINATION RIGHTS

OPTION OF TENANT TO TERMINATE LEASE

A.   Subject to the conditions set forth below, Tenant shall have the right to terminate this Lease effective as of the last day of the _____ (__) Lease Year, which right must be exercised by written notice to Landlord no later than the last day of the _____ (__) Lease Year.

B.   Tenant shall pay to Landlord at the time that Tenant delivers the notice exercising its right to terminate, a fee (the "Termination Fee") of $ _____ plus the unamortized cost of any allowances, broker's commissions or rent concessions Landlord incurs because Tenant has exercised its right(s) to expand the Premises pursuant to Section 30 or 31.

C.   If on the date that Tenant exercises its termination option or the effective date of such termination, Tenant is in Default hereunder or otherwise in default in the performance of any of the terms, covenants or conditions contained in this Lease (including, without limitation, payment of the Termination Fee), then Landlord shall have the option, upon written notice to Tenant, to declare Tenant's election to terminate this Lease void and of no effect.

EXHIBIT 8

DETERMINATION BY ARBITRATION.

In the event of the failure of the parties to agree as to the Market Rent or as to any other matter which under the terms of this Lease is to be determined by arbitration, such matter shall be submitted to arbitration as hereinafter provided. Landlord and Tenant shall each appoint a fit and impartial person as arbitrator who shall have had at least ten (10) years' experience in the commercial real estate industry. Such an appointment shall be signified in writing by each party to the other. The arbitrators so appointed shall appoint a third arbitrator within ten (10) days after the appointment of the second arbitrator. In the case of the failure of such arbitrators (or the arbitrators appointed as hereinafter provided) to agree upon a third arbitrator, such third arbitrator shall be appointed by the American Arbitration Association, or its successor, from its qualified panel of arbitrators, and shall be a person having at least ten (10) years' experience in the commercial real estate industry. In case either party shall fail to appoint an arbitrator within a period of ten (10) days after written notice from the other party to make such appointment, then the American Arbitration Association shall appoint a second arbitrator having at least ten (10) years' experience in the commercial real estate industry. The two (2) arbitrators so appointed shall appoint a third arbitrator within ten (10) days after the appointment of the second arbitrator.

The arbitrators shall proceed with all reasonable dispatch to determine the question submitted; provided, however, that in determining the Market Rent in any situation the arbitrators shall select either Landlord's estimate or Tenant's estimate of the Market Rent, and in no event shall the arbitrators have the right (i) to average the Market Rent estimates submitted by Landlord or Tenant or (ii) to choose another number. The decision of the arbitrators shall in any event be rendered within thirty (30) days after their appointment, or within such other period as the arbitrators shall order or the parties shall agree, and such decision shall be in writing and in duplicate, one counterpart thereof to be delivered to each of the parties who appointed them. The arbitration shall be conducted in accordance with the rules of the American Arbitration Association (or its successor) and applicable Illinois law, and the decision of a majority of the arbitrators shall be binding, final and conclusive on the parties. Each party hereto shall pay one-half (1/2) of the fees of the arbitrators and each party shall pay (i) the fees of counsel engaged by such party, and (ii) the fees of expert witnesses and other witnesses called for by such party.

Notice of appointment of the arbitrators shall be given in all instances to any mortgagee who prior thereto shall have given Tenant a written notice specifying its name and address. If a dispute shall be submitted to arbitration as hereinabove provided, such mortgagee shall have the right to be present at such arbitration proceedings; provided, however, that such presence shall be in association with Landlord and shall not be deemed to entitle such mortgagee to appoint an additional arbitrator or present evidence, nor to enlarge Landlord's rights in such arbitration proceeding, it being the intention of the parties that such mortgagee shall have solely the right to be present at the arbitration proceedings.

NOTES

6

FIRE-CASUALTY AND INSURANCE

Alan M. DiSciullo

Reprinted from the PLI course handbook, Current Issues in Negotiating Commercial Leases 1996. No. N4-4600

§ 11.02 Destruction by Fire or Casualty

The parties interests must be protected in the event the property is destroyed or damaged in whole or in part by fire or other casualty. A well-drafted office lease should anticipate and clearly provide for the handling of such events.

[1]—Insurance [1]

[a]—Full Value Insurance. Under many office lease forms, a landlord does not automatically obligate itself to rebuild the premises in the event of fire or casualty. Under certain situations, the landlord may agree to rebuild, but the obligation is generally limited to those instances where the insurance proceeds are sufficient to cover the costs of the rebuilding. Furthermore, these clauses do not limit a tenant's liability in the event it causes a loss to the landlord by fire or casualty although such liability may be mitigated to the extent of insurance proceeds actually received by the landlord. A tenant, therefore, has a vested interest in seeing that a landlord maintains full insurance coverage for the building so that any short fall resulting from deductibles, under value insurance or negligence exclusions do not cause the insurance proceeds to be so limited that the liability of the tenant is increased.

Traditionally, landlords maintain building insurance that is either fully paid by the tenants or with escalations that cause the tenants to pick up the costs over a certain base period. Consequently, there is little reason for a landlord not to fully insure the building to full replacement value. [2] Moreover, issues revolving around who has an insurable interest and who owns what property may present obstacles if the tenant attempts to obtain its own insurance coverage protection. For example, if a tenant installs tenant improvements into a demised premises but specifies that they are the property of the landlord upon installation, it might prove difficult for

---

[1]   This discussion of insurance is by no means intended to be a treatise on the subject, but hopefully, when read in conjunction with later chapters, it will assist the reader in identifying liabilities and risks and serve as a practical objective guide to negotiation of the subject. See Chapter 25 *infra*.

[2]   Quite frankly, any shortfall under the "no fault" scenario discussed later would be the loss to the underinsuring party.

the tenant to insure those installations for loss from fire or casualty on its own.[3]

[b]—"No Fault." One of the more fundamental issues with respect to insurance between landlords and tenants is whether commercial insurance should operate on the theory of "no fault."[4] That is, should principles of negligence and fault be disregarded? Under "no fault" insurance, each party fully insures its insurable property interest to the fullest extent that it wishes protection. In the event of loss, damage or destruction, the party looks to its own insurance for its full recovery. Each party waives the right to take direct action against the other even if the other party's actions or negligence caused the loss. In addition, each party waives in advance its insuring company's rights of subrogation against the party who caused the damage.

[c]—Self-Insurance. Self-insurance by an landlord can expose both a landlord and the tenant to resultant liability. Some attorneys feel that the waiver of rights of subrogation is all that is needed to absolve their clients of any liabilities that are in excess of insurance. What they fail to realize is that this only absolves the client to the extent of insurance. The client will still risk exposure to direct actions for the amount of the loss not covered by insurance.

[d]—Requirement of Minimum Coverage. Office leases generally require the tenant to maintain a certain level of insurance to cover destruction or casualty. Provided the tenant maintains that minimum level of insurance, most landlords will waive any direct action against the tenant except as otherwise set forth in the lease and will see to it that its insurance company waives its subrogation rights as well.

Two other requirements are typically used to assist a landlord in the event of loss. The first is to require the tenant to carry fire legal liability insurance to cover the landlord's deductible under its casualty policy in the event a fire or other casualty is caused by a tenant. It is not unusual to see the lease require a $5 million stated liability coverage for fire legal liability risk underwriting. The second is to require the tenant to carry both indemnity liability and business interruption coverage.

---

[3]   While it is increasingly easier to assume away the insurable risk issues and write the insurance coverage, it should not be automatic. Additionally, insuring to the full value is no longer an easy task.

[4]   See § 25.07 *infra* for a discussion of "no fault" insurance in the office leasing field and a sample clause illustrating same.

[e]—Waiver of Subrogation Rights. There has been a general concern that insurance companies or state regulators will require large premium increases in order to have an insurance company waive its rights of subrogation against a party causing the damage to the insured building. Some commentators have been concerned that the right to waive the insured's subrogation rights may go away all together. In either event, office leases generally provide that if there is a charge for the waiver of subrogation, the party requesting and benefiting from the waiver must pay the cost. Some leases require that in the event waivers from either landlord or tenant's insurance carrier are unobtainable, the other party to the lease agrees not to benefit from a waiver as well. This does not seem rational although it is somewhat symmetrical.

There are other ways to receive the equivalent benefit of waivers of subrogation, such as being named as an additional insured or a coinsured, whether or not a loss payee. In these instances, both parties are insured and, provided certain statutory or policy requirements are met, negligence by one party will not limit the payment or invalidate insurance with respect to that loss. In some states, such as New York, there is a requirement of a joint tort fee or endorsement waiver in order to make sure that the party causing the damage, who is an additional named insured, does not invalidate the insurance entirely.

[f]—Business Interruption Insurance. Landlords have a considerable interest in the health and well being of their tenants and their credit worthiness. Business interruption insurance is especially helpful to landlords and tenants in the event of fire or casualty. This form of insurance generally covers the tenant's costs to move out of its premises into temporary quarters and then move back to the building after restoration. In addition, business interruption insurance may cover the double rentals that sometimes result from a casualty. Double rentals occur when a landlord does not abate rent in the event of fire or casualty and the displaced tenant has to pay for temporary space as well. Business interruption insurance not only pays rent at the damaged building, but covers loss of profit and inventory as well. Shifting these burdens to the tenant lowers the landlord's insurance considerably. This can be considered a definite benefit to a tenant on a lease with escalations.

Requirements for this kind of insurance may also be imposed by mortgagees who ultimately look to the tenants for the viability of any debt reduction program under the mortgage of the building.

[g]—Rent Abatement and Rent Value Insurance. Mortgagees also tend to require landlords to carry rent value insurance for at least fifteen months. Rent value insurance assures the landlord and the mortgagee that there will be rental flow equal to the rent role preceding the destruction whether or not the tenant pays rents or has business interruption insurance.

Leases generally allow rent to abate during fire and casualty in the event the tenant is unable to occupy the premises. These provisions usually contain a caveat requiring that the abatement will only occur so long as the casualty or damage is not caused by the tenant or so long as landlord has casualty insurance covering the particular loss. Arguably the abatement should not be conditional, provided each party has fully insured. Some commentators (including the authors) believe that tenant's abatement should not be conditioned at all on whether landlord maintains insurance.

[h]—Loss in Value of the Lease. If the destruction in the office building is of a magnitude that the landlord does not have to restore the building but can terminate the lease, the tenant stands to suffer a loss in the value of its lease. For example, a tenant that occupies a demised premises in a valued location with a twenty-five year lease will more than likely find that after several years it will be paying less than if it had to go into the market for commercial office space and acquire a new lease. The difference in the rentals and additional rentals to be paid under the existing lease by the tenant and what the tenant would have to pay if it went to the market and acquired a new lease is generally referred to as the lease value. Tenants should consider insuring over the loss of an office lease due to fire and casualty in an effort to protect itself against loss of its lease value.

[i]—Conditions Attached to Coverage. As previously stated, it is common for a landlord to condition rental abatements and waivers of actions upon the presence of insurance and the tenant's lack of negligence. A tenant, for its part, may also prescribe a minimum amount of insurance to be held by a landlord on the building and may state that any shortfall in insurance will not be the responsibility of the tenant. This will not mean that the battle is entirely won. Tenant must look behind the landlord's insurance certificate to ascertain the conditions and limitations of the insurance policy for the building. For example, a close reading of the landlord's insurance clauses might reveal an exclusion for acts of war or terrorism. Arguably, in some instances, the landlord would be maintaining the prescribed insurance. However, a particular casualty may be caused by terrorism, thus invalidating the coverage entirely and causing all the tenants to be in a position of possibly losing their abatement and, in some instances, losing their rights for damages against the landlord. These conditional clauses bear considerable scrutiny as does the representation of insurance, the value of the insurance and the presence of self-insurance.

[j]—**Third Party Issues.** Landlords generally require that insurance policies of the tenant not only name the landlord as an additional insured, but also name managing agents for the project, mortgagees and sometimes ground lessors. There may also be additional named insureds on a tenant's policy. The concern exists in these situations that joint tortfeasors or negligence committed by these third parties does not invalidate or limit insurance recovery.

Third parties present other problems as well. Assuming the landlord has specific requirements for insurance levels for the tenant and the lease requires the landlord to maintain full value insurance on the building, third parties can still disrupt an otherwise reasonable arrangement. It is not unusual that tenants on one floor will leak water or other liquids down to another floor, causing considerable damage. Or tenants may leave their windows open in winter and freeze the building pipes.

The landlord has an interest in trying to avoid damage claims and disharmony among tenants in the building. Landlords have attacked this problem in a variety of ways. The authors think the simplest way is to require all tenants in the building to have water and emission damage insurance and to waive their rights of subrogation against other co-occupants of the building. Landlords often go farther, asking tenants to waive all direct actions and any liability for damage caused by other tenants, whether or not the other tenants carry insurance that may cover damage caused by the first tenant against the other tenant. This type of agreement, which excludes one of the parties, is dangerous. It is not necessarily in the best interest of the landlord or the occupants unless the landlord assures the other occupants that the landlord's insurance covers all of these contingencies without limitation or exclusions.

[2]—Landlord's Obligation to Restore

There is no affirmative obligation for a landlord to restore a project in the event of destruction by fire or casualty unless required to do so in the lease. If a landlord does not undertake the obligation, fire or destruction may prove to be an ultimate frustration of the essential purpose, ending the term of a lease.

Most office leases reviewed by the authors do not contain an obligation for the landlord to restore the demised premises or the building improvements. If it is possible to restore the demised premises and the landlord or the tenant would like to maintain its interest in the lease and the benefit of the long term bargain, the lease must be structured to continue in the event of damage. In addition, the demised premises or the building housing the demised premises must be required to be rebuilt. In the event a tenant so desires, it is helpful to assure such goal by requiring the landlord to maintain adequate insurance to make the restoration and to carry sufficient rent income insurance during the restoration period to keep itself going and to pay its ongoing responsibilities for the building project.

There are many issues to consider when structuring a restoration obligation. It is not enough to provide that a landlord will restore a demised premises and maintain full value replacement insurance to permit it to do so. This alone will not solve the problem. All contingencies flowing from destruction, damage or casualty must be dealt with in the lease and the time frame for restoration set forth. For example, the demised premises themselves may not actually be damaged by the fire or casualty in the first place. Instead, a significant portion of the building or a portion of an essential area such as service, equipment or parking may be destroyed, rendering use of the demised premises no longer viable. The restoration provision should be drafted to contemplate such an occurrence.

Other superior interests in the property have to be taken into account when negotiating a restoration obligation, even if sufficient insurance exists.[5] If there is a ground lease or a fee mortgage, for example, restoration is not automatic. Sometimes a ground lease will terminate in the event of a partial substantial destruction of the building as well as full destruction. Tenant's counsel should require the landlord to maintain the right to restore the property under any other leasehold or fee mortgage, as well as under any existing ground lease. When such rights exist, it is generally the case that there are time periods for restoration. The landlord should be required to undertake to satisfy all such time periods and all conditions for restoration.

If the tenant expects that the landlord is also going to restore any of the contents, furniture or fixtures within the demised premises, it must prescribe this obligation in the lease. Further, if the lease is for a significant amount of space in the building, the tenant should negotiate with

---

[5] See Chapter 20 *infra* discussing superior interests.

the landlord to obtain an agreement from the ground lessor or the holder of any fee interest or leasehold mortgage, clearly granting the tenant the right to perform any of the conditions necessary to allow restoration and quite possibly even the right to restore the improvement itself and seek rent reduction or other compensation thereafter.

Restoration rights may interact with subordination provisions or other conditions in superior documents, as well as with subrogation rights of insurance companies. A lease provision that requires the landlord to restore, but does not take into consideration superior document holders or ownership rights of other entities in insurance proceeds is not sufficient to protect the interests of the landlord or a tenant if the parties are under a long term lease that either or both of them would like to preserve during a restoration period.

In sum, for purposes of negotiating a restoration provision, the party should carefully analyze the position it desires to maintain. For example, if a tenant views its lease as one with favorable rates, a prime location, enhanced services and a long term, the tenant may choose a negotiation strategy that requires the landlord to promptly restore any damage or destruction under almost all circumstances. In addition, the tenant may consider negotiating a right to assist the landlord in the event the landlord does not have the resources to complete the restoration or the right to partially undertake some of the obligations of the landlord to restore the property and the improvements itself in order to continue the lease.

[3]—Liability

Liability for fire, casualty or other destruction is a distinct issue from the ability to pay, any obligations to restore, the existence of rent abatements or the presence of insurance. In the best of all worlds, responsibility or liability for causing damage or destruction would be dealt with in absolute terms. It would not be affected by impairment of insurance due to joint negligence or the failure to have waived the rights of subrogation. Unfortunately, the ideal does not prevail.

Ideally, under the concepts of "no fault" insurance, if a tenant is unable to utilize its premises, it should receive an abatement for all rentals and costs. Such an abatement would not be contingent upon the absence of liability or other actions on the part of the tenant or others that might impair the ability of the landlord to be compensated by insurance. Even if the damage or casualty was caused by the tenant's negligence or that of its agents, employees, officers or contractors, under "no fault," there would be no assessment of liability and each party would look to its own insurance to cover its particular risk. This would be the case whether or not the insurance was impaired due to acts of either party or whether or not the damaged party had insurance. Each party would waive direct liability for any damage resulting from the destruction. Each party would agree to waive the rights of subrogation of its insurance companies as against the other party.

The provisions of the lease dealing with these issues should not be conditioned upon the existence of insurance, the impairment of insurance, the joint negligence of the insured or the presence of any type of insurance policy at all. For instance, if an entity elects to be partially or fully self-insured, it should not impact the waivers of direct liability or subrogation rights of insurers in the event any insurance company exists in the equation. If the provisions are drafted properly, all parties should be fully insured for insurable events and look to their own coverage to be made whole. In the case of uninsurable events, the parties would be on their own.

[4]—Damage or Destruction Clause

Although it is difficult to locate a representative clause in the office leasing industry that deals with many of the issues raised in this chapter, the following example attempts to cover some of the major issues: (1) mandatory obligation of the landlord to rebuild; (2) time periods for reconstruction; (3) continuation of abatement periods; (4) appropriate "what ifs" in the event portions of the premises cannot be restored and are deemed to be indispensable; and (5) circumstances when the landlord or tenant can elect to terminate the lease.

Many issues are *not* covered in the example, however, including the obligation of the landlord to restore the property of the tenant within the premises. Clauses generally tend to require the tenant to insure its personal property. Typically, the building fire casualty insurance only covers the fixtures and tenant installation that become a portion of the real property.

Example 2:

Section 11.01. If the Building or the Demised Premises shall be partially or totally damaged or destroyed by fire or other cause (and if this Lease shall not have been terminated as in this Article 11 hereinafter provided), the Landlord shall repair the damage and restore and rebuild the Building and/ or the Demised Premises, except for Tenant's Work and Tenant's personal property, at its expense with reasonable dispatch in accordance with good construction practice after notice to it of the damage or destruction.

Section 11.02. If the Building or the Demised Premises shall be damaged or destroyed by fire or other cause, then the rents payable hereunder shall be abated to the extent that the Demised Premises shall have been rendered untenantable or inaccessible for the reasonable conduct of Tenant's normal business operations for the period from the date of such damage or destruction to the earlier to occur of (x) 180 days following the date on which Landlord substantially completes the repair and restoration work that Landlord is required to perform under this Article 11 and (y) the date of Tenant's occupancy of the Demised Premises for the conduct of its normal business following such casualty, such abatement to be granted on a pro rata basis if only a portion of the Demised Premises is so rendered untenantable or inaccessible; provided, however, that should Tenant reoccupy a portion of the Demised Premises as to which the abatement is in effect during the period the restoration work is taking place and prior to the date that the whole of said Demised Premises are made tenantable, Basic Annual Rent and Additional Rent allocable to such portion shall be payable by Tenant from the date of such occupancy. Landlord shall be deemed to have substantially completed the repair and restoration work that Landlord is required to perform under this Article 11 notwithstanding that (i) Punchlist Work remains to be performed, the non-completion of which does not unreasonably interfere with Tenant's ability to perform Tenant's Work and (i) portions thereof are incomplete which under good construction scheduling practice should be done after the completion of the still incomplete portions of Tenant's Work (which Punchlist Work will be diligently completed by Landlord as soon as reasonably practical). Notwithstanding anything to the contrary contained herein, in the event that substantial completion by Landlord of such repair and restoration work is delayed by reason of any delays caused or occasioned by Tenant, its agents, servants, employees, architects, engineers, servants, contractors or subcontractors, then Tenant (in addition to paying the costs and damages Landlord may sustain by reason thereof) agrees that substantial completion by Landlord of such repair and restoration work shall be deemed to have occurred on the date on which substantial completion of such work would have occurred had not the completion of such work been so delayed by Tenant, *et al.*

Section 11.03. (a) If the Building shall be so damaged or destroyed by fire or other cause (whether or not the Demised Premises are damaged or destroyed) as to require a reasonably estimated expenditure made by Landlord or a reputable contractor designated by Landlord of more than forty percent (40%) of the full insurable value of the Building immediately prior to the casualty (or ten percent (10%) if such casualty occurs during the last two years of the Term) then Landlord may terminate this Lease by giving Tenant notice to such effect within one hundred eighty (180) days after the date of the casualty and upon such notice this Lease and the estate hereby granted, whether or not the Term shall have theretofore commenced, shall terminate as if that date was the Expiration Date.

(b) In case of any damage or destruction mentioned in this Article 11 which Landlord is required to repair and restore, if (1) more than thirty-five percent (35%) of the rentable square footage of the Demised Premises shall be damaged or destroyed and rendered untenantable or inaccessible or (2) Tenant's main computer room or main mail room shall be damaged or destroyed and rendered untenantable or inaccessible (each a "Substantial Casualty") and, in the reasonable good faith opinion (the "Estimate") of an independent licensed architect or engineer selected by Landlord having at least five (5) years' experience in such matters, the repair and restoration required to be performed by Landlord pursuant to this Article 11 cannot be substantially completed within fifteen (15) months after the Adjustment Date (as hereinafter defined) then Tenant shall be entitled to terminate this Lease on sixty (60) days' notice to Landlord given within thirty (30) days after receipt of the Estimate, and upon delivery of such notice and the expiration of such 60-day period, this Lease and the Term shall expire as fully and completely as if such date were the date set forth above for the termination of this Lease and Tenant shall forthwith quit, surrender and vacate the Demised Premises in accordance with the provisions of this Lease. The Estimate shall set forth the date (the "Estimated Date") by which it is reasonably estimated that the repair and restoration required to be performed by Landlord pursuant to this Article 11 will be completed and the Estimate shall be provided by Landlord to Tenant within sixty (60) days after such fire or casualty. For purposes hereof the "Adjustment Date" is the date which is (i) ninety (90) days after the date of such Substantial Casualty if the estimated time to perform such repair and restoration is fifteen (15) months or less or (ii) one hundred eighty (180) days after the date of such Substantial Casualty if the estimated time to perform such repair and restoration is greater than fifteen (15) months.

(c) In addition, and notwithstanding anything herein to the contrary, in the event of any Substantial Casualty, if ninety percent (90%) (as reasonably estimated by said independent architect or engineer) of such work of repair or restoration to both the Demised Premises and the Building required to be performed by Landlord pursuant to this Article 11 is not substantially completed by the Outside Restoration Date (as hereinafter defined), as such Outside Restoration Date may be extended due to Force Majeure Clauses (not to exceed six (6) months in the aggregate) and delays caused or occasioned by Tenant, its agents, employees, contractors, subcontractors, architects, engineers or servants, then, if Landlord shall have failed to substantially complete the repair and restoration by the ninetieth (90th) day following the Outside Restoration Date, subject to Force Majeure Causes (not to exceed six (6) months in the aggregate) and such delays of Tenant *et al.*, Tenant shall be entitled to terminate this Lease on sixty (60) days' notice to Landlord given within thirty (30) days after the expiration of said 90 day period following the Outside Restoration Date and, upon the giving of such notice and the expiration of such 60 day period, this Lease and the term shall expire as provided in Section 11.03(b). For purposes hereof the Outside Restoration Date is the date which is later to occur of (1) fifteen (15) months after the Adjustment Date and (2) the Estimated Date if the Estimated Date was greater than fifteen (15) months after the Adjustment Date and Tenant did not elect to terminate this Lease as provided above.

Section 11.04. Except for the rent abatements expressly provided for in Section 11.02, no damages, compensation or claim shall be payable by Landlord for inconvenience, loss of business or annoyance arising from any repair or restoration of any portion of the Demised Premises or of the Building or of the Complex arising from damage or destruction caused by fire or other casualty and Landlord shall not be required to do any such repair or restoration except on Business Days from 9:00 A.M. to 5:00 P.M.

Section 11.05. Notwithstanding any of the foregoing provisions of this Article 11, if Landlord or the lessor of any superior lease or the holder of any superior mortgage shall be unable to collect all of the insurance proceeds (including rent insurance proceeds) applicable to damage or destruction of the Demised Premises or the Property by fire or other cause by reason of some wrongful action or inaction after the date of the damage or destruction on the part of Tenant or any of its officers, partners, directors, employees, agents or contractors, then, without prejudice to any other remedies which may be available against Tenant, there shall be no abatement of Tenant's rent, but the total amount of such rent not abated (which would otherwise have been abated) shall not exceed the amount of uncollected insurance proceeds.

Section 11.06. Landlord will not carry separate insurance of any kind on Tenant's property (including, without limitation, any property of Tenant's which shall become the property of Landlord as provided in Article 6), and, except as provided by law, shall not be obligated to repair any damage thereto or replace or clean the same, or any decorations, installations, equipment or fixtures installed by or for Tenant at Tenant's expense.

Section 11.07. The provisions of this Article 11 shall be considered an express agreement governing any cause of damage or destruction of the Demised Premises by fire or other casualty and any law providing for such a contingency now or hereinafter erected shall have no application in such case.

Section 11.08. In the event that either Landlord or Tenant terminates this Lease pursuant to this Article 11, the parties hereto agree that (i) Tenant shall have no obligation to restore or repair the Demised Premises and (ii) Tenant shall have the sole right to make a claim for and retain the proceeds of any insurance carried by Tenant on Tenant's Work and Tenant's property.

314

§11.03 Mortgagee's Interest in Insurance Proceeds

In the event of fire, casualty, destruction, as well as condemnation, mortgagees generally require that the proceeds of any insurance be awarded to the mortgagee to reduce the outstanding mortgage principal. Requirements of this sort will deplete the available funds that a landlord can draw upon to restore the project and maintain the lessees' interests under their leases.

In a perfect world, the application of the insurance funds to reduce the fee mortgage might not signal the death of the project. One might argue that land that is free and clear of underlying debt with an ability to produce income from leases continues to be viable for development and financing. Many times this assumption is not accurate. For instance, it may be impossible to rebuild certain improvements under existing zoning laws or variances. It is also not a foregone conclusion that real estate improvements can be financed.

In order to preserve the interests of any tenants the landlord might have as well as its own interest in the ongoing operation of the building as it existed before any casualty occurred, the mortgagor should require its mortgagee under the terms of its mortgage document to agree to allow it to reinvest all insurance proceeds in order to restore the improvements [1] and allow the continuation of the operation and performance of the property in its pre-casualty condition. A prudent tenant will check the mortgage documents during the performance of its due diligence before the lease is signed to make sure that its prospective landlord has obtained such a right from the mortgagee. If the mortgage does not contain such a provision, the tenant should require the landlord to obtain such a right at that time. [2] For its part, the mortgagee typically conditions this type of obligation upon the leases remaining in full force and effect throughout the restoration period and the tenants returning to the building. Therefore, careful attention must be given in the lease to preserving the lease obligations during the rebuilding period. [3]

---

[1]   This assumes that the building improvements will remain viable.

[2]   In addition, of course, the tenant should require the landlord to rebuild "entirely" in the event of casualty or other types of damages or destruction.

[3]   See § 11.02[4] *supra* for a clause dealing with many of these issues, including a provision in which the tenant has the right, after a prolonged period, to terminate the lease in the event of fire or casualty.

These lease preservation clauses have a circuitous logic and may depend on how the tenants' termination rights are structured under their long term leases in the event of fire, casualty and condemnation. All things being equal, a mortgagee should be able to rely on the unconditional continuation of the existing leases for which it is underwriting its original loan and upon which it relied in order to commit to allow the application of insurance proceeds from fire casualty or condemnation to be reinvested in the project.

An agreement from the mortgagee to permit the insurance proceeds to be used for restoration is essential to a tenant with a long term lease. The tenant might want to exercise some flexibility with regard to the conditions required or the time periods set for the restoration of the building project and the continuance of its lease. A tenant can maintain business interruption and rent payment insurance for at least a year and a half to two years. Consequently, a provision requiring the tenant to return to the building after restoration of the demised premises may not be an onerous one, provided the remainder of the term of its lease is sufficiently long to warrant the return.

Arguably there is an inconvenience to the tenant whether or not it returns to its demised premises. In addition, temporary space usually is just that. More permanent space will generally have to be acquired within six months to a year after the initial casualty if the tenant is still awaiting the completion of the restoration. When weighed in the balance, however, these problems are only small annoyances in the event the tenant has a significant going concern with respect to its previous location and good will and a value worth preserving under the terms of its old lease where it is presumably paying lower rentals than currently found in the market.

§ 11.04 Rent Abatements During Condemnation or Destruction

There are as many different variations on rent payments and abatements during casualty and condemnation as there are office leases. For example, many office lease forms provide for a conditional rent abatement in the event of fire, casualty, condemnation or other destruction, provided that the tenant is not responsible for causing such an event or that the insurance for rental value of the landlord is not impaired by the acts of the tenant. Under many leases, the rent abatement requirement is conditioned upon its being an insurable event under the insurance maintained by the landlord for the building improvements. These conditions and assumptions seem fair unless you have an actual event where the building owner is partially self-insured, where the form of insurance may be invalidated for negligent acts of the owner or co-insured or because there is a peculiar exception, such as for acts of state-sponsored terrorism.

Rent abatements are not absolute under most circumstances. Some leases do not allow rent to abate regardless of who is responsible or liable for the actual damage. Under those types of leases, there is usually a requirement for a tenant to maintain business interruption and rent payment insurance for a certain period of time to cover its duplicate obligations to pay rent in the building (even though it cannot use the premises), in addition to paying rent for temporary space during the restoration of the destruction.

Rent abatements that are tied to the liability of the tenant for the damage or destruction do not necessarily speak to the issue of the ultimate responsibility and liability for the actual damage to the improvements by fire or other casualty. Such responsibilities and liabilities are usually stated, separately indemnified and insured over under varying criteria. When reviewing the lease, the party should not expect to find all the responsibilities and liabilities in one paragraph. A hunting expedition through the entire document may be required to locate all of the issues, such as whether rent abatement exists or not in the event of casualty; which party is responsible for the damage; and to what extent, if any, insurance proceeds affect the existence of rent abatements or any of the liabilities or responsibilities.

Ideally, in the event of fire or casualty, it seems only reasonable to expect the following: (1) rent should abate and the landlord should be obligated to restore if the demised premises are unusable, regardless of whether they are actually damaged; (2) the landlord's obligation to restore should not be predicated on the existence of sufficient insurance proceeds; (3) the rent should abate whether or not rent value or rent income insurance exists; (4) the landlord and tenant should fully insure their own interests, without condition or negligence of either invalidating or impairing collectibility of insurance; (5) each party should look to insurance for its loss; (6) the landlord should waive direct liability against a tenant in the event the landlord under insures or self-insures; and (7) both parties should waive their insurance company's rights of subrogation over as against the other party in the event negligence caused the damage or destruction. Under this scenario, abatements would occur and sufficient funds would be available for rebuilding. Through rent value insurance and payments under the tenant's business interruption policies, the landlord would be able to maintain itself during the reconstruction process and the tenant would be able to operate and have no loss of profits. Abatements would therefore not be conditioned upon the absence of negligence, the landlord's insurance proceeds or the landlord's ability to afford them.

§ 11.05 Length of Restoration Period

Very little time and energy is focused on establishing an outside date for the completion of restoration work to repair the damages from a fire or casualty or to restore the loss of a portion of the premises from a partial condemnation. [1] Restoration rights and the extension of a lease term during the restoration period are not as of right. They must be negotiated and clearly provided for in the lease. In addition, the parties should set some parameters for the length of time that is reasonable to complete the restoration work.

Some restorations can take years. Whether or not the landlord is required to restore and irrespective of the presence of insurance proceeds, as a practical matter, the adjustment process, the permit process for demolition and the actual restoration can seem interminably long. The logistics of a restoration may be daunting, causing many tenants to end the relationship and move on rather than come back to the premises, even if good will may be present at that location and a favorable lease is in place.

Each tenant must assess its individual position to determine how long it can afford to wait to move back into its premises. For instance, if the lease is considerably below market it may be in the tenant's best interest to stick it out and return to the premises after the work is finished, even if that takes years. Provided that the tenant is able to cause the term of the existing lease (and construction abatement periods during initial fit-up) to move into abeyance and not to erode during the rebuilding process, the longer the process takes, the more valuable the leasehold interest may become. For instance, consider a brand new lease with the space under initial alterations, at $20 per square foot and with a six month free rent period during construction, a $50 per square foot market and a building that is destroyed. During the three years it might take to rebuild the building, at the end of the restoration the tenant may still have a considerable amount of time remaining in its term and an uneroded initial construction abatement period. If the costs in the market have increased at a normal compounding rate and the outside costs [2] are considerably higher, the tenant might realize an even greater saving if its lease survives and extends.

---

[1]   If the parties have elected a "no fault" insurance scheme, this should be the only practical and material issue at stake. Under "no fault," if a tenant expects to return to its valuable leasehold premises, the only question is when.

[2]   Outside costs include additional rentals such as taxes and operating expenses.

The following issues should be addressed: (1) the obligation of the landlord to restore within a reasonable time period; (2) the time frame in which the work will be completed and what work will be completed, such as landlord's and tenant's installations; (3) the right of the tenant to elect to terminate if restoration does not occur on a timely schedule; (4) the right of the tenant to keep its termination rights in place if it elects to wait for the work to be done even if the work is taking longer than expected; (5) preservation of and extension of all free rent and construction periods and replenishment of the construction fund; (6) the right of the tenant to elect to extend the term of the lease to make up for the time lost to the casualty or destruction; and (7) conclusion of the build out of the shell and of landlord's work in compliance with then existing laws and the certificate of occupancy.

§ 11.06 Summary

There are many interests and values in real estate worth preserving, even in the event of a loss due to fire, casualty or condemnation. Any landlord that spends the time and effort necessary to fill a building with operating leases upon which it can obtain financing and any tenant who has a long term lease at below current market value will appreciate the significance of being able to continue that arrangement after restoration. The viability of the landlord's project as well as the viability of the tenant's business may depend on the choices made in the office lease negotiation with regard to these issues. Nothing should be assumed. All contingencies, conditions, rights and obligations should be clearly drafted, knowledgeably reviewed and carefully imposed in accordance with the expectations of the parties.

CHAPTER 25

Casualty and Insurance

Chapter Contents [1]

---

[1] Portions of this chapter are reprinted from A. DiSciullo, "A Guide to Subrogation in Commercial Leases," Real Estate L.J. (Spring 1992). Reprinted by permission of Warren, Gorham & Lamont.

25-1

---

§ 25.01 Common Law Standards

One of the major issues arising under an office lease is the allocation of the risks and responsibilities for casualties, injuries, damage or destruction on the leased premises. Until the advent of modern insurance, the responsibility for these occurrences under most leases was governed by the common law. To a certain extent, the harshness of the common law standards imposed upon a tenant for repairing the premises has been carried forward in modern insurance provisions.

At common law, the landlord was not responsible for repairing the premises or leased improvements. The medieval tenant typically rented agricultural lands. The improvements on these lands, such as a barn or a shed, were merely incidental to the leased property. Most often, the landlord lacked the necessary tools and skills for repairing and maintaining these structures. As such, the tenants took the leasehold in an "as is" condition, with the rule of *caveat emptor* applying.

Under the common law, the tenant was under no legal obligation to restore a structure damaged by fire, flood or other casualty. However, the tenant was frequently economically compelled to rebuild the damaged or destroyed structure if it wanted to receive the maximum benefit and use of the land and the premises it was leasing. Therefore, a tenant assumed considerable risk and liability in entering into a common law lease.

This scenario no longer applies in quite the same fashion. Most modern leases involve urban and suburban offices and retail shops where the improved space is the main focus of the lease agreement rather than the underlying land. Moreover, most tenants do not have the time, skill or tools necessary to maintain and keep up a building or premises.

A few states have refused to follow this common law rule. In addition, recent cases have tended to repudiate the common law standard on the theory of commercial frustration. [2] In New York, for instance, a tenant may surrender possession of the premises and will be relieved of further rental obligations so long as the casualty was not the tenant's fault.

While most courts and modern leases are moving away from these standards, a few jurisdictions still retain these common law rules. Due to the variety of case law among the states, a tenant cannot be fully assured of what its obligations will be in a particular situation unless it is thoroughly familiar with the laws and cases of the jurisdiction governing the lease. It is a tedious job for a user with multiple operations in numerous states to keep abreast of the applicable law, but it is nonetheless extremely important.

---

[2]   See *Friedman on Leases* at 133, 473, 1404 (3d ed. 1990) for an extensive discussion on the case law and application and theory of commercial frustration and frustration of tenant's use. See also Rasch, *Landlord and Tenant* § 19.1 *et seq.* (3d ed. 1988) for an examination of the common law and current obligations of the parties with respect to transferring control of and repairing the premises.

§ 25.02 Modern Liability

[1]—In General

Tenants usually assume considerable casualty and liability risk when entering into a commercial lease. Both the common law and more modern theories impart a large amount of risk for casualties upon a tenant that typically is not fully realized until a disaster occurs. States differ greatly from one another in apportioning responsibility upon a landlord or tenant for a casualty loss.

By way of illustration of these risks, case law has not done much to clarify the liability of each party in a fire damage claim. [1] The holdings even vary with respect to the theories of liability which should be applied. The practitioner should be familiar with the current law in each state where his or her client has office leases and must find methods of limiting casualty liability that is acceptable in those jurisdictions.

A tenant may incur liability to its landlord for casualty damage to the premises or structure under four theories: (1) tort; (2) contract or lease covenant; (3) application of indemnification; or (4) vicarious liability.

[2]—Tort

A tenant's liability will be considered tortious if its negligence or that of its agents or employees, causes the casualty or damage. Tortious liability arises apart from any lease covenant or other written agreement whereby the tenant assumes this liability. Several cases have held that this liability is not necessarily excused by the landlord's covenant to repair fire damage [2] nor by the owner's or landlord's receipt of insurance proceeds obtained at that party's own cost. [3] The theory applied in these cases is that a tenant's liability is excusable only if (1) the landlord is contributorily negligent; (2) the landlord has agreed in writing or by actions to insure the premises and building on behalf of both the land-

---

[1] For an extensive citation of authority on this point, see *Friedman on Leases* at 525-528 (3d ed. 1990). See also E. Grant, "Subrogation, Indemnification and Exculpation in the Context of Commercial Leases," from "Enforceability of Subrogation and Indemnity Clauses," Chair, A. DiSciullo, American Bar Association program, Aug. 12, 1991.

[2] See, e.g., National Motels, Inc. v. Howard Johnson, Inc., 373 F.2d 375 (4th Cir. 1967); Maiatico v. Hot Shoppes, Inc., 287 F.2d 349 (D.C. Cir. 1961).

[3] See, e.g., Precisionware, Inc. v. Madison County Tobacco Warehouse, Inc., 411 F.2d 42, 48 (5th Cir. 1969).

lord and tenant; or (3) the tenant is able to prove that a substantial portion of the landlord's insurance premiums have been paid for by the tenant or are attributable to payments in operating expenses and other rents made by the tenant. [4]

[3]—Contract or Lease Covenant

Contractual liability arises quite apart from tort liability but may originate from the same events. The tenant's responsibility for fire and other casualty damage may arise from a lease covenant to surrender or "yield-up" possession of the premises in good condition. The covenant may also provide an obligation for the tenant to repair the premises at lease expiration or termination. The covenant is obviously breached if the premises or building are destroyed and cannot be restored in a timely manner. [5]

[4]—Indemnification

A landlord's or tenant's liability may similarly spring from an indemnification or exculpatory clause in the lease [6] requiring one party to hold the other harmless from casualties caused by the first party, its agents, employees, invitees or third parties. The exculpatory clauses typically protect the landlord from liability to the tenant even for the landlord's own negligence.

[5]—Vicarious Liability

A tenant may be vicariously liable for any casualty or damage caused by the subtenant, licensee or assignee whose performance the tenant guarantees. Liability has been found under the theory of *res ipsa loquitur* ("the thing speaks for itself"), [7] as well as under the theories of liability discussed above.

[6]—Fraud or Misrepresentation

Absent fraud or misrepresentation, both landlords and tenants have insurable interests in the premises and building structure. Without that

---

[4]   *Id.* See also *Friedman on Leases* § 9.9 at 526 (3d ed. 1990).

[5]   Taylor v. ROA Motons, Inc., 114 Ga. App. 671, 152 S.E.2d. 631 (1966).

[6]   See discussion of indemnification and exculpatory clauses at § 25.06 *infra*.

[7]   See Annotation, "*Res Ipsa Loquitur* as a Cause of Liability for Real Property Fires," 21 A.L.R.4th 929-1074 (1983); *Friedman on Leases* § 9.9 at 527-528 (3d ed. 1990).

insurable interest, a fire or casualty policy is void and invalid. Unless there is a subsequent waiver or estoppel, an insurer may elect to void a fraudulently obtained policy.

A landlord or tenant will be charged with any misrepresentations made by their agents as if these fraudulent statements were their own. Under these circumstances, the insured landlord or tenant is excused and coverage restored only if (1) the insured can prove that the agent's statements are unauthorized, and (2) insured is able to defeat the *prima facie* case for avoiding a policy obtained by misrepresentation or fraud. To defeat a *prima facie* case, the insured must show the *scienter* of the party making the representation, [8] that the intent was to deceive the insurer, and that the insurer relied upon the false or misleading statements to its detriment. [9] This is an exceptional situation. Generally, once an insurable interest has been established and there is no fraud or misrepresentation in obtaining the policy, either the landlord or tenant can obtain coverage.

---

[8]   The party must be shown to have made the representation knowingly.

[9]   44 C.J.S. *Insurance* §§ 179, 362.

§ 25.03 Types of Coverage

Typical insurance in office leasing transactions involves two types of broad coverage: property and liability. The tenant may be responsible for procuring these and additional types of coverage or endorsements depending on the nature of the tenancy, such as a "net" or "triple net" lease.

[1]—Property Coverage

[a]—**Direct Losses.** Property insurance for an office lease generally encompasses fire insurance, fire and extended coverage and "all-risk" insurance. This insurance includes such specialized coverages as boiler and machinery insurance and electronic data processing (EDP) insurance. Property insurance pays claims directly to the insured party. As such, it is "first-party" insurance. Property insurance coverage is narrowly defined. The policies pay for only named, covered perils and generally exclude flood, earthquakes and hazardous waste coverage. These perils can be insured for in special riders, but they are expensive to obtain.

A common form of coverage carried by landlords is a fire insurance policy with "extended coverage endorsement" (ECE). ECE perils are named perils, that is, risks specifically listed in the policy. Typical ECE perils are fire, smoke, explosion, windstorm, civil commotion or hail. High risk events such as nuclear explosions, state sponsored terrorist attacks and steam boiler and pipe explosions are excluded.

A very popular form of coverage in recent years is "all risk" property insurance. It is now unusual that any insured would purchase an ECE or other specified perils policy if an all risk policy were available. In an all risk policy, insurers are covered against all perils except those that are expressly and specifically excluded. [1]

There are four common but troublesome exclusions to the typical all risk policy. These exclusions are: (1) the "ordinance or law" clause, which generally denies coverage for losses due to the "enforcement of any ordinance or law regulating the construction, repair, demolition or condemnation of any building or structure; (2) the "flood or earthquake" hazards clause, which also covers damage from surface water overruns, sewer and drain backups or damage caused by sub-surface waters under hydrostatic

---

[1] All-Risk exclusions may be similar to those situations not covered in an ECE or other Specified Perils policies, but the premise of the types of coverage is the opposite.

pressures; (3) the "computer-related or electronic data processing" (EDP) damages clause; and (4) the "boiler and machinery" clause. [2] When one or more of these clauses are in force, the following events may not be covered by an all risk policy: electronic disturbances (except when attributable to a sudden event such as lighting); mechanical breakdown and damages caused by sudden temperature changes; and damages caused by atmospheric conditions or extremes, to name but a few.

An all risk policy may cover damages differently depending upon the circumstances. For instance, in the recent World Trade Center blast, all risk coverage paid for the cleaning of soot, dust and electromagnetic residue on thousands of computers from the explosion and smoke generated from the blast, but did not cover any subsequent mechanical breakdown of the computers from the accumulated soot if left untreated.

Property coverage varies despite the existence of standardized Insurance Service Office (ISO) forms. Coverage also depends upon what the parties negotiate. Usually the landlord will bargain for the tenant to carry a contents policy with the landlord reserving its rights to carry its property coverage under a blanket policy if it owns several properties. Where the landlord is an insurance company or large net worth entity, it may bargain to self-insure its risk. In that instance as a self insurer, the landlord acts as its own insurance carrier for the property and may have to establish reserves for losses. Alternatively, and less risky, the landlord may carry insurance, but maintain a large deductible equal to a set amount of loss per incident.

The ISO form defines "Covered Property" as the "Building (including additions, permanent and outdoor fixtures and personal property used to maintain and service the building), Business Personal Property located in or on the Building or within 100 feet of the Building and Personal Property of Others in the insured's care, custody or control." [3] "Business Personal Property" is defined to include furniture and fixtures, "stock," machinery and equipment and all other materials, labor or services furnished or arranged by the insured or other party's personal property. For a tenant, "Business Personal Property" may also cover the permanent improvements the tenant has made in the building. One commentator has warned, however, that personal property or con-

---

[2] See C.S. Ferrell, Property and Liability Insurance in Lease Transactions at 4 (Faegre & Benson, Minneapolis, MN) (1991).

[3] I.S.O. "Building and Personal Property Coverage Form," § A.1.a.

tents coverage may not include these "tenant improvements." [4] Even if these improvements are included, coverage may be for an inadequate amount or reimbursed only for their unamortized or depreciated value rather than replacement value. [5]

Even though "Covered Property" has a broad meaning, boiler and machinery "objects" and perils will typically be excluded under policies and will need to be covered under a separate policy. While most policies broadly describe covered personal property, the standard ISO policy may either specifically exclude a particular coverage or the amount of recovery elsewhere in the policy. A complete reading of the policy is necessary to know what is included or excluded and the amount of recovery that will be obtained in a loss.

As firms and companies become increasingly dependent upon computers and computer media for record retention and data processing, an insured should exercise a great degree of care in insuring for these losses in the event of a casualty at its premises. While "Covered Property" typically includes "valuable papers and records and computer equipment and media", there are coverage limitations with each. "Valuable papers and records coverage" will typically insure for the cost of replacing computer disks, CDs and microfilm in blank form. However, it will not cover the expenses of reproducing the lost data on the microfilm, disk or CD, a far more expensive process than the costs of replacing blank materials. Similarly, computer equipment and media will be covered, but with the several limitations of coverage attributable to the "specified perils" discussed elsewhere.

[b]—Indirect Losses. Loss coverage is usually only for direct losses covered under the general insuring agreement. Alternatively, there is no coverage for consequential or indirect losses. Thus, unless there is specific coverage for earnings losses, extra expenses or the costs of replacing a favorable lease that is terminated as a result of a direct loss, there is no coverage for these costs and expenses.

There is another problem associated with indirect losses. Under most standard property policies, a covered direct loss must first trigger any indirect loss coverage a party may have. Direct damage coverage, how-

---

[4]   See C.S. Ferrell, Property and Liability Insurance in Lease Transactions at 4 (Faegre & Benson, Minneapolis, MN) (1991).

[5]   Id.

ever, is usually limited to property that the insured owns at the scheduled premises. If the circumstances that trigger indirect loss originate from an incident that occurs off the insured's premises or from property not owned by the insured, the insured will not even be able to recover for the indirect losses. For example, a fire in an adjoining anchor store in a shopping mall may result in an insured tenant losing a substantial amount of customer traffic leading to a substantial loss of resulting revenues. The insured, however, will not recover from these loss revenues unless it has negotiated contingent business interruption coverage. [6]

In some instances, indirect damages may not trigger coverage for business interruption or extra expense coverage. An example of this problem may arise when a business suffers damage to its computer system. The largest extent of damage attributable to a computer-related peril generally falls into the category of indirect damages, *i.e.*, damages to the data stored within the memory of the physical equipment itself. However, because the insured may not be able to collect on its direct damages, the business interruption or extra expense coverage that would constitute the overwhelming portion of an insured's loss due to a computer-related disaster may not be triggered. To avoid such consequences, the insured may attempt to negotiate to delete the applicable exclusions, particularly with respect to the "electronic data processing" related losses. In the alternative, the insured may obtain a separate "EDP" policy specifically addressing these scenarios. [7]

Several types of contingent or indirect loss coverages are tied into lease transactions. Each cover an insured for revenue losses from a disruption of business from a casualty, be it an interruption in the rent stream or in other sources of income. "Business interruption coverage" is similar to "rents coverage," but the former is often more speculative than the latter. Landlords and tenants often negotiate over which party will carry the rent coverage or rent interruption insurance. The relative ease of collecting on a rents coverage claim compared to submitting a business interruption claim is part of the reason for this negotiation.

Tenants will look to "extra expense" coverage to compensate them for additional rental expenses if temporary premises are necessary while the leased premises are being renovated or restored following a

---

[6] See C.S. Ferrell, Property and Liability Insurance in Lease Transactions (Faegre & Benson, Minneapolis, MN) (1991).

[7] *Id.* at 11.

casualty. The extra expense coverage will reimburse the tenant only for the duplicative rents incurred as a result of the loss. These reimbursements will be offset by any rent abatements the tenant has negotiated at the original premises.

In drawing upon extra expense coverage, both landlord and tenant should consider all the factors that constitute "rent." In the typical gross lease found in most office buildings, the insurer's definition of "rent" excludes the tenant's portion of taxes, operating expenses, common area expenses and amortized work allowances. "Leasehold interest insurance" would fill this gap and cover the instances where the tenant suffers the loss of a favorable lease when the landlord elects its cancellation rights under a damage and destruction clause of the lease. This coverage regards the leasehold as a valuable asset and reimburses the tenant for the difference in rent it would pay in replacement premises over the more favorable lease that was terminated. The calculation is for net extra rents and would include the expected (presumably favorable) costs in unexercised option periods in the original contract, while offsetting any favorable investment in a new lease (rent abatements, for example) that a tenant may negotiate in a new contract.

[2]—Property Endorsements

Endorsements cover the specific perils not usually covered in an all risk or other inclusionary policy. Typical endorsements include:

> • *Specific Perils* - provides for specific *inclusions* in the coverage, such as the electronic data processing (EDP) records coverage.
> • *Rental Income Insurance* - provides coverage in a business policy for the loss of rents due to a covered loss.
> • *Plate Glass Insurance* - covers damage to the glass described in the policy schedule and to the lettering and ornamentation separately described in the endorsement from covered perils. This type of endorsement is very expensive to obtain. Even though it usually applies only to a retail lease, office tenants are still required to carry it.
> • *Vandalism Endorsement* - covers willful and malicious damages to the insured's property. It may be necessary due to the relief from liability that landlords typically want in the event of theft at the premises. Most tenants do not realize that they have assumed the risk for property losses from theft or vandalism since the exculpatory clause is usually buried in the rules and regula-

tions section rather than in the main body of the lease.

• *Agreed Amount Endorsement* - works like a "friendly" liquidated damages provision. The insurance company agrees to pay an undisputed stated amount in the event of a loss. The difficulty occurs in ascertaining the amount at the time the endorsement is obtained, especially taking into consideration the replacement value of the lost property at the time of the occurrence of a possible loss.

• *Inflation or Replacement Value Endorsement* - may be the possible solution to the problem in the previous endorsements in determining the value of a loss at time of occurrence. This endorsement will automatically increase the amount of property loss coverage to reflect the increased replacement cost of the building or premises.

• *Changed Conditions Endorsement* - covers perils not usually insured in an all risk policy, including the expenses that an insured may incur due to building code regulations enacted after the original construction and to which the insured must comply if it does any additional alterations.

• *Contractual Liability* - covers the insured for any indemnity obligations to which it has agreed in the lease. It assures the indemnified party that it will receive the contracted protection to which the insured has obligated itself under a lease indemnification provision. This endorsement is more typical of a liability rather than a property policy.

• *Rent or Business Interruption* - serves two purposes. First, it covers a landlord for the interruption of its rental income stream due to a casualty loss and, conversely, covers a tenant for any resulting business losses from the same event. Second, if correctly drafted, it avoids the problems associated with such losses being uncovered indirect losses, although this coverage may vary from policy to policy.

[3]—Liability Coverage

[a]—**In General.** Liability insurance, also known as commercial general liability (CGL), public liability and comprehensive general liability insurance, pays claims to the injured party and not the insured. Due to this feature, it is known as third party insurance. Both landlord and tenant will insist that the other carry a commercial general liability policy with, quite possibly, the other party being listed as an insured on the other's policy.

Coverage is more extensive under a liability policy than under the previously described property policies since the liability policy insures for both the third party's bodily injuries and property losses. Under the 1986 ISO Commercial General Liability Policy (CGL) currently in use today, *bodily injury* refers to sickness, disease or death, as well as physical injury. *Property damage* refers to physical injury to tangible property, including the loss of use of property that is either physically damaged or still intact but unusable due to the injury or casualty.

[b]—Claims-Made Coverage. CGL coverage insures against losses that occur during the time in which the policy is in place, even if the event or action that triggers the loss occurred prior to the effective date of the coverage. Under such a policy, the triggering issue for coverage is whether the liability policy was in effect when the claim was made. This is known as a "claims-made policy."[8]

Under claims-made coverage, the insured and claimant avoid the exercise of going back in time to identify the policy in effect at the time of the injury. The insurer, on the other hand, incurs the risk that it will have to pay out on claims submitted during the coverage period that occurred years before the policy began. The injured party may not know it has a loss until some time after the event or may not know the full extent of its losses until months or even years after the incident. Moreover, even after the claim has been identified and losses reasonably ascertained, the insured and injured party may spend a considerable period negotiating the loss before it is presented to an insurance carrier.[9]

Usually, a CGL policy includes contractual liability coverage although such a policy should be examined for its exclusions. However, contractual liability coverage is broad and a leased premises may fall under one of the covered insured contracts. Contractual liability coverage is typically complicated. This coverage may create various defenses, raise enforcement issues and exceed policy limits, thereby limiting the cover

---

[8] The claims-made policy is to be distinguished from the "occurrence policy." Under an occurrence policy, the injury or damage must have happened during the period in which the coverage was in effect. In an occurrence policy, the parties will look to the policy in effect at the time of injury or damage when the claim is later brought, even if that policy has subsequently lapsed.

[9] This is one of the main reasons why the occurrence basis policy still predominates over claims-made coverage even though there are instances such as directors and officers and errors and omissions liability where claims-made policies predominate.

age anticipated when the lease was negotiated. Because of these complexities, most parties negotiate to have the other name it as an insured or other beneficiary under its liability policy. [10]

[c]—**Common Beneficiary Designation.** The "named insured" is the party who pays the premiums and is specifically designated by name as the insured in the policy. If a landlord bargains for this designation in a tenant's policy, the insurer can hold the landlord jointly responsible with the tenant for the payment of premiums. Alternately, the landlord may wish to be named an "additional insured" under the policy. An additional insured has less protection than a named insured, but has no obligations under the policy nor is it responsible for paying premiums. [11]

There is a hierarchy to additional beneficiary status. Each has its own benefits and responsibilities. Insurers will frequently require that a party be designated as an "additional named insured." The additional named insured frequently is treated as a named insured for policy exclusions, but may not be accorded the same benefits as an additional insured. CGL policies usually have exclusions that apply only to named insureds, but not to an additional insured. Thus, the latter may actually have more protection under the policy than the party that takes out the policy and is paying the premiums. Moreover, underwriters typically are less likely to include a party as an additional named insured, making the inclusion of the party more difficult from the onset. [12]

Named insured and additional named insured status for a stranger to the policy will result in an adjustment of premiums since the insurer will want to include the risk record of the landlord or tenant requesting such designation in valuating the policy. The premiums will most likely increase since the insurer is effectively writing two policies.

---

[10] Landlord and tenant may negotiate to have the right to access the other party's liability policy. This can be done in two ways, the first being under the CGL Contractual Liability Coverage and the latter by including the other as an insured or other beneficiary under its liability policy.

[11] Together with "hold harmless clause" protection in the lease, additional insured status is a powerful contractual protection from lease liability. Each work hand in hand with the other since additional insured status alone is responsive only to limits and extent of the CGL policy accessed.

[12] C.S. Ferrell, Property and Liability Insurance in Lease Transactions at 25 (Faegre & Benson, Minneapolis, MN) (1991).

The last common designation is the "loss payee." The loss payee is the party to whom payment is made. A loss payee receives neither the benefits nor the responsibilities that a named, additional or additional named insured incur, but is simply the recipient of payments from a claim or loss.

[d]—**Policy Limits.** Policy limits provide another constraint on coverage. Even if a landlord or tenant obtains preferred status on the other party's policy, claims will be subject to whatever policy limits the insured contracted for with the carrier.

The 1986 CGL policy added a policy aggregate for insured incidences. Like its predecessors, the 1986 CGL contains "per occurrence" limits. Unlike the prior policies, the new CGL pays out claims subject to a total policy limit called the "general aggregate." For the landlord who is an additional insured under the policy of its tenant or any other party, its ability to collect under a liability policy is subject to the remaining coverage under the CAL's limits. Umbrella (or excess layer) policies will cover liability losses that exceed the insured party's primary CGL's liability policy's aggregate limits. Coverage under the umbrella policy is triggered after the primary or precedent policy's aggregate coverage is exceeded.

Umbrella policies serve to reduce premium costs. As insurance coverage becomes more expensive and difficult to obtain and there exists a good probability that an insured will not be covered for a significant portion of an expected or actual loss, landlords and tenants frequently work with one another to obtain two or more policies to assure their reimbursement from casualty losses. The umbrella policies kick in after the primary insurance limits have been reached. These excess policies provide the same coverage as primary policies, but increase the primary policy's limits at lower premium costs. Surplus insurance is also available to cover high and substandard risks, such as flood and earthquake losses, not normally insured for in the usual property or liability policies.

§ 25.04 Coinsurance

There are two common applications of the term "coinsurance." Both of these applications result in insurance protection and recoveries, but from quite different approaches.

[1]—Express Coinsurance

In the first application, expressly stated coinsurance requirements in the policy act to limit the amount that an insured can recover for an underinsured property. Property policies will contain a coinsurance limit on recovery in order to force an insured to keep its policy limits at or near the full value of the insured property. The property owner who fails to maintain its coverage at or near the current property value will be penalized in an amount proportionate to the underinsured value of the property.

The effect of a coinsurance penalty is illustrated as follows:

Example 1: [1]

$$\$ \text{ Loss} \times \frac{\text{Amount of Insurance Carried}}{\text{Amount of Insurance Required}} = \$ \text{ Recovery}$$

Hypothetical: An insured landlord owns a building with a replacement cost value of $2,500,000, but elects to insure the building under a policy with a $1,500,000 limit and an 80% coinsurance requirement. A fire occurs with a $700,000 loss. The landlord would recover $525,000 subject to its policy deductibles.

$$\$700,000 \times \frac{\$1,500,000}{\$2,500,000 \times (80\%)} = \$525,000$$

If a policy contains an "agreed amount" endorsement provision, however, such a provision would eliminate the need for coinsurance requirements. These endorsements are more important in instances

---

[1] See C.S. Ferrell, Property and Liability Insurance in Lease Transactions at 14-15 (Faegre & Benson, Minneapolis, MN) (1991).

where a landlord is dependant upon the tenant's insuring the full value of an office building in a triple net arrangement than in multi-tenant situations where the landlord will be maintaining its own insurance coverage.

[2]—Implied Coinsurance

[a]—In General. The second application of the term "coinsurance" should properly be referred to as "implied coinsurance" to distinguish it from the coinsurance discussed above. Implied coinsurance coverage of both landlord and tenant occurs when a court determines that upon its examination of facts and circumstances, the actions or words of one party to a lease (usually the landlord) or the requirements imposed upon the other party (usually the tenant) resulted in the second party's inclusion under the first party's insurance policy. Stated more simply, if at the time a lease was negotiated, a landlord made representations to the tenant that reasonably led the tenant to believe it would be covered under the landlord's insurance policy or imposed certain financial conditions upon the tenant so that the tenant was effectively paying for all or part of the landlord's insurance coverage, the tenant may prevail on a claim that it was entitled to reimbursement for losses covered by the landlord's policy under the doctrine of coinsurance. This is the so-called *Goldman* effect.

In *General Mills v. Goldman*, [2] one of the employees of the tenant negligently set off a destructive industrial plant fire. The owner's insurance carrier paid him the value of the land and building and then, as subrogee, intervened in the owner's suit against his tenant, General Mills. While the Eighth Circuit found that a lease provision relieved the tenant of the obligation to deliver or yield back the premises "in good condition" at the end of the term if the premises were destroyed by fire, it stretched its reasoning to bar the subrogation action by the landlord's insurer. [3] In ruling for the tenant, the *Goldman* court stated:

> "It is very clear that in light of all the provisions of the lease, the circumstances of its execution and the understanding about fire insurance coverage to which the lease was related that by the provision that on termination of the lease the tenant would return the property in good condition 'loss by fire ... excepted' the parties meant a loss by fire such as is always meant when men are talking about or figure on the risk

---

[2] 184 F.2d 359 (8th Cir. 1949).

[3] In the absence of the "yield up" clause in the lease, the tenant would have been otherwise liable to the landlord's insurer under the subrogation claim.

of it in business dealings— i.e., 'the loss by fire' — which always is insured against in ordinary course and against which the landlords intended here and did take out insurance in an amount greater than the owner's investment." [4]

The lease in *Goldman* required the tenant, General Mills, to return the premises in good condition (loss by fire and ordinary wear excepted) and barred the tenant from doing anything that might lead to an increase in insurance premiums. However, the lease did not specifically require the tenant to obtain fire insurance. The *Goldman* court found that it was the parties' understanding at the time the lease was negotiated that the landlord would assume responsibility for obtaining insurance and that the landlord had indeed insured the premises and had recovered under the policy. [5] In other words, the court held that the tenant was a coinsured under the landlord's policy.

Initially, *Goldman* opened the gates for insurers to bring actions for recovery of fire damage cases caused by negligent tenants. A series of cases followed *Goldman* in which insurers were able to recover against tenants on the basis of a subrogation action. [6] Negligent tenants, and even third parties who sold potentially dangerous materials to tenants, were all targets of these insureds' actions. [7]

Landlords have not been spared either. In *Western Fire Insurance Co. v. Milner Hotels, Inc.*, [8] the tenant's insurer recovered against a landlord-hotel operator for damage to the tenant's restaurant in the hotel from a fire started in the hotel. Other cases following the *Western Fire Insurance* case have had similar results.

Goldman's rationale of finding a party as a coinsured under the other's policy has been followed by many jurisdictions. Many of these

---

[4]　General Mills v. Goldman, 184 F.2d 359, 366 (8th Cir. 1949).

[5]　*Id.* at 365-66.

[6]　See, e.g., Home Ins. Co. v. Hamilton, 295 F.2d 108 (6th Cir. 1968); Hanover Insurance Co. v. Jacobson-Young, Inc., 294 So. 2d 564 (La. App. 1974); Bayley Products, Inc. v. American Plastics Products Co., 30 Mich. Ct. App. 590, 186 N.W.2d 813 (1971). For a more exhaustive compilation of cases and authority, see *Friedman on Leases* §9.9 at 529 n.20 (3d ed. 1990).

[7]　See, e.g., American Guaranty & Liability Insurance Co. v. Little, 328 So. 2d 708 (La. Ct. App. 1976) (sale of stereo receiver without adequate warning that its placement could cause a fire by blocking vents).

[8]　232 F.2d 779 (8th Cir. 1956).

cases have involved leases that expressly required the landlord to furnish insurance for the premises. Some of these cases have protected the negligent tenant even without the expressed requirement that the landlord secure fire insurance.

A number of cases have followed the holding in *Rizzuto v. Morris,* [9] in which the court reasoned that (1) it would be an unfair hardship to require a tenant to insure against its own negligence when it is paying, through its rent, for the fire insurance that covers the premises in favor of the landlord; (2) insurance companies expect to pay their insureds for their negligently caused fires and they adjust their rates accordingly; [10] and (3) the ordinary and usual meaning of "loss by fire" includes fires of negligent origin. The *Rizzuto* court concluded,

> "We do not mean our opinion states that a lessor may never shift to the lessee the burden of insurance against the lessee's negligence. We state only that; [where] there is no clear language or other admissible evidence showing an agreement to the contrary, a lease agreement should be read to place upon the lessor the burden of insuring the premises (as distinguished from a lessee's personal property) against a lessor's and lessee's negligence. Moreover, where the lease has been drawn by the lessor, the language will be strictly construed against the lessor and its insured." [11]

[b]—Commentary. [12] If a tenant is included in the landlord's policy as a named insured, the tenant is also insured under that policy. An insurance company has no subrogation claim against its own insured. To allow otherwise would permit the insurer to pass losses through to its insured and evade its obligations to cover its insured. [13] If it is later determined that insurance was obtained for the mutual benefit of tenant and landlord,

---

[9]   22 Wash. App. 951, 592 P.2d 688 (1979).

[10]   In effect, the tenant stands in the shoes of the insured landlord for the limited purpose of defeating a subrogation claim.

[11]   Rizzuto v. Morris, 22 Wash. App. 951, 592 P.2d 688, 690 (1979).

[12]   This subsection appeared in substantially identical form in A. DiSciullo, "A Guide to Subrogation In Commercial Leases," Real Estate L.J. (Spring 1992), and is reprinted herein with permission of Warren, Gorham & Lamont.

[13]   Chenoweth Motor Co. v. Cotton, 2 Ohio Misc. 123, 124, 207 N.E.2d 412, 413 (1965).

the subrogated insurer may not sue the tenant for fire damage resulting from the tenant's negligence. [14] This finding does not require a lease clause or any other writing to support it. However, it is necessary for the court to look at the parties' intent and find some agreement between them to include the tenant under the owner's policy. [15] In some instances, even if the parties merely discussed insurance generally, without any specific reference to fire insurance, the courts have concluded that the lease intended to cover the tenant was to be covered in the owner's fire policy. These findings have undoubtedly caused apoplexy for landlord's insurers and their agents.

Experts differ greatly from one another on whether a tenant is presumed to be a coinsured under an owner's policy. Even when the courts have found the tenant to be a coinsured under the landlord's policy for its own leasehold interest, the tenant may still be liable for damage to other parts of the landlord's property. [16] The cases are virtually indistinguishable from one another and serve as equally authoritative precedent for completely opposite conclusions.

In those instances where the tenant is presumed to be a coinsured, the courts' reasoning has been based on the theory that a landlord's expressed covenant to insure is for the benefit of both landlord and tenant. The basis for this conclusion is that the landlord would not have a section in the lease covering insurance if the insurance were only for the

---

[14] See, e.g.,West American Insurance Co. v. Pic Way Shoes of Cent. Mich., Inc., 110 Mich. Ct. App. 684, 313 N.W.2d 187, 188 (1981), *citing* Woodruff v. Wilson Oil Co., 178 Ind. Ct. App. 428, 382 N.E.2d 1009 (1978); Page v. Scott, 263 Ark. 684, 567 S.W.2d, 101, 103 (1978). See also Pendlebury v. Western Casualty & Surety Co., 89 Idaho 456, 406 P.2d 129, 136 (1965) (insurer barred from subrogation action against own insured).

[15] See, e.g, General Mills, Inc. v. Goldman, 184 F.2d 359 (8th Cir. 1949); Acquisto v. Joe R. Hahn Enter., 95 N.M. 193, 619 P.2d 1237, 1239 (1980); Rizzuto v. Morris, 22 Wash. App. 951, 592 P.2d 688, 690 (1979); Page v. Scott, 263 Ark. 684, 567 S.W.2d 101, 103 (1978). See also 49 Am. Jur. 3d *Landlord and Tenant* § 272, at 287 (1970); 51C C.J.S. *Landlord and Tenant* § 374, at 1000 n.68 (1968).

[16] Aetna Ins. Co. v. Craftwall of Idaho, Inc. 757 F.2d 1030 (1985); Agra-By-Products, Inc. v. Agway, Inc. 347 N.W.2d 142, 152 (N.D. 1984) (even where the tenant is a coinsured, it is still liable for amounts in excess of insurance). *Cf.*, Bonneville on the Hill Co. v. Sloane, 572 P.2d 402 (Utah 1977) (once the tenant is found to be a coinsured, it will escape liability for all portions of the landlord's property).

landlord's benefit. [17] Several decisions have taken this reasoning even farther. In the absence of an expressed agreement to the contrary, the landlord is presumed to carry insurance for the tenant's benefit. [18] A prominent expert has even suggested adopting a rule barring a landlord's insured from proceeding against a negligent tenant when the lease is ambiguous and the insurance policy is either silent or unclear. [19]

Such presumptions certainly will be disputed and a number of other courts have rejected this reasoning. There are a host of cases that have rejected this presumption of coinsurance and found the tenant liable for damage resulting from its own negligence in the absence of an expressed provision to the contrary. [20]

These cases and authorities seem to indicate that if the lease does not have a clause naming the tenant as a coinsured, the tenant is responsible for the damages it causes. At least one leading authority agrees. [21] Policy differences, then give a practitioner no clear direction in determining how a court will decide the issue of whether a tenant is a coinsured when the lease does not expressly provide for this. Almost each case becomes a test case, requiring expensive and time-consuming discovery to determine the parties' intent on whether the tenant is covered by the owner's policy.

The published cases on this issue are not easily reconciled. [22] Generally, the courts in the earlier decisions were reluctant to find the tenant to

---

[17] Monsanto Chemical Co. v. American Bitumuls Co., 249 S.W.2d 428, 432 (Mo. 1952); Fry v. Jordan Auto Co., 224 Miss. 445, 80 So. 2d 53, 58 (1955). *Accord* Newport News Shipbuilding & Drydock Co. v. United States, 34 F.2d 100, 106 (4th Cir. 1929). See generally Friedman, "Landlords, Tenants and Fires-Insurers' Right of Subrogation," 43 Cornell L.Q. 225, 228 & n. 12 (1957).

[18] See, e.g., Alaska Ins. Co., v. RCA Alaska Communications, Inc. 623 F.2d 1216, 1218 (Alaska 1981).

[19] R. Keeton, *Insurance Law* § 4.4(b) at 210 (1971).

[20] See, e.g., Acquisito v. Joe R. Hahn Enter., 95 N.M. 193, 619 P.2d 1237, 1239 (1980) (holding tenant liable because "[i]n the absence of an agreement between the parties specifying which of them will carry fire insurance for the benefit of both parties, or an express clause in the lease relieving a party from his own negligence, each party must bear the risk of loss for his own negligence.").

[21] Million, "Real and Personal Property," 33 N.Y.U. L. Rev. 552, 585 (1985).

[22] Aetna Ins. Co. v. Craftwall of Idaho, Inc., 757 F.2d 1030, 1033 (1985).

be a co-insured, especially if there was no expressed contractual agreement. [23] This position was consistent with the common law principles that the tenant was liable for its own negligence when the lease did not transfer the responsibility for repairs over the landlord. [24] Cases have been slowly rejecting this position and finding ways to have the tenant considered the landlord's co-insured, taking their cue from the *Goldman* court, which found a way to have the tenant covered for its employee's negligence when there was insurance covering the loss.

A novel theory holds that by paying its rent, the tenant has paid for its possible negligence in advance. These cases reason that the rent payments have somehow been adjusted to cover the landlord's expected fire insurance expenses. [25] Some courts have also accepted the notion that when the landlord has insured its building against "losses by fire," its tenants may reasonably expect that all fire losses caused by ordinary negligence will be covered by the owner's insurance even if the lease is silent on the issue of coinsurance. [26] As specious as this reasoning may seem to be, a number of courts have adopted this argument on the grounds that holding a tenant liable would encourage multiple insurance policies on the same building by the landlord and each of its tenants. [27]

---

[23] See, e.g., Maistico v. Hot Shoppes, Inc., 287 F.2d 349, 351 (D.C. Cir. 1961); Acquisto v. Joe R. Hahn Enter. 95 N.M. 193, 619 P.2d 1240 (1980). See generally Matan, "Liability for Loss by Fire Among Insurer, Tenant and Landlord," 18 Ohio St. L.J. 423, 425-426 (1957).

[24] United States v. Bostwick, 94 U.S. 53, 68, 24 L. Ed. 65 (1876); Miller v. Miller, 217 Miss. 650, 64 So. 2d 739 (1953). See also Annot., 10 A.L.R.2d 1023 (1950).

[25] Liberty Mutual Fire Insurance Co. v. Auto Spring Supply Co., 59 Cal. App. 3d 860, 131 Cal. Rptr. 211, 214-215 (1976); Sutton v. Jondahl, 532 P.2d 478, 482 (Okla. Ct. App. 1975). See also Rizzuto v. Morris, 22 Wash. App. 951, 592 P.2d 688, 692 n.3 (1979) (rejecting argument that public policy is violated by allowing a tenant to exculpate himself from liability for his own negligence); Page v. Scott, 263 Ark. 684, 567 S.W.2d, 101, 103-104 (1978). See Matan, "Liability for Loss by Fire Among Insurer, Tenant and Landlord," 18 Ohio St. L.J. 423, 432 (1957).

[26] Alaska Ins. Co., v. RCA Alaska Communications, Inc. 623 F.2d 1216, 1219 (Alaska 1981); Rizzuto v. Morris, 22 Wash. App. 951, 592 P.2d 688, 691 (1979); Sutton v. Jondahl, 532 P.2d 478, 482 (Okla. Ct. App. 1975).

[27] *Friedman on Leases* §§ 9.9-9.10 (3d ed. 1990).

Several noted insurance and leasing authorities have seized upon the reasoning of *Rizzuto v. Morris,* [28] that insurance companies write their policies with the expectation that they will have to pay their insureds for negligently caused fires and adjust their rates accordingly. These experts believe that subrogation is, essentially, a profit center for insurance companies, since the expected value of the fire losses have already been discounted in the premium charged to the insurer's clients. According to these authorities, subrogation is a windfall for the insurer. It plays no part in the rate schedules (or only a minor one) and no reduction is made in insuring interests, such as that of a secured creditor, when the subrogation right will obviously be worth something. Hence, in such a case, no reason appears for extending subrogation rights to the insurer. Even in the instances when casualty damage is caused by a negligent party, these authorities argue that the insurer should not shift the loss to the tortfeasor since the insurer has already been paid by the insured to cover the risk of any losses caused by the insured's negligence. [29]

A tenant relying upon the theory of coinsurance will encounter numerous pitfalls, the first being that with the split in authority, no tenant can reasonably expect to be able to predict the outcome of a casualty claim before an exhaustive trial and, at least, an initial appeal. Moreover, releasing the tenant from liability under a coinsurance theory may relieve a tenant for repaying casualty losses in its landlord's building but may not afford protection for damage to adjoining buildings. [30] Finally, the coinsured tenant only receives benefits to the extent of the limits of the landlord's policy. Damage over and above these limits is the tenant's responsibility. The measure of damages assessed against the tenant in at least one case included the replacement cost of rebuilding a building as well as lost profits and other consequential expenses. [31]

---

[28] 22 Wash. App. 951, 592 P.2d 688 (1979).

[29] E. Patterson, *Essentials of Insurance Law* 122 (1935). Accord Liberty Mutual Fire. Insurance Co. v. Auto Spring Supply Co., 59 Cal. App. 3d 860, 865, 131 Cal. Rptr. 211, 214 (1976) cited in *Friedman on Leases* § 9.9 at 542 (3d ed. 1990). See also Agra-By-Products, Inc. v. Agway, Inc. 347 N.W.2d 142, 152 (N.D. 1984) ("insurers expect to pay their insureds for negligently caused fires, and they adjust their rates accordingly").

[30] Hardware Mutual Insurance Co. v. C.A. Snyder, Inc., 242 F.2d 64 (3d Cir. 1957); Sannit v. Aarona, 297 F. Supp. 798 (D. Del. 1969); Agra-By-Products, Inc. v. Agway, Inc., 347 N.W.2d (N.D. 1984).

[31] Brown v. Aaron Rents. Inc. 414 F.Supp. 653 (W.D. Ok. 1975).

§ 25.05 Subrogation and Waivers of Subrogation [1]

Subrogation is a relatively static area in commercial leasing. The few cases on point address the issues of (1) whether the parties have effectively waived subrogation in trying to block an insurer of a casualty victim from proceeding in a subrogation claim against the defending party; (2) the clarity of the terms and the waiver of subrogation; and (3) whether other clauses in the lease can be construed in effect to bring about either a waiver of subrogation or a co-insurance situation.

[1]—Principles of Subrogation Law

Subrogation is the substitution of a party in place of a lawful claimant with regard to a demand, claim or right. [2] It is a derivative right and, as such, the party in whose favor subrogation is exercised (the subrogee) succeeds to the creditor's rights (the subrogor) in relation to the debt. [3] Subrogation is an equitable doctrine. A subrogated party stands in the shoes of a creditor and has no greater rights than those that the creditor initially had. The subrogated party is also subject to all defenses that a third-party tortfeasor might assert against a creditor. Under general equitable rules, when one person is substituted for another then that person is subrogated or succeeds to all of the other's rights as a creditor. The debtor is then obligated to pay the debt to the person to whom the creditor's rights have been subrogated. [4]

Only after its early applications in debtor-creditor law and surety law, were subrogation principles applied to insurance law with the injured insured party standing in the shoes of the original creditor and the insurance company being the party to whom the insured's rights were assigned. The rules with respect to subrogation and work of subrogation are fairly well-settled. Generally an insurance company will be able to bring a subrogation action against the party causing the injury or damage unless the parties have completely and clearly waived the subrogation rights of their insurers.

---

[1]   § 25.05 appeared in substantially identical form in A. DiSciullo, "A Guide to Subrogation in Commercial Leases," Real Estate L.J. (Spring 1992), and is reprinted herein with permission of Warren & Lamont, Boston, MA.

[2]   *Black's Law Dictionary* (4th ed. 1972).

[3]   83 C.J.S. *Subrogation* § 1.

[4]   See Verdier v. Marshallville Equity Co., 70 Ohio App. 43, 446 N.E.2d 636 (1980).

Two New Jersey cases at the turn of the century established the principle that if the insurance company settled for less than the full amount of the alleged liability, subrogation rights were not barred by a settlement with a tortfeasor. [5] These cases also established the principle that when an insurance company failed to recognize a waiver, an insurer was not prevented from proceeding against a tortfeasor even though subrogation had been waived in the contract. [6]

[2]—Waivers of Subrogation

Waivers of subrogation are generally recognized. They must, however, be clear and the insurance company given adequate notice of this contractual waiver. Protecting against a subsequent subrogation action is too important to be left later to judicial interpretation. The office lease should clearly cover wavier of an insurer's subrogation rights. Since insurers contemplate the parties waiving subrogation, this waiver is already reflected in the expected risks to be encountered by the insurer and encompassed in its premiums. With waivers of subrogation being generally accepted practice in commercial transactions, risk taking by landlord and tenant becomes more predictable; risk-shifting that otherwise would have eventually gone to the negligent party is ultimately absorbed by the insured's carrier. Waiver of subrogation has considerable benefits for the insurance companies as well. They need only to calculate the expected probability of their own insured's losses and the additional cost of the losses they might incur in subrogation claims against their insureds.

Most fire policies contain an endorsement that allows the insured to waive in advance its rights to recover against third parties for losses to its insured property. Such an endorsement means that the landlord's right to recover for its tenant's fault will rest with the landlord. Presumably, the landlord has required the tenant to obtain a fire policy with a similar endorsement so that any rights the tenant might have to recover from the landlord stay with the tenant.

This alternative, however, does not prevent the insurer from asserting any right it might have to recover its losses from a tortfeasor. A better

---

[5] Camden Fire Ins. Ass'n v. Prezioso, 93 N.J. Eq. 318, 116 A. 694 (1924); Fire Ass'n of Philadelphia v. Wells, 83 N.J. Eq. 484, 90 A. 244, *rev'd* 84 N.J. Eq. 484, 94 A. 619 (1915).

[6] *Id.*

approach would be to pass responsibility over to the insurer. This can be done by both obtaining an endorsement from the insurance company to waive its recovery rights and by inserting a clause in the lease to this effect. The following is an example of such a clause:

Example 2:

To the extent not prohibited by or violative of any policy of fire or extended coverage insurance issued to Landlord or to Tenant, Landlord and Tenant hereby waive the right to maintain a direct action against the other for damages arising out of such other's negligence or otherwise tortious acts or omissions, but only to the extent that the cost of repairing such damage is covered by insurance or would have been covered by insurance proceeds payable under any policy required to be maintained under this Lease, but not so maintained. Each policy of such insurance shall, if obtainable from the insurer without additional expense either, (i) contain a waiver of subrogation by insurer against Tenant and Landlord, as the case may be, or (ii) include the name of the Landlord or Tenant, as the case may be, as an additional insured, but not as a party to whom any loss shall be made payable. If the inclusion of either said provisions would involve an additional expense, either party, at its expense, may require such provisions to be inserted in the other's policy. In the event a party is unable to obtain such a waiver, it shall immediately notify the other of this inability. In the absence of such notification, each party shall be deemed to have obtained such waiver of subrogation.

Under the suggested clause, the landlord and tenant each waive their respective rights against one another and are required to obtain a waiver of subrogation from their insurance companies. Alternatively, a landlord and tenant may elect to have the other named as an additional insured in its own policy, effectively preventing the insurer from bringing a subrogation action since the insurer is barred from collecting against its own insured. In the last two sentences, the paragraph creates the presumption of the existence of a waiver of subrogation in the absence of notification to the other that a party is unable to obtain such an endorsement. While this last portion is intended to give a party the comfort that it will not face a subrogation action by the other party's insurer, the clause has not been litigated extensively. Presumably, the party that fails to notify the other will be liable under a breach of contract theory for any damages awarded to a subrogee. However, the effectiveness of this cause of action may be questionable if the defaulting party is either bankrupt or insolvent.

A properly drafted waiver of subrogation clause will ideally rule out a later subrogation action by an insurance company against a negligent party and thoroughly cover all instances in which coverage is intended. Several decisions have upheld these clauses.

Most cases involving waiver of subrogation clauses arise when insurers unsuccessfully attempt to go after a tortfeasor. In *Safeco Insurance Co. v. Capri,*[7] the owner recovered from his insurance company for the loss caused by fire damages to the tenant's leased premises. The insurer then sued the tenant in a subrogation claim for negligently causing the fire. The tenant argued that he could not be sued because the owner had taken out a policy to protect himself and the tenant. The court ruled that the tenant was an implied co-insured under the insurance policy.[8] As such, the insurer could not sue him. Insofar as the tenant had expected to be covered by the owner's policy when he signed the lease, nothing in the lease made him liable for negligently causing the fire.[9]

More recently, however, not all courts have followed this theme. In *Zurich-American Insurance Co. v. Eckert,*[10] the federal district court held that the insurer was entitled to subrogation against a tenant despite a lease provision requiring a waiver of subrogation. The insurer had no knowledge of such a provision in the lease, while its policy specifically provided for subrogation. The lease stated that each party's insurance policy would "contain waivers of the right of subrogation against Lessor and Lessee."[11] The lease, however, did not address this situation where the insurers were not notified of the waiver.

---

[7] 101 Nev. 429, 705 P.2d 659 (Nev. 1986).

[8] See § 25.04 *supra* for a discussion of co-insurance.

[9] See also Crowell v. Housing Authority of Dallas, 495 S.W.2d 8887 (1973); Fishel's Fine Furniture v. Rose Fruit Market, 474 S.W.2d 539 (1971); International Insurance Co. v. Medical-Professional Building of Corpus Christi, 405 S.W. 2d 867 (1966). These particular courts found generally that a waiver of subrogation rights between the parties precluded the insurer from exercising a subrogation claim.

[10] 770 F. Supp. 269 (E.D. Pa. 1991).

[11] *Id.* at 270.

The *Zurich* case gives rise to concern to protected parties that they cannot merely rely on a lease provision requiring waiver of subrogation if the insurer has not agreed. The rule in the states where this issue has been
determined, seems to be that the insurer is not bound by a waiver of subrogation to which it is not a party and of which it is not aware. [12] A simple solution for this anomaly is that each protected party should obtain a certificate from its insurer stating that the insurer has agreed to the waiver of subrogation similar to the representations commonly contained the certificate of insurance.

Insurers generally do not charge landlords or tenants extra for the waiver of subrogation endorsement. These clauses give the most extensive protection possible. A tenant should, however, be aware that a waiver of subrogation will not protect it from damage to another tenant's property and should insure itself for this possibility. On the other hand, if a landlord obtains waivers from all of its tenants, it should be fully protected.

---

[12] See I.C.C. Industries v. GATX Terminals Corp., 690 F. Supp. 1282, 1286 (S.D.N.Y. 1988).

§ 25.06 Indemnification and Exculpatory Clauses

Even before *Goldman*, [1] landlords and tenants contracted away their liability through exculpatory and indemnification clauses. In the typical clause, the landlord requires the tenant to indemnify or protect the landlord against losses or damages for any actions that may be brought later against the landlord by third parties due to activities on the tenant's premises or due to the tenant's activities. [2]

Indemnification provisions are usually triggered by actions brought by customers, contractors, employees and invitees using or working at the tenant's leased premises. These actions typically name both the tenant and the landlord with the tenant assuming the costs of the landlord's defense. *Exculpatory clauses* take this concept even farther. They require the tenant to absolve a landlord from any fault with regard to damages or injuries to the tenant even if they are due to the landlord's own negligence or willful actions. [3] Together, these clauses are an attempt by landlord and tenant to protect themselves from liability from direct or vicarious actions.

As expected, tenants and courts have not universally accepted these provisions. An indemnification clause can be dangerous for a tenant since a tenant's indemnification of its landlord may be tantamount to being an exculpatory clause. This will result in closer and stricter examination of the clause but, if enforceable, will result in the tenant waiving away almost all of its property and liability protection.

Indemnification clauses have other problems as well. It is doubtful whether indemnification covers a protected party's liability for punitive damages. Because the courts have not definitively ruled in this area, the respective liability of the protected party (the indemnitee) and protecting party (the indemnitor) for their shared activities has to be determined on a case-by-case basis.

In *Hartford Fire Insurance Co. v. Chicago Travel Terminal Co.*, [4] the court found the tenant liable to the landlord's insurer for a fire and explosion of unknown origin. The tenant's liability was based upon its agreement in the lease to indemnify and hold the lessor harmless from all losses

---

[1]   General Mills v. Goldman, 184 F.2d 359 (1949). See § 25.04[2][a] *supra.*

[2]   Tenants may also ask for a similar protection from their landlords.

[3]   Often, there are mutual indemnification provisions in a lease, but exculpatory clauses almost always run to the landlord's benefit.

[4]   12 Ill. App. Ct. 2d 539, 139 N.E.2d 770 (1956).

irrespective of the cause of the fire. Taken with the potential exculpatory effects of an indemnification clause, a tenant who is then agreeing to indemnify and hold a landlord harmless from third party liability may unwittingly become virtually an insurer for the landlord. The result would make the tenant liable for casualties for which it was not even remotely responsible.

When the indemnification provisions work properly, the tenant will usually hold the landlord harmless for the landlord's costs of defending a lawsuit and for any judgment arising from the action or will itself assume the defense of the action. These provisions are usually accompanied by an agreement to defend the landlord against any claims covered by the indemnity.

Frequently, the tenant will request the same protection from the landlord. Commentators are divided as to the effectiveness of this mutual indemnification. One commentator who criticizes the proponents of mutual indemnification points out that (1) these proponents do not fully consider the unfairness of the landlord shifting liability to the tenant by an indemnity clause; (2) there may be better standards than using a negligence standard in this risk shifting; and (3) carving exceptions to the indemnity for injury or damage caused by the landlord's negligence is superficial and may be counterproductive. [5]

If indemnification provisions, even mutual ones, give tenants and landlords pause for concern, then exculpatory clauses are even more troublesome. The usual exculpatory clause goes much further than an indemnification provision. Accordingly, it can be that much more damaging to a tenant if used to support an insurer's subrogation action against a lessor for fire damages or other casualty. The typical exculpatory clause attempts to relieve the landlord from all fault and any liability to the tenant. This waiver includes damages and injuries that are usually the landlord's responsibility, such as damages from leaking roofs, as well as from causes that are both within and beyond the landlord's control. These clauses address both tort and contractual liability.

It is long-standing law that the landlord can contractually exculpate itself from liability in commercial office leases. Even so, these clauses will be strictly construed against the landlord or other exculpated party. It is therefore important that the lawyer drafting the clause do so care-

---

[5]   E. Grant, "Subrogation, Indemnification and Exculpation in the Context of Commercial Leases," (Enforceability of Subrogation and Indemnity Clauses program, ABA, Atlanta, Georgia 1991).

fully to avoid any gaps in the protection. For instance, it has been held that where an exculpatory clause in a lease exempts the landlord for liability for damage resulting from the landlord's carelessness, negligence or improper contract, but fails to exculpate the landlord for liability for damage resulting from the defective design and construction of major structural components of the building, the landlord is not protected from liability for water damage to its tenant's computer system caused by the defective design of the roof. [6]

Some recent industry studies appear to indicate that state laws vary on whether a landlord may specifically avoid liability for its own negligence by relying solely upon an exculpatory clause. While most states either fully enforce or have placed only minor restraints upon the enforcement of exculpatory clauses in commercial leases, a few states have decided either by statute [7] or through case law [8] that these clauses are against public policy.

Recent decisions have not clarified the direction that the courts or legislatures will take in enforcing or interpreting these clauses. [9] There appears to be a slight trend for legislatures to invalidate these clauses. There is also equally strong authority in other states where the courts have voided exculpatory clauses for an owner's "active, willful or gross negligence." [10] A number of other states' highest courts have refused to enforce these clauses in commercial leases under an unequal bargaining position theory that is usually used only in turning these clauses aside in residen-

---

[6]   E. Grant, "Subrogation, Indemnification and Exculpation in the Context of Commercial Leases," at 11 (Enforceability of Subrogation and Indemnity Clauses program, ABA, Atlanta, Georgia 1991) *citing* Ultimate Computer Services, Inc. v. Biltmore Realty Co. 183 N.J. Super. 144, 443 A.2d 723, 30 A.L.R. 4th 963 (1982).

[7]   See, e.g., Ga. Code Ann. § 13-8-2; Ill. Ann. Stat. ch. 80, ¶ 91; Md. Code Ann., Real Prop. § 8-105; Mass. Gen. Laws Ann. ch. 186, § 15; N.Y. Gen. Oblig. Law § 5-321 (examples of statutes specifically prohibiting owners from entering exculpatory clauses in specific instances).

[8]   Tangere v. Manston, 127 N.H. 572, 503 A.2d 834 (1986) (struck down an exculpatory clause even though the state had no statute voiding such clauses).

[9]   E. Grant, "Subrogation, Indemnification and Exculpation in the Context of Commercial Leases," (Enforceability of Subrogation and Indemnity Clauses program, ABA, Atlanta, Georgia 1991).

[10]   Superior Cos. v. Kaiser Cement Corp., 733 P.2d 1158 (Ariz. 1986); Cregg v. Minister Ventures, 148 Cal. App. 3d 1107, 194 Cal. Rptr. 724 (1983); Gabl v. Alaska Loan & Investment Co., 6 Wash. App. 880, 496 P.2d 548 (1972); Talley v. Skelly Oil Co., 199 Kan. 767, 433 P.2d 425 (1967); Dalrey, Inc. v. Western Oil & Fuel Co., 148 N.W.2d 377 (Minn. 1967); Queens Insurance Co. of Am. v. Kaiser, 27 Wis.2d 571, 135 N.W.2d 247 (1965).

tial tenancies. [11] State cases have similarly held that an exculpatory clause will not be enforced if the owner's negligence involves his breaking the law or violating public interest. [12] However, it appears that the crest has been reached where state legislatures will void these clauses by statute. The courts have also left some doors open for enforcing these clauses in certain limited circumstances. [13] Except in the states where these cases and statutes are well-settled, a tenant cannot rely upon the courts to overturn an indemnification or exculpatory clause in its lease. Several recent cases, however, indicate the importance of clearly drafted and unambiguous exculpation clauses if these provisions are to be enforced. [14]

Are exculpatory clauses necessary in office leases? One would think not even though most states still enforce them. Given the inequities involved in requiring a tenant who may have little or no leverage in a lease negotiation contractually to exonerate a landlord from even its own actions, the comparative ease in achieving the same result from the insurance protection previously mentioned and the no fault indemnification discussed below, exculpatory provisions are archaic, inequitable and out of line with an office leasing transaction that is trying to achieve even a modicum of fairness.

---

[11] Johnson v. Mobil Oil, 405 F. Supp. 264 (E.D. Mich. 1976); Princeton Sportswear Corp. v. H&M Assoc., 507 A.2d 339 (Pa. 1986); Fireman's Fund Insurance Co. v. BPS Co., 23 Ohio Ct. App. 56, 491 N.E.2d 365 (1985); Porter v. Lumbermen's Investment Corp., 606 S.W.2d 715 (Tex. Ct. App. 1980); Smith v. Smith, 375 So. 2d 1041 (Miss. 1979); Weaver v. American Oil Co. 276 N.E.2d 144 (Ind. 1971); Mayfair Fabrics v. Henley, 48 N.J. 483, 226 A.2d 602 (1967).

[12] Trailmobile, Inc. v. Chargen, 370 S.W.2d 840 (Tenn. Ct. App. 1980); John's Dass Seafood Co. v. Weber, 369 So. 2d 616 (Fla. Dist. Ct. App. 1979).

[13] See, e.g., Hogeland v. Sibley, Lindsay & Curr. Co., 42 N.Y.2d 161, 397 N.Y.S.2d 602, 366 N.E.2d 263 (1977) (indemnification clause may be enforced if it requires both parties to be insured). See also Metropolitan Art Assoc. v. Wexler, 499 N.Y.S.2d 164 (1986) (indemnification clause void since violates Gen. Oblig. Law § 5-321).

[14] Topp Copy Products Inc. v. Singletary, 591 A.2d 298 (Pa. Sup. Ct. 1991) (water had leaked from above tenant's space, damaging its inventory; exculpatory clause provided that landlord was discharged "from and all liability for damages that might have resulted from the bursting or leakage of water pipes or other plumbing;" clause of this nature would not be enforced to protect landlord from its own negligent acts, unless the negligence was expressly stipulated in the clause; court found that exculpatory clause in the lease was ambiguous and could not be read to exculpate the landlord based on his own negligent conduct), relying on Rizzi v. Butler Petroleum, 588 A.2d 1 (1991).

§ 25.07 The "No Fault" Approach

[1]—In General

Recently, some notable authorities in the commercial leasing field have advanced the position that by combining certain lease provisions on insurance, indemnification and subrogation, the parties can achieve a "no fault" indemnification in the lease. The "no fault" scheme essentially shifts liability and property damage risk (without regard to fault) to the parties most able and willing to carry these risks, namely the landlord and tenant's insurance carriers. While the no fault indemnification is not absolute (some liability still remains), it is clearer, much fairer and more user friendly than the shifting of risk for liability and damage that typically occurs in most office lease negotiations.

One prominent commentator and commercial real estate attorney speaks most eloquently on this topic. He states: "A simple solution to the problem of negotiation on indemnity clauses is to convert the lease, as to indemnity, to no fault. Resistance to this proposition—as efficacious as it sounds—is nearly universal. Some day, I hope to have the reasons explained to me." [1]

The theory of "no fault" is simple. The risk of loss for any given damage or claim of damage falls on the party who is obligated to carry the insurance for such a loss under the terms of the lease. For example, as one commentator explains, if the landlord is obligated to carry an "all risk" policy for the building, it does not matter why the building burned down. [2] Except for certain exclusions, the landlord is then declared to be the responsible party.

"No fault" has clear advantages to both parties, particularly the landlord, since most of the insurance obligations rest with the tenant. Liability, property and insurance for tenant's improvements installed by the tenant are typically all a tenant's obligations. The landlord is usually obligated to carry property insurance only for the building and will be obli-

---

[1]   M. Zangel. *Negotiating Commercial Real Estate Leases* at 157 (1991). The authors could not agree more. If a risk is insurable at commercially acceptable rates, carefully and fully insure it, waive direct actions and claims one against the other, waive subrogation rights and get on with it. Look only to insurance. Nothing seems clearer than when each party is required to maintain insurance and there is a huge reservoir of insurers who most likely calculated in their premiums the cost of covering catastrophic damage caused by either its insured or the other party. That many still resist no fault protection does not make sense.

[2]   M. Zangel. *Negotiating Commercial Real Estate Leases* (1991).

gated to indemnify the tenant from any claims arising out of damage to the building. Except for the common areas, which the landlord is required to keep and maintain, the parties should be able to have simple "no fault" handling of normally insurable claims. Excluded from normal insurance are those casualties that are caused by gross negligence and those that the courts in a particular state will forbid indemnification of, such as a party's own acts of negligence or injuries and damage caused by a party's willful acts.

There may be some types of exculpatory clauses that have the potential to defeat even a "no fault" approach. Landlords may attempt to completely exculpate themselves or excessively limit the extent of their liability even for the negligence of their own work, for failure to respond to the tenant's needs or fulfill their own obligations under the lease.[3] Take, for example, the situation where a plumber negligently tightened a value on a high pressure water column, therefore shutting off pressure on lower floors. As a result, a valve exploded, flooding several floors. Due to an exculpatory clause in the lease, the landlord was able to avoid paying for the resulting damage.[4]

What are some of the reasons mitigating against no fault? Some carriers claim that premiums are based on the landlord's loss history. With a switch to "no fault," the party takes on the obligation for losses that may not be its fault, but rather are the fault of another party. However, a protected party can protect itself against this result by providing examples of its own exemplary loss record and stipulating that the "no fault" provisions will not apply if the other protected party does not keep an exemplary loss record.

One of the leading commercial leasing lawyers in the country makes one of the few persuasive arguments for retaining exculpatory clauses.[5] He states that due to the IRS regulations, landlords use partnership and non-corporate entities to enter into leases. Under these types of structures, the landlords are not able to avail themselves of the protection of the corporate shield. Therefore, they need the protection of exculpatory clauses against a tenant that might be able to bring an

---

[3] J. Wood, Navigating the Dangerous Shoals of Commercial Leases at 39-40 (1991) (on file with author). (Available in supplemental materials to "Analyzing Commercial Leases," Y64.3030-001, Assistant Adjunct Professor A. DiSciullo, New York University Graduate School of Real Estate, New York University Bookstore, New York, NY).

[4] Id.

[5] E. Halper, "Can You Find a Fair Lease?," The Real Estate L.J., vol. 14, no. 2 (Fall 1985).

Richards Lumber V Town of Mount Kisco

action or obtain a judgment against a landlord, possibly decimating the landlord vehicle and going against the individual partners comprising the ownership. [6]

The better, clearer and easier way, however, is the "no fault" scheme. A mutually satisfactory end can be achieved by clearly stating the intent of the parties to the lease, setting up a scheme of mutual waiver of subrogations and mutual indemnifications for items that can be indemnified, by striking out exculpation clauses and setting up strong insurance clauses.

[2]—A Sample "No Fault" Clause _)Sid Saltz drafted this clause_

The following is an example of a "no fault" clause prepared by a prominent real estate attorney: [7]

Example 3:

VI. RISK ALLOCATION AND INSURANCE

6.0. Allocation of Risks. The parties desire, to the extent permitted by law, to allocate certain risks of personal injury, bodily injury or property damage, and risks of loss of real or personal property by reason of fire, explosion or other casualty, and to provide for the responsibility for insuring those risks. It is the intent of the parties that, to the extent any event is insured for or required herein to be insured for, any loss, cost, damage or expense, arising from such event, including, without limitation, the expense of defense against claims or suits, be covered by insurance, without regard to the fault of Tenant, its officers, employees or agents ("Tenant Protected Parties"), and without regard to the fault of Landlord, its beneficiaries (if Landlord is an Illinois land trust), Agent, their respective partners, shareholders, members, agents, directors, officers and employees ("Landlord Protected Parties"). As between Landlord Protected Parties and Tenant Protected Parties, such risks are allocated as follows:

---

[6] _Id._ In the exculpatory clause to which this commentator refers (which may in many respects be a limitation of liability clause going to judgment rather than liability in the first place), the most serious harm a lawsuit ever does is to take the landlord's interest in the real estate. He suggests inducing the tenant to go along with the clause by providing "that the tenant will have the right to make deductions from rent to recoup the cost of curing a failure by the landlord to comply with his obligations under the lease." He notes, however, that this concession should be limited to protect the landlord.

[7] Excerpts from "no fault" clause prepared by Sidney G. Saltz, Esq. of Chicago, IL. Copyright 1995. Reprinted with permission of the author.

(a) Tenant shall bear the risk of bodily injury, personal injury or death, or damage to property, of third persons occasioned by events occurring on or about the Leased Premises, regardless of the party at fault. Said risks shall be insured as provided in Section 6.1(a).

(b) Landlord shall bear the risk of bodily injury, personal injury, or death or damage to the property of third persons occasioned by events occurring on or about the Real Estate (other than premises leased to tenants), provided such event is occasioned by the wrongful act or omission of any of Landlord Protected Parties. Said risk shall be insured against as provided in Section 6.2(a).

(c) Tenant shall bear the risk of damage to Tenant's contents, trade fixtures, machinery, equipment, furniture and furnishings in the Leased Premises arising out of loss by the events required to be insured against pursuant to Section 6.1(b).

(d) Landlord shall bear the risk of damage to the building on the Real Estate arising out of loss by events required to be insured against pursuant to Section 6.2(b).

Notwithstanding the foregoing, provided the party required to carry insurance under Section 6.1(a) or Section 6.2(a) hereof does not default in its obligation to do so, if and to the extent that any loss occasioned by any event of the type described in Section 6.0(a) exceeds the coverage or the amount of insurance required to be carried under said Sections or such greater coverage or amount of insurance as is actually carried, or results from an event not required to be insured against or not actually insured against, the party at fault shall pay the amount not actually covered.

6.1. Tenant's Insurance. Tenant shall procure and maintain policies of insurance, at its own cost and expense, insuring:

(a) the Landlord Protected Parties (as "named insureds"), and Landlord's mortgagee, if any, of which Tenant is given written notice, and Tenant Protected Parties, from all claims, demands or actions made by or on behalf of any person or persons, firm or corporation and arising from, related to or connected with the Leased Premises, for bodily injury to or personal injury to or death of any person, or more than one (1) person, or for damage to property in an amount of not less than $3,000,000.00 combined single limit per occurrence/aggregate. Said insurance shall be written on an "occurrence" basis and not on a "claims made" basis. If at any time during the term of this Lease, Tenant owns or rents more than one location, the policy shall contain an endorsement to the effect that the aggregate limit in the policy shall apply separately to each location owned or rented by Tenant. Landlord shall have the right, exercisable by giving written notice thereof to Tenant, to require Tenant to increase such limit if, in Landlord's reasonable judgment, the amount thereof is insufficient to protect the Landlord Protected Parties and Tenant Protected Parties from judgments which might result from such claims, demands or actions. If Tenant is unable, despite reasonable efforts in good faith, to cause its liability insurer to insure the Landlord Protected Parties as "named insureds", Tenant shall nevertheless cause the Landlord Protected Parties to be insured as "additional insureds" and in such event, Tenant will protect, indemnify and save harmless the Landlord Protected Parties from and against any and all liabilities, obligations, claims, damages, penalties, causes of action, costs and expenses (including without limitation reasonable attorney's fees and expenses) imposed upon or incurred by or asserted against the Landlord Protected Parties, or any of them, by reason of any bodily injury to or personal injury to or death of any person or more than one person or for damage to property, occurring on or about the Leased Premises, caused by any party including, without limitation, any Landlord Protected Party, to the extent of the amount of the insurance required to be carried under this Section 6.1(a) or such greater amount of insurance as is actually carried. Tenant shall cause its liability insurance to include contractual liability coverage fully covering the indemnity hereinabove set forth.

(b) All contents and Tenant's trade fixtures, machinery, equipment, furniture and furnishings in the Leased Premises to the extent of at least ninety percent (90%) of their replacement cost under Standard Fire and Extended Coverage Policy and all other risks of direct physical loss as insured against under Special Form ("all risk" coverage). Said insurance shall contain an endorsement waiving the insurer's right of subrogation against any Landlord Protected Party, provided that such waiver of the right of subrogation shall not be operative in any case where the effect thereof is to invalidate such insurance coverage or increase the cost thereof (except that Landlord shall have the right, within thirty (30) days following written notice, to pay such increased cost, thereby keeping such waiver in full force and effect.

(c) Tenant Protected Parties from all worker's compensation claims.

(d) Landlord and Tenant against breakage of all plate glass utilized in the improvements on the Leased Premises.

6.2. Landlord's Insurance. Landlord shall procure and maintain policies of insurance insuring:

(a) All claims, demands or actions made by or on behalf of any person or persons, firm or corporation and arising from, related to or connected with the Real Estate, other than premises leased to tenants, for bodily injury to or personal injury to or death of any person, or more than one (1) person, or for damage to property in an amount of not less than $3,000,000.00 combined single limit per occurrence/aggregate. Said insurance shall be written on an "occurrence" basis and not on a "claims made" basis. If at any time during the term of this Lease, Landlord owns more than one location, the policy shall contain an endorsement to the effect that the aggregate limit in the policy shall apply separately to each location owned by Landlord.

(b) The improvements at any time situated upon the Leased Premises against loss or damage by fire, lightning, wind storm, hail storm, aircraft, vehicles, smoke, explosion, riot or civil commotion as provided by the Standard Fire and Extended Coverage Policy and all other risks of direct physical loss as insured against under Special Form ("all risk" coverage). The insurance coverage shall be for not less than 90% of the full replacement cost of such improvements with agreed amount endorsement. Landlord shall be named as the insured and all proceeds of insurance shall be payable to Landlord. Said insurance shall contain an endorsement waiving the insurer's right of subrogation against any Tenant Protected Party, provided that such waiver of the right of subrogation shall not be operative in any case where the effect thereof is to invalidate such insurance coverage or increase the cost thereof (except that Tenant shall have the right, within thirty (30) days following written notice, to pay such increased cost, thereby keeping such waiver in full force and effect).

(c) Landlord's business income, protecting Landlord from loss of rents and other charges during the period while the Leased Premises are untenantable due to fire or other casualty (for the period reasonably determined by Landlord).

(d) Flood or earthquake insurance whenever, in the reasonable judgment of Landlord, such protection is necessary and it is available at commercially reasonable cost.

6.3. Form of Insurance. All of the aforesaid insurance shall be in responsible companies. As to Tenant's insurance, the insurer and the form, substance and amount (where not stated above) shall be satisfactory from time to time to Landlord and any mortgagee of Landlord, and shall unconditionally provide that it is not subject to cancellation or non-renewal except after at least thirty (30) days' prior written notice to Landlord and any mortgagee of Landlord. Originals of Tenant's insurance policies (or certificates thereof) satisfactory to Landlord, together with satisfactory evidence of payment of the premiums thereon, shall be deposited with Landlord at the Commencement Date and renewals thereof not less than thirty (30) days prior to the end of the term of such coverage.

This clause achieves a number of desired goals when drafting an office lease. It is very well written and clear in its intent. Section 6.0, entitled "Allocation of Risks," explicitly states the parties' intent to allocate the risks normally incurred in a commercial leasing transaction between the parties, and where possible, to shift those risks to an insurer.

This opening section achieves several purposes. First, by clearly stating the contractual intent of the parties at the outset, the provision reduces the possibility of the clause being misinterpreted by strangers to the deal or by the parties themselves at some later date. Second, a clearly drafted clause stating the intent of the parties reduces the possibility of ambiguity in the interpretation of the entire provision. Thus, the parties may avoid the need later to find the persons who originally negotiated the deal, if indeed they can be found, in order to determine what the parties intended to do when they negotiated this provision. In the authors' experience, even if the original negotiators later surface for depositions or trial testimony, their recollections of a particular transaction are often so vague that their testimony is of little or no use in interpreting a particular clause. Even if this testimony is supported by notes or memoranda made contemporaneously with the transaction, it is the authors' experience that a clearly drafted provision is much more useful in constructing the contractual intention of the landlord and the tenant than later recollections that can become muddied or biased with the passage of time.

Having acknowledged the risk allocation that is inherent in any lease negotiation, Section 6.0 then defines the risks that will be apportioned between the landlord and tenant and the manner in which those risks will be shared. Overall, subsections 6.0(a) through (d) attempt to apportion the risk fairly to the party most able to bear that risk or the party who receives the most beneficial use of the area or property for which it is responsible. Thus, the tenant bears the risk for injury and damage occurring on or about the leased premises (of which the tenant is the sole occupant and beneficiary under subsection (a)), as well as for damages to its contents, trade fixtures and other property on the leased premises under subsection (c). Similarly, the landlord bears the risk of loss for injuries and damages arising out of events in the "building" (outside the leased premises) and on the "property" under subsections (b) and (d). Each party agrees to indemnify the other for third party claims in the areas for which they are responsible under subsections (a) through (d). The result of this clause is that each party has the responsibility of bearing the risk or expense for property or events most within control of that party.

This is the first step in establishing a "no fault" framework. In the acknowledgment of risk allocation, the identification of risks that a party can best handle and by setting a mutual indemnification scheme, the parties have begun the process of shifting the casualty and liability risk to the parties in the business of handling such risks—the insurers. So long as the landlord and tenant maintain the insurance required in Sections 6.1 and 6.2, subject to periodic review for adequacy of coverage, the parties should not have to worry about incurring any liability beyond that for which they have contracted. [8]

---

[8] Note that the insurance amounts should be adequate to cover any claims since there is an exception for this preliminary "no fault" scheme. In the last paragraph of Section 6.0, the party at fault is responsible for paying the amount of any damages or claims not actually insured.

The parties' insurance requirements are remarkably similar in the spirit and intent of a "no fault" scheme. Each party is required to insure the other party and itself from liability and property damage claims with at least a $3 million combined single limit policy. The insurance is to be written on an occurrence basis rather than a claims made basis so that the protection runs from the originating event. Each party is also required to at least ask its insurer to name the other party as the "named insured" or, being unable to do that, as an "additional insured." The effect of adding the other as an insured is to cut off any possibility of a subrogation action against a party responsible for generating the claim by an insurer paying out on a claim, thus ending the action at the insurer's doorstep. Subsections 6.1(b) and 6.2(b) mirror one another in requiring the tenant's and landlord's property carrier to include an endorsement in which the insurer waives any subrogation rights against the other party, achieving the same result on property claims as is achieved in liability claims under subsections 6.1(a) and 6.2(a).

The insurance requirements are not exact mirror images of one another, however. Under Section 6.1(a), the landlord has the right to require the tenant to increase its liability limits if the amounts are insufficient to cover the parties from possible claims, damages or actions, in the landlord's reasonable judgment. The tenant does not have a reciprocal right to have the landlord increase its insurance. The provision is also not clear as to the extent of protection that a tenant receives from exposure for damage to the entire building or property due to a fire or other casualty caused by the negligence of the tenant or one of its employees, contractors, customers or agents. It is in this area that the real exposure can occur to the tenant. If the building or property are not adequately insured by the landlord, then the tenant may find itself liable for paying the balance of the costs to replace or restore the building or property not covered by the landlord's policy.

Overall, this risk allocation and waiver of claims provision is a thorough attempt at creating a fair apportionment of the risks and liability between the parties in the event of fire or other casualty. The provision clearly states its intent, allocates responsibilities and finds ways to place the liabilities on the parties intended by the landlord and tenant to incur it.

§ 25.08 Summary

In striving to reach a "no fault" position with respect to liability for fire damage or other casualties, landlords and tenants should be aware of the numerous steps necessary to achieve this result. Each party must realize the pitfalls of such devices as indemnification and exculpatory provisions and, especially, the ramifications of a subrogation action in the event of a casualty.

While a growing number of states have placed restrictions on unrestrained exculpation and indemnification provisions in commercial transactions, neither a tenant nor a landlord should rely upon a court overturning an exculpatory or indemnification clause in a commercial lease in order to defeat a claim for damages from the protected party. The courts and legislatures are still not uniformly clear on their interpretation of these clauses and have, in some instances, retreated from their former positions of viewing these provisions with a jaded eye.

A tenant who believes that it is automatically covered on a landlord's policy as a coinsured when the lease does not expressly provide this coverage is not entitled to any sympathy when it is later liable for fire loss. The cases are much too sparse on the point to find such comfort. If a common thread is apparent from these cases, it is that the courts may stretch their reasoning to extend fire coverage to a tenant whose negligence has caused fire damage to a building when the building is insured by the owner. However, the courts will not always do this.

While this reasoning is partially based on some experts' opinion that subrogation presents a windfall to the insurance companies, the application of coinsurance is better suited for residential leasing situations. [1] Subsequent cases may start to chip away at this notion of coinsurance in commercial leases, however, tenants should take notice and structure their insurance and casualty clauses accordingly.

Subrogation can still defeat all precautions taken by landlords and tenants in establishing a "no fault" liability scheme in their leases. Insurers can still swoop in after a casualty on a subrogation claim and

---

[1] In residential leasing, the bargaining positions are usually mismatched and the resulting liability is much more catastrophic to the negligent tenant than in commercial transactions where the parties have relatively equal bargaining positions, better access to competent representations, and better opportunities for comprehensive insurance coverage.

recoup their losses against a negligent party. The only sure way of deflecting these actions is through (1) a waiver of subrogation clause in the lease; (2) a clear and concise waiver of direct actions or claims of landlord and tenant against each other; and (3) obtaining certificates of mutual waiver of the insurer's rights of subrogation recovery from each insurance carrier. The waivers must, however, be clear, explicit, and binding upon the landlord's and tenant's respective insurance companies. Only then will the ominous threat of a subrogation action be dissipated as it properly should in a risk free commercial transaction rather than later taking center stage after casualty strikes.

NOTES

7

COMMERCIAL LEASES AND INSURANCE: A PRIMER FOR LAWYERS

Jay L. Paxton
Jodi B. Fedor

I. INTRODUCTION

Many lawyers who draft and negotiate commercial leases have only at best a general knowledge of insurance coverages, in part because insurance markets, policies and practices evolve over time. Unfortunately, the usually slow pace of that evolution may sometimes abruptly hasten in response to mounting losses from previously unanticipated or underappreciated risks, often escaping the notice of the inattentive lawyer.

Many leases prepared today contain insurance provisions drafted years before and carried from transaction to transaction without careful analysis. For example, some such provisions still require "fire and extended coverage insurance," although that form of policy is no longer in wide use. In many cases, by the use of outdated and broadly stated insurance requirements, leases may unintentionally require one or the other of the parties to obtain coverages which are not commonly available or which are available only with exclusions that render the coverage significantly narrower than the broadly described coverage required by the lease.

In addition to problems resulting from changes in coverages caused by the evolution of the insurance markets, difficulties may also arise from the fact that insurance policies and coverages in many states may vary from company to company. Some standardization may be achieved through legislation, however, and through the fact that many policies are based on forms prepared by the Insurance Services Office (known as the "ISO").

Given the limited familiarity of many leasing lawyers with insurance law and practices generally, and most importantly with the specific coverages maintained by their clients, it is prudent (perhaps essential) for counsel to consult with the client's insurance broker or risk manager regarding the insurance obligations in a lease, and to have him or her review not only the provisions regarding insurance, but also the provisions pertaining to

-1-

damage and destruction, indemnification, waivers and releases, and obligations for
compliance with laws.

II.   PROPERTY INSURANCE

Overview

Description of Policies. Property insurance is referred to as first party
insurance, which of course simply means the insurer pays proceeds to the insured party.
There are two general types of property insurance coverage: (1) named-perils coverage,
which identifies the specific risks insured against, and includes ISO standard forms for
"basic" and "broad" coverage, and (2) all-risk coverage, which covers all direct physical loss
unless it is caused by a peril specifically excluded from coverage under the terms of the
policy. All-risk insurance is the form more commonly required in commercial leases today.

All-risk insurance does not cover losses from earthquakes or floods. Other
exclusions cause all-risk insurance not to cover code-mandated upgrades to property required
to be added in the course of rebuilding after a casualty, damage to computer and electronic
data processing equipment, or damage to boilers and machinery. Endorsements to the all-
risk policy, or separate policies of insurance, can usually be obtained to cover those excluded
losses.

A significant change in the use of the insured property, or a breach of
conditions to coverage contained in the policy, may create a defense in the insurer under a
property insurance policy. In addition, property insurance policies may provide that a
substantial increase in hazardous activities at the premises will give the insurer a defense
against liability for losses occurring during those activities, regardless of whether the loss
resulted from the activity. The insurer's defense against liability may be limited, however,

-2-

370

to increased hazards of which the insured was aware.

The "loss-payee" under a property insurance policy is the party to whom insurance proceeds will be paid by the insurer. Generally, it makes sense to designate the party who will be responsible for restoration and repair as the loss-payee. However, if the casualty affects the building or improvements which are owned by the landlord, the landlord may believe it has a legitimate interest in controlling the disbursement of the proceeds in order to assure that reconstruction will occur, even if the tenant is responsible for the work. In those circumstances, the landlord may insist that it be the loss-payee. Also, a lender often may require that it be named as the loss-payee in order to control the application of the proceeds in accordance with the loan documents.

Lease provisions establishing the amount of insurance to be carried should use the term "full replacement cost," rather than "actual cash value," since the latter would result in a deduction of depreciation and obsolescence from the value of the property insured. To further assure that the policy will cover the full cost of repair and to avoid co-insurance problems, an agreed amount endorsement or guaranteed replacement cost coverage (discussed below) is generally also advisable.

Endorsements. Additional coverage can be added to insurance policies by endorsements, many of which simply add categories of covered losses, but only to the extent those losses result from perils insured against by the underlying policy. For example, coverage under a business interruption or rental income endorsement is ordinarily limited to income or rent lost due to perils covered by the policy. Some endorsements for property insurance policies that may be appropriate in a leasing context (in addition to endorsements adding coverage for excluded perils such as earthquake, flood, boiler and machinery or

-3-

computer damages), are discussed below.

Rental Income:

Rental income insurance (also known as rent loss or rent continuation insurance) reimburses the landlord for lost rents (which may include pass-throughs and other recurring charges, in addition to base rent) resulting from a covered peril. Cost savings realized by the landlord while the tenant is not using the premises, such as savings in energy usage or janitorial services, may be deducted from rent in determining available proceeds of the policy. Often, rental income insurance may be most easily obtained in connection with a property insurance policy, which also provides an incentive to the insurer to reduce the period of rental loss by cooperating to assure that reconstruction occurs without delay.

Lenders typically require the landlord to carry rental income insurance. Even without this requirement by a lender, the landlord often carries it because its cost is relatively low and can often be passed through to the tenant.

Rental income insurance is usually limited to a set period (typically 12 months) after the casualty.

Rental income insurance does not typically include denial of a tenant's use of the premises due to landlord's voluntary acts, such as interruption in services or alterations to the building (as opposed to casualty), but coverage for denials of use (such as utility interruptions) may be added by a rider to the rental income endorsement.

Business Interruption/
Additional Expense:

Business interruption insurance reimburses the tenant for its inability to use the premises and loss of business resulting from a peril insured against by the underlying policy. Business interruption insurance coverage may also be extended to cover loss of business resulting from a casualty occurring outside the premises, such as a fire in an anchor store that the tenant relies upon for customer traffic. Extra expense insurance covers additional expenses incurred by tenant after a casualty for such things as temporary replacement space (offset by any rent abatement received by tenant) and relocation costs.

-4-

372

Agreed Amount:	An agreed amount endorsement provides an agreement by the insurer that the full amount of any loss (up to the policy limits) will be paid, even if the property is underinsured. This addresses the coinsurance concerns discussed below.
Guaranteed Replacement Cost:	This endorsement goes beyond the agreed amount endorsement, providing for payment of the lesser of the replacement cost or the amount actually incurred to repair or replace, without regard to the policy limit.
Ordinance or Law:	An ordinance or law endorsement may be appropriate for leases of older buildings. If the insured property is rebuilt under updated codes, required upgrades will not be covered under standard policies, absent this endorsement.
Inflation Guard:	An inflation guard endorsement will automatically increase liability limits to account for the effects of inflation.
Leasehold Interest:	This endorsement compensates the tenant for any difference between rent incurred for replacement space and the rent under the insured lease if the insured lease is terminated after a casualty. This endorsement is not necessary unless the lease is particularly favorable to the tenant.

Other commonly used endorsements cover plate glass, vandalism, extended indemnity periods, service interruption, builders' risk, earthquake sprinkler leakage (eliminating the exclusion from sprinkler leakage coverage for earthquakes when earthquake insurance is not obtained), and reproduction cost endorsement (for historic buildings being restored to a particular condition).

Property Insurance Leasing Issues

Coverage Under a Lease. Regardless of which party actually obtains the insurance policies required under a lease, the tenant often ultimately pays for it, either directly, as a component of rent, or through the landlord's pass-throughs of operating

-5-

expenses. Therefore, the responsibility for carrying property insurance should be determined by considering such factors as: which party can obtain the best price; whether the landlord wants to retain control over the insurance being obtained; which party is responsible for repairs; lender requirements; and the parties' existing insurance programs.

In office leases, deductible amounts paid by the landlord often will be passed through to the tenant as operating expenses. It is therefore in the tenant's interest to make certain any policies carried by the landlord do not have excessive deductibles, so that if a casualty occurs the expense that is passed through to the tenant is not excessive. Because of the usually very high deductibles which are common in earthquake insurance coverage, the tenant should consider negotiating for a limit on the amount of any deductible expense which can be passed through.

Typically, the landlord insures the building shell and common areas, and the tenant insures its personal property and fixtures. A tenant in a multi-tenant building will not have an insurable interest in the whole building, but only in the premises and perhaps those portions of the building which affect them. However, in a single-tenant building it may be appropriate for the tenant to insure the building shell, as well as the tenant improvements, particularly if the tenant is managing the building and is responsible for any repair or restoration after a casualty.

Tenant improvements may be insured by either party, but it is usually preferable for the party insuring the building shell to include tenant improvements in its property insurance policy, for several reasons. In multi-tenant buildings, it is usually significantly less expensive for the landlord to insure the tenant improvements than for each tenant to individually insure their own. In addition, if a casualty occurs, the rebuilding process is complicated if multiple insurers are involved. A further complication can arise if

-6-

the delineation between the shell and tenant improvements is not clear, which can be avoided by having a single insurer cover both.

If a tenant in a multi-tenant building is insuring its own tenant improvements, it should of course try to exclude premiums for insurance on other tenants' leasehold improvements from the operating cost pass-throughs.

Significant issues of fairness may also exist, however, where the levels of tenant improvements vary widely from premises to premises within a building. A tenant having only building standard improvements will not want to see its share of operating expenses include premiums on luxury improvements of other tenants. That issue may be addressed by having the landlord insure the tenant improvements to a certain level of replacement cost (perhaps the cost of replacing only building standard improvements), with the tenant separately insuring the remainder of the replacement cost of any above-standard improvements which it may have in its premises.

Whatever the allocation of obligations as between the tenant and the landlord, it is always important to clearly designate in the lease the responsibility for insuring each portion of the premises and building, including the tenant improvements, to avoid overlapping insurance. There is no reason for landlord and tenant to both insure the same property, and in fact, if the same casualty is insured under multiple policies it can create potential coinsurance and allocation issues.

If property insurance is carried by a party that does not own the property being insured, the property owner should be named an "additional insured" under the policy.

Coinsurance. Property insurance should always be written on a full replacement cost basis. If it is not, and an actual cash value policy is instead obtained, the

-7-

insurer may deduct the building's depreciation and obsolescence from the replacement cost of the building when calculating insurance proceeds. In addition, if the property insurance policy does not cover the full replacement cost and the insurance includes a 100% coinsurance clause, the insured may be a coinsurer for the deficiency. For example, if the building is insured for 80% of its replacement value, the insurance proceeds will only be 80% of the loss, even if the loss is a partial loss. Any increased value resulting from tenant improvements or alterations to a building should be taken into account in the liability limits on property insurance policies in order to avoid coinsurance penalties.

Rent Abatement. A tenant will want its rent to abate under certain circumstances which temporarily prevent or restrict the tenant's use of the premises, such as casualty or interruption of services. If the landlord agrees to abate rent under the lease, the landlord should attempt to limit the abatement right to rental income insurance proceeds received by landlord. As discussed above, rental income insurance is commonly obtained as an endorsement to a property insurance policy, and it will be limited to perils covered by the underlying insurance policy. For example, if there is no earthquake insurance on the building, rental income insurance will not be available for lost rents resulting from an earthquake.

Willful Misconduct Exclusion. If a loss results from the willful misconduct of the party obtaining the property insurance, the insurance policy may be invalidated. For example, if the tenant obtains the property insurance for the building, and then commits arson, the resulting loss would not be covered by the property insurance. Such an exclusion is usually applicable only if the party obtaining the insurance and committing the misconduct (i) is an

-8-

individual, or (ii) specifically authorized the misconduct by corporate or partnership act (and

not just committed negligence by not supervising employees). That problem can be

addressed by the parties indemnifying one another for property damage caused by their

willful misconduct, and willful misconduct can be excluded from any waiver of claims,

although the credit of the party committing the misconduct may limit the value of such an

indemnity.

III. COMMERCIAL LIABILITY INSURANCE

Overview

        Description of Policies. Commercial general liability ("CGL") insurance is

third party insurance, which means the insurer pays proceeds directly to third parties making

claims against the insured parties. The basic CGL policy is "primary," covering loss from

bodily injury, property damage and personal injury to third parties, with set liability limits.

An "excess" liability policy, which increases the liability amount but not the scope of

coverage, may be added to the primary policy. An "umbrella" policy is somewhat similar to

an excess policy, but may offer broader coverage on one or more primary or excess policies.

If the different layers of policies vary as to their effective dates, as to their exclusions, or as

to whether or not they are issued on an occurrence basis, serious gaps in coverage may

occur. Accordingly, if an excess or umbrella policy is to be relied upon to provide coverage

required under the lease, the lease should require that all policies be concurrent and that the

excess and umbrella policies provide coverage that is at least as broad as the primary policy.

        Two ISO-created commercial general liability forms are currently in

widespread use: the 1986 and 1988 forms. The new forms include coverage for "contractual

liability," which was previously available only through an endorsement such as a Broad Form

Comprehensive General Liability Endorsement. Contractual liability insurance provides protection against claims by third parties for personal injury or property damage as to which an indemnity obligation is contractually assumed by the tenant under the lease. Such coverage is of course subject both to the policy limits and to the exclusions from the CGL policy, the most significant of which may be the pollution exclusions, and applies to contractually assumed tort liability only. It does not cover breaches of the lease itself. It is also important to note that the extent of insurance coverage will be limited by the scope of the indemnity itself.

The new ISO CGL forms contain broad pollution exclusions. If appropriate to the tenant's use, special pollution coverage may be available for particular pollution risks.

There is some potential overlap between property and CGL insurance. However, CGL policies are written to prevent the insured from relying on them for coverage that would typically be included in property policies. For example, many CGL policies contain exclusions for tenant's negligence with respect to property in the "care, custody and control" of the insured (for example, landlord's property which is maintained by the tenant under the lease). In addition, CGL policies may include by endorsement fire liability coverage, covering fires caused by the insured tenant. However, the liability limits for this coverage are typically low, and landlords instead should rely on property insurance for coverage of these losses.

Currently, it is common for CGL policies to be written on a "combined single limit per occurrence" basis, which means that all claims for personal injury or property damage that arise from a single occurrence are covered by the same liability limit. In addition, the new ISO CGL forms include a separate "general aggregate" amount that limits the total amount the insurer will pay in one year for all claims by the insured. This limit

-10-

378

may apply to multiple locations of the tenant. Older policies often did not include a general aggregate limit. Liability amounts should be determined by the client's risk manager or insurance broker based on the nature of the tenant's business, size of the leased premises, and other factors. It is generally advisable to require a general aggregate limit that is a multiple of the per occurrence limit, depending on the number of locations covered by the general aggregate limit and the per occurrence liability amount.

Additional Insureds, Primary Insurance and Cross-Liability. The landlord should be included as an "additional insured," as opposed to a "named insured" (or "additional named insured"), on the tenant's CGL policy. An additional insured is not responsible to the insurer for premiums, but it generally is extended the benefits of the policy, although with less rights with respect to directing the defense and settlement of claims. Some policies also contain additional limitations on the coverage available to an additional insured that do not apply to a named insured, however, so the lease should specify that the coverage extended to an additional insured is at least as broad as the coverage extended to the named insured. The premium should not be affected by adding an additional insured. The tenant's CGL policy should be "primary" to avoid any proration between the tenant's and landlord's CGL policies. CGL policies should include an endorsement to provide "cross-liability" coverage, which means that an additional insured and named insured will be covered by the policy in connection with any claims against each other. In addition, CGL policies should provide for severability of interests, which treats each insured as though it had a separate policy, although all are together subject to the limits of the policy.

Claims vs. Occurrence. Commercial general liability insurance is written on

-11-

either an occurrence basis or a claims-made basis. A claims-made policy covers liability of the insured for third-party claims that are made during the effective period of the insurance policy, regardless of when the events giving rise to the claim occurred. An occurrence policy covers claims arising from events that occurred during the policy period, regardless of when the claim is made. In order to avoid a gap in coverage after the termination of a lease, the lease should require that the tenant's commercial general liability insurance is written on an occurrence basis.

Endorsements. Some endorsements to CGL policies that may be appropriate in a leasing context are discussed below.

Per Location: A per location endorsement specifies that the "aggregate" limit for the CGL policy applies separately to a specific location owned or rented by the tenant. This endorsement should be required by the landlord whenever a tenant has multiple locations insured under a blanket policy.

Additional Insured: An additional insured must be added to a commercial liability policy by endorsement. The form of endorsement varies, so it should be reviewed by the landlord and, if necessary, modified. For example, the additional insured may only be covered to the extent of the premises leased to the tenant. This should be expanded to cover losses in the common area which are caused by the tenant. The endorsement may also exclude third party claims resulting from alterations, construction or demolition conducted by or on behalf of the landlord, so the landlord's liability policy should address this risk. That is of particular concern where the landlord constructs the tenant improvements.

Primary Insurance: An insurance policy must be designated as primary by endorsement.

Other endorsements to CGL policies that may be applicable to certain leases include liquor liability, automobile, errors and omissions and garage keepers legal liability.

-12-

380

IV. GENERAL INSURANCE AND INDEMNIFICATION ISSUES

Waiver of Subrogation. Every lease should include a mutual waiver of subrogation. The purpose behind a mutual waiver of subrogation is to assure that, to the extent any loss is covered by a property insurance policy, the insurer should bear the risk of loss, regardless of any fault on the part of one or both of the parties to the lease. Another purpose is to prevent a potential windfall to an insurer subrogated to the rights of the insured against the other party to the lease. Because the insurer presumably has taken the risk of loss into account in establishing its premiums, the insurer should not have the ability to recoup the loss by subrogation. Most property insurance policies now include a provision allowing the insured to waive the insurer's subrogation rights against the other party to a lease. In addition, if a party is named as an additional insured under an insurance policy, a waiver of subrogation is not required because an insurer may not subrogate against its own insured. However, a mutual waiver of subrogation should be included in any lease, and acknowledged by each insurer, to avoid unintended liability. This is important not only to a tenant, but also to a landlord. In addition to limiting its own exposure to unintended risk, the landlord will not want its tenant to incur liability for damage that is covered by the landlord's insurance policy and, therefore, be impaired in its ability to fulfill its obligations under its lease. A waiver of subrogation also is important if one or both parties is self-insured, to be effective to the same extent as if a policy existed, although in some jurisdictions anti-exculpation statutes or policies (which prohibit a party from being released from or indemnified against its own negligence) may make such waiver unenforceable if there is no third party insurer.

Indemnification. Indemnification provisions in leases should be drafted in consideration of the insurance requirements. Generally, indemnities should cover claims by

-13-

third parties, and not between the landlord and tenant. Landlord oriented leases often include indemnities from tenant to landlord, but not from landlord to tenant. Tenants will often ask for a fully reciprocal indemnity from the landlord. Neither approach is entirely appropriate. In multi-tenant buildings, the landlord should be willing to indemnify the tenant for liability for which it has CGL insurance, such as landlord's acts or negligence with respect to common areas. However, the landlord should not indemnify the tenant for liability arising from the premises, since the landlord may not have liability insurance coverage to back up this indemnity and since the tenant is more likely to be aware of dangerous conditions in the premises during the term of the lease. In leases of single-tenant buildings, the landlord may not carry CGL insurance at all, in which event it would be appropriate for the tenant to fully indemnify the landlord for any third party claims, regardless of fault.

If the landlord is named as an additional insured under the tenant's commercial general liability policy, the policy will cover the landlord's negligence, so it need not be excluded from the tenant's indemnity (except, perhaps, to the extent a loss resulting from landlord's negligence exceeds the policy limits for the tenant's insurance or to the extent such insurance is subject to a material deductible). However, some jurisdictions prohibit or limit the ability to be released from, or indemnified against, one's own active negligence, either by statute or common law. Therefore, regardless of whether it is specifically excluded, the tenant's indemnity may automatically exclude losses resulting from the landlord's active negligence. In many jurisdictions, these rules do not apply if the indemnitor specifically and expressly includes the indemnitee's negligence in the indemnity. It is thus generally good practice to specifically include the landlord's negligence in the tenant's indemnity, to the extent that the claim relates to the premises, the tenant improvements or any breach of the

-14-

lease by the tenant.

An indemnity should specifically provide an obligation to defend and should cover "liability" incurred by the indemnitee (and not just losses, damages, etc.) in order to trigger the indemnification obligation before actual losses are incurred. In addition, an indemnity should cover the acts and omissions of the indemnitor (and not just its negligence or willful misconduct) to cover any strict liability claims. This also avoids defenses by the indemnitor to its obligation to indemnify or defend based on failure to establish its negligence.

Indemnities should cover employees, agents and contractors of both the indemnitor (because the indemnitor's CGL policy should cover these parties) and of the indemnitee (to avoid a gap in the mutual indemnities and, consequently, require the indemnitee to make a claim on its own policy to cover claims by its employee, agent or contractor for a loss caused by the indemnitor which should be covered by the indemnity).

Finally, all leases should specifically provide that the indemnification obligations of each party are not limited by insurance, to avoid any defense based on exclusions from insurance policies, deductibles or claims in excess of liability limits.

The "No-Fault" Approach to Claims and Losses. In recent years, there has been movement toward a "no-fault" approach to indemnification and exculpation provisions in leases. This approach suggests that, rather than focusing on the cause of a loss in allocating risk, the parties should look to their respective insurance policies to absorb the loss. A true no-fault lease includes mutual waivers of claims for any property losses, and modified waivers for losses covered by the parties' CGL policies. Each party is responsible for carrying insurance on its own property and takes the risk of any exclusions, deductibles or

-15-

other limitations in its insurance coverage.

Most advocates of the no-fault approach limit it to property losses. There are some advantages to this approach. The parties avoid lengthy negotiations over carve-outs from exculpation or waiver of claims provisions and indemnities (for example, exclusions for the indemnified party's negligence or misconduct). If a loss occurs, litigation or other legal actions to determine fault are avoided. Limitations on recourse against the party at fault (whether due to limitations on liability included in the lease, or the applicable party's financial capacity) are irrelevant, because the insurance company will be the source of recovery for any losses. Finally, if the lease is completely no-fault (including a complete waiver of claims), and clearly designates the ownership of all portions of the premises and property located on the premises, the parties do not need to review the other party's property insurance policies, or even require that the other party carry property insurance.

However, a pure no-fault approach to risk allocation has at least two drawbacks. First, the loss may not be covered by insurance, either because it is excluded from the insurance policy (such as by reason of the pollution or other exclusion), or because it is below the policy's deductible or exceeds policy limits, or because the party incurring the loss is self-insured. Second, a party's insurance premium may increase as a result of claims made against the policy, even if the party paying the premium was not at fault in creating the claim.

The no-fault approach also does not work if the tenant is required by the lease to insure the landlord's property, such as in a single-tenant building in which the tenant is responsible for insuring the entire property. A full waiver of claims by the landlord against the tenant is not appropriate in this situation, because the landlord is relying on the tenant to insure the landlord's property. If the tenant does not provide adequate insurance or there are

-16-

any gaps in coverage, and a casualty occurs, it is appropriate for the tenant to be liable to the landlord for damage to the landlord's property.

Perhaps a more satisfactory approach to indemnification and exculpation is to acknowledge the advantage of using insurance to cover most losses, but still preserve the concept of fault, where appropriate, in allocating risk. First, clearly designate the party responsible for insuring each portion of the building, and clearly describe the required scope and amount of coverage. This, combined with the modified waiver of claims described below, should avoid most overlapping insurance. Second, include a mutual waiver of subrogation for insured losses, and either obtain a waiver from all insurers or ascertain that each policy contains a provision permitting a waiver of subrogation by the insured. Third, include a waiver of claims by landlord and tenant against each other (and their respective agents, employees and contractors), covering damage to the parties' property to the extent covered by insurance. Consider including a threshold for the size of claims in the waiver, so that the party at fault is responsible for minor claims which are below the deductible and/or are so small that making a claim on the insurance policy is not worthwhile. The waiver of claims should not include damages to the property of third parties (including the parties' employees or contractors), or personal injury or other third party claims. The waiver of claims also should exclude any claims or losses which are excluded from the insurance policies. Since many states restrict or limit indemnification against a party's own negligence unless expressly provided by contract, the waiver should specifically include negligence.

One drawback to limiting the waiver of claims to losses covered by insurance is that parties need to monitor each other's insurance coverage and take the risk of any exclusions or limits, or a lapse in coverage. One solution is to limit the waiver to claims that would be covered by the insurance required under the lease. Then, each party will incur

-17-

the risk of any gaps or lapse in its own insurance coverage. If this approach is taken, it is even more critical to be sure that the lease clearly describes all required insurance coverage, and that the parties' insurance broker carefully reviews these provisions to confirm that all required coverage is obtained.

A no-fault approach may be appropriate for certain leases, if the risk of an uninsured loss is small relative to the costs the parties expect to incur to negotiate appropriate waivers and indemnities regarding fault. However, before incorporating a no-fault approach into any lease, the client should be clearly advised of the risks. If a tenant under a no-fault lease causes serious contamination of the property not protected by the property insurance due to the operation of a pollution exclusion, the landlord probably will be surprised to learn that it has no recourse against the tenant for the loss to its property, and will not be comforted to learn that this risk was taken to avoid the legal fees necessary to negotiate an appropriate limitation on the waiver of claims in the lease.

Certificates of Insurance. In many leases, landlords only require the tenant to provide certificates of insurance, and not a copy of the tenant's insurance policies. However, certificates of insurance often state that they do not confer any rights in the recipient and also may not adequately reveal whether the tenant has obtained the endorsements required by the lease. Certificates often will provide that the insurer is not obligated to notify the recipient of any cancellation, nonrenewal or material change in the insurance coverage, notwithstanding any requirements in the lease. To the extent possible, a certificate of insurance should be revised to correct those deficiencies.

At a minimum, the landlord should review both a certificate of insurance and copies of all endorsements that are required by the lease before delivering possession of the leased

-18-

premises to the tenant. To be safe, the landlord should review the tenant's entire insurance policies, confirming that all required endorsements are attached and are effective for the current year.

Self-Insurance. The tenant may request permission to self-insure for some or all of its insurance responsibilities. If the landlord allows the tenant to partially or fully self-insure, the lease should condition the self-insurance on the tenant maintaining a certain net worth and providing landlord with periodic financial reports to monitor this requirement. The landlord may also require that the tenant provide guaranties or security to back up its self-insurance program if the tenant's financial capacity to cover potential losses is questionable.

The acceptability of self insurance for losses that would be covered by property insurance will depend not only on the party's financial capacity, but also on the nature of the insurance obligations. For example, if the landlord carries insurance on the building shell and the tenant improvements, and the tenant self insures its personal property, there is relatively little risk to the landlord, unless the viability of the tenant's business is highly dependent on its personal property. However, if the tenant is responsible for insuring the building shell or substantial tenant improvements or both, self-insurance presents more obvious risks to the landlord.

Self-insurance provisions should provide that the self-insured party has the same obligations in respect of a claim or loss for which it self insures as an insurance carrier would have if a policy had been obtained. Such a provision would create a fiduciary relationship and help to avoid the assertion of offsets or defenses arising from alleged defaults under the lease on the part of the other party.

-19-

Interaction with Other Lease Provisions. The lease requirements for repair and restoration should be consistent with its insurance provisions. Typically, the party responsible for restoring a particular portion of the premises should obtain the insurance for it. Repair and restoration requirements, and use of insurance proceeds, should be subject to the requirements of any lender. In addition, if the lease provisions regarding the condition in which the tenant is obligated to return the property to the landlord at lease termination are subject to any casualty, this may be interpreted as the landlord's intent to waive casualty damage to the property. Lease provisions regarding indemnification, waivers, alterations, repairs and maintenance, compliance with laws and landlord's liability for entry also need to be consistent with the insurance requirements.

V.   Conclusion

Lease provisions relating to indemnity and insurance are often left by the landlord and tenant to its lawyers to negotiate. While counsel need not shy away from that burden, he or she should obtain the assistance and advice of the risk manager or insurance broker of the client and should make certain that the client has a reasonable understanding of the agreements reached.

Insurance and indemnity issues may vie with condemnation as the least interesting parts of a lease, but, in the event a catastrophe occurs, they may be the most important provisions in the entire document.

NOTES

8

INSURANCE AND INDEMNIFICATION ISSUES IN CONTRACTS & LEASES

Jennifer A. Fox

NEAR NORTH
INSURANCE
BROKERAGE

CHICAGO
John Hancock Ctr.
875 N. Michigan
Suite 2000
Illinois 60611
(312) 280-5600
(800) 859-6719
Fax: (312) 280-5602

DALLAS
1 Galleria Tower
13355 Noel Rd.
Suite 1010
Texas 75240
(214) 866-6900
Fax: (214) 866-6944

LONDON
Shepperton Studios
Studios Road
Shepperton
Middlesex
TW17 OQD
England
(011 44) 1932 562611
Fax: (011 44) 1932
572524

LOS ANGELES
1840 Century Park East
Suite 1100
California 90067
(310) 556-1900
Fax: (310) 556-4702

NEW YORK
777 Third Avenue
New York, NY 10017
(212) 935-7373
Fax: (212) 702-3333

TAMPA
550 N. Reo
Suite 300
Florida 33609
(813) 287-5082
Fax: (813) 287-5194

WASHINGTON D.C.
1600 Wilson Blvd.
Suite 800
Arlington VA 22209
(703) 312-6400
Fax: (703) 524-9850

TABLE OF CONTENTS

393

OVERVIEW

HOLD HARMLESS/INDEMNIFICATION AGREEMENTS AND WHAT THEY ACCOMPLISH

- An assumption, by contract, of another's liability
- Agreement to "indemnify" (make whole) another party
- The obligation is either transferred or assumed
- Effort to make the "mutual understanding" part of the consideration for the contract
- Transfer of financial burden not liability

THE INSURANCE CONTRACT

Advantages

- A financial resource for the indemnitor
- A guarantee of source of funds to cover the obligation assumed under the contract

Disadvantages

- Coordinate insurance requirements with the hold harmless clause to avoid
  - ~ uninsured exposures and
  - ~ placing the indemnitee in a needless breach of contract situation

INSURANCE REQUIREMENTS AND WORDING

COVERAGES

- Usual and customary to protect the financial interests of the tenant
- Particular emphasis to endorse the Commercial General Liability
- Provide coverage for contractually assumed liability

ADEQUATE LIMITS

- Difficult risk to ascertain
- Guidelines to evaluate exposure:
  - ~ identify types and amounts of coverages carried by others in similar business operations or industry groups.
  - ~ review case law which predicates successful suits and the damages awarded
  - ~ consult with a knowledgeable insurance broker to perform a comprehensive risk management assessment of exposures

INSURANCE REQUIREMENTS AND WORDING, continued

POLICY TERMS

- Additional Insured
- ~ provides policy rights
- ~ protects against vicarious liability
- ~ provides coverage if the hold harmless/indemnification provision is not enforceable
- ~ primary and non-contributory coverage for the additional insured
- ~ eliminates possibility of subrogation

POLICY NUMBER: COMMERCIAL GENERAL LIABILITY

THIS ENDORSEMENT CHANGES THE POLICY.
PLEASE READ IT CAREFULLY.
ADDITIONAL INSURED—DESIGNATED PERSON OR ORGANIZATION

This endorsement modifies insurance provided under the following:

COMMERCIAL GENERAL LIABILITY
COVERAGE PART
SCHEDULE

Name of Person or Organization:

(If no entry appears above, information required to complete this endorsement will be shown in the Declarations as applicable to this endorsement.)

WHO IS AN INSURED (Section II) is amended to include as an insured the person or organization shown in the Schedule as an insured but only with respect to liability arising out of your operations or premises owned by or rented to you.

CG 20 26 11 85 Copyright. Insurance Services Offices, Inc., 1984

OTHER ISSUES TO CONSIDER

- ~ Waiver of Negligence

  In accordance with Illinois Statute, negligence cannot be waived

- ~ Essential Elements of Negligence Liability

  Generally, a defendant will be held liable for negligence only if the plaintiff can sustain the burden of proof that:

- ~ a defendant owed a legal duty to the plaintiff
- ~ the defendant breached the legal duty it owed to the plaintiff,
- ~ the plaintiff suffered actual damages, and there was a "proximate" or close causal connection between the defendant's negligent act or omission and the resulting damages to the plaintiff

INSURANCE REQUIREMENTS AND WORDING, continued

ADDITIONAL COVERAGES AND EXPOSURES

Business Income Coverage Form, Property.

Defined

A commercial property form providing coverage for "indirect Losses" resulting from property damage, such as loss of business income and extra expenses incurred. It has replaced earlier Business Interruption and Extra Expense forms. Provides rents insurance determined by the amount of insurance that should be carried including but not limited to the sum of:

Landlord

- Total anticipated gross rental from tenants
- All costs and expenses assumed by the tenant that are normally the owner's obligation.
- The rental value of the property.
- The amount of anticipated rental income including, i.e., taxes, maintenance costs, assessments, and other costs that are the obligation of the tenant.
- In the event the rent and additional rent abates, the landlord will be able to recover its true income and expenses that necessarily must continue.

Tenant

Must consideration the amount of rent payable in the event the rent does not abate, and the additional rent costs that necessarily continue for the period of the loss.

SEE APPENDIX G FOR BUSINESS INCOME FORM

399

INSURANCE REQUIREMENTS AND WORDING, *continued*

ADDITIONAL COVERAGES AND EXPOSURES

Plate Glass

Glass Coverage

Commercial property forms combined with the causes of loss (basic, broad, or special) form, provides coverage subject to sublimits for glass damage by fire and other perils.

Sample Wording
Lessee Responsible For Glass

> Lessee shall also keep the Lessor insured with responsible insurance companies against loss or damage by breakage or otherwise to all plate glass on the Premises.

> 12. **Breakage of Glass** that is a part of a building or structure. This cause of loss does not include breakage of neon tubing attached to the building or structure.
> We will not pay more than:
> a. $100 for each plate, pane multiple plate insulating unit, radiant or solar heating panel, jalousie, louver or shutter; or
> b. $500 in any one occurrence.

CP 10 20 10 91 Causes of Loss Broad Form

Improvements & Betterments

Insurance covering the use interest of a tenant or lessee in improvements, alterations, and additionals against damage or destruction by a covered peril is commonly available as an automatic coverage feature of some commercial property policies. When coverage is desired separately and /or for protection on a broader peril basis, insurance can be written as a separate policy or as a separate item under various forms.

- Criteria of coverage

- Exposures not within coverage scope

- Considerations of coverage

- Builder's Risk vs. Commercial Property

- Owner's Contractor's Protective

> (6) Your use interest as tenant in improvements and betterments. Improvements and betterments are fixtures, alterations, installations or additions:
> (a) Made a part of the building or structure you occupy but do not own; and
> (b) You acquired or made at your expense but cannot legally remove;

CP 00 10 06 95 – Section A, b(6)

INSURANCE REQUIREMENTS AND WORDING, continued

ADDITIONAL COVERAGES AND EXPOSURES, continued

Leasehold Interest

- A financial loss beyond loss of rental value if the lease is canceled.

- A principal reason for cancellation of a lease – substantial damage or destruction to the building occupied by the tenant.

- Most leases contain a fire clause – describes the conditions that would permit the landlord to cancel.

> **b. Leasehold Interest Coverage Form**
> (1) paragraph B.1.a. Ordinance or Law, does not apply to insurance under this Coverage Form.
> (2) We will not pay for any loss caused by:
>   (a) Your cancelling the lease;
>   (b) The suspension, lapse or cancellation of any license; or
>   (c) Any other consequential loss.

- Lease cancellation options – based on possibly a 50% damage or upon a certain amount of time required to repair or replace damaged property.

CP 10 30 10 91–Special Exclusions

- The amount of the loss suffered by the tenant depends on the unfulfilled portion of the lease. The values exposed will continue to decline as the lease runs.

The leasehold interest policy is written for the total amount of net leasehold interest of the insured for the unexpired months of the lease at the inception of the policy. Generally, the Commercial Property insurance policy combined with a causes of loss form excludes this coverage which can be purchased under a separate leasehold Interest Coverage Form.

INSURANCE REQUIREMENTS AND WORDING, continued

ADDITIONAL COVERAGES AND EXPOSURES, continued

Property Damage Liability

The Commercial General Liability policy includes an exclusion for property of others held in your care, custody and control. This exclusion amends the policy to provide for coverage for fire damage to property of others. The tenant (lessee) must be legally liable for fire damage to property of others for this coverage to respond.

> **J. Damage to Property**
>
> "Property damage" to:
>
> (1) property you own, rent, or occupy;
>
> (2) premises you sell, give away or abandon, if the " property damage" arises out of any part of these premises.
>
> (3) property loaned to you;
>
> (4) Personal property in the care, custody or control of the insured;
>
> (5) That particular part of real property on which you or any contractors or subcontractors working directly or indirectly on your behalf are performing operations, if the "property damage arises of those operations; or
>
> (6) That particular part of any property that must be restored, repaired or replaced because "your work" and incorrectly performed on it.
>
> Paragraph (2) of this exclusion does not apply if the premises are "your work" and were never occupied, rented or held for rental by you.
>
> Paragraphs (3), (4) (5) and (6) of this exclusion do not apply to liability assumed under a sidetrack agreement.
>
> Paragraph (6) of this exclusion does not apply to "property damage" included in the "products-completed operations hazard"

> Exclusions c. through n. do not apply to damage by fire to premises while returned to you or temporarily occupied by you with permission to the owner. A separate limit of insurance applies to this coverage as described in LIMITS OF INSURANCE (Section III).

Commercial General Liability – Occurrence Form CG 00 01 10 93

INSURANCE REQUIREMENTS AND WORDING, continued

Boiler & Machinery Insurance Policy

Provides coverage which is specifically excluded under the Commercial Property Causes of Loss form

<u>Electrical Arcing</u>

<u>Mechanical Breakdown</u>

<u>Steam Explosion</u>

The lessee should maintain a separate policy when they are responsible to restore or replace the boiler and related machinery in accordance with the terms and provisions in the lease.

Please see exclusion 2 a, d (6), 2 e. of the Causes of Loss -Special Form Appendix G, Sample Policy Forms.

INSURANCE REQUIREMENTS AND WORDING, continued

ADDITIONAL COVERAGES AND EXPOSURES, continued

Liquor Liability

The commercial general liability policy contains a liquor liability exclusion which is directed at firms in the business of manufacturing, distributing, selling, serving or furnishing alcoholic beverages. The exclusion precludes coverage for bodily injury and property damage claims for which the insured may be held liable. Therefore, a seller of alcoholic beverages confronted with a liquor liability suit does not have any protection under an unendorsed commercial general liability policy.

The general purpose of the dram shop acts or alcoholic beverage control acts is to provide a person, when injured by an intoxicated adult or by a minor who is served alcoholic beverages, a right of action against the dispenser of the beverages.

If the insured is not considered to be in the business, then by inference the insured could be considered a host and covered by exception to the exclusion. This coverage is sometimes referred to as host liquor liability coverage.

> 2. Exclusions
>
> c. Liquor Liability
>
> "Bodily Injury" or "property damage" for which any insured may be held liable by reason of:
>
> (1) Causing or contributing to the intoxication of any person;
>
> (2) The furnishing of alcoholic beverages to a person under the legal drinking age or under the influence of alcohol; or
>
> (3) Any statue, ordinance or regulation relating to the sale, gift, distribution or use of alcoholic beverages.
>
> This exclusion applies only if you are in the business of manufacturing, distributing, selling, serving or furnishing alcoholic beverages.

Commercial General Liability Occurrence Coverage Form – CG 00 01 10 93

SAMPLE CONTRACTS–CASE STUDIES

SAMPLE CONTRACTS–CASE STUDY (1)

ARTICLE 14. *Insurance.*

Tenant agrees to maintain, at its own expense, during the Term hereof commencing no later than the date Tenant takes possession of the premises for the purpose of doing Tenant's Work, the following insurance coverage (with such subsequent increases in coverage as Landlord may reasonably request) with respect to the premises in companies and with policies satisfactory to the Landlord: (I) public liability and property damage on a comprehensive general liability form, in the minimum amount of One Million Dollars ($1,000,000) for injury to or death of any one person; Three Million Dollars ($3,000,000) for the injury to or death of more than one person arising out of any one accident or occurrence; and One Million Dollars ($1,000,000) for damage to property, all such insurance to include Landlord, its employees and agents as assured parties and to include all claims for damage or injury occurring in, upon or about the premises; and (II) fire, extended coverage, vandalism and malicious mischief with all risk endorsements, on contents and business property, including all Tenant's Work and endorsed to cover improvements and betterments, in an amount not less than the actual replacement cost thereof and naming Landlord and Tenant as insured parties as their interests shall appear. Tenant shall provide Landlord with copies of policies or certificates of insurance prior to the date Tenant takes possession of the premises for the purpose of commencing Tenant's Work and from time to time thereafter as required by Landlord evidencing that the aforesaid insurance is in full force and effect.

> Article 14 Comments
>
> Paragraph #1
>
> (i) Match Commercial General Liability Requirements to how insurance is typically purchased.
>
> General Liability
>
> | | |
> |---|---|
> | General Aggregate | $ 2,000,000 |
> | Products Aggregate | $ 2,000,000 |
> | Broad Form Property Damage or Fire Legal Liability | $ 1,000,000 |
> | Any one occurrence | $ 1,000,000 |
>
> Umbrella Liability
>
> | | |
> |---|---|
> | Any one occurrence | $ 3,000,000 |
>
> • Request to be added as additional insured–Lessor as evidenced by an endorsement.
>
> • Add primary and non-contributory wording.

> (ii) Property Insurance
> • Stipulate level of deductible that you feel is appropriate.
> • Rent Insurance/Rent Abatement
> • Replacement Cost Coverage
> • Certificate should indicate improvements and betterments are covered

> For both property and casualty coverages you might want to dictate that a carrier must have a Bests' rating of at least an A-.

Tenant agrees to deliver or cause to be delivered to Landlord at least ten (10)

SAMPLE CONTRACTS–CASE STUDIES,
CASE STUDY (1), continued

days prior to the commencement of Tenant's Work under Article 4 hereof or the commencement of any work under Articles 10 or 11 hereof a policy of insurance in a company satisfactory to Landlord providing public liability and property damage coverage in the minimum amounts set forth in Exhibit B hereto or in such greater amounts as Landlord may hereafter from time to time advise Tenant in writing, naming Tenant, its general contractor, all subcontractors, and Landlord, its employees and agents as assured parties endorsed so as to cover any and all liability arising out of or in any manner connected with the work to be performed on the premises by the Tenant and a policy evidencing workmen's compensation coverage in the minimum amount set forth in Exhibit B hereto.

All policies shall provide that Landlord shall be given a minimum of thirty (30) days written notice by any such insurance company prior to the cancellation, termination or change of such coverage. All insurance herein required shall be deemed to be additional obligations of the Tenant and not in discharge of or limitation to Tenant's obligation to indemnify Landlord, and its employees and agents under Article 17 hereof.

> Article 14 Comments
> Paragraph #3
> Illinois statutes require insurance companies to provide sixty (60) days notice of cancellation.

Landlord and Tenant each hereby waive any and every claim for recovery from the other for any and all loss of or damage to the Building or the premises, or any portion of either, or to the contents thereof, which loss or damage is covered by valid and collectible fire and extended coverage insurance policies, to the extent that such loss or damage is recoverable under said insurance policies, inasmuch as this mutual waiver will preclude the assignment of any aforesaid claim by the way of subrogation (or otherwise) to an insurance company (or any other person), Landlord and Tenant each agree to give to each insurance company which has issued to it policies of fire and extended coverage insurance written notice of the terms of this mutual waiver, and to have said insurance policies properly endorsed if necessary, to prevent the invalidation of said insurance coverages by reason of said waiver.

> Article 14 Comments
> Paragraph #4
> • There is a school of thought that mutual waiver of subrogation does not transfer liability. Also, there are no insurance products to address this situation

SAMPLE CONTRACTS–CASE STUDIES,
CASE STUDY (1), continued

ARTICLE 16. *Fire or Casualty.*

In the event the premises are damaged by fire, explosion, or other casualty or occurrence, the damage thereto (excluding damage to stock in trade, fixtures, furniture, furnishings, carpeting, floor covering, wall covering, drapes, equipment and all Tenant's Work) shall be repaired and restored by Landlord with reasonable promptness, subject to reasonable delays for insurance adjustments and matters beyond Landlord's reasonable control. Such repair and restoration shall be at Landlord's expense; provided, however, that Landlord in no event shall be required to expend for such repair an amount in excess of the insurance proceeds recovered or recoverable as result of such damage. In the event of damage by fire, explosion or casualty or occurrence in which (a) the level of the Mall in which the premises is located, the Mall, or the Building is **damaged to the extent of 50%** or more of its respective insurable value, or (b) the damage is caused by any occurrence not covered by Landlord's insurance and is in excess of $100,000, or (c) the premises or the level of the Mall in which the premises is located is damaged within the last three years of the Lease term to the extent of 25% or more of its respective insurable value, then

Article 16 Comments

1. If building is deemed untenable or damaged more than 50% of its insurable value, the tenant (since they are responsible for tenant's work on improvements & betterments) should make sure they have an adequate limit to cover undamaged improvements & betterments.

2. Contains a Rent Abatement Clause therefore tenant does not have to purchase business income insurance to cover rent: however, the landlord typically carries loss of Rents.

3. Also, the tenant is responsible for repairing/replacing leasehold improvements and should purchase coverage on a full replacement basis.

Landlord may elect to repair or rebuild the premises or the level of the Mall in which the premises are located or the Mall, as the case may be, or to terminate this Lease upon giving notice of such election in writing to Tenant within 120 days of the happening of the event causing the damage; provided, however, that Landlord in no event shall be required to expend for such repair an amount in excess of the insurance proceeds recovered or recoverable as a result of such damage. The amount of insurance proceeds recoverable as a result of such damage shall be determined by Landlord's insurance carrier, which determination shall be binding as between Landlord and Tenant. If, in Landlord's reasonable determination, the casualty or the repairing or rebuilding shall render the premises untenantable in whole or in part, a proportionate **abatement of the Minimum Rent**, and all Additional Rent shall be allowed from the date when the damage occurred until the date when the premises are made tenantable, or until the effective date of termination as herein provided, said abatement to be computed on the basis of the relation which the Rentable Area of the space rendered untenantable bears

SAMPLE CONTRACTS–CASE STUDIES,
CASE STUDY (1), continued

to the aggregate Rentable Area of the premises. There shall be no abatement of Rent if such damage results directly or indirectly from the negligence or willful act or omission of Tenant, its agents or employees. If Landlord is required or elects to rebuild the premises as herein provided, **Tenant shall at its expense, repair or replace its leasehold improvements**, including its fixtures, furniture, furnishings, carpeting, floor coverings, wall covering, drapes and equipment, stock in trade, and all Tenant's Work. If Tenant has closed, Tenant shall promptly reopen for business upon completion of such repairs. For purposes of this Article 16, the extent of any damage and the insurable value of the premises or any portion of the Mall or Building shall be determined by the replacement cost thereof.

ARTICLE 17. *Waiver of Claims and Indemnity.*

Except as and to the extent prohibited by law, Tenant waives all claims against Landlord and its agents and employees for injury to persons or damage to property, including trade fixtures, sustained by Tenant or any person claiming through Tenant resulting from any occurrence in or upon the Building, including, but not limited to such claims for damages resulting from: (a) any equipment or appurtenances becoming out of repair; (b) injury or damage done or occasioned by wind, water, flooding, freezing,

> Article 17 Comments
> Paragraph #1
> * The commercial property form contains a blanket waiver of subrogation.
> * Are perils consistent with that of the property insurance purchased by tenant

fire, explosion, earthquake, excessive heat or cold, vandalism, riot or disorder or other casualty; (c) any defect in or failure of plumbing, heating or air conditioning equipment, electric wiring or installation thereof, water, steam, gas or sewer pipes, stairs, railings or walks; (d) broken glass; (e) the backing up of any sewer pipe or downspout; (f) the bursting, leaking, overflowing, stopping or running of any tank, tub, washstand, water closet, water pipe, drain, cooling coil or any other pipe or tank in, upon or about the Building; (g) the escape of steam or hot water; (h) water, snow or ice being upon or coming through the roof, skylight, trapdoor, stairs, walks or any other place upon or near the Building or otherwise; (i) the falling of any fixture, plaster, stucco or other object; (j) any act, omission, or negligence of co-tenants or of other persons or occupants of the Mall or of the Building or owners of adjacent or contiguous property; (k) damage to or loss by theft or otherwise of property of Tenant or others; and (l) any negligence of Landlord, its agents and employees.

Except as and to the extent prohibited by law, Tenant agrees to indemnify, defend and hold harmless Landlord and its agents and employees, from and against all

SAMPLE CONTRACTS–CASE STUDIES,
CASE STUDY (1), continued

claims, liabilities, losses, suits, fines, proceedings, and expenses (including those arising out of the negligence of Landlord, its agents and employees), including reasonable attorneys' fees, for injury to or death of any person or loss of or damage to property in or upon or about said premises and including the person and property of Tenant, its employees, agents, invitees, licensees or others, it being understood and agreed that all property kept, stored, maintained in or upon the premises, shall be at the risk of Tenant. The foregoing shall be in addition to Tenant's obligation to supply insurance as required by this Lease and not in discharge of or substitution for same.

Except as otherwise herein provided, if any damage to the premises or other property of Landlord results from any act or neglect of Tenant, its agents, employees, invitees or licensees, Landlord may at its option repair such damage, and Tenant shall promptly on demand reimburse Landlord for the cost thereof.

SAMPLE CONTRACTS–CASE STUDIES, continued

CASE STUDY (2)

18.   INSURANCE

18.01 Tenant, at Tenant's expense, agrees to maintain in force during the Term: (I) Comprehensive General Liability Insurance on an occurrence basis with limits of liability in amounts not less than: (a) $3,000,000 for bodily injury, personal injury or death; and (b) $500,000.00 with respect to damage to property, including water and sprinkler damage; (ii) Hazard Insurance, with extended coverage and vandalism and malicious mischief endorsements, in an amount adequate to cover the full replacement value of all leasehold improvements and all fixtures, contents and wall and floor coverings in the Premises; and (iii) **Rental insurance to cover at least one (1) year's Rent.**

18.02 The policies referred to in Section 18.01(I) and 18.01(iii) shall name Landlord, the Manager and their respective agents and employees as additional insureds and shall not provide for deductible amounts. The policy referred to in Section 18.01(ii) shall not provide for deductible amounts in excess of $1,000. Each policy referred to in Section 18.01 shall be issued by one or more responsible insurance companies reasonably satisfactory to Landlord and shall

General Aggregate	$2,000,000
Products Aggregate	$2,000,000
Personal Injury and Advertising	$1,000,000
Broad Form Property Damage or Fire Legal Liability,	$1,000,000
Any One Occurrence	$1,000,000
Umbrella Liability	$5,000,000

Any one occurrence to follow form over the Commercial General Liability

b.Delete this wording as it implies that the tenant is responsible for damage to the leased premises, which is typically handled through a waiver of subrogation. If there will be no waiver of subrogation, then tenant must carry Property Legal Liability.

(ii)Insurance on personal property, leasehold improvements, all fixtures, wall and floor coverings and business income insurance to cover at least one year's rent. The coverage will be equivalent or better than the Causes of Loss - Special Form (CP1030) as published by the Insurance Services Offices (ISO).

Comment: Is it necessary to include a requirement for the tenant to carry insurance on the loss of rental income. Typically, office leases contain a rent abatement clause.

18.02 - The policies referred to in 18.01 (I) shall name landlord, the manager and their respective agents and employees as additional insureds with respect to liability. The liability coverage shall be written on a first dollar basis without a deductible. The policy referred to in 18.01 (ii) shall contain a maximum deductible of $1,000. All insurance policies shall be written with insurance companies carrying a minimum Best's rating of A-. The policies shall provide that insurance may not be canceled without thirty days prior written notice to landlord and manager except for 10 days notice for non-payment of premium... Tenant shall provide landlord with a Certificate of Insurance showing lessor, manager and their respective agents and employees as additional insureds on a providing waiver of subrogation... Policy shall be endorsed to apply on a primary basis.

410

SAMPLE CONTRACTS–CASE STUDIES,
CASE STUDY (2), continued

contain the following provisions and endorsements: (I) that such insurance may not be canceled or amended without thirty (30) days' prior written notice to Landlord and the Manager; and (ii) an express waiver of any right of subrogation by the insurance company against Landlord, the Manager and their respective agents and employees.

18.03 Tenant shall deliver to Landlord, certificates of insurance of all policies and renewals thereof to be maintained by Tenant hereunder, not less than ten (10) days prior to the Commencement Date and not less than ten (10) days prior to the expiration date of each policy.

18.04 Provided that the insurance policies of Tenant will not be invalidated nor will the right of the insured to collect the proceeds payable under such policies be adversely affected by the waiver contained in the following portion of this sentence, each party hereby expressly waives all rights of recovery which the party making this waiver might otherwise have against the other party, its Manager or their agents, and employees, for loss or damage is covered by valid and collectible insurance policies, notwithstanding that such loss or damage may result from the negligence of the party making this waiver, its Manager or their agents or employees. Each party shall use its best efforts to obtain from its insurer the right to waive claims as set forth in the preceding sentence without thereby invalidating its insurance or affecting its right to proceeds payable thereunder.

18.04 - In the event of fire or other loss or damage to the premises, the landlord and tenant mutually waive their rights of subrogation and recovery against each other, their agents, and employees to the extent that they are insured or are required to carry insurance for said loss.

The landlord agrees to maintain insurance against loss or damage to the building and personal property owned by the landlord including loss of rental income. The coverage shall be equivalent or better than the Causes of Loss - Special Form (CP1030) as published by the Insurance Services Office (ISO) and shall be on a replacement cost, no coinsurance basis.

The tenant shall maintain insurance on personal property owned by the tenant on a replacement cost basis, no coinsurance basis and will also carry business income insurance. The coverage will be equivalent or better than the Causes of Loss - Special Form (CP1030) as published by the Insurance Services Office. Both landlord and tenant will maintain said coverage with limits equal to the full replacement cost of building and/or personal property as the case may be and with limits equal to the full 12 month loss exposure for loss of rental income and business income and extra expense.

411

SAMPLE CONTRACTS–CASE STUDIES,
CASE STUDY (2), continued

18.05 Prior to engaging in any service of any alcoholic liquor whatsoever, the Tenant shall obtain and deliver to Landlord a liquor

> 18.05 - This Clause can be eliminated from the lease. Liquor Liability only applies in circumstances when a company is selling alcohol.

liability policy or policies of insurance under the Illinois Liquor Control Law with limits of not less than:

(i) One Million Dollars ($1,000,000.00) for bodily injury (fatal or non-fatal) to any person and Three Million Dollars ($3,000,000.00) for bodily injury to more than one person;

(ii) One Million Dollars ($1,000,000.00) for means of support; and

(iii) One Million Dollars ($,1000,000.00) for injury to property; and

(iv) Five Million Dollars ($5,000,000.00) excess liability for bodily injury and property damage.

SAMPLE CONTRACTS–CASE STUDIES, continued

CASE LAW

Failure to Name Additional Insured

In the case of *Olympic Inc. v. Providence Washington Insurance Company of Alaska, 648 Pac.2d 1008 (1982)*, a tenant signed a lease and agreed to procure liability insurance for a limit of $300,000 naming the landlord as an additional insured. The tenant obtained the liability insurance but forgot to amend the policy with the foregoing requirement.

During a fire at the rental property, a firefighter was killed allegedly because of various building code violations. The estate of the decedent sued for $600,000 in damages which were paid by the landlord's insurance company. Having paid that sum, the landlord's insurer then sought contribution of the $300,000 limit from the tenant's insurer, particularly since the landlord required the tenant to procure liability insurance on its behalf. However, the tenant's insurer denied payment of indemnity because of the absence of the landlord's name on the tenant's policy. The landlord's insurer objected to this and maintained that coverage applied for such breach of contract under the term "incidental contract," as defined in the tenant's liability policy.

The court held that the tenant's insurer was not required to contribute to the settlement amount. One reason for the denial was that the tenant's contractual obligation to procure insurance for the landlord was not a "hold harmless" or "indemnification" agreement. Or, to say it another way, the liability that is assumed under contract or agreement, for purposes of coverage under a liability policy, refers to liability incurred when one promises to indemnify another person. Such assumption of liability does not refer to liability that results from a breach of contract. Another reason the court denied relief to the landlord's insurer was that the tenant's liability policy did not expressly cover the tenant's failure to procure the liability insurance.

Relying on Coverage of Others—Shortfalls

The lessor who wants to save on insurance costs by cancelling its own liability insurance and relying, instead, on the insurance of the lessee must tread carefully because there are pitfalls in doing so. Take the case, for example, of National hills Shopping Center Inc. v. Liberty Mutual Co. 551 F.2d 655 (1977). National Hills was the lessor of a shopping center which carried its insurance with INA, and White Stores was the lessee which was insured by Liberty Mutual.

413

SAMPLE CONTRACTS–CASE STUDIES, continued

CASE LAW, continued

One day the roof over the area occupied by White Stores collapsed, damaging its goods. After payment of the claim, the lessee's insurer commenced a subrogation action against the lessor. However, the lessor maintained that it was an additional insured under the lessee's liability policy and therefore should be outside the scope of the insurer's subrogation action.

While the lessor was an additional insured under the lessee's liability insurance policy, the coverage of the later contract was limited to liability arising out of the business of the named insured (lessee). And, since the damage arose from the liability of the lessor, the lessor was held not to be protected under the lessee's policy.

For the lessor to have been protected under the lessee's insurance policy, the insurance policy provision would have had to be written so as to encompass the independent liability of the lessor. Unfortunately, great pains sometimes are taken to draft a broad lease agreement but very little attention is paid to whether the insurance corresponds to the requirements of that contract. It therefore makes good sense for a lessor to maintain its own insurance in the event the transfer of attempted liability fails.

On the other hand, sometimes lease agreements are more limited in scope than the drafter realizes until it is too late. Take the case of *Travelers Indemnity Co. v. The Hanover Insurance Company. 470 F.Supp. 630 (1979)*, which involved the City of Norfolk, Virginia, as a lessor, and Cellar Door Concerts, Inc., promoters of a concert, as lessee. The lessor owned and operated an auditorium that it leased to the lessee. The lease provided that the lessee would indemnify and hold harmless the lessor for any claims made against the lessor "occasioned by the negligence of the lessee in connection with the use of the lessor's premises". The certificate of insurance issued by the lessor's insurer, Hanover, named the lessor as an additional insured regarding the activities of the lessee.

Following the death of one of the spectators, suit was filed against the lessor and lessee. While there are allegations of negligence against the lessor for its own acts or omissions (as well as allegations of negligence against the lessee), there were no allegations that the lessor was obligated to the decedent's estate as a result of any negligence on behalf of the lessee. So when the lessor called upon the lessee's insurer for defense, the insurer refused. Travelers, the

SAMPLE CONTRACTS–CASE STUDIES, continued

CASE LAW, continued

insurer of the lessor, settled the suit and then sought to recover from the Hanover.

It was clear to the United States District Court for the Eastern District of Virginia that the lease and lessee's liability insurance only protected the lessor for any of its obligations arising out of the negligence of the lessee. Since the allegations did not come within the purview of the risks assumed by the Hanover, the lessee was held not to be obligated to provide defense or indemnification to the lessor.

The Matter of Other Insurance

One important reason why a person or entity, such as the landlord, will request to be an additional insured on the insurance policy of a tenant is to rely on the tenant's insurance policy first and its own policy as the last resort. It makes good risk management sense to do so. Unfortunately, this intent, while commonly implied, is not always understood. An example is the case of *Deerfield Management Co., et al. v. Ohio Farmers Insurance Company. 1989 C.C.H. (Fire and Casualty) 2890.*

Briefly, the facts are as follows: A hotel building was owned by a bank as land trustee and managed by an agent. Part of that building was leased to an occupant in the cleaning business. This occupant, as lessee, agreed to the following provision in its lease agreement with the lessor:

> Lessee hereby indemnifies and holds lessor and its agents and employees harmless from all claims and any costs, including attorney's fees, related thereto, made by any person arising out of the lessee's use and operation of the leased premises. Lessee shall carry comprehensive public liability insurance with a policy limit of at least $500,000 per individual or occurrence. Such insurance shall be carried with a financially sound carrier and shall name lessor as an additional insured. Lessor shall be furnished with a certificate of insurance requiring at least ten days prior written notice to lessor of cancellation of such insurance.

In compliance with the lease the cleaner (lessee) carried insurance with Ohio Farmers as named insured and the managing property agent (lessor) as an additional insured.

What prompted the litigation was a fire loss allegedly caused within the premises of the lessee that spread and killed a number of persons within the hotel occupancy. The parties agreed that if the lessor were held to be liable for the losses resulting from the fire, then both the lessee's liability policy

415

SAMPLE CONTRACTS–CASE STUDIES, continued

CASE LAW, continued

with Ohio Farmers and the lessor's policy with Unigard would provide coverage. The dispute, however, was over which of the two policies was to provide primary and excess protection.

The other insurance provisions of both policies revealed that the one written for the lessee was excess, whereas the policy written for the lessor was primary. However, the lessee maintained that the terms of the lease indicated that the lessee's liability policy was to apply on a primary basis. The court, however, found the lease absent of any requirement that the lessee's insurance was to be primary. The lessee countered by arguing that lessor's insurance policy was to serve as primary because of the indemnification clause of the lease. The court refused to consider this argument because the lease agreement was not at issue here. It was the matter of how the insurance was to be applied.

The court ultimately held that it was the lessor's liability policy that applied as primary and the lessee's as excess. In so holding, the court explained that the lessor is provided with all of the protection it obviously intended to obtain when it signed the lease and purchased its own liability insurance. Thus, it was the lessor's policy which applied as primary, and the lessee's policy, which named the lessor as an additional insured, that applied as excess. In addition, since the lease agreement between the two parties required the lessee to "indemnify" the lessor, the lessee's insurer had no duty to defend the lessor, only a duty to reimburse the lessor for defending any covered claims.

Based on court decisions of this nature, it certainly would behoove lessors or parties that require lease agreements to be more specific about the accountability of liability when it comes to priority of insurance (damages and legal costs).

APPENDIX A - GLOSSARY OF INSURANCE TERMS

INSURANCE TERMS

Actual Cash Value	Replacement Cost less depreciation
Additional Insureds	Entity, other than the named Insured, who is protected under terms of the insurance contract. (i.e. Landlord named on tenant's policy.)
Additional Named Insureds	Have the same rights under the policy but not the same obligations as the first named insured(s).
Agreed Amount	Insured and Insurer agree the amount of insurance carried will automatically satisfy the co-insurance clause.
All Risk	Implies no exclusions subject to misinterpretation - do not use.
Binder	Temporary Insurance Contract - subject to terms, conditions & limitations of policy in current use by the insurance company.
Boiler and Machinery	Insures accidents to Boilers & Machinery as well as HVAC equipment, motors, compressors, miscellaneous electrical. apparatus.
Building Ordinance	Coverage will protect you against loss due to enforcement of existing building or zoning laws that results in additional costs to rebuild or demolish an insured building. Coverage for loss of any undamaged portion of such building can also be insured. Recommended on older buildings.

417

APPENDIX A – GLOSSARY OF INSURANCE TERMS, continued

INSURANCE TERMS, CONTINUED

Business Income incl.
Extra Expense

Insures Loss of income and extra expense from an insured loss. Rents can be included. Important that tenant carries Business Income including Rents if no abatement clause in lease. Typically, Landlord insures for loss of rents.

Certificate of Insurance

Provides information only and confers no rights to the Certificate Holder. The certificate does not amend, extend or alter the coverage afforded by the policies shown.

Commercial General Liability

Insurance carrier pays sums that the insured becomes legally obligated to pay as damages because of Bodily Injury, Property Damage, Personal Injury, Advertising Injury that insurance applies to subject to policy exclusions. Reference should be made to Occurrence Form CG 00 01 10 93.

Employers Liability

Coverage B on standard Workers Compensation policy. It provides coverage against common law liability of an employer for injuries to employees as distinguished from liability imposed by Worker's Compensation law.

Excess Liability

Additional Limits over Primary Liability insurance.

Lenders Loss Payable

Provides creditor of the insured the same rights and duties that a mortgagee clause gives a Mortgagee. It may be used to protect a creditors interest in personal property.

418

APPENDIX A – GLOSSARY OF INSURANCE TERMS, continued

INSURANCE TERMS, CONTINUED

Liquor Liability	Host Liquor included in General Liability for those with incidental exposures. (Not in Liquor Business)
Loss Payable Clause	Provision in property policy that authorizes payment to persons other that the insured to the extent that they have insurable interest.
Mortgagee Clause	Establishes that payment for covered loss will be made to Mortgage holder. Mortgagee's right of recovery shall not be denied by any act or neglect of the insured. Mortgagee will receive written notice of cancellation.
Named Insured	Person of organization to whom the policy is issued. Entity specifically designated in the policy declaration.
Property Legal Liability	If no Waiver of Subrogation in lease tenant must insure against damage to landlord's property in tenant's care, custody and control.
Rents	Loss of Rental Income arising from an insured loss.

NOTES

9

LENDER'S VIEW OF THE LEASE - DISAPPEARING INK OR HIDDEN ASSET

Andrew L. Herz

LENDER'S VIEW OF THE LEASE - DISAPPEARING INK OR HIDDEN ASSET

By Andrew L. Herz
Richards & O'Neil, LLP
New York, New York

I. Lender's Analysis of Commercial Space Leases and Ground Leases

A. Financing of Fee or Landlord's Interest

    1. Purpose of Lender's Analysis

        a. Amount of loan is determined by capitalization of net rental income payable under leases. Lender must review business terms of leases (e.g., base rent, escalations, etc.)

        b. Leases must provide sound basis for underwriting.

            1. Lease income is primary source of funds for servicing debt.

            2. Lease income is especially critical if loan is non-recourse.

        c. Lender may become the landlord under the leases if the borrower defaults.

            1. Lender must look for typical landlord's protections.

            2. Lender must confirm that it can enforce tenants' essential obligations and not be unduly burdened by landlord's obligations.

    2. Lease Review

        a. Lender's review may be "after the fact". Lease may already be executed or lender may have committed to loan without complete review.

        b. Lease may include provision requiring tenant to make changes subsequently required by lender. Provision may be limited by requiring only good faith negotiation of changes or only changes that are industry standard.

c. In multi-tenant gross lease situations, only major tenants are relied upon by lender. However, all leases must be reviewed, primarily to determine if they are subordinate to the mortgage.

3. Review of Specific Lease Provisions

    a. Parties

        1. Lender must consider credit-worthiness of tenant and guarantors. Questions relevant in this regard include whether tenant is a sole purpose subsidiary or if tenant's credit is being relied upon.

        2. Following of formalities - proper names, designations and authority

    b. Description of premises

        1. All of the leased premises must be encumbered by mortgage for lender to control performance by landlord.

        2. If not, the following problems may arise: 1) lender may be unwilling or unable to cure landlord's defaults to the extent cure requires entry or expenditures as to non-mortgaged property, 2) permitting tenant to cure and set off may create charges to rent unrelated to mortgaged property and 3) lender may be unable to perform after assuming ownership.

    c. Landlord's covenants

        1. Lender must determine if there are affirmative covenants in the leases as to which compliance would

be difficult or burdensome, particularly if landlord's breach permits offsets against rent or termination under relevant state law.

2. Lender cannot cure covenants that are personal to landlord (e.g., landlord must continue in a certain business).

3. Landlord may not be able to employ a certain name for the building.

4. Lender cannot permit a provision in the lease requiring the landlord's compliance with loan requirements or the cross-defaulting with loan documents.

5. Possible solutions for lender with respect to over-inclusive covenants include the following: 1) tenant may not terminate the lease based on their violation, 2) any such covenant is void if lender succeeds to interest of landlord, or 3) such covenants do not apply to successor owners or are restricted so as to be reasonably performable by successor owners.

6. Expansion, construction or alteration obligations by landlord

    a. Lender will seek to avoid such obligations for lease terms that have not commenced.

    b. Lender's potential financial obligations must be factored into appraisal.

7. Landlord obligation to "takeover" old lease - Lender may be willing to accept such an obligation if (i) the existing lease to be assumed by landlord is of short

duration or already sublet to a good credit entity and (ii) tenant agrees that (a) the "take-over" obligation is personal to landlord and will not survive foreclosure and (b) tenant cannot terminate new lease but may only sue for damages if landlord defaults under "take-over" lease.

d.   Lease term

1.   Commencement and termination dates should be confirmed. Occupancy and/or inception of rent payments may be required before loan is funded.

2.   Lender ordinarily will not approve a provision permitting tenant to terminate upon landlord's default (e.q., time limit on buildout), except in certain limited circumstances (total or substantial destruction or damage or condemnation).

e.   Rent

1.   Lender must consider rent-free periods, expense caps, services provided without charge, compensation for moving and other expenses, tenant improvement allowances, and landlord's assumption of existing lease.

2.   Assurance of Rent Payments - Tenant must covenant to pay rent. Rent should be paid "without deduction, abatement, set off or demand".

3.   Lenders very strongly resist abatement of rent, but may permit it (i) if landlord materially defaults (e.g., real estate taxes) and notice and opportunity to cure is given to landlord and separately to lender,

especially if curable by payment of money or (ii) during restoration or repair of casualty damage, if landlord furnishes adequate rental value insurance.

4. Tenant's right to cure landlord defaults by payment of money and offsetting against rent generally is not acceptable to lender.

   a. If tenant may pay debt service or other liens or charges which are subordinate to lender's mortgage, tenant's lien in effect could become senior to mortgage.

   b. Tenant should waive any set-off right if lender (or its successors) own the property.

5. Lenders always prefer true net leases, or at least a dollar stop or base year without a maximum or "cap," requiring Tenant to pay its share of increases in operating expenses and real property taxes. If base year method is used, parties' assumptions as to potential costs should be reviewed.

   a. Expense definitions must be clear and should broadly cover actual increases as opposed to use of fixed indices or factors, unless they can be demonstrated to be more profitable.

   b. Proportionate shares should be based on rentable square footage relative to building as a whole to assure that sum of parts equals the whole. "Gross-up" provision for adjustment of expenses to a 95-100% leased amount is necessary for tenants to pay fair shares in a partially occupied building.

c. Lender may require periodic escalations of base rent for long-term leases. Use of index such as CPI may be unacceptable substitute for market value-based increases. A "floor" equal to the most recent rent would protect lender.

6. Percentage Rent

a. Percentage rent provisions must be considered differently. Without minimum fixed rent, lender's appraiser may not be able to determine value, and debt service coverage cannot be assured.

b. Any confidentiality requirements for tenant's books should permit mortgagee's right to review and landlord's right to audit.

c. Lender's identity should be considered - certain nonprofit entities may not share in profits under applicable tax laws.

d. Percentage rent should be based upon gross rent, not net, and should be paid at least quarterly.

e. Lease should require tenant to conduct business in a diligent manner.

f. The propriety of the exclusions from gross rent should be examined.

7. Timing

a. Timing of rent payments, including base rent, expense passthroughs and percentage rent, should be sufficiently early to allow for appropriate cash flow.

b. Lender also will prohibit prepayment more than one month in advance to assure that, upon default or foreclosure, landlord will not receive funds that should be payable to lender or are necessary to operate the property.

f. Environmental Compliance and Indemnities

   1. Potential Liability of Lender/Landlord

      a. Lender is particularly concerned about landlord's potential joint and several liability with tenant for cleanup under CERCLA due to status as operator and owner, respectively. Lender may inherit this obligation as landlord's successor.

      b. Lender also has potential liability to the government, despite no affirmative or intentional engagement in hazardous activities. Super lien for cleanup costs may affect priority of lender's lien.

      c. Lender is more attractive target for government and other third parties. Lender also may not be able to realize upon landlord or tenant indemnity - tenant or landlord may be single purpose corporation or otherwise judgment proof or bankrupt even if the non-recourse provision has a carveout.

2. Avoidance of Environmental Problems

    a. Lender should receive a written disclosure of the details of any operation involving hazardous materials, including what quantities and types of hazardous materials are involved, what permits are required, and what storage and/or transportation mechanisms are used.

    b. Lender will require strict landlord obligations to comply with applicable reporting, removal and other requirements. Lender should require landlord to assure and monitor the existence of and compliance with safety programs for all tenants in a multi-tenant building, especially in premises that are already potentially contaminated, _e.g._, restrictions on alternations that might disturb asbestos-containing materials.

    c. Lender may require landlord to impose restrictions on use of hazardous materials beyond mere compliance with government regulation to absolute restriction against using or disposing of hazardous substances except as specified.

    d. Lease should also provide for monitoring of compliance with covenants during lease term, including environmental audits. As a practical matter, these continuing covenants may permit landlord (and lender) to look to tenant when tenant and its assets are available.

e. Lease should provide for express reaffirmation of representations and warranties relating to hazardous materials usage, as well as regular reporting of use, storage and disposal.

f. Landlord should require tenant's submittal of copies of licenses and other permits, tenant's responses to reporting obligations, and workers' compensation reports on an ongoing basis.

3. Financial Safeguards

a. Creditworthiness analysis may be very different for a tenant using hazardous materials that pose substantial risks.

b. Additional safeguards may be required - upgraded fire and hazard insurance; additional improvements such as drainage, storage pads, and improved sprinkler system; and any environmental insurance available.

c. Increased operational and testing costs resulting from contamination, costs of monitoring of status, and tenant's particular use should be passed through to individual tenant.

4. Special Improvement Requirements

a. Tenant's improvement requirements may be very expensive. Even if landlord were able to finance improvements, there may be concern with respect to usefulness to other tenants, amortization of costs in rent, and additional security.

       b.   Tenant may need special design requirements (e.g., extra fire systems, floor pad reinforcement, additional sewage, heavy duty elevators). Tenant may have much greater need for utilities.

       c.   Insurance requirements may impose special obligations based on tenant's use. Tenant should pay increased insurance costs and may be required to obtain own insurance.

5.   Indemnity by Tenant

       a.   Landlord may seek to shift entire environmental liability to tenant.

       b.   Tenant should be responsible for defense of and indemnity for any site contamination for which tenant or its agents, employees or contractors is responsible, not only to the extent tenant is in violation of laws.

       c. Indemnity should cover not only the cost of remediation but also investigation costs, attorneys' fees, fees and costs of governmental authorities, and third party claims resulting from any contamination, disposal or discharge.

       d.   Tenant's obligations must survive lease termination and benefit successors of landlord as well as lender.

g.   Assignment and Subletting

   1.   Consent required

a. Tenant identity may be critical.

b. Lease must expressly restrict assignment or subletting without landlord's consent, including by indirect stock transfer and merger. If lease provides time limitations for landlord's response, sufficient time should be allowed for lender to decide.

2. Reasonable Consent

a. Should lender be obligated to be reasonable?

b. Is it reasonable for landlord to withhold consent if lender does not approve?

3. Liability

a. A tenant should not be released from primary liability if lender is relying upon that tenant's credit.

b. Assignee should assume all liability under the lease arising from and after the effective date of assignment.

4. Other Remedies - Ability to recapture the premises and/or recover share of excess proceeds may be critical to lender, especially in states where landlord's disapproval rights are restricted.

h. Tenant's Ownership or Control of Improvements

1. If lease provides that tenant owns any improvements, their value should be discounted or removed from appraisal.

2. Landlord's obligation to purchase, or tenant's right to remove
or alter, improvements will be binding on lender.

i. Damage and Destruction - Lender's
principal concern is the effect of such
provisions upon the value of the property. The three main issues are lease
termination rights of landlord and tenants, landlord's obligation to repair,
and rent abatement.

1. Insurance Proceeds

a. Lender may permit proceeds to
be used for reconstruction, but
may require repayment of loan at
lender's option.

b. Lender's and tenant's rights
usually conflict since lease
usually requires reconstruction
in some circumstances. A prior
lease that is not subordinate or
possibly a nondisturbance agreement may require lender to abide
by the terms of the lease. Even
if lease is truly subordinate or
an express agreement allows lender's discretion in application of
proceeds, lender will negotiate
to assure continuation of necessary leases.

2. Duty to Repair

a. Landlord's duty to repair
should be limited to (i) insured
losses which can be repaired
within a certain time period
(typically 180 days) or (ii) a
maximum amount of damage (percent
of replacement value or area
covered).

b. Lender may not want reconstruction requirement during
final years of lease term.

3. Landlord's Termination - Landlord should have right to terminate
lease based on damage to building as
whole. The fact that one tenant's
space is unaffected should not be
determinative.

4. Tenant's Termination

a. Tenant's right to cancel
lease should be limited to substantial destruction of premises,
perhaps during the final years of
lease term.

b. Standards may include maximum
time period for repair or minimum
portion of the premises.

5. Insurance

a. Insurance should not be able
to be cancelled or modified.
Insurance proceeds should be payable to or controlled by lender.

b. The tenant should be prohibited from obtaining other fire
insurance on the premises which
contributes in the event of a
loss.

c. All policies should state
that they will not be invalidated
by any act or neglect of a tenant
or any subtenant.

d. The tenant should waive all
rights to recover against the
landlord for loss or damage to
tenant's contents.

6. Abatement of Rent - Any abatement of rent must be covered by rental value insurance, which must be required under mortgage documents.

7. Subrogation Waivers

   a. If tenant is released from liability for fire damage, landlord should obtain waiver of subrogation from its insurer to avoid nonpayment to landlord if tenant was responsible for fire. Landlord also should be released by tenant.

   b. Landlord's obligation to obtain waiver should be conditioned upon ability to obtain coverage from companies approved by mortgagee.

8. Consistency - Restoration and termination clauses in various leases must be consistent to avoid requirement of restoration for one tenant while others may terminate.

j. Condemnation

1. Tenant's Termination - Lender may accept termination rights by tenant if a certain amount of tenant's space is taken. Possible standards include percentage of square footage or tenant's ability to operate. Latter is more vague but may be more limited.

2. Duty to Repair - Lender has similar concerns as with damage. Duty to repair should be related to landlord's business judgment as to entire building and should be consistent among leases. Obligation to restore should be tenant's, with landlord's obligation limited to

making that portion of the proceeds
of the condemnation award attributable to the improvements available.
Landlord may want to opt to apply
condemnation award to debt reduction.

3. Condemnation Award

   a. Lender will not permit tenant
   to receive any portion of award
   (including any value attributable
   to lease) except amounts allocable to removable trade fixtures.

   b. Lender may require lease to
   be expressly subordinate to mortgage, but subordination will not
   protect lender after foreclosure
   if lease stays in effect.

4. Rent Abatement

   a. Rent reductions (permanent or
   temporary) should be proportionate to reduction in rental value
   which, hopefully, is recouped in
   condemnation proceeding.

   b. For a permanent taking, debt
   principal may need to be reduced
   to permit lower rent to support
   debt service.

5. Temporary Taking - Lender may
prefer tenant to pay rent and receive award to avoid landlord's
downside risk. If temporary taking
extends beyond lease term, landlord
is entitled to portion attributable
to period after lease term.

k. Landlord's Remedies Against Tenant

1. Any remedies that must be specifically provided for under applicable law should be included.

2. Minimally, landlord's rights should include termination of lease in expedited proceeding and acceleration and recovery of any loss.

3. Lender will seek to avoid responsibility for reletting or mitigation.

l.   Tenant's Remedies Against Landlord

1. Rights to terminate or offset are strictly scrutinized.

2. Some lenders will insist that any recovery by tenant be limited to landlord's interest in the property.

3. A subordinate tenant may request the right to receive notice of and cure landlord's defaults under mortgage. Lender may agree if tenant's cure does not create offset or lien priority issues.

4. Lender may be at risk for security deposits after foreclosure even if it does not receive them from the borrower. Lender may require special deposit of the funds to assure availability, particularly if the security deposit is substantial. Subordination agreement may provide for no liability of lender absent actual receipt.

m.   Lender's Right to Cure Landlord's Defaults

1.   Notice of Default

a.   Notice of landlord default should be provided to lender, and lender should have the right but

17

not the obligation to cure. A
separate agreement by tenant may
be required.
b. Notices of landlord default
should be sent by tenant simultaneously to lender in order to be
effective. Formal notice of
lender address should be provided
by landlord.

2. Period to Cure

a. Lender requires longer period
to cure than allotted to landlord
along with an extension of such
cure period to proceed with foreclosure.

b. Tenant, as well as landlord,
should prefer that landlord's
cure period run first. If lender
cures, landlord is probably in
default under loan.

3. Cure by Foreclosure - Commencement of foreclosure action may be
necessary for lender to obtain legal
right to enter premises, or lender
may desire legal title before taking
action involving substantial costs.

n. Estoppel Certificates

1. Purpose - Confirm terms and
status of lease for benefit of lender and prevent tenant from later
claiming prior default, amendment,
etc. Lender should require an estoppel certificate at the outset of
transaction and have the right to
seek such a certificate on other
occasions.

2. Elements

    a. Key Elements of Estoppel - Lease is in full force; lease is entire agreement (consider attaching a copy); tenant has accepted premises and is in possession; and there are no defaults, defenses or offsets (or events that could become such after notice and expiration of cure period) or rights to any rebates on part of landlord or tenant.

    b. Lease should require that tenant will provide an estoppel certificate.

3. It may be advisable to (i) agree on minimum form in advance and attach to lease and (ii) indicate whether any sublease or assignment is in effect.

4. If subordination agreement will not be used, estoppel may include agreements in favor of lender, e.g., obligation to provide notice and right to cure to lender and agreement not to amend, extend, pay rent in advance, terminate or release.

5. Estoppel must be directed to lender and should acknowledge that loan is being made in reliance thereon.

4. Notice to Tenant of Landlord's Assignment of Lease

    a. Purpose

    1. Advise tenant that lease has been assigned for security purposes and that landlord has agreed that lender may receive rents if landlord in default under loan.

2. If lender does not obtain tenant's estoppel certificate or agreement, notice may also reference
restrictions upon landlord's actions
in relation to lease, e.g., landlord's agreement not to modify, extend, collect advance rents, or
waive provisions without lender's
consent.

b. Form

1. Notice should authorize tenant
to pay rent to lender upon loan
default.

2. If loan provides for a trust/
escrow account for rents or security
deposits, notice should reference,
and tenant should agree, to direct
deposit of rents.

5. Lease Subordination and Priority

a. Priority

1. Lease will be prior to mortgage
if lease is prior in time and does
not contain a subordination provision, as long as tenant has not
executed a separate subordination
agreement.

2. Lender's notice of prior lease
or tenant's occupancy alone will be
sufficient to assure priority.

3. Prior lease is not affected in
foreclosure of mortgage.

b. Subordination

1. Lease will be subordinate if
later in time, if lease includes
subordination provision, or if subordination agreement is executed.

2. There should be no affirmative requirement in the lease to be met by the mortgagee (e.g., notice of default must be sent to tenant, a limit on the terms of any mortgage to which the lease is subordinate, or the mortgagee is obligated to allow the tenant to cure a default).

3. If lease states that it may be subordinated or is subordinate if a nondisturbance agreement is delivered by lender, an executed agreement is required.

4. A subordinate lease without an attornment clause causes automatic termination in foreclosure in many states, at least in nonjudicial foreclosure, and provides lender with an option to terminate lease in most jurisdictions.

c. Decision as to whether to subordinate

1. Lender must analyze the economics of each lease to consider whether a particular lease is necessary for viability of the project. Factors include whether the rent is market, present and projected market conditions, if project is single or multiple tenant, whether landlord's obligations are too onerous for lender to fulfill, and if tenant is affiliated with the borrower.

2. Lender may prefer tenant to subordinate its rights under lease in order to permit later evaluation of the market.

3. Tenant may require a nondisturbance agreement if tenant has made a significant investment in its premises or the market generally requires this concession.

4. If lender does not want lease to terminate on foreclosure, lender may nevertheless require subordination agreement to provide the following: 1) lender is not liable for, and tenant cannot set off against lender for, prior landlord defaults, 2) lease amendment and assignment or sublease by tenant is not effective without lender's consent, 3) lease termination is not effective without notice to and opportunity to cure by lender, 4) tenant may not prepay rent more than one month in advance, 5) express subordination of certain provisions (e.g., lender has first claim to condemnation and insurance proceeds), 6) lender is not liable for constructing improvements or for particular warranties made by land-lord, and 7) lender's liability is limited to its interest in the prop-erty. Lender may prefer subordina-tion with nondisturbance to priority in order to override conflicting lease provisions (e.g., rights to and use of condemnation and insur-ance proceeds).

5. Tenant should agree not to sub-ordinate to junior liens or lease could be terminated pursuant to foreclosure of junior lien.

d. Preservation of lease

1. For a tenant to ensure that its lease will not be terminated in foreclosure, lease must be prior in time and there cannot be a subordi-nation clause.

2. Nondisturbance clause must be used with attornment provision or tenant will have option to termi-nate.

3. If mortgagee desires to preserve lease upon foreclosure rather than providing the tenant with the option to vacate, the tenant and mortgagee must enter into a nondisturbance and attornment agreement which will also benefit a purchaser at a foreclosure sale.

e. Options and Rights of First Refusal to Purchase

1. The most significant issue is lien priority. In most jurisdictions, prior lease which includes an option to purchase must be subordinated in order for mortgage not to be extinguished by exercise of option.

2. To avoid enforceability against lender, lender may require agreement not only to subordinate the lease/option but to provide that the option is extinguished on foreclosure or deed in lieu.

3. If lease is junior to mortgage, and lender permits sale of the property to tenant, exercise of option will result in new borrower and terminate lease. Lender may want fee and leasehold not to merge and/ or tenant to assume borrower's mortgage obligations (landlord may request a release). If lease does merge (or as a practical matter, probably even if it does not), lender must assume for valuation purposes that lease terminates on first date that exercise of option is permitted. Lender should also consider landlord's (or lender's) possible inability to abide by option, and whether breach will enable tenant to terminate lease.

4. If lease is prior, lender may require tenant to agree in lease amendment that purchase price will be paid to lender to extent of indebtedness, including any prepayment charge.

5. Even if lease is subordinate, if tenant can exercise the option and the loan will be repaid, lender may restrict exercise of the option during "lock-in" or prepayment penalty period to avoid issues regarding prepayment charge, acceleration and foreclosure. Option purchase price must be sufficient to pay prepayment charge and full loan amount during the term.

6. Option to purchase a portion of the property is even more problematical, even if subordinate. Exercise will create two owners/borrowers and frequently a need for reciprocal easements. Lender may require partial prepayment and release.

7. Landlord/seller obligations (delivery of title or otherwise) must be analyzed. Lender will want to avoid making representations, including warranties of title (by deed or otherwise) or other covenants.

B.   Leasehold Mortgages on Ground Leases

1.   General Considerations

a. It is imperative in negotiating any ground lease to endeavor to satisfy leasehold financing requirements even if the leasehold mortgagee is not known in advance. The potential penalty for having to negotiate at a later stage is that the landlord may exact some further concession. Even the participation of the leasehold mortgagee in the initial negotiation will not, however, obviate all such problems for the tenant due to the possibility of refinancing at a later time with a different leasehold mortgagee.

b. Almost every ground lease provision is of potential concern to the leasehold mortgagee if examined from the viewpoint that the leasehold mortgagee might at some time find itself taking over the estate or trying to resell the leasehold after default.

c. Leasehold Mortgagees

1. Traditionally, life insurance companies and pension funds have had the leading role in the long-term financing of major leaseholds.

2. Many institutional lenders are circumscribed in making leasehold mortgage loans by statutory requirements or the strictures of regulatory bodies.

a. A national bank, for example, can lend on leasehold security only if the lease term extends beyond the maturity date of the loan by at least ten years.

b. New York Insurance Law §1404(a)(6)(A)(ii)(II) provides that a domestic insurer may make leasehold mortgage loans if

1. The lease provides for a term of at least 21 years.

2. The property underlying the leasehold shall be subject to no prior liens except for liens for nondelinquent ground rents, taxes, assessments, and similar charges, and there shall be no condition or right of reentry or forfeiture not

insured against under which
the insurer is unable to continue the lease in force for
the duration of the loan.

3. The loan shall provide for
such payment that at any time
during the period of the loan,
the aggregate payment of principal to be made will be sufficient to repay the loan
within the lesser of 40 years
or a period equal to 80% of
the term of the lease, through
payments of interest only for
5 years and equal payments
applicable first to interest
and then to principal at the
end of each year thereafter.
The term "term" herein refers
to the unexpired term of the
lease at the date of the loan,
in addition to any term which
may be provided by options to
renew.

2. Legal Investment Requirements

a. Loan-to-Value Ratio - The amount of
the loan may not exceed a specified
ratio of the appraised fair market value
of the leasehold.

b. Amortization - The loan must fully
amortize within a major fraction of the
unexpired lease term, and interest-only
payments are permitted for a limited
time.

c. Term of Lease - Remaining term must
meet minimum requirements.

3. Particular provisions

a. Initial Term of the Lease

1. Leasehold Mortgagee's Objective
- If the leasehold mortgagee fore-

closes or otherwise acquires title after a default, there must be a sufficient term remaining to recoup the loan balance and interest, either through operation or resale.

2. Protective Provisions - The initial term must either be sufficiently long at the start or the tenant must exercise sufficient renewal options. In the latter case, the lease must require such renewal far in advance of the start of the renewal term.

b. Use of the Demised Premises

1. Leasehold Mortgagee's Objective - The leasehold mortgagee seeks maximum flexibility. Over a period of years, the most desirable use of property may change and any use limitations reduce marketability.

2. Protective Provisions

a. The lease should require the landlord to grant or join in easements, covenants, restrictions, reciprocal easement agreements, permits, and applications reasonably necessary for the development of the property.

b. The lease should permit additions to and alterations in the improvements (and, under prescribed conditions, the demolition, removal and replacement thereof) to meet changed conditions and requirements, so long as all costs incurred thereby are promptly and fully paid for by the tenant.

c. If the landlord requires the tenant to remove improvements and clear, grade and restore the land at the end of the lease term, such obligations should be carefully negotiated.

c. Fixed Rent and Adjustment of Rent

   1. Leasehold Mortgagee's Objectives

     a. The leasehold mortgagee must be able to determine in advance the cost to its borrower of holding a leasehold rather than a fee. As a result, the rent to be paid must be fixed or at least determinable. These amounts must be paid to keep the lease alive if the leasehold mortgagee takes over the tenant's position.

     b. Rental readjustments during the term must be reasonable and limited.

   2. Protective Provisions

     a. Indexing the fixed rent by the Consumer Price Index or some other formula is normally unacceptable. In such an instance, the amount which will be payable obviously cannot be known in advance.

     b. Reappraisal of rent tied to market value presents similar problems because of the uncertainty.

d. Security Deposits

   1. Leasehold Mortgagee's Objective - Security deposits are unusual under long term ground leases and if required, would normally not extend beyond completion of the initial improvements.

   2. Protective Provisions

a. The landlord should recognize the security assignment by the tenant to the leasehold mortgagee of the tenant's interest in the deposit, subject to the landlord's rights under the lease.

b. The leasehold mortgagee may want the security deposit held in trust.

e. Taxes and Other Impositions

1. The tenant must pay all taxes and comply with all legal requirements and instruments of record affecting the property.

2. With respect to each of the above, the tenant must be given reasonable time to contest their application.

3. With respect to taxes, the tenant must be permitted to institute and control tax certiorari proceedings. The landlord should be obligated to join in such proceedings or should empower the tenant to do so in the landlord's name.

4. If the tenant fails to exercise certain critical rights, such as contesting a tax assessment, the landlord should give notice of the tenant's failure to the leasehold mortgagee, who should have additional time and the right to act in the tenant's stead.

f. Fee Mortgages and Other Encumbrances on Title

1. Leasehold Mortgagee's Objective - All subleases and other interests which derive from the leasehold and provide the economic basis for oper-

ating the property must be prior to all interests except the lease.

2. Protective Provisions

a. The lease and all renewals and replacements thereof, including any new lease issued under the leasehold mortgaging provisions, must be and remain prior to any fee mortgage or other major lien or encumbrance.

b. It is not acceptable to the leasehold mortgagee for the lease to be subject to a fee mortgage whose holder merely provides the tenant with a non-disturbance agreement.

c. Where the leasehold mortgage is responsible for materially improving the property to the landlord's ultimate benefit, there is little justification for the landlord to mortgage the fee on a priority basis if there is any possible prejudice to the leasehold lender's security.

d. A fee mortgage, if permitted, must be subordinate to the lease, subleases, etc. in all respects.

1. The subordination does not extend to such matters as claims to insurance proceeds and condemnation awards unless specifically stated.

2. Neither the tenant nor the leasehold mortgagee wishes to discover, for example, that the lease and mortgage permit almost unlimited alterations which are non-structural, but a fee mortgage, although sub-

ordinate, requires consent for every $5,000 change.

g. Insurance

1. Leasehold Mortgagee's Objective - The leasehold mortgagee wants the property properly insured and is concerned that it participates in or controls the adjustment process with insurers, and that it holds and controls the disbursement of insurance proceeds to be used in the process of restoration.

2. Protective Provisions

a. The leasehold lender must be protected under a standard non-contributory mortgagee endorsement and must have advance notice from the insurer of any cancellation or material change.

b. The leasehold lender will normally require possession of the original policies.

c. The insurance should not be invalidated as to the leasehold mortgagee by any act of the insured.

d. Neither party to the lease should have an enforceable option to terminate unless the loan is paid in full.

h. Damage/Destruction and Condemnation Provisions

1. Purposes

a. The value, condition and utility of the property will be preserved and restored.

b.   In the event of a total destruction or condemnation, the
mortgage loan will be paid in
full.

2.   Protective provisions for damage
and destruction

a.   The leasehold mortgagee must
have the right to participate in
the adjustment of losses.

b.   The leasehold mortgagee must
have the right to supervise and
control the receipt of insurance
proceeds.

c.   Consequences of a total or
partial destruction

1.   Total destruction (actual
or constructive)

a.   If the insurance proceeds are sufficient to
repay the loan, the lease
terminates.   If not, the
lease continues and the
tenant must restore.

b.   A negotiated formula
must be specified to allocate insurance proceeds,
with the leasehold mortgagee receiving sufficient
funds to satisfy the leaseh
old mortgage.

c.   Often, there is no
concept of total destruc-
tion permitting termination
of the lease.   In these
circumstances, the tenant
must always restore and all
insurance proceeds are
applied therefor.

2.   Partial destruction

a. The lease continues.

b. All insurance proceeds are applied to the restoration of the property, with any excess being paid to the tenant, although the leasehold mortgagee may require the right to elect to apply the excess to the mortgage.

3. Protective provisions for condemnation

a. The leasehold mortgagee must be able to participate in all condemnation proceedings and settlement discussions.

b. The leasehold mortgagee must have the right to supervise and control the receipt of awards.

c. Consequences of a total or partial taking

1. Total taking

a. The lease terminates.

b. A negotiated formula must be specified to allocate awards. The landlord wants to receive the value of the land (considered to be unimproved but subject to the lease), the tenant wants to receive the value of the lease and improvements, and the leasehold mortgagee wants to receive sufficient funds to pay off the leasehold mortgage.

2. Partial taking

a. The lease continues.

b. The entire award is applied to restoration with any excess allocated according to a negotiated formula designed to provide for the landlord's receipt of that portion of the award allocable to the land that is taken.

c. There is a pro-rata reduction in the rent based upon the percentage of land that is taken.

d. Alternatively, any excess after restoration belongs to the tenant, and rent is not reduced. This approach is appropriate only for a very long term ground lease.

3. Temporary taking - The lease continues and the entire award is applied to current rent and then to current debt service.

4. Protective provisions for restoration

a. Except for total destruction, total condemnation, or temporary taking, all insurance proceeds and condemnation awards are applied to the restoration of the property.

b. There must be adequate time to restore, including force majeure provisions.

c. The leasehold mortgagee or a depositary normally is entitled to receive and disburse the insurance proceeds or condemnation

awards periodically as the restoration proceeds.

i. Defaults and the curing of defaults

    1. Leasehold Mortgagee's Objectives

        a. Three categories

            1. Monetary defaults or de-
faults which may be cured by
the payment of money

            2. Curable non-monetary de-
faults such as failure to
repair

            3. Non-curable non-monetary
defaults such as a bankruptcy
or an assignment in violation
of lease restrictions

        b. The leasehold mortgagee wants
to (i) eliminate defaults it cannot cure, (ii) have sufficient
time to cure non-monetary defaults, and (iii) have some additional time even as to monetary
defaults both to avoid expiration
of the grace period and to decide
upon a course of action.

    2. Protective provisions

        a. Notice

            1. The landlord must give
notice of all defaults to the
leasehold mortgagee.

            2. No notice to be given to
the tenant is effective unless
a copy is also given to the
leasehold mortgagee.

            3. All notices given by the
landlord or the tenant to each
other or received by either of

them from any governmental authority must also be given to the   leasehold mortgagee.

4. A notice of default is valid only if (i) mailed by certified or registered mail, return receipt requested and (ii) the nature of the default is specified therein in con-siderable detail.

b.   Right to cure

1. Landlord should not have any extraordinary remedies.

2. The ground lease should contain standard provisions for notice to and cure by the tenant. The tenant's right to cure should provide for a longer cure period due to force majeure or the occur-rence of a bona fide dispute about whether the state of facts alleged by the landlord actually is a default under the ground lease.

3. Leasehold mortgagee has the right and opportunity to cure all defaults by tenant.

a. The leasehold mort-gagee's right to cure should not run concurrently with the tenant's.

b. The leasehold mortgagee should receive a second notice of default and the opportunity to cure after the expiration of the ten-ant's cure period.

4. Monetary defaults or de-faults that may be cured by

the payment of money should have a specified grace period (after the expiration of any grace period afforded to the tenant) in which the leasehold mortgagee may, after notice, cure the default.

5. Nonmonetary defaults that are not susceptible of cure by the leasehold mortgagee should not permit the landlord to terminate the lease so long as the leasehold mortgagee is diligently proceeding to foreclose and take possession and cures any monetary default while doing so. Nonmonetary defaults may not be curable by the leasehold mortgagee, which cannot be assured of obtaining physical possession of the property until foreclosure proceedings have been completed.

6. For nonmonetary defaults that may be cured by the leasehold mortgagee, the ground lease must provide for a significant cure period allowing leasehold mortgagee to cure (and even foreclose and take possession if necessary). During this period, the leasehold mortgagee must diligently proceed to cure the nonmonetary default in addition to curing any monetary defaults that occur, and the landlord must refrain from exercising its remedies under the ground lease.

7. The ground lease may not be terminated by a default of the tenant that is not curable by the leasehold mortgagee

(e.g., bankruptcy, requirement of continued corporate existence, continued ownership requirements, prohibitions on assignment).

8. Length of cure period for a leasehold mortgagee must consider institutional slowness.

c. Right to a new lease

1. The lease must provide for the right to a new lease between the landlord, as landlord, and the leasehold mortgagee or a nominee, as tenant, if the original ground lease is terminated due to the tenant's default. Although this provision is problematical (see below), most leasehold mortgagees insist upon such a clause, primarily due to a concern that the leasehold mortgagee may inadvertently misplace a notice of default and never attempt to cure the tenant's default within the time period allotted therein.

2. The new lease should incorporate the same terms and conditions as the original ground lease except that (i) the term of the new lease should be reduced in order to take into account the portion of the term of the original ground lease which will have expired and (ii) if the leasehold improvements have already been constructed, those clauses relating thereto should be inapplicable.

3. The leasehold mortgagee must pay delinquent back rent and landlord's expenses incurred in evicting the tenant in addition to curing any other default.

4. Required elements of new lease provision

a. The leasehold mortgagee should have the right to notify the landlord within a certain period of time after termination of the original ground lease (at least 60 days) that the leasehold mortgagee elects to enter into a new ground lease.

b. The new lease should have the same priority as the original lease. If there is more than one leasehold mortgagee, the right to a new lease should be exercised according to priority.

c. Title to the improvements must automatically vest in the leasehold mortgagee.

d. The landlord must assign to the leasehold mortgagee all subleases whose tenants have attorned to the landlord.

e. All rents collected by the landlord during the period between the termination of the original ground lease and the commencement of the new lease should be

credited against ground
rent.

5. The new lease provision
should be referenced in the
recorded short form or memorandum of lease for any assistance that may provide under
local law with respect to
claims against the property
arising after recordation.

6. Problems with new lease
provision

    a. The new lease is an
executory contract that may
be disaffirmed by the trustee in any bankruptcy of
landlord.

    b. The right to receive a
new lease may violate the
rule against perpetuities
due to the possible remote-
ness in vesting.

    c. The new lease may be
subject to intervening or
preexisting but previously
subordinate liens, e.g.,
fee mortgages. Any liens
arising after execution of
the original ground lease
but prior to execution and
recording of the new ground
lease are likely to be
superior to the new lease.
A possible solution to this
dilemma would be for the
ground lease to prohibit
the landlord from mortgaging his fee interest or to
require any such fee mortgage to be subordinate not
only to the original ground
lease but to any new ground

lease executed pursuant to the new lease provision.

d. A new lease provision may interfere with the tenant's right of redemption following termination of the original ground lease.

7. A new lease may be useful in the case of a bankrupt tenant where the lease is not assumed or where a ground lease is terminated but the tenant is not in bankruptcy. In the latter instance, a leasehold mortgagee may acquire the security without the expense and delay of foreclosure.

8. As an alternative to a new lease provision, a leasehold mortgagee may execute a "back-up" lease. A back-up lease is presumably more likely to be enforceable than a new lease provision since the leasehold mortgagee is committing to leasing the property upon an early termination of the ground lease. However, enforceability of the back-up lease is unclear if the leasehold mortgagee has not taken possession of the property thereunder prior to the landlord's bankruptcy.

j. Assignment, Mortgaging and Subletting

1. Leasehold Mortgagee's Objective - The leasehold mortgagee requires the maximum freedom not only to resell the leasehold in case of default but to be certain of the va-

lidity of the original lending transaction.

2. Protective Provisions

    a. Legal considerations

        1. If the lease is silent, the lease may be mortgaged or assigned.

        2. Some statutes regulating leasehold mortgagees will not permit disposition to be subject to third party control after a default. Accordingly, the lease should provide an absolute right of the tenant and each subsequent tenant to assign without consent or other limitation, although this right is sometimes drafted to become effective only for the leasehold mortgagee and its successors after a default occurs.

    b. Provisions regarding assignability

        1. The lease must be freely assignable to the leasehold mortgagee and, after default, by an assignment in lieu of foreclosure or otherwise by a leasehold mortgagee, particularly at a foreclosure sale or after receiving a deed in lieu of foreclosure.

        2. The lease must be freely assignable by the purchaser at a foreclosure sale.

        3. Upon assignment, the tenant thereunder should be released of all liability thereafter accruing under the lease

and the successor should become liable, if at all, only as to obligations accruing from the effective date of assignment. Generally, a tenant should be liable only for obligations to be performed during its ownership of the leasehold estate.

4. The lease should be nonrecourse with respect to the tenant except to the extent of the tenant's interest in the property and for any removal of improvements and land restoration work to be performed at the end of the lease term.

c. Provisions regarding subleases

1. Purpose - Restrictions must be minimized so as not unduly to restrict the economics of operation and the value on resale.

2. Required provisions

a. The lease should expressly permit subleases.

b. The landlord should be required to grant nondisturbance agreements to subtenants provided that certain criteria are met.

d. Restrictions on mortgaging must be non-existent or based on minimal tests with which the leasehold mortgagee can easily comply, such as providing notice of its interest to the landlord and furnishing copies of the mortgage documents and an official notice address.

1. If only institutional lenders may lend upon the leasehold, future refinancing may be inhibited if the definition of institutional lender is too narrow.

2. Purchase money mortgages should be specifically permitted.

e. Ground leases vary as to whether the benefits inure to only one leasehold mortgagee or to several. If only one is initially permitted, the lease should require an additional exception for purchase money mortgage financing in case the leasehold mortgagee takes over the leasehold and subsequently sells. The restriction should apply to one leasehold mortgagee rather than one mortgage to protect tenants in those states where mortgages are consolidated to preserve mortgage recording tax benefits.

k. Special Leasehold Mortgagee Protections

1. Leasehold Mortgagee's Objective - The leasehold mortgagee wishes to the extent possible to freeze the characteristics of the leasing relationship upon which the initial decision to lend was based and, in the event of default, to have time to determine a course of action and then to act.

2. Protective Provisions

a. The ground lease may not be amended, modified, cancelled or surrendered without the leasehold mortgagee's prior written consent. Any such action without such consent is void.

b. The landlord will accept performance by the leasehold mortgagee as if it were performance by the tenant.

c. All of the leasehold mortgagee's rights may be exercised directly or through a designee or nominee, provided the leasehold mortgagee remains financially responsible for any undertaking to cure defaults.

1. Renewal/Arbitration

1. Leasehold Mortgagee's Objective - As in the case of renewal rights, the leasehold mortgagee does not want valuable tenant rights to lapse due to inaction by the tenant.

2. Protective Provision - The lease provides the leasehold mortgagee with an additional period to that given to the tenant to appoint an arbitrator for the tenant and the right to participate in the proceedings.

m. Estoppel Certificates

1. Leasehold Mortgagee's Objective - The leasehold mortgagee should be able to establish from time to time by written certificate from the landlord that the lease is still in good standing and that no material defaults exist or at least that none is known to the landlord.

2. Protective Provision - Upon request by the leasehold mortgagee, the landlord will certify the status of the lease to the leasehold mortgagee within a specified number of

days after request, which certificate shall include the following:
i) the date to which rent has been
paid, (ii) statements that (a) the
lease is in full force and effect
and has not been altered, amended or
modified and (b) no default notices
have been sent, and (iii) whether,
to the knowledge of the landlord,
there are any existing defaults
under the lease.

n. Notices

1. Leasehold Mortgagee's Objective
- The form of notices to be given to
the leasehold mortgagee should be
described precisely.

2. Protective Provision

a. A well-drafted notice clause
specifically related to the
leasehold mortgagee should be
included.

b. The leasehold mortgagee,
however, may wish to provide that
certain notices to it are not
effective until received and that
certain notices provided by it
are effective if given by counsel
or certain administrative officers.

o. Bankruptcy of Landlord

1. The lien of the leasehold mortgage should be extended to include
the tenant's right to remain in
possession and the tenant's right to
exercise §365(h) rights.

2. The tenant must obtain the consent of the leasehold mortgagee
before electing to treat the lease
as terminated.

3. All claims for damages arising out of the landlord's rejection of the lease should be assigned to the leasehold mortgagee.

4. The leasehold mortgagee should control any rent offsets and all bankruptcy litigation.

p. Non-Merger and Spreader - If title to the fee and leasehold estates become combined in one person or entity or affiliates thereof, (i) the estates are nonetheless to remain separate to facilitate resale of the ground lease and to avoid merger of subleases, unless the leasehold mortgagee consents in writing, and (ii) the lien of the leasehold mortgage should be extended to the fee to provide greater security.

II. Subordination and Non-disturbance Agreements ("SNDA") (This portion of the outline is based upon the Report of the Subcommittee on Nondisturbance Agreements of the Commercial Leasing Committee of the Real Property Section of the New York State Bar Association, published in Volume 22, No. 1 (Winter, 1994) of the NYSBA Real Property Law Section Newsletter. Those who are interested in obtaining a copy of the full report should contact the New York State Bar Association, 1 Elk Street, Albany, New York, 12207).

A. Introduction

1. Reason for a SNDA

a. Most commercial leases provide that the tenant's estate is subordinate to the landlord's mortgage. Therefore, if the landlord's mortgagee were to foreclose and name the tenant as a party defendant in the foreclosure action, the foreclosure would terminate the tenant's lease and the tenant's right of occupancy.

b. Most commercial tenants do not understand why, if their landlord defaults on its mortgage, the mortgagee or anyone else should have the right to terminate the tenant's occupancy if the tenant is not in default.

2. State laws regarding termination of subordinate leases

a. In some states, a foreclosure automatically terminates subordinate leases regardless of any agreement between the parties.

b. In other states (including New York), a tenant's rights in a subordinated lease are not automatically extinguished unless the tenant is specifically joined in the foreclosure proceeding.

3. Functions of a SNDA

a. If the mortgagee forecloses, the mortgagee will respect and recognize the tenant's lease and not disturb the tenant's rights thereunder. In addition, the tenant agrees to attorn to the mortgagee as the new landlord.

b. The SNDA addresses issues about the relationship between the mortgagee and the tenant, usually resolving those issues within a predictable range of outcomes.

4. Overall approach

a. The SNDA is ancillary to the basic contract between the mortgagee and the mortgagor, which is the mortgage, and the basic contract between the landlord and the tenant, which is the lease.

b.   The parties should insure that the mortgage and the lease provide each party with the relevant protections, rather than rely on the SNDA to repair problems and fill gaps in the landlord-tenant or mortgagor-mortgagee relationship.

5.   Tenants successful in obtaining a SNDA

    a.   1980's

        1.   Mortgagees generally granted SNDAs only to nationally recognized tenants or other tenants with significant leverage and creditworthiness, and then only after careful review of the proposed lease.

        2.   These SNDAs would generally limit the tenant's rights and protect the mortgagee's interests in every possible way.

        3.   Mortgagees would also sometimes try to use a SNDA as an occasion to renegotiate leases, adding such provisions as environmental indemnities from the tenant.

b.   1990's - Mortgagees are more willing to grant a tenant a SNDA.   A tenant that might not have been able to obtain a SNDA in 1986 will routinely ask for one, and is more likely to receive it, in 1997.

c.   Overall - Commercial tenants that are leasing a considerable amount of space, intend to make a substantial investment in tenant improvements, or otherwise have significant negotiating strength.

6. Exhibit A - Model SNDA ("Model Agreement") drafted by Commercial Leasing Committee of the New York State Bar Association Real Property Section

B. Issues commonly resolved in SNDAs

1. Subordination

   a. Lease should be subordinated to present and future mortgages and any refinancing.

   b. All of the property that is to be mortgaged should be indicated.

   c. Subordination should be automatic.

   d. Power of attorney should be granted to execute necessary documents to confirm subordination.

   e. Fixtures that may be removed by tenant at the expiration of the lease should be excluded.

2. Attornment

   a. Tenant's attornment should cover judicial and non-judicial foreclosures as well as the voluntary or involuntary sale or assignment of landlord's interest in the premises.

   b. Power of attorney should be granted to execute all necessary documents confirming attornment.

3. Non-disturbance

   a. In any foreclosure proceeding, tenant possession will not be disturbed and tenant will not be named as a party.

   b. Mortgagee will affirmatively assume landlord obligations.

4. Basic Economic Terms of Lease

    a. Issue - Should the mortgagee honor the business terms that the tenant negotiated with the landlord or should the mortgagee override extension or expansion options, representations and warranties, or other such terms?

    b. Resolution in Model Agreement

        1. The tenant should be entitled to the basic economic and possessory benefits of the lease. The favorable outcomes of these negotiations were presumably reflected in the rent the tenant agreed to pay, thereby creating the value to support the loan.

        2. This approach forces the mortgagee to carefully review the lease to identify specific objectionable provisions and to renegotiate them with the tenant.

5. Security Deposit

    a. Issue - Should the mortgagee or tenant bear the risk that the landlord will misapply the tenant's security deposit?

    b. Resolution in Model Agreement

        1. §4.3 places the risk on tenant. The mortgagee is not responsible for security deposits unless actually received by the mortgagee.

        2. This approach is consistent with the normal negotiated outcome in most SNDAs and the New York statute requiring

actual delivery of security
deposits to a purchaser for
the purchaser to incur liability for them (N.Y. Gen. Oblig.
Law § 7-105(2)).

c. If the parties decide to place
such risk on the mortgagee, the
mortgagee would effectively be required to hold all security deposits
from the inception of the loan.

6. Construction Work

a. Issue - Should the mortgagee be
required to finish construction that
the landlord failed to complete
(including even initial fixturiza-
tion)?

b. Treatment of this issue in mortgagee's form of SNDA - The mortgagee is excused from any obligation to
complete such construction yet is
permitted to collect rent after
foreclosure that is premised on the
space being delivered in the condition required by the lease.

c. Resolution in Model Agreement

1. The Model Agreement leaves
the matter for negotiation
between the mortgagee and the
tenant, to be memorialized in
each case in a separate "schedule" to the Model Agreement.

2. If the parties do not
specifically address the issue
and the mortgagee names the
tenant as a defendant in the
foreclosure action, the mortgagee will, after foreclosure,
have no obligation to complete
or pay for the tenant's construction and the tenant will

have no recourse against the mortgagee (§4.6).

d.   Possible Resolution

1.   One possible solution - If the initial improvements to the premises are not completed and the mortgagee, after attornment, does not agree in writing within a certain period to complete such work within a reasonable time, the tenant may either terminate the lease or complete such work and offset the expenses thereof against rent.

2.   Sample language - "If Former Landlord has failed to perform Landlord's Construction-Related Obligation(s) with respect to Tenant's initial occupancy of Tenant's Premises and Successor Landlord does not agree in writing within 30 days after Tenant's demand after the date of attornment to complete such Construction-Related Obligation(s) within a reasonable period, then Tenant, as its sole remedy, shall have the right to elect either to terminate the Lease by written notice to Successor Landlord, or to complete and pay for such Construction-Related Obligations and offset all reasonable costs thereby incurred (the "Construction Cost"), together with interest on the unrecovered balance of Construction Cost, against any Rent thereafter payable, until Tenant shall have so recovered the entire Construction Cost."

7.   Casualty and Condemnation Repairs

   a.   Issue - To what extent should
   the mortgagee perform casualty and
   condemnation repairs?

   b. Resolution in Model Agreement

      1.   §§1.1 and 3.2 require the
      mortgagee to perform casualty
      and condemnation repairs to
      the extent that such repairs
      would be required of landlord.

      2.   Rationale

         a.   If the mortgagee's
         obligation is limited to
         the amount of insurance
         proceeds received, the
         mortgagee would be re-
         ceiving a better deal
         than that negotiated by
         the landlord and tenant.

         b.   This approach pre-
         vents the mortgagee from
         seizing upon the build-
         ing's misfortune as the
         basis for early prepay-
         ment, except to the
         extent expressly contem-
         plated by provisions in
         the lease.

         c.   A mortgagee, by
         properly drafting and
         administering the mort-
         gage, can control the
         level of insurance, the
         insurance adjustment
         process, and the appli-
         cation of insurance
         proceeds. The tenant
         should not be adversely
         affected if the mortgag-
         ee fails to do its job.

8. Deed in Lieu of Foreclosure

    a. Issue - When should mortgagee protections be triggered?

    b. Resolution in Model Agreement

        1. Mortgagee protections in SNDAs are triggered not only by an actual foreclosure, but also by a deed in lieu of foreclosure delivered by the landlord to the mortgagee (or its designee or nominee) (§1.2).

        2. This resolution is consistent with industry norm.

        3. Possible argument by tenant - A tenant may argue that by accepting a deed in lieu of foreclosure, a mortgagee should succeed to exactly the same rights and obligations as the landlord, and the landlord's delivery of a deed in lieu of foreclosure should not be an occasion for any change in the landlord-tenant relationship.

9. Options

    a. Issue - Should mortgagee be bound by options to purchase, expand, contract, renew, etc.?

    b. Resolution in Model Agreement

        1. Tenant should be entitled to preserve any options expressly provided for in the lease, and the mortgagee should take free only of those options not set forth in the lease.

2. §§ D, 3.2, 7.1 of the Model Agreement

> a. These provisions state that the lease is the entire agreement between landlord and tenant and the only agreement by which the mortgagee will be bound.
>
> b. No particular discussion of options is required to effectuate the above resolution.

c. Tenant's counsel should insure that the SNDA expressly recognizes (and defines as part of the "Lease") any side letters, option agreements, or other ancillary documentation providing the tenant with valuable rights that should survive foreclosure.

10. Amendments and Modifications

a. Issue - To what extent may landlord and tenant amend the lease?

b. Resolution in Model Agreement - The Model Agreement permits landlord and tenant to amend the lease as they wish, but states that the mortgagee will not be bound by any amendments made without the mortgagee's consent (§4.4).

c. Mortgagee's standard position is a prohibition on all amendments

d. Intermediate position - The tenant might agree that any amendment reducing rent or increasing the space, the term or landlord's obligations requires the mortgagee's consent, since such an amendment would impair cash flow and therefore adversely affect the mortgagee even before foreclosure.

11. Offset Rights

    a. Issue - To what extent may the tenant offset against the mortgagee?

    b. Resolution in Model Agreement

        1. The Model Agreement prohibits offsets against the mortgagee based on events that occurred before the date of attornment (§§1.4, 4.1), which is consistent with industry norm. Therefore, if a tenant negotiates an offset right in a lease, the tenant should assert that right promptly because such right will not survive foreclosure as to those offsets that accrued prior to foreclosure.

        2. After foreclosure, the Model Agreement requires the Successor Landlord to accept the lease according to its terms, including any express offset rights (but only as to matters occurring after foreclosure) (§§3.2, 4.1).

        3. The Model Agreement defines "Offset Right" broadly (§ 1.4). The parties may prefer to limit the term to any "offset, defense, or counterclaim."

12. Estoppel Certificate

a. Model Agreement

1. The Model Agreement includes a full estoppel certificate (§ 7).

2. This estoppel certificate
will often need to be tailored
to the particular lease, including (a) whether the landlord has completed construction work and the tenant has
taken possession; (b) identification of any presently
determinable important dates,
such as the "Commencement
Date" or the "Rent Commencement Date"; (c) the status of
any tenant termination options
that may no longer exist if
certain time periods lapse or
certain conditions are satisfied; and (d) the extent of
the tenant's obligations under
the lease to deliver an estoppel certificate.

b. It may be more customary to omit
the estoppel provisions or put them
in a separate document. Either way,
tenant's counsel should carefully
review the accuracy of any estoppel
provisions with the tenant.

13. Opportunity to Cure Landlord's Default

a. Resolution in Model Agreement

1. The Model Agreement provides the mortgagee with a
fairly generous cure period
for landlord's defaults. This
period, longer than the norm
in many SNDAs, is similar to
the mortgagee's cure period
available under a ground lease
(§§ 6.2, 6.3).

2. This cure period is tempered somewhat by language stating that once a receiver is appointed, the mortgagee must cause the receiver to cure the landlord's default within a reasonable time (§ 6.3), which may be quite difficult, particularly as to nonemergency matters.

b. A tenant may regard the mortgagee's cure period in the Model Agreement as excessive and may, for example, require the right to suspend or offset rent or exercise self-help during the cure period.

14. Nonrecourse

   a. Resolution in Model Agreement

      1. The Model Agreement provides that any "Successor Landlord" is automatically exculpated from personal liability under the Lease (§ 5).

      2. This position is consistent with industry standard.

      3. Most tenants will accept this provision because they are accustomed to seeing such a clause run to the benefit of the landlord.

   b. If a lease did not contain such a clause, a mortgagee could always achieve the same result by having a shell corporation bid at the foreclosure sale.

15. Landlord's Payment Obligations - If the lease requires the landlord to make payments relating to matters beyond the premises, such as "takeover payments" with

respect to a tenant's existing lease, tenant's counsel should modify the SNDA to make sure this obligation survives foreclosure.

16.   Future Advances

a.   Issue - A tenant may prefer to subordinate (even with nondisturbance rights) only to a mortgage securing a known loan amount, and not to any future advances or loans that the same mortgage might later secure.

b.   Resolution in Model Agreement

1.   The mortgage to which the tenant subordinates includes future advances and increases (§§ C,2).

2.   This result reflects industry standards.

17.   Bankruptcy of Landlord

a.   Issue

1.   Many SNDAs provide that a tenant's nondisturbance rights cease if the lease terminates without excluding a lease termination that occurs because the tenant's lease is rejected in the landlord's bankruptcy under 11 U.S.C. § 365(h).   Although the Bankruptcy Code permits the tenant to remain in possession in such circumstances, the tenant's lease has probably still been "terminated."

2.   This termination of the tenant's lease may allow the mortgagee, during or after foreclosure, to deny the ten-

ant nondisturbance rights
(because the lease has terminated) and simply remove the
tenant under the subordination
clause of the SNDA. Thus, a
mortgagee may be able to avoid
a nondisturbance covenant by
manipulating the landlord's
bankruptcy.

b. Resolution in Model Agreement -
The Model Agreement solves this
problem by providing that the tenant
loses nondisturbance rights only if
the lease was terminated due to a
default by tenant.

C. Additional Issues to Consider (The following
issues are not addressed in most SNDAs and thus
do not appear in the Model Agreement. However,
they may be appropriate to consider in particular transactions).

1. Payment of Rent to Mortgagee

a. Issue - A mortgagee may want the
tenant to agree in the SNDA to pay
rent directly to the mortgagee on
request.

b. Such provisions are not included
in the Model Agreement.

1. They are not (yet) industry practice.

2. The landlord and tenant
can reasonably tell the mortgagee to rely on the standard
legal rights and remedies in
this area (e.g., appointment
of a receiver, New York Real
Prop. Law § 291-f).

c. Sample provision

Tenant's Covenant. Add the
following covenant by Tenant

(breach of which would cause
Tenant to lose nondisturbance
rights or trigger other remedies):

> Rent Payment Notices.
> From and after Tenant's
> receipt of written no-
> tice from Mortgagee (a
> "Rent Payment Notice"),
> Tenant shall pay all
> Rent to Mortgagee or as
> Mortgagee shall direct
> in writing, until such
> time as Mortgagee di-
> rects otherwise in writ-
> ing. Tenant shall com-
> ply with any Rent Pay-
> ment Notice notwith-
> standing any contrary
> instruction, direction
> or assertion from Land-
> lord. Mortgagee's de-
> livery to Tenant of a
> Rent Payment Notice, or
> Tenant's compliance
> therewith, shall not be
> deemed to: (a) cause
> Mortgagee to succeed to
> or to assume any obliga-
> tions or responsibili-
> ties as Landlord under
> the Lease, all of which
> shall continue to be
> performed and discharged
> solely by Landlord un-
> less and until any at-
> tornment has occurred
> pursuant to this Agree-
> ment; or (b) relieve
> Landlord of any obliga-
> tions under the Lease.

Landlord's Acknowledgment.
Add the following to Landlord's acknowledgment at the
end of the Model Agreement:

Landlord irrevocably
directs Tenant to comply
with any Rent Payment
Notice, notwithstanding
any contrary direction,
instruction, or asser-
tion by Landlord! Ten-
ant shall be entitled to
rely on any Rent Payment
Notice. Tenant shall be
under no duty to contro-
vert or challenge any
Rent Payment Notice.
Tenant's compliance with
a Rent Payment Notice
shall not be deemed to
violate the Lease.
Landlord hereby releases
Tenant from, and shall
indemnify and hold Ten-
ant harmless from and
against, any and all
loss, claim, damage,
liability, cost or ex-
pense (including payment
of reasonable attorneys'
fees and disbursements)
arising from any claim
based upon Tenant's
compliance with any Rent
Payment Notice. Land-
lord shall look solely
to Mortgagee with re-
spect to any claims
Landlord may have on
account of an incorrect
or wrongful Rent Payment
Notice. Tenant shall be
entitled to full credit
under the Lease for any
Rent paid to Mortgagee
pursuant to a Rent Pay-
ment Notice to the same
extent as if such Rent
were paid directly to
Landlord.

   2.   Tenant Exculpation - If the lease
includes a tenant nonrecourse clause, the tenant
may wish to incorporate the same clause, verba-
tim, in the SNDA.

   3.   Bankruptcy of Mortgagee

        a.   Issue - A SNDA probably consti-
        tutes an executory contract that the
        mortgagee could reject in its own
        bankruptcy proceeding or similar
        proceedings for failed financial
        institutions.

        b.   Possible resolution

             1.   At least in cases where
             the lease is executed prior to
             the mortgage, the tenant may
             insist on deleting the stan-
             dard subordination clause in
             the lease and instead require
             that subordination be ad-
             dressed only in the SNDA, with
             a proviso stating that the
             subordination is effective
             only so long as the SNDA is
             effective against the mortgag-
             ee.

             2.   Therefore, even if the
             SNDA were rejected, the lease
             itself and Bankruptcy Code
             § 365(h) should provide a
             degree of protection, although
             no case law directly supports
             this proposition.

   4. Miscellaneous

        a.   A mortgagee might want the same
        periodic deliveries that the land-
        lord receives under the lease, such
        as updated financial information or
        estoppel certificates.
        b.   A mortgagee might want the right
        to participate in legal proceedings
        relating to the determination of the

rights of parties to the lease
(e.g., arbitration).

c.   If the transaction involves out-
of-state parties, a consent to jurisdiction might be included.

d.   To prevent a desirable lease
from terminating if a junior mortgagee forecloses, a first mortgagee
may want the tenant to agree not to
subordinate to the lien of any junior mortgage.

e.   Recordation

> 1.   Every SNDA should be re-
> corded whether or not the
> lease or a memorandum thereof
> has been, although it is com-
> mon practice not to record
> SNDAs.
>
> 2.   If the lease prohibits
> recordation, tenant's counsel
> should consider whether re-
> cording a SNDA might violate
> that prohibition.
>
> 3.   In arranging execution of
> a SNDA, tenant's counsel
> should also prepare any ancil-
> lary affidavits, tax returns,
> a copy of the tenant's lease,
> and similar documentation that
> the recording office may re-
> quire.

f.   If the Model Agreement is used
in an "automatic cut-off" state, the
mortgagee may require leases to be
prior to the mortgage on all of the
same terms and conditions set forth
in the Model Agreement.

EXHIBIT A

_____

_____

_____ ("Mortgagee")

and

_____ ("Tenant")

_____

SUBORDINATION, NONDISTURBANCE
AND ATTORNMENT AGREEMENT

_____

_____, 199

_____

_____

This instrument affects real property situated,
lying and being in the County of _____,
State of New York, known as follows:

Section:
Volume:
Block(s):
Lot(s):

Street Address:
[New York City Only]

RECORD AND RETURN TO: NO MORTGAGE RECORDING
TAX IS PAYABLE WITH
RESPECT TO THIS AGREE-
MENT. NOTHING IN THIS
AGREEMENT IS INTENDED TO
_____, New York   EVIDENCE OR SECURE ANY
INDEBTEDNESS OR TO CRE-
ATE ANY LIEN.

Att'n:

File No.:
Document No.:

SUBORDINATION, NONDISTURBANCE
AND ATTORNMENT AGREEMENT

This SUBORDINATION, NONDISTURBANCE, AND ATTORNMENT AGREEMENT (this "Agreement") is entered into as of _____, 199_ (the "Effective Date"), between _____, a _____, whose address is _____ ("Mortgagee"), and _____, a _____, whose address is _____ ("Tenant"), with reference to the following facts:

A. _____, a _____, whose address is _____ ("Landlord"), owns the real properly located at _____ (such real property, including all buildings, improvements, structures and fixtures located thereon, "Landlord's Premises"), as more particularly described in Schedule A.

B. Mortgagee has made a loan to Landlord in the original principal amount of $_____ (the "Loan").

C. To secure the Loan, Landlord has encumbered Landlord's Premises by entering into that certain <u>Mortgage, Consolidation and Modification Agreement</u> dated _____, 19__, in favor of Mortgagee (as amended, increased, renewed, extended, spread, consolidated, severed, restated, or otherwise changed from time to time, the "Mortgage") [to be] recorded [on _____, at Book _____, Page _____,] in the Official Records of the County of _____, State of New York (the "Land Records").

D. Pursuant to a ___<u>Lease</u>___ dated as of _____, 19__, as amended on _____, 19__ and _____, 19__, (the "Lease"), Landlord demised to Tenant [a portion of] Landlord's Premises ("Tenant's Premises"). Tenant's Premises are commonly known as _____ .

[E. A memorandum of the Lease [is to be recorded in the Land Records prior to the recording of this Agreement.] [was recorded in the

Land Records on _____, at Book ___,
Page _____.]

    F.   Tenant and Mortgagee desire to agree
upon the relative priorities of their interests
in Landlord's Premises and their rights and
obligations if certain events occur.

    NOW, THEREFORE, for good and sufficient
consideration, Tenant and Mortgagee agree:

1. Definitions.

    The following terms shall have the follow-
ing meanings for purposes of this Agreement.

    1.1.   Construction-Related Obligation. A
"Construction-Related Obligation" means any
obligation of Landlord under the Lease to make,
pay for, or reimburse Tenant for any alterations, demolition, or other improvements or work
at Landlord's Premises, including Tenant's Premises. "Construction-Related Obligations" shall
not include: (a) reconstruction or repair following fire, casualty or condemnation; or (b)
day-to-day maintenance and repairs.

    1.2.   Foreclosure Event. A "Foreclosure
Event" means: (a) foreclosure under the Mortgage; (b) any other exercise by Mortgagee of
rights and remedies (whether under the Mortgage
or under applicable law, including bankruptcy
law) as holder of the Loan and/or the Mortgage,
as a result of which Successor Landlord becomes
owner of Landlord's Premises; or (c) delivery by
Landlord to Mortgagee (or its designee or nominee) of a deed or other conveyance of Landlord's
interest in Landlord's Premises in lieu of any
of the foregoing.

    1.3.   Former Landlord. A "Former Land-
lord" means Landlord and any other party that
was landlord under the Lease at any time before
the occurrence of any attornment under this
Agreement.

    1.4.   Offset Right. An "Offset Right"
means any right or alleged right of Tenant to

any offset, defense (other than one arising from actual payment and performance, which payment and performance would bind a Successor Landlord pursuant to this Agreement), claim, counter-claim, reduction, deduction, or abatement against Tenant's payment of Rent or performance of Tenant's other obligations under the Lease, arising (whether under the Lease or other applicable law) from Landlord's breach or default under the Lease.

     1.5. <u>Rent</u>. The "Rent" means any fixed rent, base rent or additional rent under the Lease.

     1.6. <u>Successor Landlord</u>. A "Successor Landlord" means any party that becomes owner of Landlord's Premises as the result of a Foreclosure Event.

     1.7. <u>Termination Right</u>. A "Termination Right" means any right of Tenant to cancel or terminate the Lease or to claim a partial or total eviction arising (whether under the Lease or under applicable law) from Landlord's breach or default under the Lease.

2.   <u>Subordination</u>.

     The Lease shall be, and shall at all times remain, subject and subordinate to the Mortgage, the Lien imposed by the Mortgage, and all advances made under the Mortgage.

3.   <u>Nondisturbance, Recognition and Attornment</u>.

     3.1. <u>No Exercise of Mortgage Remedies Against Tenant</u>. So long as the Lease has not been terminated on account of Tenant's default that has continued beyond applicable cure periods (an "Event of Default"), Mortgagee shall not name or join Tenant as a defendant in any exercise of Mortgagee's rights and remedies arising upon a default under the Mortgage unless applicable law requires Tenant to be made a party thereto as a condition to proceeding against Landlord or prosecuting such rights and remedies. In the latter case, Mortgagee may join Tenant as a defendant in such action only for such purpose and not to terminate the Lease or otherwise adversely affect Tenant's rights under the Lease or this Agreement in such action.

3.2. _Nondisturbance and Attornment_. If the Lease has not been terminated on account of an Event of Default by Tenant, then, when Successor Landlord takes title to Landlord's Premises: (a) Successor Landlord shall not terminate or disturb Tenant's possession of Tenant's Premises under the Lease, except in accordance with the terms of the Lease and this Agreement; (b) Successor Landlord shall be bound to Tenant under all the terms and conditions of the Lease (except as provided in this Agreement); (c) Tenant shall recognize and attorn to Successor Landlord as Tenant's direct landlord under the Lease as affected by this Agreement; and (d) the Lease shall continue in full force and effect as a direct lease, in accordance with its terms (except as provided in this Agreement), between Successor Landlord and Tenant.

3.3. _Further Documentation_. The provisions of this Article shall be effective and self-operative without any need for Successor Landlord or Tenant to execute any further documents. Tenant and Successor Landlord shall, however, confirm the provisions of this Article in writing upon requests by either of them.

4. _Protection of Successor Landlord_

Notwithstanding anything to the contrary in the Lease or the Mortgage, Successor Landlord shall not be liable for or bound by any of the following matters:

4.1. _Claims against Former Landlord_. Any Offset Right that Tenant may have against any Former Landlord relating to any event or occurrence before the date of attornment, including any claim for damages of any kind whatsoever as the result of any breach by Former Landlord that occurred before the date of attornment. (The foregoing shall not limit either (a) Tenant's right to exercise against Successor Landlord any Offset Right otherwise available to Tenant because of events occurring after the date of attornment or (b) Successor Landlord's obligation to correct any conditions that existed as of the date of attornment and violate Successor Landlord's obligations as landlord under the Lease.)

4.2. <u>Prepayments</u>. Any payment of Rent that Tenant may have made to Former Landlord more than thirty days before the date such Rent was first due and payable under the Lease with respect to any period after the date of attornment other than, and only to the extent that, the Lease expressly required such a prepayment.

4.3. <u>Payment; Security Deposit</u>. Any obligation: (a) to pay Tenant any sum(s) that any Former Landlord owed to Tenant or (b) with respect to any security deposited with Former Landlord, unless such security was actually delivered to Mortgagee. This paragraph is not intended to apply to Landlord's obligation to make any payment that constitutes a "Construction-Related Obligation."

4.4. <u>Modification, Amendment, or Waiver</u>. Any modification or amendment of the Lease, or any waiver of any terms of the Lease, made without Mortgagee's written consent.

4.5. <u>Surrender, Etc.</u> Any consensual or negotiated surrender, cancellation, or termination of the Lease, in whole or in part, agreed upon between Landlord and Tenant, unless effected unilaterally by Tenant pursuant to the express terms of the Lease.

4.6. <u>Construction-Related Obligations</u>. Any Construction-Related Obligation of Former Landlord, except as expressly provided for in Schedule B (if any) attached to this Agreement.

5. <u>Exculpation of Successor Landlord</u>.

Notwithstanding anything to the contrary in this Agreement or the Lease, upon any attornment pursuant to this Agreement the Lease shall be deemed to have been automatically amended to provide that Successor Landlord's obligations and liability under the Lease shall never extend beyond Successor Landlord's (or its successors' or assigns') interest, if any, in Landlord's Premises from time to time, including insurance and condemnation proceeds, Successor Landlord's interest in the Lease, and the proceeds from any sale or other disposition of Landlord's Premises by Successor Landlord (collectively, "Successor Landlord's Interest"). Tenant shall look exclusively to Successor Landlord's Interest (or that of its successors and assigns) for payment or discharge of any obligations of Successor Landlord under the Lease as affected by this Agreement. If Tenant obtains any money judgment against Successor Landlord with respect to the Lease or the relationship between Successor Landlord and Tenant, then Tenant shall look solely to Successor Landlord's Interest (or that of its successors and assigns) to collect such judgment. Tenant shall not collect or attempt to collect any such judgment out of any other assets of Successor Landlord.

6.   Mortgagee's Right to Cure.

6.1. Notice to Mortgagee. Notwithstanding anything to the contrary in the Lease or this Agreement, before exercising any Termination Right or Offset Right, Tenant shall provide Mortgagee with notice of the breach or default by Landlord giving rise to same (the "Default Notice") and, thereafter, the opportunity to cure such breach or default as provided for below.

6.2. Mortgagee's Cure Period. After Mortgagee receives a Default Notice, Mortgagee shall have a period of thirty days beyond the time available to Landlord under the Lease in which to cure the breach or default by Landlord. Mortgagee shall have no obligation to cure (and shall have no liability or obligation for not curing) any breach or default by Landlord, except to the extent that Mortgagee agrees or undertakes otherwise in writing.

6.3. <u>Extended Cure Period</u>. In addition, as to any breach or default by Landlord the cure of which requires possession and control of Landlord's Premises, provided only that Mortgagee undertakes to Tenant by written notice to Tenant within thirty days after receipt of the Default Notice to exercise reasonable efforts to cure or cause to be cured by a receiver such breach or default within the period permitted by this paragraph, Mortgagee's cure period shall continue for such additional time (the "Extended Cure Period") as Mortgagee may reasonably require to either (a) obtain possession and control of Landlord's Premises and thereafter cure the breach or default with reasonable diligence and continuity or (b) obtain the appointment of a receiver and give such receiver a reasonable period of time in which to cure the default.

7. <u>Confirmation of Facts</u>.

Tenant represents to Mortgagee and to any Successor Landlord, in each case as of the Effective Date:

7.1. <u>Effectiveness of Lease</u>. The Lease is in full force and effect, has not been modified, and constitutes the entire agreement between Landlord and Tenant relating to Tenant's Premises. Tenant has not interest in Landlord's Premises except pursuant to the Lease. No unfulfilled conditions exist to Tenant's obligations under the Lease.

7.2. <u>Rent</u>. Tenant has not paid any Rent that is first due and payable under the Lease after the Effective Date.

7.3. <u>No Landlord Default</u>. To the best of Tenant's knowledge, no breach or default by Landlord exists and no event has occurred that, with the giving of notice, the passage of time or both, would constitute such a breach or default.

7.4. <u>No Tenant Default</u>. Tenant is not in default under the Lease and has not received any uncured notice of any default by Tenant under the Lease.

7.5. <u>No Termination</u>. Tenant has no commenced any action nor sent or received any notice to terminate the Lease. Tenant has no presently exercisable Termination Right(s) or Offset Right(s).

7.6. <u>Commencement Date</u>. The "Commencement Date" of the Lease was _____, 199_.

7.7. <u>Acceptance</u>. Except as set forth in Schedule B (if any) attached to this Agreement: (a) Tenant has accepted possession of Tenant's Premises; and (b) Landlord has performed all Construction-Related Obligations related to Tenant's initial occupancy of Tenant's Premises and Tenant has accepted such performance by Landlord.

7.8. <u>No Transfer</u>. Tenant has not transferred, encumbered, mortgaged, assigned, conveyed or otherwise disposed of the Lease or any interest therein, other than sublease(s) made in compliance with the Lease.

7.9. <u>Due Authorization</u>. Tenant has full authority to enter into this Agreement, which has been duly authorized by all necessary actions.

8. <u>Miscellaneous</u>.

8.1. <u>Notices</u>. All notices or other communications required or permitted under this Agreement shall be in writing and given by certified mail (return receipt requested) or by nationally recognized overnight courier service that regularly maintains records of items delivered. Each party's address is as set forth in the opening paragraph of this Agreement, subject to change by notice under this paragraph. Notices shall be effective the next business day after being sent by overnight courier service, and five business days after being sent by certified mail (return receipt requested).

8.2. <u>Successors and Assigns</u>. This Agreement shall bind an benefit the parties, their successors and assigns, any Successor Landlord, and its successors and assigns. If Mortgagee assigns the Mortgage, then upon delivery to Tenant of written notice thereof accompanied by the assignee's written assumption of all obligations under this Agreement, all liability of the assignor shall terminate.

8.3. <u>Entire Agreement</u>. This Agreement constitutes the entire agreement between Mortgagee and Tenant regarding the subordination of the Lease to the Mortgage and the rights and obligations of Tenant and Mortgagee as to the subject matter of this Agreement.

8.4. <u>Interaction with Lease and with Mortgage</u>. If this Agreement conflicts with the Lease, then this Agreement shall govern as between the parties and any Successor Landlord, including upon any attornment pursuant to this Agreement. This Agreement supersedes, and constitutes full compliance with any provisions in the Lease that provide for subordination of the Lease to, or for delivery of nondisturbance agreements by the holder of, the Mortgage. Mortgagee confirms that Mortgagee has consented to Landlord's entering into the Lease.

8.5. <u>Mortgagee's Rights and Obligations</u>. Except as expressly provided for in this Agreement, Mortgagee shall have no obligations to Tenant with respect to the Lease. If an attornment occurs pursuant to this Agreement, then all rights and obligations of Mortgagee under this Agreement shall terminate, without thereby affecting in any way the rights and obligations of Successor Landlord provided for in this Agreement.

8.6. <u>Interpretation; Governing Law</u>. The interpretation, validity and enforcement of this Agreement shall be governed by and construed under the internal laws of the State of New York, excluding its principles of conflict of laws.

8.7. <u>Amendments</u>. This Agreement may be amended, discharged or terminated, or any of its provisions waived, only by a written instruments executed by the party to be charged.

8.8. <u>Execution</u>. This Agreement may be executed in any number of counterparts, each of which shall be deemed an original and all of which together shall constitute one and the same instrument.

8.9. <u>Mortgagee's Representation</u>. Mortgagee represents that Mortgagee has full authority to enter into this Agreement, and Mortgagee's entry into this Agreement has been duly authorized by all necessary actions.

IN WITNESS WHEREOF, this Agreement has been duly executed by Mortgagee and Tenant as of the Effective Date.

Its: _____

Dated:_____, 19__

Attachments:

    Acknowledgments
    Schedule A = Description of Landlord's
                  Premises
    Schedule B = Landlord's Construction-
                  Related Obligations

ACKNOWLEDGMENTS

[Individual General Partner]

STATE OF NEW YORK)
) ss
COUNTY OF   )

      On the _____ day of _____, 199_,
before me personally came _____, to me
known, who, being by me duly sworn, did depose
and say that (s)he resides at _____, that
(s)he is a general partner of _____, the
partnership named in the foregoing instrument;
and that (s)he executed such instrument as the
act and deed of, and on behalf of, said partnership.

_____
Notary Public

[Corporation]

STATE OF NEW YORK)
) ss
COUNTY OF   )

      On the _____ day of _____, 199_, be
fore me personally came _____, to me known,
who, being by me duly sworn, did depose and say
that (s)he resides at _____, that
(s)he is the _____ of _____, the
corporation described in and which executed the
foregoing instrument; and that (s)he signed h__
name thereto by authority of the board of directors of said corporation.

_____
Notary Public

[Individual]

STATE OF NEW YORK)
) ss
COUNTY OF   )

On the _____ day of _____, 199_,
before personally came _____, to me known
to be the individual described in and who executed the foregoing instrument, and acknowledged
that (s)he executed the same.

_____
Notary Public

[Corporate General Partner of Limited Partner-
ship]

STATE OF NEW YORK)
) ss
COUNTY OF   )

On the _____ day of _____, 199_, before me personally came _____, to me known,
who, being by me duly sworn, did depose and say
that (s)he resides at _____; that (s)he
is the _____ President of _____, the
corporation described in and which executed the
foregoing instrument as general partner of _____
_____, the limited partnership named in the
foregoing instrument; that (s)he signed h__ name
thereto by authority of the board of directors
of said corporation; and that (s)he executed
such instrument as the act and deed of, and on
behalf of, said limited partnership acting
through its corporate general partner.

_____
Notary Public

Schedule A

Description of Landlord's Premises

ALL THAT CERTAIN REAL PROPERTY lying, being and situated in the City of _____, County of _____, and State of New York, more particularly described as follows:

Schedule B

Construction-Related Obligations

A.   Construction-Related Obligations Remaining to Be Performed as of Effective Date.

     [Summarize and Describe]

B.   Successor Landlord's Construction-Related Obligations After Attornment.

     [Negotiate and Describe]

III. Estoppel Certificates (a sample form of estoppel certificate is appended at the end of this section)

A.   An estoppel certificate is a signed state-ment by a tenant certifying for the bene-fit of another party that a particular statement of facts with respect to a lease is accurate as of the date of the state-ment.

B.   Its purpose is to "estop" or preclude a tenant from asserting a claim that is contrary to statements made by the tenant in its estoppel certificate. If a tenant has not carved out an exception in the estoppel certificate indicating that the landlord is in default in performing a particular obligation, the estoppel cer-tificate may be interposed by the landlord as the tenant's representation that the

landlord is not in default under the lease
or has cured all lease defaults as of the
date the estoppel certificate was executed, even if at the time such statement was
not true. A tenant must also be diligent
in examining the representations it is required to make in the estoppel certificate
with respect to the amounts of rent and
other monies it certifies it is paying the
landlord pursuant to the lease.

C.   Landlords have the most use for estoppel
certificates when they wish to sell their
building or finance their interest therein, since nearly all prospective purchasers and lenders will insist upon receiving
an estoppel certificate from most major
tenants before purchasing a building or
making a loan. It is important for the
lender that the estoppel certificate incorporate all of the documents related to
or that are a part of the lease. If there
are amendments or side agreements that are
not included in the lease itself, they
must be identified in the estoppel certificate. An estoppel certificate identifies
the entire lease deal, gives the lender
comfort that it has performed its due
diligence in making the loan and shifts
the burden of identifying the lease documents onto the tenant.

D.   The failure to provide an estoppel certificate from an important tenant can frustrate a financing or sale. In order to
avoid the consequences of a delayed or
denied certificate, the estoppel certificate provision in a lease should state
that (i) a proffered certificate will be
presumed to be correct if a response is
not received within a particular period or
(ii) the landlord is empowered to act as
the tenant's attorney-in-fact in executing
the estoppel certificate if the tenant
fails to do so.

E.   In order to avoid any disagreement about
the form of the estoppel certificate, many

landlords attach the form to their leases and negotiate at the time of execution of the lease any objections that the tenant raises. This practice makes it easier to prove that the tenant understood the ramifications of not signing the estoppel certificate and that the tenant was aware of what it was expected to sign when the certificate arrived.

F.   Tenants may attempt to use an estoppel certificate as a wedge with the landlord in order to obtain additional concessions or to compel a landlord to perform obligations that the tenant feels the landlord has failed to perform. A landlord must attempt to avoid a dispute with one of its tenants that may give rise to unspecified amounts of liability or a potential termination of a lease and rent stream that the lender or purchaser plans to rely upon in making the loan or purchase.

G.   If the tenant fails to timely return the estoppel certificate, the landlord may declare the tenant in default under the lease. This gives rise to a material breach of the lease, with all the rights and remedies set forth in the lease when the tenant is in default. Unless the lease provides otherwise, at the end of the review period, the landlord may be required to give the tenant an additional period of time before the tenant can actually be declared in default.

H.   An estoppel certificate can also be used by a landlord as a wedge. A landlord is generally not limited to presenting a tenant with an estoppel certificate solely in connection with a sale or financing. A landlord may present a certificate periodically in order to determine if the tenant is complying with the terms of its lease or the time period turnarounds. A landlord with the right to act as a tenant's attorney-in-fact may also use it as a means of amending a lease.

TENANT ESTOPPEL CERTIFICATE

To:

Re: _____

_____

Suite _____

Gentlemen:

The undersigned, (**"Tenant"**), as tenant under that certain lease dated _____-_, 19__ (said lease as same has been amended, supplemented or changed is hereinafter referred to as the **"Lease"**) between Tenant, as lessee, and _____, as lessor (**"Landlord"**), affecting the captioned premises (the **"Premises"**), does hereby certify, that as of the date hereof:

1. Attached hereto as Exhibit A is a true, correct and complete copy of the Lease, together with all amendments thereto, if any, all of which are in full force and effect on and as of the date hereof.

2. The Lease represents the entire agreement between the parties with respect to the leasing and occupancy of the Premises, and there are no other agreements or representations of any kind between Landlord and Tenant with respect thereto.

3. Tenant acknowledges that no obligation of Landlord to Tenant in connection with the Premises is unperformed as of the date hereof.

4. The term of the Lease has commenced on _____ and shall expire on _____ unless sooner terminated in accordance with the terms of the Lease or as may be extended for _____ in accordance with the terms of the Lease.

5. The current rent under the Lease is $_____ per month and has been paid

up to and including _____. All additional rent and other charges under the Lease have been paid in full for the current periods.

6. No default, or event that with the passing of time or the giving of notice, or both, would constitute a default on the part of Tenant or Landlord, exists under the Lease, and Tenant and Landlord have well and truly performed all of the terms, covenants and conditions of the Lease respectively required to be performed by it.

7. Tenant has no charge, lien or offset against the enforcement of the Lease by Landlord, or against rentals or other charges due or to become under the Lease.

8. No prepayments of rents due under the Lease have been made and no security or deposits as security have been made, except the sum of $_____.

9. There are no actions, whether voluntary or otherwise, pending against Tenant under the bankruptcy or insolvency laws of the United States or of any state or territory of the United States.

10. To the best of Tenant's knowledge, no hazardous wastes have been treated, stored or disposed of on the premises, and no petroleum or other hazardous substances have been disposed of on the Premises.

11. Tenant does not have any rights of first refusal for additional space or options to increase its space or options to purchase the Premises, except as specifically set forth on Schedule A, annexed hereto, and Landlord does not have any obligations to, or agreements with the Tenant regarding the Premises (including, without limitation, obligations to build or make additional improvements for Tenant) except as contained in the Lease.

12. Tenant confirms and agrees that the Lease is and shall at all times be

subject and subordinate to any mortgages now or hereafter affecting the land, building and/or air rights relating to the premises in which the Premises are located, including, without limitation, any mortgage now or hereafter held by the Bank encumbering such premises and any amendments, modifications, consolidations, substitutions, replacements, additions, renewals, extensions or re-advances thereof.

     13.   Tenant covenants and agrees as follows:

    (a)   to provide the Bank at its offices set forth above with copies of any notices of default (i) given by Tenant to Landlord or (ii) received by Tenant from Landlord; and

    (b)   not to modify, amend, restate and/or cancel the Lease without the Bank's prior written consent in each instance.

     14.   Tenant understands and acknowledges that the Bank is relying upon the declarations, covenants, representations and warranties contained herein and is entitled to do so.

_____ -

_____

(Tenant)

Dated: _____, 199_

IV.   Guaranties

    A.   Guarantees (See Exhibit A)

        (a)   Consideration
        (b)   Limitations
        (c)   Continuing effectiveness
        (d)   Right to be released

            Upon Tenant creditworth-
            iness
            Upon posting security
            Upon substitute guaran
            tor

    B.   Good guy guarantees (See Exhibit
No. 2)

        (e)   Usefulness
        (f)   Limitations

Exhibit A: Guaranty of Lease

In order to induce Landlord (as hereinafter defined) to execute that certain Lease
("Lease"), dated as of _____, 199_, between
_____ ("Landlord") and _____
("Tenant"), the undersigned ("Guarantor"), does
hereby absolutely and unconditionally guarantee
the full performance and observance of all the
terms, covenants and agreements provided to be
performed and observed by Tenant therein, including, without limitation, the prompt payment
of the Fixed Rent and Additional Rent and all
other amounts provided therein to be paid by
Tenant. The Lease is hereby incorporated by
reference as if herein set forth in its entirety. Guarantor represents and warrants to Landlord that prior to Guarantor's execution of this
Guaranty, it received and reviewed a true, complete, and correct copy of the Lease. All capitalized terms not otherwise defined herein shall
have the meaning ascribed thereto in the Lease.

The Guarantor expressly agrees that its obligations hereunder shall in no wise be terminated, affected or impaired by reason of the granting by Landlord of any indulgences to Tenant or by reason of the assertion against Tenant of any of the rights and remedies reserved to Landlord pursuant to the provisions of the Lease. Moreover, in the event that Tenant is relieved of a portion of its obligations under the Lease by operation of law or otherwise, the Guarantor expressly agrees that its obligations under this Guaranty regarding Tenant's remaining obligations under the Lease shall in no way be terminated, affected or impaired.

This Guaranty is an absolute and unconditional guaranty of payment (and not of collection) and of performance. The liability of Guarantor is coextensive with that of Tenant and this Guaranty shall be enforceable against Guarantor without the necessity of any suit or proceeding on Landlord's part of any kind or nature whatsoever against Tenant and, except as provided in the last sentence of this paragraph, without the necessity of any notice of non-payment, non-performance or non-observance or of any notice of acceptance of this Guaranty or of any other notice, proof, or demand to which Guarantor might otherwise be entitled, all of which Guarantor hereby expressly waives. Guarantor hereby expressly agrees that the validity of this Guaranty and the obligations of Guarantor hereunder shall in no way be terminated, affected, diminished or impaired by reason of (a) the assertion or the failure to assert by Landlord against Tenant of any of the rights or remedies reserved to Landlord pursuant to the terms, covenants and conditions of the Lease, or (b) any non-liability of Tenant under the Lease on account of insolvency or bankruptcy. Guarantor shall be entitled to copies of all notices required to be given to Tenant under the Lease at the same time such notices are delivered to Tenant.

This Guaranty shall be a continuing guaranty, and, except for actual payment and performance by Guarantor or payment or performance by

Tenant, in each case to the extent the same
would result in commensurate reductions of liability under this Guaranty and the liability of
Guarantor hereunder shall in no way be affected,
modified or diminished by reason of (a) any
assignment, renewal, modification, amendment or
extension of the Lease, or (b) any modification
or waiver of or change in any of the terms,
covenants and conditions of the Lease by Landlord and Tenant, or (c) any extension of time
that may be granted by Landlord to Tenant, (d)
any consent, release or indulgence under or in
respect of the Lease, or (e) any dealings or
transactions or matter or thing occurring between Landlord and Tenant, or (f) any bankruptcy, insolvency, reorganization, liquidation,
arrangement, assignment for the benefit of creditors, receivership, trusteeship or similar
proceeding affecting Tenant, whether or not
notice thereof is given to Guarantors.

Notwithstanding anything herein to the
contrary, should Landlord be obligated by any
bankruptcy or other law to repay to Tenant or to
Guarantor or to any trustee, receiver or other
representative of either of them, any preferen-
tial payments or other similar amounts previously paid, this Guaranty shall be reinstated in
the amounts of such repayments.

No waiver or modification of any provision
of this Guaranty nor any termination of this
Guaranty shall be effective unless in writing,
signed by Landlord; nor shall any such waiver be
applicable except in the specific instance for
which given.

All of Landlord's rights and remedies
under the Lease and under this Guaranty, now or
hereafter existing at law or in equity or by
statute or otherwise, are intended to be distinct, separate and cumulative and no exercise
or partial exercise of any such right or remedy
therein or herein mentioned is intended to be in
exclusion of or a waiver of any of the others.

No such payment or performance by Guarantor pursuant to any provision hereof shall enti-

tle Guarantor by subrogation or otherwise to the rights of Landlord to any payment by Tenant or out of the property of Tenant, except after payment of all sums or fulfillment of all covenants, terms, conditions or agreements to be paid or performed by Tenant.

Without regard to principles of conflicts of laws, the validity, interpretation, performance and enforcement of this Guaranty shall be governed by and construed in accordance with the internal laws of the State of _____ ___.

If Guarantor fails to pay any amount payable under this Guaranty when due, interest on such amount shall accrue at the rate set forth in Section ___ of the Lease.

Guarantor agrees that this Guaranty shall inure to the benefit of and may be enforced by Landlord, its mortgagees and their respective transferees, successors and assigns. This Guaranty shall not be assigned in whole or in part by any Guarantor.

Any notice, demand, request or other communication required or permitted to be given under this Guaranty shall be deemed given (a) upon written confirmation of hand delivery, (b) one (1) business day after deposit with Federal Express or other commercially recognized courier for overnight delivery, charges prepaid, (c) three (3) business days after mailing registered or certified United States mail, postage prepaid, return receipt requested, or (d) upon written confirmation of facsimile transmission and in each case addressed as follows:

(i)   If intended for Guarantor:

_____
_____
_____

(ii) If intended for Landlord

_____
_____
_____

with a copy to:

_____
_____
_____

or at such other address as the party to be served notice may have furnished in writing to the party seeking or desiring to serve notice as a place for service of notice. Notices given in any other fashion shall be deemed effective only upon receipt.

Until such time as all of the obligations under the Lease have been fulfilled, the Guarantor waives and releases any claim (within the meaning of 11 U.S.C. § 101) which Guarantor may have against Tenant arising from a payment made by Guarantor under this Guaranty and agrees not to assert or take advantage of any subrogation rights of Guarantor or any right of Guarantor to proceed against Tenant for reimbursement. It is expressly understood that the waivers and agreements of Guarantor set forth above constitute additional and cumulative benefits given to Landlord for its security and as an inducement for its execution of the Lease.

If any term, provision, or condition of this Guaranty shall be invalid, illegal or unenforceable in any respect, the remainder of this Guaranty shall be construed without such provision and the application of such term or provision to persons or circumstances other than those as to which it is held invalid, illegal or unenforceable, as the case may be, shall not be affected thereby, and each term and provision of this Guaranty shall be valid and enforced to the fullest extent permitted by law.

IN WITNESS WHEREOF, this Guaranty is executed by a duly authorized officer of Guarantor as of this _____ day of _____, 199_.

By:_____

Its_____

Exhibit B: "Good Guy" Guarantee

"Premises"   Portions of the _____
                          floor in the building known as

                          _____

"Landlord"   _____ -

_____

                                    _____ -

_____   _____ -

"Tenant"   _____

                                    _____

                                    _____ -

_____

                                    _____ -

_____

"Lease"   That certain lease,
                          dated _____,
                          between Landlord and
                          Tenant and covering the
                          Premises, as the same
                          may be hereafter modi-
                          fied or amended

        As an inducement for the execution of the
Lease, the undersigned, _____,
an individual having an address at _____-
_____, and _____,
an individual having an address at _____-
_____ (collectively, "Guarantor",
which term shall be deemed to include any successors and assigns), hereby **[jointly and sever-
ally]** absolutely, unconditionally and irrevocably guarantee to Landlord (which term shall be
deemed to include the named Landlord and its
successors and assigns) the full and prompt
payment of all fixed rent and additional rent
and all other charges and sums (including, without limitation, Landlord's reasonable attorneys'

fees and disbursements) payable by Tenant through the date the Premises shall be surrendered to Landlord vacant and broom clean (the "Surrender Date"), together with all of Landlord's costs of collection under this Guaranty (including, without limitation, Landlord's reasonable attorneys' fees and disbursements). Guarantor shall not be liable for any fixed rent, additional rent or other charges accruing under the lease from and after the Surrender Date.

[Add customary other guaranty terms]

Dated:_____   ——

                                        ——

STATE OF _____   )
) ss.:
COUNTY OF _____   )

          On the __ day of _____
before me came _____ and _____-
_____, to me known and known to me to be
the individuals described in, and who executed
the foregoing instrument and duly acknowledged
to me that they executed the same.

                                        ——

Notary Public

_____
Mr. Herz is the senior real estate partner in
the New York City law firm of Richards & O'Neil,
LLP. In addition, he served as chair of the
American Bar Association's Real Estate Asset
Management Committee and chair of the Commercial
Leasing Committee of the Real Property Section

of the New York State Bar Association. Mr. Herz
wishes to thank Lawrence Lenzner for his assistance in the preparation of this article.

NOTES

10

THE LENDER'S VIEW OF THE LEASE

Mary G. Murphy

THE LENDER'S VIEW OF THE LEASE

1.   **Background.** The lender has a critical interest in reviewing and understanding the existing and future leases of any property that secures a debt. The leases help to define the value of the property, which is critical to determining the loan to value ratio. They also give rise to net rental income of the property thereby providing the cash flow which will be used by the borrower to service the debt. Further, the lender must understand the risks and obligations imposed by the leases in the event it forecloses. In the process of performing its due diligence and documenting the loan, the lender must attempt to protect its interests from certain risks.

The loan documents creating the lender's security interest should provide the lender certain rights as against the borrower to protect the cash flow from the leases in the event of a default. Some of these protections should also be set forth in the lease as a covenant between the landlord and tenant. For example, both the lease and the Assignment of Leases typically contain covenants prohibiting the payment by tenant or the acceptance by landlord of more than one month's prepaid rent at any time.[1] The loan documents also provide the lender with some degree of control over future leases and amendments of existing leases. For example, the lender usually requires its approval of matters involving leases of a size over a certain square footage. The lease size that triggers lender's approval rights varies from loan to loan, depending on the make up of the property at issue. In the same way, the lender can use the estoppel certificates obtained from tenants in the course of its due diligence to ascertain and confirm the status of the leases and to protect itself from certain risks upon foreclosure. Attached as Exhibit A are some typical lease provisions addressing the landlord's need to satisfy the lender's requirements.

2.   **Lease Provisions of Concern to Lenders.**

(a)   Basic Facts. The lender should, as a matter of course, ascertain that the basic formalities of the lease are correct, for example, that the borrower is the same entity as the landlord and that the leasehold premises are fully encumbered by the lender's lien. The primary due diligence vehicle for reviewing all basic lease information is the estoppel certificate (see Exhibits B and C for examples). The estoppel certificate protects the lender from claims of landlord default through the date of the certificate and confirms critical facts about the lease. Because the certificate specifically provides that it runs to the lender's benefit and that the lender may and will rely on it, the tenant should be estopped from making contrary claims in the future. The estoppel certificate provides assurance from the tenant to the lender that the lease documents are complete, correct and in force and that landlord (and sometimes, tenant) is not in default under the lease. It also sets forth the fundamental lease terms, such as term of the lease, the size of the premises, extension options, rights of first refusal or similar rights, the basic rent payable under the lease, as well as operating expense details. The certificate should also address whether landlord has any outstanding monetary obligations to tenant, such as an unpaid tenant improvement allowance or pending construction obligations.

---

[1]   A similar covenant is also often found in a Subordination, Nondisturbance and Attornment Agreement, as discussed below.

(b)   <u>Rent and Other Economic Terms.</u> In addition to understanding the basic rent payable, the lender should review the operating expense provisions of the leases to confirm that all appropriate expenses of operating the building are being passed through consistently to all tenants. In a fully-serviced lease context, this includes evaluating the lease's base year or expense stop assumptions. Ensuring the full pass through of operating expenses may also entail understanding the recovery of costs associated with building amenities or parking facilities and the possible bifurcation of retail from office space in a building. In performing this evaluation, the lender must factor in such items as rent-free periods, expense caps, tenant improvement allowances, and services for which tenant is not charged. In a retail context with a percentage rent clause, the landlord must pay focus on any minimum fixed rent, definitions of gross or net profits, appraisal rights, and other provisions that effect or address profit generation, such as continuous operation clauses and operating hour requirements.

(c)   <u>Abatement, Offset, Deduction of Rent.</u> After coming to an understanding of the true economics of any lease, the lender must assess the risks of defensible nonpayment by tenant. All leases should contain some formulation such as "tenant shall pay rent without offset, recoupment or deduction" or "tenant shall pay rent without offset, deduction, abatement, or demand". Notwithstanding this language, the lender must review the lease for instances in which tenant may rightfully refuse or fail to pay rent. Rightful nonpayment can occur for more than one reason. Sometimes the tenant refuses to pay or seeks actual reimbursement from the landlord because of a landlord default. A common situation is one in which tenant executes a landlord repair obligation and offsets the costs against rent otherwise owed and payable. The lender should review the lease for any such rights on the part of tenant, as well as for waivers of any applicable statutory repair rights granted to tenant. In California, then, the lender should see if the lease contains an affirmative waiver of California Civil Code Section 1942.[2] The circumstances in which a right of abatement typically arises are: (1) damage and destruction; (2) utilities interruption; and (3) condemnation. Provisions granting tenants abatement rights in such circumstances also often contain termination rights for both landlord and tenant. The lender must require that landlord carry rental interruption insurance to protect against the tenants' abatement rights under the leases.

(d)   <u>Use Provisions.</u> The lender should attempt to understand how use provisions of the leases effect the overall character of the property (and hence, its value) as well as the manner in which the use clauses possibly preclude certain subletting and assignments. Lease provisions limiting the uses of the leased premises typically protect and are favored by, the lender. On the other hand, exclusivity clauses which prohibit the landlord from leasing to tenants' competitors limit the possible future leasing of the project and should be reviewed carefully.

(e)   <u>Assignment and Subletting.</u> The identity of tenants in any project, whether office or retail, is very important and the lender must carefully review the assignment and subletting provisions of the leases. In California, an extensive statutory framework governs

---

[2] Civil Code Section 1942 provides that the tenant may, within a reasonable time of written notice to landlord of dilapidation rendering the premises untenantable, may repair (up to an amount equal to one month's rent) and deduct the expenses of the repairs from rent when due.

2

the parties' rights in this area, and the lender should have some familiarity with those provisions.[3] The California Civil Code provides that in the absence of a contractual provision restricting transfer rights, the tenant,s rights under the lease include the unrestricted right to transfer the tenant's interest in the lease. California Civil Code Section 1044 and 1995.210(b). The Code also permits the parties, by contract, to completely prohibit any transfer. However, this is not a preferred alternative, because a complete prohibition results in the loss of the landlord's rights under California Civil Code Section 1951.4(a) (which permits the landlord to continue the lease in effect after the tenant's default and abandonment and collect rent as it becomes due). See California Civil Code Section 1951.4(b). In keeping with the statutory framework, the lease should require landlord's consent and specifically enumerate the reasons or circumstances under which landlord's refusal to consent will be deemed reasonable. The lender should review these provisions to ensure that matters of concern to lenders (such as the crediworthiness of the proposed assignee) are listed among landlord's reasonable grounds for denial.

(f)   Damage and Destruction; Condemnation. As discussed above, these provisions are of concern to lender because they often give rise to tenant rights to abate rent as well as rights on the part of both landlord and tenant to terminate the lease. The lease should provide the landlord flexibility to decide whether to repair or to terminate in the event that the costs or time to repair are prohibitive in the landlord's judgment. Where the lease imposes a duty on the landlord to repair, it may be in conflict with the lender's rights to require that insurance proceeds be used to repay the loan.

(g)   Environmental Issues. Recent amendments to the Comprehensive Environmental Response, Compensation and Liability Act ("CERCLA") now provide lenders with a greater measure of comfort regarding their potential liability for environmental problems arising on properties securing debts. The purpose of the amendments was to nullify the decision in United States v. Fleet Factors Corp., 901 F.2d 1550 (11th Cir. 1990), cert. denied, 11 S.Ct. 753 (1991), which held that a mere capacity to assert control over contaminated property could be sufficient to give rise to lender liability. The amendments provide that the lender loses its exemption from liability if it participates in management, which means "actually participating in the management or operational affairs of a vessel or facility; and does not include merely having the capacity to influence, or the unexercised right to control, vessel or facility operations." (to be codified at 42 U.S.C. Section 9601(20)(F)(i)). Notwithstanding this change in CERCLA, environmental problems are of grave concern to lenders because they may completely nullify the value of the property as security for the debt. Although the lender will probably require a separate environmental indemnity from the borrower/landlord, it also should look for protections against tenants in the leases. The tenant should be prohibited from handling hazardous materials without landlord's approval (with the possible exception of standard office materials, such as copy machine toner, in customary amounts and manners). Strict compliance with all applicable laws and regulations should be required for any handling of hazardous materials approved by landlord and the landlord should have inspection rights. All costs associated with tenant's

---

[3] The California Civil Code also address use provisions in a manner similar to the statutory framework governing assignment and subletting. See California Civil Code Sections 1997.010-1997.270.

handling of hazardous materials, whether with or without landlord approval, should be recoverable by landlord and such rights should survive termination of the lease.

      3.   <u>Subordination.</u> Subordination issues arise with respect to all leases, whether the leases were entered into before the lien is placed on the property or after. A lease is a lien against the property, just like the lender's deed of trust, and is treated in accordance with the first in time, first in right priority rule set forth in California Civil Code Section 2897. See also California Civil Code Section 1214. The lender's lien will be subordinate to pre-existing leases, whether or not a memorandum of lease was recorded, provided the tenant is in possession of the leased premises. Subordination is an extremely important issue because of the long-standing rule that foreclosure of the senior lien "wipes out," or extinguishes, junior liens in the absence of an agreement to the contrary.

      (a)   <u>Automatic Subordination.</u> Most leases contain some provision regarding subordination. An example is attached as Exhibit A. As in the attached example, leases most often state that the lease is subordinate to existing and future encumbrances, although the example specifically conditions subordination to future encumbrances on agreement by the holder of the future encumbrance not to disturb a non-defaulting tenant. California case law in this area is currently somewhat contradictory. In <u>Dover Mobile Estates v. Fiber Form Products, Inc.,</u> 220 Cal. App. 3d 1494, 270 Cal. Rptr. 183 (1990), the court held that the automatic subordination clause of a pre-existing lease operated to make the lease junior to a subsequent lien. When the lienholder foreclosed, the lease was deemed terminated by operation of law. In <u>Dover</u>, the foreclosing lender sought to enforce a lease which contained an automatic subordination clause. Like many of these clauses, the one at issue also provided that the lender could elect to treat the lien of the lease as superior to the lender's lien, but the court found that the lender had never elected to do so. Against the lender's wishes, then, the tenant walked away from what appears to have been an above-market lease. See also <u>R-Ranch Markets 2, Inc. v. Old Stone Bank</u>, 16 Cal. App. 4th 1323, 21 Cal. Rptr. 2d 21 (1993) (lease made prior to deed of trust not extinguished by foreclosure, but amendment to that lease made after deed of trust extinguished). By contrast, <u>Miscione v. Barton Development Company,</u> 52 Cal. App. 4th 1320, 61 Cal. Rptr. 2d 280 (1997), the court held that a lease made after the deed of trust that contained an automatic subordination provision seemingly quite similar to that found in <u>Dover</u> was not wiped out by foreclosure because the tenant also covenanted in the lease to attorn to the new owner. The court in <u>Miscione</u> found that the lender's notices to tenant directing the tenant to pay rent to it were evidence of the lender's acceptance of the lease and that tenant had agreed to attorn to any new owner that "acquire[d]" and "accept[ed] the Premises subject to th[e] lease." The dissent in <u>Miscione</u> points out that the attornment provision appeared in a fairly standard lease subordination provision, addressing subordination as well as attornment and nondisturbance, and criticizes the majority's distinguishing of <u>Dover</u> on the basis that it did not discuss the attornment clause of the lease's subordination provision.

      (b)   <u>Subordination, Nondisturbance and Attornment Agreements.</u> The lesson to be drawn from <u>Dover</u> and <u>Miscione</u> is that if the parties clearly wish to establish their rights on foreclosure, they should not rely on the automatic subordination provisions of the lease (and a court's subsequent interpretation thereof), but should enter into a separate Subordination,

4

Nondisturbance and Attornment Agreement ("SNDA"). A sample SNDA is attached as Exhibit D. In the SNDA, the lender agrees not to disturb the tenant in the absence of defaults and the tenant agrees to attorn to lender. As seen in Exhibit D, the lender usually requires the tenant to waive its rights of offset and absolves lender from responsibility for landlord's defaults prior to lender's foreclosure.

5

ENCUMBRANCES.

(a)   Subordination. This Lease is expressly made subject and subordinate to any mortgage, deed of trust, ground lease, underlying lease or like encumbrance affecting any part of the Property or any interest of Landlord therein which is now existing or hereafter executed or recorded ("**Encumbrance**"); provided, however, that such subordination shall only be effective, as to future Encumbrances, if the holder of the Encumbrance agrees that this Lease shall survive the termination of the Encumbrance by lapse of time, foreclosure or otherwise so long as Tenant is not in default under this Lease. Provided the conditions of the preceding sentence are satisfied, Tenant shall execute and deliver to Landlord, within ten (10) days after written request therefor by Landlord and in a form reasonably requested by Landlord, any additional documents evidencing the subordination of this Lease with respect to any such Encumbrance and the nondisturbance agreement of the holder of any such Encumbrance. If the interest of Landlord in the Property is transferred pursuant to or in lieu of proceedings for enforcement of any Encumbrance, Tenant shall immediately and automatically attorn to the new owner, and this Lease shall continue in full force and effect as a direct lease between the Purchaser and Tenant on the terms and conditions set forth in this Lease.

(b)   Mortgagee Protection. Tenant agrees to give any holder of any Encumbrance covering any part of the Property ("**Mortgagee**"), by registered mail, a copy of any notice of default served upon Landlord, provided that prior to such notice Tenant has been notified in writing (by way of notice of assignment of rents and leases, or otherwise) of the address of such Mortgagee. If Landlord shall have failed to cure such default within thirty (30) days from the effective date of such notice of default, then the Mortgagee shall have an additional thirty (30) days within which to cure such default or if such default cannot be cured within that time, then such additional time as may be necessary to cure such default (including the time necessary to foreclose or otherwise terminate its Encumbrance, if necessary to effect such cure), and this Lease shall not be terminated so long as such remedies are being diligently pursued.

ESTOPPEL CERTIFICATES AND FINANCIAL STATEMENTS.

(a)   Estoppel Certificates. Within ten (10) days after written request therefor, Tenant shall execute and deliver to Landlord, in a form provided by or satisfactory to Landlord, a certificate stating that this Lease is in full force and effect, describing any amendments or modifications hereto, acknowledging that this Lease is subordinate or prior, as the case may be, to any Encumbrance and stating any other information Landlord may reasonably request, including the Term, the monthly Base Rent, the date to which Rent has been paid, the amount of any security deposit or prepaid rent, whether either party hereto is in default under the terms of the Lease, and whether Landlord has completed its construction obligations hereunder (if any). Any person or entity purchasing, acquiring an interest in or extending financing with respect to the Property shall be entitled to rely upon any such certificate. If Tenant fails to deliver such certificate within ten (10) days after Landlord's second written request therefor, Tenant shall be liable to Landlord for any damages incurred by Landlord including any profits or other benefits from any financing of the

1

Property or any interest therein which are lost or made unavailable as a result, directly or indirectly, of Tenant's failure or refusal to timely execute or deliver such estoppel certificate.

(b)   Financial Statements. Upon request by Landlord, not more than once a year, Tenant shall deliver to Landlord a copy of Tenant's financial statements (including at least a year end balance sheet and a statement of profit and loss) for each of the three most recently completed years, prepared in accordance with generally accepted accounting principles (and, if such is Tenant's normal practice, audited by an independent certified public accountant), all then available subsequent interim statements, and such other financial information as may reasonably be requested by Landlord or required by any Mortgagee.

EXHIBIT B

TENANT ESTOPPEL CERTIFICATE

TO: [Buyer]   [Lender]

_____   _____

_____   _____

_____   _____

Re: Suite _____, _____, _____ _____ (the "Premises")

This estoppel certificate is delivered by the undersigned ("Tenant") to _____ ("Buyer") in connection with its contemplated purchase of certain real property commonly known as _____ _____, _____ (the "Property"), and to _____ ("Lender") in connection with its making of a loan to Buyer to finance Buyer's purchase of the Property. Tenant hereby certifies the following information on which Buyer may rely in connection with its purchase of the Property and Lender may rely in connection with its making a loan secured by the Property:

1.   The undersigned is the tenant in possession of the Premises under a written lease with _____ as landlord ("Landlord") dated _____, 19__, [as amended by _____], which lease [as amended] (the "Lease") is in full force and effect and is a valid and binding obligation of Tenant, has not been modified or amended except as specifically set forth above, and contains the entire understanding and agreement between tenant and landlord concerning the Premises.

2.   The Premises consist of approximately _____ [net rentable] or [gross] square feet of [office] [retail] space.

3.   The term of the Lease commenced on _____ and terminates on

_____.

4.   Current monthly base rent under the Lease is _____. [Percentage rent of _____ is due [annually or quarterly]]. Base rent has been paid through the period ending _____. The Lease provides for the monthly rent to increase as follows: _____. There are no agreements concerning free rent, partial rent, rent rebate, credit for improvements, or other rental concessions except as follows: _____.

5   The Lease requires Tenant to pay its pro rata share of increases in real estate taxes and operating expenses for the Property over the [base year] or [expense stop] amount of $_____. Tenant's pro rata share is _____. For the calendar year 1994, Tenant is obligated to pay monthly estimated amounts for real estate taxes and operating expense increases of $_____, and has paid such estimates through the period ending

1

_____. Tenant is owed no refund of real estate taxes or operating expense payments made for prior calendar years.

6. The Lease contains no option to renew the Lease term, right of first refusal, option to expand, right of first refusal, option to purchase, or option to terminate, except as follows:

_____

_____.

7. The landlord is holding a security deposit of $_____. The landlord holds no other funds for Tenant's account.

8. Tenant is not, and to the best of Tenant's knowledge Landlord is not, in default under any provision of the Lease nor has any event occurred which with the passage of time or giving of notice, or both, would constitute a default on the part of Tenant or Landlord, both parties having performed the obligations required to be performed by each party thereunder through the date hereof. Tenant asserts no claim of default or offset or defense (against Landlord or any other person) against the payment of rent or other charges payable by Tenant or the performance of any other obligations by Tenant under the Lease.

9. The space required to be delivered by the landlord to Tenant has been so delivered in accordance with the terms of the Lease, and landlord has fully completed any obligation it may have had to construct improvements to the Premises or to finance or provide an allowance to construct any improvements.

10. The Lease entitles Tenant to the [non-exclusive] use of _____ parking spaces.

11. Tenant has not assigned its rights under the Lease or sublet any portion of the leased premises.

12. There are no actions, whether voluntary or otherwise, pending against Tenant under any insolvency, bankruptcy or other debtor relief laws of the United States or California.

The statements made herein shall be binding upon us, our successors and assigns, and shall inure to your benefit and the benefit of your successors and assigns. The officers executing this letter have been duly empowered to do so on behalf of the undersigned.

Each of you may consider this certificate and the information contained herein accurate as of any date that is within 45 days after the date hereof set forth below, except to the extent we notify you in writing at your address set forth above of changes to the within-described information.

2

Dated:_____

Very truly yours,

By: _____

Name: _____

Its: _____

3

EXHIBIT C

TENANT ESTOPPEL CERTIFICATE

TO: [Buyer]   [Lender]

_____   _____

_____   _____

_____   _____

Re: Suite _____, _____, _____ _____ (the "Premises")

This estoppel certificate is delivered by the undersigned ("Tenant") to _____ ("Buyer") in connection with its contemplated purchase of certain real property commonly known as _____ _____, _____ (the "Property"), from _____ ("Landlord") and to _____ ("Lender") in connection with its making of a loan to Buyer to finance Buyer's purchase of the Property which loan will be secured by a deed of trust (the "Deed of Trust") on the Property. Tenant hereby certifies the following information on which Buyer may rely in connection with its purchase of the Property and Lender may rely in connection with its making a loan secured by the Property:

1.   The undersigned is the tenant in possession of the Premises under a written lease with _____ as landlord ("Landlord") dated _____, 19__, [as amended by _____], which lease [as amended] (the "Lease") is in full force and effect, each provision of which is binding on Tenant in accordance with its terms, has not been modified or amended in writing or orally except as specifically set forth above, and contains the entire understanding and agreement between Tenant and Landlord concerning the Premises. A true, complete and accurate copy of the Lease is attached hereto as Exhibit A.

2.   The Premises consist of approximately _____ [net rentable] or [gross] square feet of [office] [retail] space.

3.   The term of the Lease commenced on _____ and terminates on _____.

4.   Current monthly base rent under the Lease is _____. [Percentage rent of _____ is due [annually or quarterly]]. Base rent has been paid through the period ending _____. The Lease provides for the monthly rent to increase as follows: _____. There are no agreements concerning free rent, partial rent, rent rebate, credit for improvements, or other rental concessions except as follows: _____.

5.   The Lease requires Tenant to pay its pro rata share of increases in real estate taxes and operating expenses for the Property and appurtenant property over the [base year 199__ real

1

estate taxes and operating expenses of $_____] or [expense stop of
$_____]. Tenant's pro rata share is _____. For the calendar year 19____,
Tenant is obligated to pay monthly estimated amounts for real estate taxes and operating expense
increases of $_____, and has paid such estimates through the period ending
_____. Tenant is owed no refund of real estate taxes or operating expense payments
made for prior calendar years.

6. Tenant has no option to extend or to renew the term of the Lease except as
follows: _____
_____.

7. The Lease contains no right of first refusal to lease additional space, option to
expand, option to terminate the Lease, or right of first refusal or option to purchase the Property
or any interest therein, except as follows:_____
_____.

8. The landlord is holding a security deposit of $_____. The landlord
holds no other funds for Tenant's account.

9. Tenant is not, and to the best of Tenant's knowledge Landlord is not, in default
under any provision of the Lease nor has any event occurred which with the passage of time or
giving of notice, or both, would constitute a default on the part of Tenant or Landlord, both
parties having performed the obligations required to be performed by each party thereunder
through the date hereof. Tenant asserts no claim of default against Landlord or any other person
or offset or defense against the payment of rent or other charges payable by Tenant or the
performance of any other obligations by Tenant under the Lease.

10. The Premises have been delivered to Tenant in accordance with the terms of the
Lease, Tenant has accepted the Premises, and Landlord has fully completed all construction and
improvements to the Premises required to be completed by Landlord under the Lease. Landlord
has fulfilled all obligations to finance or provide an allowance for improvements to the Premises.

11. The Lease entitles Tenant to the [non-exclusive] or [exclusive] use of
_____ parking spaces.

12. Tenant has not assigned its rights under the Lease or sublet any portion of the
premises.

13. There are no actions, whether voluntary or otherwise, pending against Tenant
under any insolvency, bankruptcy or other debtor relief laws of the United States or of any state.

14. All insurance required of Tenant under the Lease has been obtained by Tenant and
all premiums have been paid.

2

532

15.   Tenant has no notice of any prior assignment, hypothecation or pledge by Landlord of the Lease or the rents due thereunder. Tenant has not assigned, hypothecated or pledged its interest in the Lease to any person or entity.

16.   From the date hereof until the Deed of Trust is reconveyed, Tenant will not consent to or enter into any modification or termination of the Lease without the prior written consent of Lender, unless such consent is not required under the terms of the Deed of Trust.

17.   From the date hereof until the Deed of Trust is reconveyed, in the event of a default by Landlord under the Lease, Tenant shall give prompt written notice to Lender to the address set forth above and a reasonable time (which in no event shall be less than thirty (30) days or any longer period set forth in the Lease) to cure or commence cure of such default.

18.   If Landlord's interests in the Property are acquired by Lender by foreclosure, deed in lieu of foreclosure or any other method, Lender shall not be liable for any act of omission of Landlord or any prior landlord.

19.   Tenant's current address for Notices is:

_____

_____

_____

The statements made herein shall be binding upon us, our successors and assigns, and shall inure to your benefit and the benefit of your successors and assigns. The officers executing this letter have been duly empowered to do so on behalf of the undersigned.

Each of you may consider this certificate and the information contained herein accurate as of any date that is within 45 days after the date hereof set forth below, except to the extent we notify you in writing at your address set forth above of changes to the within-described information.

Dated:_____

                    Very truly yours,

                    By: _____

                    Name: _____

                    Its: _____

3

EXHIBIT D

RECORDING REQUESTED BY AND
WHEN RECORDED RETURN TO:

_____
_____
_____

....

(Space above this line for Recorder's use)

SUBORDINATION, ATTORNMENT AND NONDISTURBANCE AGREEMENT

NOTE THAT THE SUBORDINATION PROVIDED FOR IN
THIS AGREEMENT RESULTS IN YOUR LEASEHOLD
ESTATE BECOMING SUBJECT TO AN INTEREST IN THE
PROPERTY CREATED BY SOME OTHER INSTRUMENT.

This Agreement is made as of _____, 19___ by and among
_____,
as lender ("Lender"), _____, a _____,
as lessor ("Lessor"), and _____, a _____,
as lessee ("Lessee").

RECITALS

A.   Lessor is the owner of the building commonly known as _____,
_____, California (the "Building"), which Building has been constructed by
Lessor on the real property described in Exhibit A attached hereto (the "Real Property").

B.   Lessor has executed or will execute a deed of trust (the "Deed of Trust") in favor
of Lender covering Lessor's interest in the Real Property and the improvements thereon to secure
a loan evidenced by a promissory note in the principal sum of $_____ dated
_____, payable to the order of Lender, which Deed of Trust has been recorded in the
Official Records of the County of _____, California, as Instrument No. _____ at
Book _____, Page _____, concurrently with the recording hereof.

C.   Lessee has entered or is entering into a lease with Lessor, dated
_____, 19___, for certain space in the Building. Such lease and any amendments,
modifications and side letters thereto shall collectively be referred to herein as the "Lease." In
order to carry out the provisions of the Lease, the parties are willing to enter into this Agreement,
subject to the conditions set forth below.

1

535

NOW THEREFORE, in consideration of good and valuable consideration, the receipt and sufficiency of which is hereby acknowledged, and of the mutual benefits to accrue to the parties hereto, Lender, Lessor, and Lessee agree as follows:

1. It is hereby declared and understood that the Lease, the leasehold interests and estates created thereby, and the rights, privileges, and powers of Lessor and Lessee thereunder are subject and subordinate to the Deed of Trust, and to any renewals, extensions, modifications, or replacements thereof. It is expressly understood and agreed that this Agreement shall supersede, to the extent inconsistent herewith, the provisions of the Lease relating to the subordination of the Lease and the leasehold interests and estates created thereby to the Deed of Trust.

2. In the event Lender or any other purchaser at a foreclosure sale or sale under private power contained in the Deed of Trust succeeds to the interest of Lessor in the Lease by reason of any foreclosure of the Deed of Trust or the acceptance by Lender of an assignment of Lessor's rights in the Real Property in lieu of foreclosure, or by any other manner or for any other reason, it is agreed that:

(a) Lessee shall be bound to Lender or such other purchaser under all of the terms, covenants, and conditions of the Lease for the remaining balance of the term thereof, with the same force and effect as if Lender or such other purchaser were the lessor under such Lease, and Lessee does hereby agree to attorn to Lender or such other purchaser, such attornment to be effective and self-operative without the execution of any further instruments on the party of any of the parties to this Agreement, immediately upon Lender or such other purchaser succeeding to the interest of Lessor under the Lease.

(b) So long as Lessee is not in default under the Lease, which default shall not have been cured or is not in the process of being cured within the applicable grace periods set forth in the Lease,

(1) Lessee shall not be evicted from its space in the Building, nor shall Lessee's rights under the Lease be affected, by reason of a default by Lessor and foreclosure, or transfer in lieu of foreclosure, under the Deed of Trust,

(2) the Lessee's leasehold estate under the Lease shall not be disturbed or terminated by reason of any default by Lessor under the Deed of Trust,

(3) Lessee shall not be joined in any foreclosure action or proceeding instituted or taken by Lender, and

(4) Lender shall assume Lessor's obligations under the Lease;

provided, however, that neither Lender nor any other purchaser at such a foreclosure proceeding shall be (i) liable for or obligated to cure any default of Lessor under the Lease occurring prior to foreclosure sale or private sale under the Deed of Trust or transfer in lieu thereof prior to the time that Lender or such other purchaser succeeded to the interest of Lessor under the Lease,

2

(ii) subject to any offsets or defenses that Lessee may be entitled to assert against Lessor, (iii) bound by any payment of Base Rent by Lessee to Lessor for more than one month in advance or by any payments of security deposits or Additional Charges unless Lessor delivers such amounts to Lender or such other purchaser, or (iv) bound by any modification or amendment of the Lease made without the written consent of Lender.

3.   The covenants and agreements contained herein shall run with the land and shall be binding upon and inure to the benefit of the respective heirs, administrators, executors, legal representatives, successors, and assigns of the parties hereto.

4.   In the event that any party fails to perform any of its obligations under this Agreement or in the event a dispute arises concerning the meaning or interpretation of any provision of this Agreement, the defaulting party or the party not prevailing in such dispute, whichever the case may be, shall pay any and all costs and expenses incurred by the other parties in enforcing or establishing their rights hereunder, including without limitation court costs and reasonable attorneys' fees.

5.   This Agreement shall not be modified or amended except by a written instrument executed by all of the parties hereto.

IN WITNESS WHEREOF, the undersigned have executed this instrument as of the day and year first above written.

NOTICE: THE SUBORDINATION PROVIDED FOR IN THIS AGREEMENT RESULTS IN YOUR LEASEHOLD ESTATE IN THE PROPERTY BEING SUBJECT AND SUBORDINATE TO RIGHTS IN THE PROPERTY CREATED BY ANOTHER INSTRUMENT.

LENDER: _____,

a _____

By: _____

Its: _____

LESSOR: _____,

a _____

By: _____

Its: _____

3

LESSEE: _____,
a _____

By: _____

Its: _____

By: _____

Its: _____

4

538

NOTES

11

LENDERS AND THEIR AGENTS: THE LANDLORD'S SHADOWS

Peter A. Sarasek

LENDERS AND THEIR AGENTS:
THE LANDLORD'S SHADOWS

November 20, 1997

By   Peter A. Sarasek
Wilson & McIlvaine
Chicago, Illinois

I.   The Lender/Landlord Relationship

    A.   When every landlord sits at the negotiating table with a prospective tenant, it brings with it an unseen party in the form of either an existing mortgage lender or a future mortgage lender.

    B.   A prudent landlord wants to make sure that in its leasing program, it is negotiating its leases in a manner that preserves and enhances the value of its asset, both from a selling standpoint as well as from a financing standpoint.

    C.   In the case of an existing lender, a landlord's negotiating ability may have already been restricted if not compromised; a future lender may similarly want to set parameters for the borrower's leasing of the asset.

II.   In conventional mortgage financing, how does the lender control the landlord's ability to lease its property?

    A.   The mortgage documents will contain specific covenants requiring that the borrower not enter into any new leases or lease renewals or amendments to leases in all or certain specified instances without the lender's prior written approval.

    B.   The lender will require that the borrower utilize a pre-approved form of commercial lease, and not deviate from that lease except for certain pre-approved lease modifications (some lenders will require that the landlord submit not only the proposed deal terms for pre-approval, but also submit the final form of lease in a blacklined format to the lender and its counsel for their final approval).

    C.   The Assignment of Leases/Rents instrument gives the lender the right to collect the rents from the property in the event of any borrower default under the mortgage loan, so that the lender at some point can step into the shoes of the landlord and realize upon the value of the asset.

III. Preserving and Enhancing Appraised Value: The Landlord's and Lender's Joint Objective

Property appraisals for financing purposes are based on the "bricks and mortar" approach, the "comparable sales" approach, and the "income" approach.

1. The bricks and mortar approach: The appraiser values the asset in its completed form from a replacement cost standpoint, and assigns basic values to the land and improvement components of the property.

2. The comparable sales approach: The appraiser will compare the property to recently-sold and similarly situated properties and assign a value to the subject asset based upon the selling prices of those properties.

3. The income approach: The appraiser will review the quality of the leases of the property, the creditworthiness of the tenants, the economics of each specific leasing transaction, and determine a rental income stream from the property which will then be capitalized at a particular cap rate in order to achieve a value for the property.

4 The more dominant and singular a particular lease, the more important it becomes for financing purposes.

   a. Ground leases: The ground lease is particularly significant in that it in itself will support the entire income stream for a particular property, giving the ground lessee the ability thereafter to enter into subleases; the terms of the ground lease which is subject to ground leasehold financing become particularly critical, since the single ground lease supports the entire income picture for the property.

   b. Industrial properties: Not unlike the ground lease, a single industrial lease will often support the single income of a property.

   c. Retail leases: Anchor tenant leases become critical from a financing standpoint, because these instruments not only support a significant stream of income, but also determine when a shopping center may or may not remain open and how the departure of other anchor tenants may affect a particular anchor tenant lease.

   d. Office tenants: A single office lease of a significant portion of the building will become critical for a lender, and the larger the tenant is in the building, the more interested the landlord will be in the terms of that particular lease.

544

IV.   What types of lease provisions are particularly important to a lender in its review?

Prefatory note: In the case of existing leases, a lender and/or its counsel will review each and every one of the leases of the particular asset to be financed, and will summarize the key terms of all of those leases. The lender will identify any particular terms of a leasing transaction or unusual lease provision which it may choose to discuss with the borrower. If a particular lease is problematic, the lender may require that the lease be clearly subordinated to the loan and the lender may not include the rental income from that lease in determining for financing purposes the appraised value of the property.

A.   The tenant's identity: The lender will want to know the strength of the particular tenant, and will be particularly pleased to find in the lease a requirement that the tenant provide financial statements to the landlord and/or its mortgagee upon request, so that the lender has a current financial picture for each tenant (see Appendix A for a sample lease clause that a landlord may want to insert in its lease for this purpose). Similarly, the lender will be concerned with a particular tenant's ability to assign the lease, and will be concerned if the original credit tenant is ever released from liability under the lease.

B.   The lease economics: The lender will insist that the lease clearly spell out the 'tenant's rental obligation and the various components of rent. If the lease is not carefully drafted and the language is in any way obscure, the lender may require that its borrower obtain an amendment to the lease to more clearly identify the rental picture of the property (or, as will be discussed later, the lender may want the tenant in an estoppel letter to address this point).

C.   Tenant termination rights: If a tenant has any ability to terminate the lease, by way of an early termination right, for example, the lender will value the lease only with respect to that portion of the term preceding the point of possible termination. In other words, for financing purposes, the lender will assume that the tenant will exercise its termination right, and value a lease only with respect to the true committed portion of the term. Lenders will be concerned if leases grant tenants any rights to terminate in unusual situations (e.g. a retail tenant in an office building is given a right to terminate if occupancy levels fall below a certain point; a law firm is permitted to terminate if the main banking tenant in the building no longer occupies the building).

D.   Set off rights: The lender needs the income stream to be solid and absolute, and will look with disfavor upon any lease that gives the tenant a right to set off against the rental income stream any claims by the tenant. For example, a key major tenant in the building may want the right of "self help" if a future absentee landlord were to allow a building to fall into a state of disrepair or permit essential services to be disrupted: the tenant might want the right to step in and cure the landlord's default and then set off against future rent payments any costs or expenses incurred by the tenant in effecting the cure. While there are ways to address that type of a situation, in general lenders frown upon any type of set off right and may require further security from the borrower in the event any such rights have been granted to any tenants in a particular property.

E.   Casualty/liability insurance: The lender will want to make sure that the insurance coverages to be maintained by each tenant are adequate and include lender protections (e.g. naming the mortgagee as an additional insured party; waiver of subrogation clauses; landlord's ability to increase the amount of liability coverage over the term of the lease).

F.   Casualty claims/insurance proceeds: The lender will want to seek consistency in casualty clauses, and will be concerned with any tenant's ability to seize upon a landlord's insurance proceeds for rebuilding purposes. The lender will want to control insurance proceeds, since in financing the property it wants to ensure that the property is rebuilt in a manner satisfactory to the lender (and not simply satisfactory to the tenant).

V.   Tenant Estoppel Certificates

A.   Before making its loan, the lender will want each of the key (if not all of the) tenants to confirm for the benefit of the lender the key components of each particular leasing transaction. Appendix B sets forth a sample form of tenant estoppel certificate which indicates the lender's primary concerns.

B.   The lender will want the tenant to identify with particularity the current rental income being paid by the tenant, and confirm the current term of the lease, whether the tenant has any options to terminate, options to expand, whether the landlord has any unfulfilled covenants, whether the tenant has any claims against the landlord.

C.   The lender is primarily concerned that it might at some point in the future step into the shoes of the landlord, and it wants to ensure that the tenant has identified for the benefit of the lender the tenant's understanding of the lease and the tenant's expectations.

D.   The lender may also want the tenant to agree that, upon receipt of notice from lender the tenant will forward all rents thereafter directly to the lender and not to the landlord (tenants will be reluctant to agree to that provision, without an acknowledgment by the landlord that the tenant in that instance should so honor the lender's demand).

E.   Tenant estoppels as quasi-lease amendments: If a lender believes a lease provision is not entirely clear, and the borrower is unwilling to obtain a lease amendment addressing the issue, the lender may utilize the estoppel as a quasi-amendment and require the tenant to agree for the benefit of the lender that a particular provision will control if the lender were to take title to the property. Since landlords are not eager to ask tenants to amend previously negotiated leases in order to address a current lender concern, this may be a realistic approach in order for a lease point to be addressed. The question is whether the particular point in the estoppel letter is thereafter binding upon any future owners of the property.

VI.   Subordination, Non-Disturbance and Attornment Agreements

A.   Just as the lender is concerned that a particular lease instrument contain terms satisfactory to the lender, the lender also wants to make sure that at the lender's option the tenant will be obligated to attorn to the lender as its new landlord if the lender or its successors and assigns were to take title to the property through foreclosure or otherwise.

B.   Subordination provisions: If a lender does not want a particular existing lease to survive a foreclosure, it may want to make sure that a prior lease is subordinated to the particular loan. Some leases contain automatic subordination provisions, whereby the tenant agrees that its rights are automatically subordinate, without further action of the tenant, to any existing or future mortgage of the property. State law may vary whether a court will recognize such automatic features, or require instead that a tenant enter into a specific subordination agreement in favor of a particular lender.

C.   On the other hand, lenders may want to ensure that specific tenant leases survive a foreclosure, and will want tenants to agree to attorn to the lender at foreclosure. Existing lease provisions may contain an attornment requirement, but lenders often require that the borrower obtain specific attornment agreements from the particular tenants of the properties.

D.   Tenants in turn will want to ensure that in the event a particular mortgage is foreclosed against the property, their lease survives the foreclosure and the favorable deal that it negotiated with the landlord is not simply subject to termination by the foreclosing lender. Such tenants will want to receive from the lender a non-disturbance agreement, whereby the lender agrees not to disturb a tenant's tenancy in the event it forecloses and takes title to the property.

E.   The subordination agreement, a recognition and attornment agreement, and a non-disturbance agreement can all be found in separate instruments or in one combined instrument, depending upon the particular situation [see Appendix C for a sample form of subordination, non-disturbance and attornment agreement (SNDA)].

VII.   Landlord's Obligation to Provide an SNDA.

Landlords are reluctant to tie their hands and commit to providing subordination, non-disturbance and attornment agreements from any lender.

A.   In the case of existing lenders, the landlord should have discussed with its lender at the time of the making of the loan under what circumstances the lender would be willing to issue SNDAs, so that the landlord would be in a position to confirm to new tenants whether an existing lender is prepared to grant a non-disturbance agreement at the time of lease signing.

B.   Landlords do not know how future lenders will react to a request for an SNDA, and landlords will therefore be reluctant to offer those agreements in consideration for a tenant's willingness to subordinate and attorn.

C.   The size and strength of a tenant and its importance to a particular property will determine the landlord's level of willingness to use "best efforts", "commercially reasonable efforts", "reasonable efforts", or to simply request (without any guarantee of success) an SNDA from a future lender as a condition to a tenant's agreement to subordinate.

VIII.   What Form of SNDA Controls?/Key Lender Concerns

A.   Some tenants want SNDAs to be in a form "reasonably satisfactory" to the tenant, and not only the lender.

B.   Landlords will want the SNDA to be in the form then in use by the particular lender.

C.   The particular lender will want the SNDA to be its form, recognizing that it may be required to negotiate parts of its form of SNDA in order to obtain a tenant's execution of the document prior to the loan funding.

D.   What are the key lender concerns in an SNDA?

1.   Tenant's acknowledgment that the lender is not liable for return of any security deposit to the extent the lender does not receive security deposit funds from the original landlord

2.   The lender is not required to recognize any lease amendment which it has not previously approved in writing.

3.   The lender is not liable for any prior landlord default.

4. The lender is not liable for any offsets against the prior landlord.

5. The lender is not responsible for any unfunded tenant improvement allowance or similar landlord concession.

6. All provisions of the lease (especially use of casualty/condemnation proceeds) are subordinate to mortgage provisions.

E. All of the foregoing are of importance not only to the lender but also to the tenant, and may require negotiation before the tenant willingly signs an SNDA in favor of an existing lender.

IX. Conclusion

A. The parties to each lease negotiation must be mindful of the concerns of any current or future lender, and each must determine how to protect its position in light of those concerns.

B. The smaller the tenant, the more likely a lender's requirements will control in the leasing negotiation and dictate the outcome of certain leasing issues.

C. The larger and more significant the tenant, the more likely the tenant's leverage will counter the lender's desire to control the lease, and ensure that the tenant's presence is similarly felt throughout the landlord/tenant/lender relationship.

Appendix A

Tenant agrees that within ninety (90) days following the end of each fiscal year, Tenant shall provide to Landlord a copy of the audited financial statement of Tenant for the preceding fiscal year.

TENANT ESTOPPEL CERTIFICATE
OF
[COMPLETE TENANT'S NAME]

To: _____ ("_____")

Re: Lease Between [complete Landlord's Name] ("Landlord") and [complete Tenant's Name] ("Tenant") for space located at _____, [Suite No._____] ("Leased Premises")
Loan #_____

Ladies and Gentlemen:

For good and valuable consideration and as an inducement to the making of a secured loan by _____ to [Fill in Name of Borrower] covering property of which the Leased Premises are a part, the undersigned, as Tenant under that certain lease dated _____ [complete date of lease and list all amendments] ("Lease") made with _____, as Landlord, hereby certifies to _____, its successors and assigns that (a) the undersigned has entered into occupancy of the Leased Premises on _____ which Leased Premises is acknowledged to contain _____ square feet; (b) the Lease is in full force and effect and has not been modified, supplemented or amended in any way; (c) the Lease represents the entire agreement between the parties as to this leasing; (d) the term of the Lease commenced on _____ and expires on _____; (e) the Tenant is presently occupying the Leased Premises and is paying rent and additional rent in accordance with the terms of the Lease; (f) there are no options to extend the term except as follows: _____; (g) there are no options to purchase the Leased Premises or any rights of first refusal except as follows: _____; (h) all conditions under the Lease to be performed by the Landlord prerequisite to the full effectiveness of the Lease have been satisfied; (i) all of the construction, repair and improvements contemplated by the Lease to be performed by Landlord have been performed by Landlord and have been completed satisfactorily in accordance with the terms of the Lease, and that no other construction, repair and improvements are contemplated under the Lease except as follows: _____ (j) there are no sums or credits due Tenant from Landlord under the Lease; (k) on this date there exists no factual circumstance or condition which, with notice or the lapse of time, or both, would give rise to any obligation on the part of Landlord, would constitute a default on the part of Landlord, would constitute a defense to the enforcement of the Lease by Landlord or an offset against the rents or other charges due the Landlord under the Lease, or would constitute the basis for a claim or cause of action against the Landlord; (l) the minimum rental obligation under the Lease in effect is $_____ per annum, the current monthly additional rental is $_____, the minimum and additional rental to _____ has been paid, and no rental has been paid in advance; (m) a security deposit in the amount of $_____ was paid by Tenant to Landlord; (n) the Tenant is not using the Leased Premises in violation of any applicable laws, rules, ordinances or regulations, including, but not limited to, any applicable environmental laws, rules or regulations (collectively "Laws"), there are no regulatory actions or other claims pending or threatened against the Tenant in connection with any such Laws, Tenant has not received any notice from any third party or governmental authority alleging a violation of any such Laws, and Tenant shall immediately notify Landlord and _____ in writing of any existing, pending or threatened action by any local, state or federal governmental authority and of any third party claims of which Tenant is aware arising out of the violation or alleged violation of any Laws; (o) there has not been filed by or against the Tenant nor, to the best knowledge and belief of Tenant, is there threatened against or contemplated by Tenant, a petition in bankruptcy, voluntary or otherwise, any assignment for the benefit of creditors, any petition seeking reorganization or arrangement under bankruptcy laws of the United States or of any state thereof, or any other action brought under said bankruptcy laws; and (p) to the best of Tenant's knowledge, there has not been any assignment, hypothecation or pledge of Landlord's interest in the Lease or rents accruing under the Lease, other than to _____ .

All notices to _____ shall be by certified mail, return receipt requested addressed to:

_____

The Tenant acknowledges having read this Certificate and understands the certifications and representations made herein, and hereby executes this Certificate, which shall take effect as a sealed instrument, intending reliance hereon by _____ , its successors and assigns. The undersigned signatory represents and warrants that he or she is duly authorized to execute this Certificate on behalf of the Tenant.

TENANT'S NAME:

BY:_____ Date:_____
   Name:

_____
Title: Its _____ President, duly authorized

W/SNDA
Pre-Closing

EXHIBIT __ TO OFFICE LEASE
FOR

SUBORDINATION, NON-DISTURBANCE AND ATTORNMENT AGREEMENT

THIS AGREEMENT is made by and among _____, an _____ ("Lessor"), _____, a _____ ("Lessee"), and _____ ("Lender").

WITNESSETH:

WHEREAS, under a certain lease dated as of _____ __, 19__ (hereinafter referred to as the "Lease"), Lessor did lease, let, and demise a portion of the Property (hereinafter called the "Premises"), as described in the Lease to Lessee for the period of time and upon the covenants, terms, and conditions therein stated; and

WHEREAS, said Lease has not been amended or modified; and

WHEREAS, by making a mortgage loan, Lender has become the owner of an indebtedness and holder of a certain Note, dated as of ____, 19__ (said Note, together with all renewals, extensions, modifications and amendments thereto and all substitutions therefor, being hereinafter called the "Note"), secured by a Mortgage, Security Agreement, Assignment of Rents and Leases, and Financing Statement dated ____, 19__, recorded in the records of ____ County, ____ on ____, 19__, as Document No. _____, which Mortgage together with any and all renewals, extensions, modifications, and amendments thereto, and all substitutions therefor is hereinafter called the "Mortgage"), constituting a valid lien upon the Property, and secured by an assignment of Lessor's interest in the Lease as more particularly set forth in a certain Assignment of Rents and Leases, dated as of ____, 19__, recorded in the records of ____ County, ____ on ____, 19__, as Document No. ____ (the "Assignment of Leases"); and

WHEREAS, Lessor and Lessee jointly and severally acknowledge and agree to the aforesaid Assignment of Leases, and more particularly, the covenants and agreements of Lessor set forth therein; and

WHEREAS, the parties hereto desire to establish additional rights of quiet and peaceful possession for the benefit of Lessee, and further to define the covenants, terms, and conditions precedent to such additional rights.

NOW, THEREFORE, in consideration of the covenants, terms, conditions, agreements, and demises herein contained, and in consideration of other good and valuable consideration, each to the other, the sufficiency and receipt of which are hereby acknowledged, the parties hereto agree, covenant, and warrant as follows:

Lender, Lessor, and Lessee do hereby covenant and agree that the Lease and any modifications and amendments subsequently approved by Lender and all rights, options, liens or charges created thereby are and shall continue to be subject and subordinate in all respects to the Mortgage and the lien created thereby, to any advancements made thereunder, to any consolidations, extensions, modifications or renewals thereof, and to any other mortgage on the Premises which may hereafter be held by Lender.

Subject to the observance and performance by Lessee of all of the covenants, terms and conditions of the said Lease or in any modification or amendment specified herein or subsequently approved by Lender on the part of Lessee to be observed and performed, Lender hereby covenants that in the event it obtains title to the Premises, either by foreclosure or by deed in lieu of foreclosure, and thereafter obtains the right of possession of the Premises, that the Lease and any modifications or amendments specified herein or hereafter approved by Lender will continue in full force and effect, and Lender shall recognize the Lease and any modifications or amendments specified herein or subsequently approved by Lender and the Lessee's rights thereunder, and will thereby establish direct privity of estate and contract between the Lender and Lessee with the same force and effect and with the same relative priority in time and right as though the Lease and any modification or amendment specified herein or subsequently approved by Lender were directly made from Lender in favor of Lessee.

Lessee agrees to give Lender by registered or certified mail, return receipt requested, notice of any default of the Lessor in the obligations of Lessor under the Lease. Lender shall have thirty (30) days following receipt of said notice (or in the case of an emergency situation, such shorter period of time as is reasonable) within which to cure such default or if such default cannot be cured within that time, then such additional time as may be necessary if, within thirty days, Lender has commenced and is diligently pursuing the remedies necessary to cure such default, in which event the Lease shall not be terminated while such remedies are being so diligently pursued. It is specifically agreed that Lessee shall not, as to Lender, require cure of any such default which is personal to the Lessor, and therefore not susceptible of cure by Lender.

That in the event the interests of the Lessor under the Lease shall be transferred to Lender by reason of foreclosure, deed in lieu of foreclosure, or otherwise, Lessee hereby covenants and agrees to make full and complete attornment to the Lender as substitute Lessor upon the same terms, covenants and conditions as provided in the Lease, except for provisions which are impossible for Lender to perform, so as to establish direct privity of estate and contract between the Lender and Lessee with the same force and effect and relative priority in time and right as though the Lease and all modifications and amendments thereof specified herein or hereafter consented to by Lender, together with all guarantees of Lessee's obligations under the Lease, was originally made directly between Lender and Lessee. Lessee will thereafter make all payments directly to Lender and will waive as against Lender only any defaults of Lessor (whether curable or non-curable) which occurred prior to Lender gaining right of possession to the Premises and becoming substitute Lessor. Lessee waives all joinder and/or service of any and all foreclosure actions by Lender under the Note or Notes and Mortgage upon the Premises, and of any actions at law by Lender to gain possession of the Premises. It shall not be necessary, except as required by law, for Lender to name Lessee as a party to enforce its rights under the Note or Mortgage, or any other instrument collateralizing the loan, or to prosecute any action at law to gain possession of the Premises and unless required by law Lender agrees not to name Lessee in any such proceeding. If the interests of Lessor under the Lease shall be transferred by reason of foreclosure of the Mortgage, deed in lieu of foreclosure, or otherwise, to any party other than Lender (hereinafter referred to as a "Transferee"), then Lessee hereby covenants and agrees to make full and complete attornment to such Transferee as substitute Lessor, upon the same terms and conditions as provided for herein in the case of attornment to Lender.

The provisions of this Agreement shall be real covenants running with the Property, and shall be binding upon and inure to the benefit of the respective parties hereto and their respective heirs, executors, administrators, beneficiaries, successors and assigns, including without limitation any person who shall obtain, directly or by assignment or conveyance, (a) any interest in the Mortgage; (b) any certificate of purchase following foreclosure of the Mortgage; (c) any certificate of redemption following such foreclosure; or (d) any interest in the Premises, whether through foreclosure or otherwise. Furthermore, the provisions of this Agreement shall be binding upon any Guarantor of Lessee's obligations under the Lease.

Notwithstanding anything contained herein to the contrary, or anything to the contrary in the aforesaid Lease or in any modifications or amendments thereto, Lessor and Lessee hereby covenant and agree that Lender and its respective assignees shall not be:

(a) Liable for any act or omission of Lessor.

(b) Subject to any offsets or defenses which Lessee might have as to Lessor, except those offsets specifically set forth in the Lease (and only to the extent that the same arise after Lessor's interest in the Lease is transferred to Lender).

(c) Required or obligated to credit Lessee with any rent or additional rent for any rental period beyond the then current rental period which Lessee might have paid Lessor, except to the extent the same is received by Lender.

(d) Bound by any amendments or modifications of the Lease made without Lender's consent, other than exercise of rights, options or elections contained in the Lease, including without limitation options to extend the term of the Lease.

(e) Bound to or liable for refund of all or any part of any security deposit by Lessee with Lessor for any purpose unless and until all such security deposit shall have been delivered by Lessor to and actually received by Lender. In the event of receipt of any such security deposit, Lender's obligations with respect thereto shall be limited to the amount of such security deposit actually received by Lender, and Lender shall be entitled to all rights, privileges and benefits of Lessor set forth in the Lease with respect thereto.

Lessee hereby acknowledges that Lessor has executed and delivered the Assignment of Leases to Lender to secure the aforesaid loan, and Lessee covenants and agrees as follows for the benefit and reliance of Lender:

(a)   That it will not, without the express written consent of Lender:

    (i)   Cancel, terminate or surrender the Lease, except as provided therein or in any modification or amendment specified herein or hereafter consented to by Lender, and then only after Lender has failed to or unsuccessfully attempted to pursue its rights and remedies as provided herein; or

    (ii)   After date hereof, enter into any agreement with Lessor, its successors or assigns, which grants any concession with respect to the Lease or which reduces the rent called for thereunder; or

    (iii)   After date hereof, create any offset or claims against rents, or prepay rent.

(b)   That it hereby acknowledges receipt of a copy of the Assignment of Leases and agrees, except to the extent prohibited by law or legal proceedings, to make rental payments according to the terms of such Assignment of Leases upon written demand by Lender in the event of any default under the Note or Mortgage.

Lessor and Lessee hereby jointly and severally agree for the benefit and reliance of Lender, as follows:

(a)   That neither this Agreement, the Assignment of Leases, nor anything to the contrary in the aforesaid Lease or in any modifications or amendments thereto shall, prior to Lender's acquisition of Lessor's interest in and possession of the Premises, operate to give rise to or create any responsibility or liability for the control, care, management or repair of the Premises upon the Lender, or impose responsibility for the carrying out by Lender of any of the covenants, terms and conditions of the Lease or of any modification or amendment specified herein or hereafter consented to by Lender, nor shall said instruments operate to make the Lender responsible or liable for any waste committed on the Premises by any party whatsoever, or for dangerous or defective condition of the Premises, or for any negligence in the management, upkeep, repair or control of said Premises resulting in loss, injury or death to any Lessee, licensee, invitee, guest, employee, agent or stranger. Notwithstanding anything to the contrary in the Lease, Lender, its successors and assigns or a purchaser under the terms of the Mortgage, shall be responsible for performance of only those covenants and obligations of the Lease accruing after Lender's acquisition of Lessor's interest in and possession of the Premises.

(b)   That in the event Lender gains title to the Premises and becomes substitute Lessor, it is agreed that Lender may assign its interest as substitute Lessor without notice to, the consent of, or assumption of any liability to any other party hereto.

Any notices to Lessee or to Lender hereunder shall be effective upon mailing to Lessee by certified mail, return receipt requested, addressed as follows:

Lessee:

         _____
         _____
         _____
         Attn: _____

Lender:

         _____
         _____
         _____

or as to each party, to such other address as the party may designate by a notice given in accordance with the requirements contained in this Section 9.

Notwithstanding anything which is or may appear to be to the contrary contained in this Agreement, neither the partners in Lessor nor the partners, stockholders, directors, officers, agents, or employees, as the case may be, in Lessor's constituent partners shall be personally liable for performance of any obligations hereunder or for the correctness of any representations or warranties contained herein, and recourse hereunder shall be limited to the assets of Lessor.

This Agreement contains the entire agreement between the parties hereto. No variations, modifications or changes herein or hereof shall be binding upon any party hereto unless set forth in a document duly executed by or on behalf of such party.

This instrument may be executed in multiple counterparts, all of which shall be deemed originals and with the same effect as if all parties hereto had signed the same document. All of such counterparts shall be construed together and shall constitute one instrument, but in making proof, it shall only be necessary to produce one such counterpart.

Whenever used herein, the singular number shall include the plural, the plural the singular, and the use of any gender shall include all genders. The words, "Lender," "Lessor" and "Lessee" shall include their heirs, executors, administrators, beneficiaries, successors and assigns.

The Lease and this Agreement have been duly authorized, executed and delivered by the Lessee and constitute legal, valid and binding instruments enforceable against Lessee in accordance with their respective terms, except as such terms may be limited by bankruptcy, insolvency or similar laws affecting creditors' rights generally.

IN WITNESS WHEREOF, the parties hereto have caused this Agreement to be signed, sealed and delivered in their respective names and in their behalf; and if a corporation, by its officers duly authorized, this _____ day of _____, 19__.

LESSOR:

_____, a _____

By:_____
Its:_____

LESSEE:

_____, a _____

By:_____
Its:_____

LENDER:

_____

By:_____
Its:_____

In the event of any act or omission by Landlord which would give Tenant the right to terminate this Lease or to claim a partial or total eviction from the Premises, Tenant shall not exercise any such right (a) until it has notified in writing the Landlord's Mortgagee of such act or omission, and (b) until a reasonable period for remedying such act or omission shall have elapsed following the giving of such notice, and Landlord's Mortgagee shall not with reasonable diligence have commenced and continued to remedy such act or omission or to cause the same to be remedied. Landlord will notify Tenant in writing of the name and address of each Landlord's Mortgagee upon the execution of this Lease and subsequently inform Tenant of any new Landlord's Mortgagee immediately upon the execution of a mortgage or deed of trust encumbering the Building. No Landlord's Mortgagee shall be bound by any cancellation, amendment or modification of this Lease, or waiver of any provision of this Lease, which has not been consented to in writing by that Landlord's Mortgagee.

NOTES

12

SYNTHETIC LEASE TRANSACTIONS AND "OFF-BALANCE SHEET" FINANCING

Evelyn Giaccio

SYNTHETIC LEASE TRANSACTIONS AND "OFF-BALANCE SHEET" FINANCING

I.   Introduction

A synthetic lease is a financing technique designed to qualify as an operating lease for financial accounting and reporting purposes and as a loan for federal income tax purposes. By complying with applicable financial accounting and tax guidelines, the synthetic lease structure permits a lessee of a property to achieve "off-balance sheet" accounting treatment for the asset and any debt used to finance the acquisition and construction thereof, while obtaining the construction and operational control and the tax benefits of property ownership.

A special purpose entity ("SPE") is formed to facilitate the transaction and acquire the real estate. The SPE then leases the property to a substantial credit corporate user under a triple net, bond-like lease. Synthetic leases are often used for build-to-suit projects. The lessee and lessor also enter into a construction agency agreement pursuant to which the lessor engages the lessee to act as its agent to construct the improvements to the lessee's specifications, at the lessor's cost and expense.

Although an investor/lessor itself may provide the entire funding for the cost of the asset, a synthetic lease is usually structured as a leveraged lease transaction. The lessor finances the cost of the acquisition and construction of the project through equity contributions and non-recourse loans. The term of the lease is structured to correspond with the maturity of the debt and the equity investment. The amount and timing of the rental payments under the lease, similarly, are formulated to match the debt service on the loans and return on equity. The lease grants

565

the lessee the option, at the end of the lease term, to acquire the facility for a fixed purchase price equal to the then outstanding amount of debt and equity. Should the lessee desire not to exercise the option, the lessee is obligated to either return the property to the lessor or market it for sale to a third party and, in either event, pay the lessor a final termination lease payment in a specified maximum amount which is sufficient to repay the outstanding debt and equity. Synthetic leases include residual value guarantees by the lessee as well as provisions allowing the lessee to participate in the appreciation of the leased asset. Credit enhancements, such as third party guarantees, letters of credit or security deposits, may be utilized to secure the lessor's residual value risk.

II.   Accounting Literature

To achieve off-balance sheet accounting treatment, a synthetic lease transaction must be structured taking into account certain standards issued by the Financial Accounting Standards Board ("FASB"), the body designated by the American Institute of Certified Public Accountants to establish generally accepted accounting principles, and certain interpretations of accounting issues addressed by the Emerging Issues Task Force ("EITF"), the group organized by FASB to resolve questions resulting from varying accounting practices. Particularly, as discussed in detail below, a synthetic lease transaction should be designed (1) to be classified as an operating lease under Statement of Financial Accounting Standards ("SFAS") No. 13, "Accounting for Leases" (November 1976, as amended through May 1988); (2) to avoid characterization as a sale-leaseback under SFAS No. 98, "Accounting for Leases: Sale-Leaseback Transactions Involving Real Estate; Sales-Type Leases of Real Estate; Definition of Lease Term; Initial Direct Costs of Direct

2

Financing Leases" (May 1988); and (3) to prevent consolidation of the lessor's and lessee's financial statements under EITF No. 90-15, "Impact of Nonsubstantive Lessors, Residual Value Guarantees, and Other Provisions in Leasing Transactions" (1990-1991) and EITF No. 96-21, "Implementation Issues in Accounting for Leasing Transactions Involving Special-Purpose Entities" (August 1996).

SFAS No. 13 (Classification of Leases)

From the perspective of a lessee, a lease is either a capital lease or an operating lease. If, at its inception, a transaction meets any of the following four criteria, it will qualify as a capital lease and, therefore, off-balance sheet financing treatment will not be available to the lessee:

1. The lease transfers ownership of the leased property to the lessee during the term of the lease or at its end.

2. The lease contains a bargain purchase option, namely, an option by the lessee to purchase the leased property for a price sufficiently lower than its expected fair value on the exercise date, so that exercise of the option appears, at the inception of the lease, reasonably assured (the "Bargain Purchase Option Test").

3. The lease term, including renewal terms, equals or exceeds 75% of the estimated economic life of the leased property (the "75% Economic Life Test").

4. The present value at the beginning of the lease term of the minimum lease payments[1] equals or exceeds 90% of the fair value of the leased

3

property (the "90% Fair Value Test"). "Minimum lease payments", for purposes of the 90% Fair Value Test, include any guarantee by the lessee or any party related to the lessee of the residual value at the expiration of the lease term, including any stated maximum deficiency in the lessor's realization of the residual value that the lessee agrees to make up.

If a lease is treated as a capital lease, the lessee records the leasehold interest as an asset and the related payment obligations as a liability on its balance sheet. Conversely, if a lease is classified as an operating lease by a lessee because none of the above-described capitalization criteria are applicable, neither the asset nor the related liability appear on the lessee's balance sheet; however, disclosure may be required in the footnotes to the lessee's financial statements. Rental payments under an operating lease are treated as operating expenses in the income statement. As a result, the lessee's balance sheet, earnings and the financial ratios (such as debt to equity and interest coverage ratios) used to evaluate the lessee are enhanced compared with a capital lease transaction.

A synthetic lease transaction is structured not to satisfy any of the capitalization criteria. The SPE/lessor of a synthetic lease acquires and holds title to the leased property and only transfers ownership of the real estate to the lessee should the lessee exercise its purchase option included in the synthetic lease. The exercise by the lessee of the purchase option is not "reasonably assured" as required by the second condition of SFAS No. 13, as the lessee may decide to surrender the property at the expiration of the lease term as discussed below. The purchase option included in a synthetic lease is fixed at a non-bargain purchase price, determined at lease inception, equal to the

4

remaining principal amount of the debt and the equity investment. In order to be classified as an operating lease under SFAS No. 13, the term of a synthetic lease may not equal or exceed 75% of the property's estimated economic life. Therefore, synthetic leases are set at short terms of a few years, typically 3-7 years. Rental payments (including any maximum residual guarantee or residual termination payment due upon lease termination) are calculated at amounts so that the present value thereof fails the 90% Fair Value Test.

SFAS No. 98 (Sale-Leaseback Accounting Treatment)

A sale-leaseback involves the sale of property by the owner and a leaseback of the property by such seller. SFAS No. 98 provides that, for a seller/lessee to qualify for operating lease treatment in a sale-leaseback transaction, the seller/lessee must transfer all of the risks and rewards of ownership as demonstrated by the absence of the seller/lessee's "continuing involvement" with the leased property (other than a "normal leaseback" relationship involving active use of the property by the seller/lessee.) SFAS No. 98 describes examples of forms of continuing involvement by the seller/lessee that result in the seller/lessee not transferring the risks and rewards of ownership to the buyer/lessor, including the following, which are specifically relevant to a synthetic lease transaction:

1. The seller/lessee has an option to repurchase the leased property.

2. The seller/lessee guarantees the buyer/lessor's investment or a return on that investment for a limited or extended period of time.

5

569

3. The seller/lessee is required to pay the buyer/lessor at the end of the lease term for a decline in the fair value of the property below the estimated residual value (i.e., the seller/lessee guarantees a minimum residual value.)

4. The buyer/lessor is obligated to share with the seller/lessee any portion of the appreciation of the property.

In addition, EITF No. 96-21 notes that, in a build-to-suit lease transaction, if a lessee incurs development costs prior to leasing a property, the lessee would be considered the owner of the construction in-progress, which asset would be recognized by the lessee in its balance sheet, and any subsequent lease arrangement would be subject to the sale-leaseback rules under SFAS No. 98. Construction activities are deemed to have commenced if the lessee has (a) broken ground, (b) incurred "hard costs" (such as site preparation, construction costs and equipment expenditures) no matter how insignificant relative to the fair value of the improvements, or (c) incurred "soft costs" (such as architectural fees, survey costs and zoning fees) that represent more than 10% of the expected fair value of the leased property.

Synthetic lease transactions contain purchase options and guarantees of residual value deficiencies that constitute "continuing involvement" as described above. Therefore, in order to avoid application of SFAS No. 98 and qualification of the transaction as a sale-leaseback, title to the property under a synthetic lease should be acquired by the lessor rather than the lessee and the lessee should not incur any development costs prior to entering into the lease agreement.

6

EITF No. 90-15 discussed whether operating lease accounting treatment is appropriate for leasing transactions which contain certain characteristics usually found in synthetic leases. The EITF reached a consensus that, the assets, liabilities, results of operations and cash flows of an SPE/lessor are required to be consolidated in the lessee's financial statements, and, therefore, off-balance sheet accounting treatment will _not_ be available to the lessee, when _all_ of the following conditions exist:

1. Substantially all of the activities of the SPE involve assets that are to be leased to a single lessee.[2]

2. The expected substantive residual risks and substantially all the residual rewards of the leased asset(s) and the obligation imposed by the underlying debt of the SPE reside directly or indirectly with the lessee[3] through means such as:

    a. The lease agreement.

    b. A residual value guarantee, for example, the assumption of first dollar of loss provisions.

    c. A guarantee of the SPE's debt.

    d. An option granting the lessee a right to (1) purchase the leased asset at a fixed price or at a defined price other than fair value determined at the exercise date or (2) receive any of the lessor's sale

7

proceeds in excess of a stipulated amount.

3. The owner(s) of record of the SPE has (have) not made an initial substantive residual equity capital investment that is at risk during the entire lease term.

EITF No. 90-15 stated that the EITF Working Group agrees that 3% is the minimum acceptable initial residual equity capital investment to constitute as "substantive" within the meaning of the third criteria. The Securities and Exchange Commission, however, believes that a greater investment may be necessary depending on the facts and circumstances of the transaction, such as the lessee's credit risk, the leased property's market risk, and the cost of borrowed funds. In addition, EITF No. 90-15 provides that an investor note payable issued to the SPE does not qualify as an initial substantive residual equity investment at risk. An investment would also not be considered at risk if an investor were provided with a letter of credit or other guarantee on the initial investment or return thereon.

The leasing arrangement described in EITF No. 90-15 included the following characteristics: (1) lessee residual value guarantees and participations in both risks and rewards associated with ownership of the leased property; (2) purchase options; (3) a non-substantive SPE/lessor; (4) improvements performed to a lessee's specifications; and (5) lease payments adjusted for final construction costs. The EITF determined that a lease containing such characteristics which does not meet the consolidation conditions described above may qualify for operating lease treatment. However, the EITF noted that the facts and circumstances of each lease transaction in relation to the requirements of SFAS

8

No. 13 will be considered in determining proper lease classification.

Synthetic lease transactions usually qualify under the first two consolidation criteria but are intended specifically to fail the third test. With respect to the first and second conditions, the use of a special purpose vehicle is central to the structure of synthetic lease transactions, as is the triple net leasing and build-to-suit arrangements, purchase option and residual value guarantee provisions and other elements of management and control. The equity investment used to finance synthetic leases is set at a minimum of 3% in order to avoid application of the third consolidation criteria of EITF No. 90-15.

III.   Tax Considerations

Synthetic lease transactions are structured to achieve different financial reporting and tax treatment. For federal income tax purposes, a synthetic lease is designed to be treated as a financing rather than a sale-leaseback, with the lessee being considered the owner of the property and the borrower of the debt. As a result, the lessee would be entitled to deduct depreciation and interest expense on its income tax return, thus producing lower income taxes. The SPE is also not taxed at the entity level as it is treated as a "conduit" under federal income tax law.

Federal income tax rulings and case law consider a number of factors in determining whether a transaction is a sale-leaseback or a mortgage, including the intention of the parties and whether the lessee or the lessor of a lease possesses the burdens and benefits of tax ownership. The parties to a synthetic lease should consult their tax counsel and advisors as to satisfaction of the tax requirements for characterization of the transaction as a financing.

9

In this regard, an important provision included in a synthetic lease is the parties' "Statement of Intention" that the lease be treated for income tax purposes only as a financing arrangement and that the lessee be recognized as the tax owner of the property, with all rent payments made by the lessee under the lease constituting payments of principal and interest on a loan by the lessor to the lessee. Inclusion of such a provision protects against recharacterization of the transaction as a sale-leaseback rather than a financing for income tax purposes.

Although the SPE/lessor of a synthetic lease transaction holds title to the property, the benefits and burdens of ownership fall on the lessee through the triple net, bond-type lease structure, the fixed purchase price option permitting the lessee to participate in the appreciation of the property, and the lessee's obligation to make up any deficiency in the sale proceeds and the outstanding debt and equity (or, conversely, entitling the lessee to any excess sales proceeds after repayment of the debt and equity) in the event the purchase option is not exercised by the lessee and the property is sold to a third party.

IV.   Detailed Description of Synthetic Lease Structure

a.   Lessee

Because the financing of a synthetic lease transaction is dependent upon the lessee's credit, the lessee is usually an investment grade company seeking build-to-suit facilities, a higher valuation of its stock and lower taxes and financing expenses.

10

b.   Lessor

       To achieve "conduit" tax treatment whereby no federal income tax is imposed at the entity level, to prevent sale-leaseback accounting treatment under SFAS No. 98, and to preclude consolidation of the lessee and the lessor in bankruptcy, a grantor trust or other bankruptcy-remote SPE is formed to take title to the real estate and be the lessor of the transaction.

c.   Construction of Improvements

       As mentioned above, it is necessary for the lessor and the lessee to enter into a construction agency agreement in order to provide the lessee with control over the construction process and design of the leased improvements. The lessee, as construction agent for the lessor, is responsible for the completion of the construction, at the lessor's cost, and for all cost overruns in connection with the work.[4] As with any construction loan agreement, the construction agency document provides procedures for construction draws, change orders and approval of plans and specifications.

d.   Debt and Equity Structure

       The lessor typically finances the acquisition of the property and the construction of the facility through a combination of equity investments and non-recourse loans. The beneficiaries of the trust/lessor or shareholders of the SPE/lessor provide at least 3% of the equity funding (i.e., the minimum acceptable substantive residual capital investment to prevent consolidation of the lessor's and lessee's financial statements under EITF No. 90-15.) The equity contributions may themselves be funded by an interest-only non-recourse loan secured by a first security interest in the beneficial interests of the lessor as well as by

11

a subordinate assignment of rents and leases. The beneficiaries/stockholders' share of the rents received under the lease are then used to repay such loan.

The remaining 97% of the cost of the project is provided by a non-recourse loan or loans to the lessor (the "97% Debt") which is secured by a first security interest in the property and by a first assignment of rents and leases. In addition to the constraints of the consolidation accounting rules, the 97% Debt is structured to prevent compliance with the 90% Fair Value Test of SFAS No. 13, as the amount of the rent payments under the lease relate to the amount of the debt service requirements under the 97% Debt. The 97% Debt may be interest-only or fully amortizing and is typically divided into two tranches, with different risks, pricing, priorities of payment and yields.[5] The equity investor(s) are compensated only after the 97% Debt has been repaid.

The lessor's residual risk amount is sometimes secured by a credit enhancement device, such as a letter of credit, security deposit or third party guaranty. The residual credit facility issuer receives a security interest in the property which is subordinate to that of the lenders of the 97% Debt [6].

V. Provisions of a Synthetic Lease

a. Triple Net, Bond-Type Lease

The lessee of a synthetic lease bears the expenses for taxes, insurance and maintenance of the property as well as the risk of casualty and condemnation. In the event of damage or destruction due to fire or other casualty or a taking by eminent domain, the lessee is not permitted a rent abatement but may have the right to

12

terminate the lease. If the lessee exercises its right of termination, the lessee is required to pay the lessor a termination payment in an amount sufficient to repay the outstanding debt and equity. Rental obligations under a synthetic lease are absolute and not subject to abatement, reduction, setoff, counterclaim, defense or deduction whatsoever. As with bond leases, the lessee must perform all of its obligations under the lease during the term and may not terminate the lease, other than in the circumstances set forth above or in connection with its exercise of the purchase option.

b.   Lease Term and Financing Term

The term of a synthetic lease, including renewal terms, must be short enough so as to fail the 75% Economic Life Test of SFAS No. 13 and must correlate to the term of the debt and equity components of the transaction.

c.   Purchase Option

The lease grants the lessee an option to purchase the property at the expiration of the lease term, provided no event of default exists or is continuing thereunder, upon payment of a fixed purchase price equal to the amount of the then outstanding debt and equity. As described above, the stated purchase price must fail the Bargain Purchase Option Test of SFAS No. 13.[7]

d.   Rights and Obligations at Lease Expiration

If the lessee does not exercise its rights to renew the lease or purchase the property, the lessee must surrender the premises at the expiration of the lease term. If the lessee elects to return the property (whether or not the property is sold through the lessee's marketing efforts as

13

described below), the lessee is obligated to pay the lessor, as additional rent, a termination payment in an amount satisfactory to repay the then outstanding debt and equity. Such termination payment is required by SFAS No. 13 to be included in minimum lease payments and, if no event of default shall exist and be continuing, is limited to a stated maximum amount (the "Specified Maximum Payment") necessary to avoid application of the 90% Fair Value Test. If the lessor does not desire the return of the asset, the lessee is required to market the property for sale to an unaffiliated third party. The lessee guarantees to the lessor, upon a sale, the residual value deficiency, up to the Specified Maximum Payment, between the proceeds of sale and the amount of the then outstanding debt and equity. However, the lessee is entitled to any excess profits made upon a sale, after repayment of the debt and equity investments.[8] The lessor is not required to accept any bids for the property obtained by the lessee if the lessor is unable to recover the lessor's residual risk amount (i.e., the difference between the amount of the then outstanding debt and equity and the Specified Maximum Payment). As discussed above, the lessor's residual risk amount may be secured by a third party guaranty or cash or letter of credit security deposit.

e.   Rent

Rental payments under a synthetic lease are fixed at amounts which relate to the required debt service under the loans and the return on equity, and so that the present value thereof fails the 90% Fair Value Test of SFAS No. 13. In addition to the Specified Maximum Payment as noted above, any structuring or administrative fees paid by the lessee to the owners of record of the SPE for structuring the transaction and arranging financing are included as part of minimum lease payments for purposes of applying the 90% Fair Value Test (but any amounts for structuring or

14

administrative fees are not included in the "fair value of the leased property" under said test).[9]

    f.   <u>Defaults</u>

Synthetic leases include default clauses customarily found in leases and loans, such as the failure to pay fixed rent within 5-7 days of the due date thereof, the failure to make any termination payments required by the lease when due, the failure to observe nonmonetary obligations under the lease after 30 days of grace, bankruptcy defaults and cross default provisions.

EITF No. 97-1, "Implementation Issues in Accounting for Lease Transactions, including Those involving Special-Purpose Entities" (1997), provides that a lease may also include default provisions that are unrelated to the lessee's use of the property, such as requiring the lessee to maintain particular financial ratios, without affecting its classification as an operating lease, if all of the following conditions are met:

(1)   The non-performance related default clause is typically found in financing transactions;

(2)   The occurrence of the event of default under the clause can be determined on an objective basis;

(3)   The determination of whether an event of default exists has been established based upon pre-defined criteria, related solely to the lessee and its operations; and

15

(4) It is reasonably unlikely, based upon facts and circumstances that exist at the inception of the lease (including recent trends in the lessee's operations), that the event of default will occur.

Remedies for default by the lessee of a synthetic lease include all traditional lease remedies, such as the lessor's right of termination, as well as the lessor's right to "put" the property to the lessee conditioned upon the lessee's payment of a stipulated amount, as liquidated damages, equal to the termination value of the property.[10]

g. Indemnities

Synthetic leases include standard indemnification and hold harmless provisions by the lessee for claims relating to the construction and operation of the premises by the lessee. Some synthetic leases also require lessee indemnification for losses and damages resulting from environmental conditions caused by the lessee during the lease term, as well as pre-existing environmental matters. Careful consideration as to the pre-existing environmental risks should be given as the accounting treatment of the lease may be affected thereby. EITF No. 97-1 states that the lessee's classification of the lease for accounting purposes will not be affected by either (1) lessee indemnification for environmental contamination caused by the lessee during the lease term or (2) lessee indemnification for pre-existing environmental contamination if, at the inception of the lease, the likelihood of loss under such pre-existing environmental conditions indemnification is remote. However, if the likelihood of loss under a pre-existing condition environmental indemnity is "reasonably possible," the lessee is treated as having entered into a sale-leaseback transaction subject to SFAS No. 98.

16

VI.   Conclusion

The structuring of a synthetic lease transaction is the product of various skills and expertise. The parties should consult their lawyers, accountants, tax advisors and financial consultants to ensure that the transaction complies with all applicable laws and guidelines in order to achieve "off-balance sheet" accounting treatment and property ownership tax benefits. In addition, because the accounting rules and tax laws may change in the future and be retroactive, parties to a synthetic lease transaction are advised to structure lease terms as short as possible in order to maintain flexibility and minimize any potential adverse exposure.

17

---

[1] The present value of the minimum lease payments shall be
computed by the lessee using, except as noted
below, its incremental borrowing rate, which is
defined by SFAS No. 13 as the rate that, at the
inception of the lease, the lessee would have
incurred to borrow over a similar term the funds
necessary to purchase the leased asset. However,
the lessee shall use the interest rate implicit in the
lease (i.e., as defined by SFAS No. 13, the discount
rate that, when applied to the minimum lease
payments and the unguaranteed residual value
accruing to the lessor's benefit, causes the present
value at the beginning of the lease term to equal the
fair value of the leased property to the lessor at the
inception of the lease) if (1) it is practicable for the
lessee to learn the implicit rate computed by the
lessor and (2) the interest rate implicit in the lease is
less than the lessee's incremental borrowing rate.

[2] In EITF No. 96-21, the EITF considered a transaction
which involved the formation of an SPE to acquire
two separate properties that were to be leased to
two unrelated lessees and to borrow on a
nonrecourse basis two loans that do not contain
cross-collateral provisions. The EITF recommended
that the use of nonrecourse debt with no cross-
collateral provisions effectively segregates the cash
flows and assets associated with the two leases,
thereby creating two SPE's, with each lessee being
considered to have satisfied the first consolidation
criteria of EITF No. 90-15. Consequently, to fail
the first condition of EITF No. 90-15, the SPE's
assets would need to be commingled such that, in

18

the event of default, both lenders to the SPE would have pari passu rights to the cash flows and assets relating to both leases.

[3] EITF No. 90-15 notes that whether a lessee would be expected to bear the substantive residual risks and rewards depends upon the specific facts and circumstances of each transaction, and is not related to the 90% Fair Value Test set forth in SFAS No. 13.

[4] The parties should consult their accountants as to the proper treatment of payments made by the lessee for cost overruns and the effect (if any) of such payments on how the lease is classified. See discussion of whether a lease should be accounted for as a capital lease or operating lease if rents are adjusted based on the final cost of the property in Issue Summary No. 90-15, "Impact of Non-Substantive Lessors, Residual Value Guarantees and Other Provisions in Leasing Transactions" (June 28, 1990), prepared by Coopers & Lybrand.

[5] For a detailed explanation of the structuring of the 97% Debt, see Nancy R. Little "Unraveling the Synthetic Lease," 11 Probate and Property 22-26 (Jan.-Feb. 1997) and James D. Bridgeman and Nancy R. Little, "The Synthetic Lease - Is it a Lease or Is It a Loan?" in Second Annual Non-Traditional Real Estate Forum: The Synthetic Lease - Is It a Lease or Is It a Loan? (Spring 1997).

[6] See Ross A. Pascal, "Synthetic Leases" included in Second Annual Non-Traditional Real Estate Forum: The

19

Synthetic Lease - Is It a Lease or Is It a Loan?
(Spring 1997).

[7] It has been suggested that an appraisal be obtained at the lease inception in order to assure that the purchase option is not considered a "bargain purchase option" under SFAS No. 13. See "Synthetic Real Estate: Corporate America goes off balance sheet," E&Y Kenneth Leventhal Real Estate Journal (Fall 1995). If the 97% Debt is interest-only or has little amortization, the purchase price stated in the purchase option should not be deemed to be a bargain. See Nancy R. Little, "Unraveling the Synthetic Lease," 11 Probate and Property 22-26 (Jan.-Feb. 1997).

[8] A lessor's participation in excess residual values is considered a contingent decrease in rental payments and should be accounted for as contingent rents. Contingent rentals are excluded from the definition of "minimum lease payments" under SFAS No. 13. See Issue Summary No. 90-15, "Impact of Non-Substantive Lessors, Residual Value Guarantees and Other Provisions in Leasing Transactions" (June 28, 1990), prepared by Coopers & Lybrand.

[9] See EITF No. 96-21. From the SPE's perspective, structuring or administrative fees are considered a return of the owner's initial equity capital investment. For purposes of applying the consolidation criteria of EITF No. 90-15, if and to the extent structuring or administrative fees reduce the equity capital investment below the minimum acceptable amount, the owners of record of the SPE would not be considered to have made a substantive

20

residual equity investment that is at risk during the entire lease term. Therefore, the transaction would require consolidation of the lessee's and SPE/lessor's financial statements.

[10] Ross A. Pascal, "Synthetic Leases" included in Second Annual Non-Traditional Real Estate Forum: The Synthetic Lease - Is it a Lease or Is It a Loan?" (Spring 1997).

21

NOTES

13

USE A TERM LETTER TO PROTECT TENANT INTERESTS

James S. Saunders
Noel M. Flagg

Reprinted with permission from Volume 4, Number 5, The Metropolitan Corporate Counsel, May 1996. Copyright © 1996 The Metropolitan Corporate Counsel, Inc. All rights reserved.

USE A TERM LETTER TO PROTECT TENANT INTERESTS

James S. Saunders and Noel M. Flagg

The negotiation of an office lease, like that of any other major transaction, can unravel at any stage of the process. If negotiations break down early in the game, little damage results. The tenant can simply move the field of play to another venue, and open discussions with another landlord for a different unit of space. If, however, this occurs in the final innings, particularly after a lease has been drafted, the tenant can incur significant financial losses and operational disruption. By this time, major sums have been invested in the deal for architectural, engineering and legal fees. Further, the range of relocation alternatives has been limited, and the time remaining to make a commitment may be running short. The passage of time invariably tends to shift the balance of negotiating power toward the landlord's side of the table.

In order to protect the tenant's interests, it is therefore critical to resolve as many issues as possible prior to the drafting of the lease. While a competent tenant representative has by then brought about agreement on such basic business terms as rent, area, escalation, options and sublease rights, dozens of issues typically surface only when the landlord's attorney presents the tenant with the first lease draft. From the tenant's point of view, this is the worst time for disagreements or misunderstandings to emerge. Increasing urgency to close the deal and get the relocation program under way can now pressure the tenant to agree to unfavorable lease provisions. In our practice, we have found that a well-crafted Term Letter can prevent this situation from occurring.

The Term Letter is a statement of intent to execute a lease based on a detailed recitation of the terms and conditions, both legal and business in nature, that the lease is to reflect. It is delivered to the landlord following the parties' agreement on the basic business terms, but before the drafting of a lease. Any issues between the parties that the Term Letter uncovers can then be negotiated several weeks sooner than is typical, with considerable savings in legal fees to the tenant (and to the landlord as well), and with an increment to the tenant's leverage due to its conservation of competing alternatives.

Comprehensiveness is crucial to the effectiveness of this strategy. The Term Letter should be drafted by the tenant's negotiating team with the same attention to detail that would go into the preparation of an actual lease. Nothing can be taken for granted. Since it must be assumed by the team that any issues omitted or inadequately addressed will ultimately be resolved in the landlord's favor, the Term Letter must encompass all significant legal and economic issues.

Among the areas covered in our standard Term Letters, and some of the provisions included, are the following:

Delivery of Premises

The condition of the premises must be brought into permittable condition at the landlord's sole cost and expense, with no deduction from the stated tenant improvement allowance. Any pre-existing violations and hazardous materials must be removed, and all base building work must be completed, including Class E, demolition and fireproofing, prior to delivery. The space must be prepared in compliance with the Americans With Disabilities Act, and all other federal, state and local laws and regulations. The building must have its Certificate of Occupancy in place, as well as a Temporary Certificate of Occupancy for the premises, so that the tenant need take no action other than the filing of plans to receive its construction permits

Tenant Construction

If the tenant is responsible for building the space, there should be no deduction from the stated tenant improvement allowance. Neither the landlord nor the landlord's contractors should be entitled to any supervision, profit or overhead charges. If the landlord is providing tenant with construction valued at a specific amount, labor and materials should be priced at the landlord's actual cost. Representations should be required that the labor and unit pricing were obtained pursuant to competitive bids, and that they reflect all necessary or reasonably implied work and materials required to prepare the space in accordance with the tenant's plans and specification. In either case, all schedules, restrictions and delay remedies should be stated in the Term Letter, and any charges by he landlord or the landlord's engineer for the review of tenant plans relating to initial construction should be specifically precluded.

Landlord Delays

A firm date is specified for the landlord to deliver the premises in condition satisfactory to the tenant. If delivery is delayed through no fault of the tenant, a financial penalty or other remedy is stated.

Electricity

If electrical consumption cannot be directly metered by the utility company, it should be charged to reflect the landlord's actual cost, based on the best service rates available. Any cost the landlord contemplates for passing current through to the tenant's premises should be included in the base rent, not as a markup on the building's electric bill. The cost of electricity usage, water and HVAC usage during construction of the premises should be absorbed by the landlord.

Options

Specific target dates, combined with specific dollar figures or verifiable financial formulae such as "Fair Market Value" percentages, with realistic definitions and strong arbitration provisions, should be linked to all expansion, contraction and renewal options. If the tenant has a termination right associated with a payment, both the timing and the calculation of that payment should be clearly specified. Without these provisions, what appears to be a tenant option is, in fact, no more than a minefield bound to explode during the term of the lease.

Specifications

The Term Letter should state the specifications and service hours for heating, ventilating, air conditioning and cleaning, the electrical connectable load, and all provisions for above-standard and after-hours service. It should specify that all non-standard utilities and costs will be priced at the landlord's actual cost; such vague terms as "reasonable charges" should be avoided.

Sublease and Assignment

While the bulk of the Term Letter contemplates the tenant's continued occupancy of the premises, equal attention must be devoted to its exit strategy. Provided that the use and the requirements of the lease are adhered to, there should be no impediments to sublease or assignment. The Term Letter should specify the formula that will govern the division of any potential future profits that may arise from such transactions. Additional typical provisions include the following:

1. Any sublease/assignment to the affiliates, parent company, subsidiaries or successor of the tenant should be as of right, with a requirement of notice, but no requirement for landlord consent.

2. The landlord's consent to a sublease/assignment to third parties may not be unreasonably withheld or delayed.

3. Tenant creditworthiness may be a requirement for assignment, but not for subletting.

4. If the landlord is to retain recapture rights, such rights should be exercised immediately after tenant's notification of intent to sublet.

Operating Expense Escalation

The Term Letter should list all landlord costs that are to be excluded from the calculation of direct operating expense escalations. Reasonable exclusions include ground lease payments, financing costs, depreciation, advertising and other leasing expenses, costs incurred to satisfy the terms of other tenant's leases, insurable losses, and many others. The tenant should only be charged for capital expenditures if they are either required by law or will reduce operating expenses. In such cases, they should be charged through straight-line amortization over their useful life, and capped at the tenant's proportionate expense prior to such improvements. All landlord operating statements should be based on Generally Accepted Accounting Principals Consistently Applied. The tenant should have a continuing right to audit these statements.

Non-Disturbance

Non-disturbance agreements should be forthcoming from all lenders and from the ground lessor, if appropriate, by a specified date. Non-delivery of such documents should entitle the tenant to nullify the lease and to be reimbursed for its costs.

Restrictive Covenants

Any specific companies, or categories of businesses that are competitive with the tenant, and are to be excluded from leasing space in the building, should be listed.

This is only a small sample of the potentially deal-breaking or otherwise costly issues that the Term Letter should address. The delivery of this document will trigger a round of intense negotiations. If the issues can be resolved to the satisfaction of both parties, the final negotiation following the drafting of the lease will be relatively swift and painless for both parties. If, on the other hand, the Term Letter process uncovers issues that cannot be resolved, the negotiations will end sooner than if it had not been written, thus allowing the tenant to preserve its options with substantial savings in costs.

Gross up provisions

Net Lease — Electricity Expense

Gross Up Variable Portion of Operating Expenses

Gross Lease / Base Year (BY)

Tenant needs to get BY as high as possible

" W/all Tenats paying foll rent "

NOTES

14

FULL BENEFIT OF THE DEAL LETTER / LETTER OF INTENT

Richard C. Mallory

[DATE]

[BROKER'S NAME AND ADDRESS]

Re: Proposal for Lease by **[NAME OF TENANT]** in building located at **[ADDRESS]**, which Building is part of the office project known as "**[NAME OF PROJECT]**."

Dear _____ :

_____ on behalf of _____ ("**Landlord**"), is pleased to submit a lease proposal for **[NAME OF TENANT]** ("Tenant") to lease space in the referenced Building on the terms and conditions set forth as follows. This proposal is submitted in order to permit the parties to engage in open and informed discussions of potential leasing terms, and is not intended as and shall not constitute an offer, an acceptance or a contract.

1.   <u>BUILDING</u>.   Office building located at _____
_____ .

2.   <u>BUILDING DESCRIPTION</u>.   **[TO BE COMPLETED]**

_____
_____
_____
_____

3.   <u>PREMISES</u>.

                                       Approximate
                Floor(s)   Square Feet

                [INSERT APPROPRIATE FIGURES]

-2-

OPTIONAL PROVISIONS RELATING TO
THE EXPANSION OF THE PREMISES:

3.1 PRE-MOVE-IN EXPANSION OPTION.

Tenant shall have the right, up until _____, to lease approximately _____ rentable square feet on the _____ (____) floor of the Building under the same terms and conditions as those set forth herein for the initial Premises, subject only to the determination by Landlord of revised dates for submission of construction drawings by Tenant relating to such space.

3.2 MUST-TAKE SPACE.

Tenant shall lease _____ rentable square feet of space on the ____ floor of the Building during _____. The exact amount of and delivery date of such space shall be determined by Landlord in its discretion. The leasing of such space shall be on the same terms and conditions as are then applicable to the initial Premises; provided that if such space has been previously improved, Tenant shall take such space in its "as is" condition, and if such space has not been previously improved, Tenant shall receive an improvement allowance equal to _____. **[NOTE - THERE ARE SEVERAL WAYS TO HANDLE THE` IMPROVEMENT ALLOWANCE - THE FOREGOING IS ONE METHOD]**.

3.3 OPTIONS FOR ADDITIONAL SPACE.

Tenant shall have the right to lease additional space ("**Option Space**") in the Building. The location and scheduled delivery dates for each increment of Option Space and the range of square footages for each such increment are as follows:

Square Footage   Floor   Delivery Date

[INSERT APPROPRIATE FIGURES]

-3-

Tenant shall give Landlord eighteen (18) months' written notice of its intention to exercise each option prior to the scheduled delivery date.

Landlord shall deliver the Option Space up to twelve (12) months prior or twelve (12) months following the scheduled delivery date at Landlord's discretion.

Terms and conditions for such Option Space shall be the terms and conditions being quoted by Landlord for comparable space in the Building as of the date of the commencement of the respective option, but in no event shall the annual base rent for the Option Space be less than the then current Annual Base Rent, plus escalations, for the Premises. The rights granted to Tenant hereunder are personal to Tenant and may only be exercised by Tenant when Tenant is in possession of the entire Premises.

3.4   **RIGHT OF FIRST OFFER.**

Landlord shall grant to Tenant a one-time right of first offer, following initial leasing, on all remaining space on the _____ (_____) floor of the Building. The terms and conditions for the lease of such space shall be those then being quoted by Landlord for the leasing of comparable space in the Building, but in no event shall the annual base rent for such space be less than the then current Annual Base Rent, plus escalations, for the Premises. Tenant must elect to lease such space within five (5) business days of Landlord's offer to lease such space. If Tenant does not timely elect to lease such space, Landlord may lease such space to anyone whom Landlord desires upon terms acceptable to Landlord. The rights granted to Tenant hereunder are personal to Tenant and may only be exercised by Tenant when Tenant is in possession of the entire Premises.

-4-

3.5 <u>RIGHT OF FIRST NEGOTIATE</u>.	Tenant shall have a one-time first right to negotiate, after initial leasing, on the space located on the ___ floor of the Building. Landlord shall notify Tenant of its intent to lease such space and Tenant shall have five (5) business days to commence good faith negotiations with Landlord concerning such space. If Tenant does not timely elect to negotiate with Landlord to lease such space, Landlord may lease such space to anyone whom Landlord desires upon terms acceptable to Landlord. The rights granted to Tenant hereunder are personal to Tenant and may only be exercised by Tenant when Tenant is in possession of the entire Premises.
4. <u>METHOD OF MEASUREMENT</u> **[SEE OPTIONAL NEGOTIATED PROVISION]**.	The rentable square footage of the Building and the Premises is calculated pursuant to the Standard Methods of Measuring Floor Area in Office Buildings, ANSI Z65.1-1980 ("**BOMA**"), provided that the rentable square footage of the Building includes, and therefore, the rentable square footage of the Premises includes a portion of, the common area of the Building, and the occupied space located within the Building and dedicated to the service of the Building **[OPTIONAL CLAUSE TO PROVIDE CAP FOR BOMA PLUS MEASUREMENT** - (collectively, the "**Additional Area**"); and provided further that the amount of the Additional Area shall not exceed an amount equal to ___ percent (___%) of the rentable footage of the Building measured pursuant to BOMA].
5. <u>PURPOSE OF USE</u> **[SEE RETAIL PROVISIONS]**.	The Premises will be used for business and professional offices in keeping with the character of a first class office building. **[RETAIL PROVISION - The Premises will be used only for [INSERT SPECIFIC RETAIL USES ALLOWED]]**.

-5-

6. <u>LEASE TERM.</u>

The term of the Lease (the **"Lease Term"**) shall be **[INSERT TERM]** years commencing upon substantial completion of the Premises, which is anticipated to be **[INSERT ANTICIPATED LEASE COMMENCE-MENT DATE]**.

<u>OPTIONAL PROVISIONS RELATING TO THE EXTENSION OR TERMINATION OF THE LEASE TERM.</u>

6.1   <u>OPTION TO RENEW.</u>

Tenant shall have _____ (____) five (5) year option(s) to renew all space then under lease by Tenant, upon first providing Landlord with eighteen (18) months' prior notice. The annual base rent for an option term shall be the base rent then being quoted by Landlord for comparable space in the Building as of the date of the commencement of such option, but in no event shall the annual base rent be less than the Annual Base Rent, plus escalations, paid by Tenant at the expiration of the then current Lease Term. The rights granted to Tenant hereunder are personal to Tenant and may only be exercised by Tenant when Tenant is in possession of the entire Premises.

-6-

6.2   TENANT LEASE CANCELLATION OPTION UPON PAYMENT OF A TERMINATION FEE **[SEE CALCULATION OF TERMINATION FEE]**.

Tenant shall have a one-time right to cancel the lease effective at the end of the ____ month of the initial Lease Term (the **"Termination Date"**). Tenant must give notice of its intention to cancel the lease not later than one-year prior to the Termination Date. In the event Tenant exercises its option to cancel, Tenant shall, at the time of such exercise, pay Landlord a cancellation fee equal to **[THE AMOUNT OF THE TERMINA-TION FEE CAN BE CALCULATED AT THE LEASE PROPOSAL STAGE AS FOLLOWS:** The Cancellation Fee is equal to the sum of the following amounts: (i) the present value (using a discount rate as low as possible, preferably seven percent (7.0%)) of the unamortized tenant improvement allow-ance, brokerage commission, free rent, and all other monetary concessions given in connection with the Lease, and (ii) an amount equal to the Base Rent, as escalated, that would have been due under the Lease during the one-year period commencing on the day after the Termination Date]. The rights granted to Tenant hereunder are personal to Tenant and may only be exercised by Tenant when Tenant is in possession of the entire Premises.

-7-

6.3   TENANT CANCELLATION OPTION UPON FAILURE OF LANDLORD TO TIMELY COMPLETE THE PREMISES.

Landlord shall use diligent efforts to cause the completion of Tenant's space to occur on or before **[INSERT A DATE PREFERABLY ONE YEAR LATER THAN THE ANTICIPATED LEASE COMMENCEMENT DATE]** (the "**Outside Date**"). In the event the delivery of the Premises is delayed beyond the Outside Date, and such delay is not caused by Tenant or by force majeure, then Tenant's sole right shall be a five (5) business day right to terminate the lease by written notice to Landlord. Notwithstanding the above, Landlord shall have the one-time right to extend the Outside Date for thirty (30) days by delivering to Tenant a certificate from Landlord that in Landlord's best good faith judgment the substantial completion of Tenant's space will occur within thirty (30) days after the Outside Date. In addition, if, at any time, Landlord determines that Landlord will be unable to deliver the Premises by the Outside Date, Landlord may notify Tenant of Landlord's good faith opinion, as to when the Premises will be delivered, and within five (5) business days thereafter, Tenant must notify Landlord as to whether Tenant will (i) terminate the Lease or (ii) agree to extend the Outside Date to the date set forth in Landlord's notice.

7.   ANNUAL BASE RENT **[SEE OPTIONAL RETAIL PROVISION]**.

The annual base rent (the "**Annual Base Rent**") per rentable square foot of the initial Premises during the Lease Term shall be as follows:

Months	Annual Base Rent

[INSERT APPROPRIATE FIGURES]

-8-

[RETAIL PROVISION - PERCENTAGE RENT - Tenant shall pay, as annual rent under the Lease, the greater of (i) the Annual Base Rent, and (ii) ___ percent (__%) of the annual gross sales for the Premises].

8.   RENT ABATEMENT.

Tenant's obligation to pay the Annual Base Rent shall be abated for the first **[INSERT FREE RENT PERIOD]** months of the Lease Term. Notwithstanding such abatement, Tenant shall pay its full share of operating expenses and real property taxes attributable to such period of time.

9.   PROPERTY TAX AND OPERATING EXPENSE ADJUSTMENTS **[SEE ALTERNATIVE PROVISIONS OF "EXPENSE STOP" VERSUS "BASE YEAR" SCENARIOS VERSUS RETAIL "N/N/N" SCENARIO]**.

[**EXPENSE STOP** - If, during the Lease Term, Tenant's proportionate share of taxes and operating expenses for the Building exceeds **[INSERT EXPENSE STOP]** per rentable square foot of the Premises, Tenant shall be responsible for such excess. Operating expenses will be calculated on a grossed-up basis reflecting variable operating expenses as if the Building was fully occupied.]

OR

[**BASE YEAR** - If, during the Lease Term, Tenant's proportionate share of taxes and operating expenses for the Building exceeds the amount of operating expenses and taxes for **[INSERT BASE YEAR]**, Tenant shall be responsible for such excess. Operating expenses will be calculated on a grossed-up basis reflecting variable operating expenses as if the Building was 95% occupied. Real property taxes will be calculated as if the Building and parking structure were fully completed and fully assessed.]

OR

-9-

608

[RETAIL PROVISION - N/N/N - During the Lease Term, Tenant shall pay its proportionate share of taxes and operating expenses for the Building. Operating expenses will be calculated on a grossed-up basis reflecting variable operating expenses as if the Building was fully occupied].

[OPTIONAL RETAIL PROVISION - Tenant shall, at its expense, directly meter the Premises for water, gas, and electrical usage, and Tenant shall pay directly for such utilities].

OPTIONAL PROPOSITION 13
PROTECTION AND PROPOSITION 13
PROTECTION BUY-OUT PROVISIONS:

9.1   TOTAL PROPOSITION 13 PROTECTION.

If during the **[INSERT NUMBER OF YEARS OF TOTAL PROPOSITION 13 PROTECTION]** years of the Lease Term, a sale or refinancing of the Building is consummated, and as a result thereof, the real property taxes for the Building increase pursuant to a reassessment under the terms of Proposition 13, then Tenant shall not be obligated to pay, during the **[INSERT NUMBER OF YEARS OF TOTAL PROPOSITION 13 PROTECTION]** years of the Lease Term, any portion of such increase.

-10-

9.2   <u>TOTAL AND PARTIAL PROPOSITION 13 PROTECTION</u>.

If during the **[INSERT NUMBER OF YEARS OF TOTAL PROPOSITION 13 PROTECTION]** years of the Lease Term, a sale or refinancing of the Building is consummated, and as a result thereof, the real property taxes for the Building increase pursuant to a reassessment (the **"Reassessment"**) under the terms of Proposition 13, then Tenant shall not be obligated to pay, during the **[INSERT NUMBER OF YEARS OF TOTAL PROPOSITION 13 PROTECTION]** years of the Lease Term, any portion of such increase (the **"Tax Increase"**). For each year occurring after the **[INSERT LAST YEAR OF TOTAL PROPOSITION 13 PROTECTION]** year of the Lease Term, Tenant shall pay an annually increasing percentage of its share of the Tax Increase, which percentage is calculated by compounding ten percent (10%), on a cumulative basis, for each year of the Lease Term which has occurred up to and including the year of the Reassessment.

-11-

610

9.3   EXAMPLE OF APPLICA-
TION OF FIVE-YEAR
TOTAL PROTECTION AND
FIVE-YEAR PARTIAL
PROTECTION.

As an illustration of the application of the terms of this provision, assume that the Building is initially fully assessed for real estate tax purposes at an amount equal to $3.00 per rentable square foot of the Building, and immediately thereafter, on the first day of the second year of the Lease Term, the Building is sold and on such day the Building is reassessed so that the real estate taxes are increased to an amount equal to $5.00 per rentable square foot of the Building. For the first five years of the Lease Term, Tenant would not pay any portion of the $2.00 tax increase attributable to such reassessment ($5.00 - $3.00). Commencing in the sixth year of the Lease Term and until the end of the Lease Term, Tenant would pay an increasing percentage of such $2.00 tax increase as follows: (i) sixth year - 77.16%, (ii) seventh year - 94.87%, and (iii) eighth through tenth years - 100%.

9.4   LANDLORD'S PROPOSI-
TION 13 BUY-OUT OPTION

Notwithstanding anything to the contrary set forth above, Landlord shall have the right to accelerate the foregoing Proposition 13 protection, and thereby eliminate the same, at any given time by paying Tenant the present value of the then-remaining Proposition 13 protection, which present value shall be calculated by using the rates payable for T-bills maturing at approximately the same time as the remaining Proposition 13 protection would have occurred plus two percent (2.0%), which T-bill rates shall be those in effect for the above time periods at such time as Landlord exercises its right to accelerate.

-12-

10. ASSIGNMENT AND SUBLEASING [SEE RETAIL PROVISION AND NEGOTIATED RECAPTURE PROVISION].

Tenant shall have the right during the Lease Term to sublease or assign all or any portion of the Premises to a related entity or affiliate (as defined in Landlord's lease form) upon notification to Landlord. In addition, Tenant shall have the right to assign or sublease to unrelated entities as provided below. Tenant shall remain liable to Landlord for performance under the Lease regardless of such sublease or assignment.

In addition, Tenant shall have the right to assign or sublease all or any portion of the Premises subject to Landlord's consent, which consent will not be unreasonably withheld or delayed. Landlord shall retain 85% of all profits paid in connection with any sublease or assignment in excess of Tenant's rent obligations hereunder. **[RETAIL PROVISION** - Tenant shall have the right to sublease or assign all or a portion of the Premises subject to Landlord's consent, which consent may be withheld by Landlord in its sole discretion. Landlord shall retain the profits from such sublease or assignment].

Upon Tenant's notice to Landlord of an intended sublease or assignment of all or any portion of the Premises, Landlord shall have the right to recapture such sublease or assignment space (except to any related entity or affiliate of Tenant). **[ALTERNATE NEGOTIATED RECAPTURE PROVISION** - If Tenant intends to sublease or assign all or any portion of the Premises, Tenant shall give Landlord notice of such intention, and Landlord may, within ninety (90) days of such notice, recapture the portion of the Premises pertaining to the intended assignment or sublease for the term of such intended sublease or assignment].

-13-

612

11. CONSTRUCTION OF TENANT IMPROVEMENTS [SEE ALTERNATIVE PROVISIONS FOR LANDLORD CONTROLLED CONSTRUCTION WITH "ALLOWANCE" VERSUS "TURN-KEY" SCENARIOS AND "TENANT CONTROLLED CONSTRUCTION WITH ALLOWANCE"].

[LANDLORD CONTROLLED CONSTRUCTION\ ALLOWANCE - Landlord shall provide Tenant an allowance of $_____ per usable square foot of Premises to be used by Tenant for permanently affixed improvements and the cost of all architecture and engineering fees, licenses and permits for the construction of the Premises].

OR

[LANDLORD CONTROLLED CONSTRUCTION\ TURN-KEY Landlord shall construct the Premises according to [INSERT PLANS AND SPECIFICATIONS], but in no event shall Landlord's contribution to the cost of the construction of the Premises exceed $____ per usable of the Premises.

Tenant shall select an interior architect of its choice who shall prepare Final Space Plans for the entire Premises by _____, 199__. Tenant shall submit drawings, specifications, quantities and purchase releases for all long-lead items and for all structural and internal stairway items and requirements to be used in connection with the construction of the tenant improvements by _____, 199__. Tenant shall submit Final Working Drawings to Landlord on or before _____, 199__. Landlord shall construct the improvements and shall be paid a construction supervisory fee by Tenant of [INSERT FEE] the total cost of such design and construction. [USE THIS PROVISION WITH BOTH LANDLORD CONTROLLED CONSTRUCTION SCENARIOS AND IN ORDER TO EXPEDITE THE DESIGN PROCESS DURING LEASE NEGOTIATIONS].

OR

-14-

[TENANT CONTROLLED CONSTRUC-TION WITH ALLOWANCE - Landlord shall provide Tenant an allowance of $_____ per usable square foot of the Premises to be used by Tenant to construct the Premises. Tenant shall retain a contractor selected from a list of contractor approved by Landlord to construct the Premises. Tenant shall pay Landlord a construction coordination fee of **[INSERT FEE]** of the total cost of the design and construction of the Premises].

12. PARKING.

Tenant shall rent parking passes in the Building parking facility at a ratio of 3.3 parking passes per one thousand (1,000) rentable space square feet of the Premises. Parking rates will be **[INSERT PARKING RATE]** per space per month. Parking rates are guaranteed for the first year of the Lease Term. Thereafter, Tenant will pay according to the Building's posted rates.

13. HEATING, VENTILATION AND AIR-CONDITIONING

[SEE OPTIONAL PROVISION].Landlord, as part of operating expenses, shall furnish heating, ventilation and air-conditioning for normal office usage, Monday through Friday, from 9:00 a.m. to 6:00 p.m., and Saturday, from 9:00 a.m. to 12:00 p.m., except for recognized national and state holidays. **[OPTIONAL** - Landlord shall provide, upon Tenant's request and at Tenant's expense, after-hours heating, ventilation and air conditioning on an hourly, full-floor basis under terms and conditions to be established by Landlord].

14. ELECTRICITY.

Landlord, as part of operating expenses, shall provide Tenant with electricity for lighting and normal office equipment to the extent such electrical consumption does not exceed four (4) watts per rentable square foot of the Premises.

-15-

614

15. **CLEANING SPECIFICATIONS.** Landlord, as part of operating expenses, will clean Tenant's premises five (5) days per week.

16. **IDENTITY.** Tenant shall be permitted to install, at its expense and subject to Landlord's consent which will not be unreasonably withheld, signage at the entrance of its premises on any full floor that it occupies. Signage on multi-tenant floors will be according to Building standard.

17. **DIRECTORY BOARD.** Landlord, at Landlord's expense, will furnish Tenant with space on the Building directory for two (2) designated names per each one thousand (1,000) rentable square feet of the Premises.

18. **BUILDING MANAGEMENT.** The managing agent of the Building shall operate the Building in a first class manner.

19. **BUILDING SECURITY.** Landlord, at Landlord's expense (to be included as an operating expense), shall provide Building security, equipment, personnel, procedures and systems. Tenant, at its own cost and with Landlord's consent, shall be permitted to install its own security system for the Premises.

20. **SECURITY REQUIREMENTS [SEE ALTERNATE PROVISIONS]**.[Tenant shall pay a security deposit equal to _____ (___) months' Annual Base Rent (calculated as of the ____ month of the Lease Term) upon execution of the Lease.]

[Tenant shall pay a security deposit equal to _____ (___) months' Annual Base Rent (calculated as of the ____ month of the Lease Term) upon execution of the Lease.]

AND\OR

[Appropriate guarantees shall be determined upon Landlord's review of Tenant's financial information.]

AND\OR

-16-

[The obligations of Tenant under the Lease shall be personally guaranteed by the principals of the firm.]

AND\OR

[It is understood and agreed that the partners of Tenant shall be personally jointly and severally liable for any claim arising out of or relating to the Lease.]

OPTIONAL MISCELLANEOUS
PROVISIONS:

21.   OPERATION OF PREMISES [RETAIL PROVISION].

Tenant shall continuously operate the Premises during the hours of _____ on _____, except national holidays.

22.   RELOCATION ALLOWANCE.

Landlord will provide Tenant up to $____ per usable square foot of the Premises for the cost of Tenant's relocation to the Premises. Such relocation costs are subject to Landlord's approval, which shall not be unreasonably withheld.

23.   NON-DISTURBANCE AGREEMENT.

Landlord shall use good faith efforts to secure and deliver to Tenant a non-disturbance agreement executed by the first trust deed holder of the Building.

24.   BUILDING PLANNING.

Upon notice to Tenant, Landlord may relocate the Premises to other space in the Building.

ADDRESS OF BUILDING
[Name of Tenant]

616

25. **TENANT'S RIGHT TO ABATE BASE RENT.** If the Premises is made untenantable for Tenant by Landlord, Tenant shall give Landlord notice, specifying such failure to perform by Landlord. If Landlord has not cured such default within five (5) business days after the receipt of the notice, Tenant may immediately abate Base Rent payable under this Lease for the portion of the Premises rendered untenantable for Tenant, until the earlier of the date Landlord cures such default or the date Tenant recommences use of that portion of the Premises so affected. Such right to abate Rent shall be Tenant's sole and exclusive remedy at law or in equity for a Landlord default.

This lease proposal is intended as an outline of the major lease provisions only and, whether or not countersigned, is not a binding agreement by either party to lease the Premises. As a result, notwithstanding the execution of this lease proposal by Landlord and Tenant, neither Landlord nor Tenant shall have any legal obligation or liability to the other with respect to the matters set forth in this lease proposal unless and until a mutually agreed upon lease document is fully executed and delivered by both parties. As such, the parties hereby acknowledge and agree that this lease proposal is nonbinding and that any acts or omissions undertaken or any costs or expenses incurred by Landlord or Tenant following the execution of this lease proposal are made or incurred at such party's sole risk and expense. Tenant hereby acknowledges that the execution of this lease proposal by Landlord does not in any way prohibit or limit Landlord's right to market the Premises or a portion thereof or to negotiate and/or consummate a lease transaction with third parties with respect to all or a portion of the Premises. This lease proposal contains all of the agreements of the parties hereto with respect to any matter covered or mentioned in this lease proposal, and no prior agreements or understanding pertaining to any such matters shall be effective for any purpose.

The undersigned acknowledges that all correspondence (including this lease proposal) and all communication between Landlord, Tenant, and the undersigned concerning information which may ultimately become or becomes part of the Lease is confidential information (collectively, the **"Confidential Information"**). Whether or not the Lease is ultimately consummated, the undersigned and Tenant shall keep the Confidential Information strictly confidential and shall not disclose the Confidential Information to any person or entity other than Tenant's financial, legal, and space planning consultants.

ADDRESS OF BUILDING
[Name of Tenant]

Please return a signed counterpart of this letter by no later than **[DATE]** to confirm your concurrence with the noncontractual terms outlined here.

Sincerely,

"[LANDLORD'S BROKER]"

By:_____

   Its:_____

"TENANT"

By:_____

   Its:_____

cc:

ADDRESS OF BUILDING
[Name of Tenant]

NOTES

Program Schedule
and
Faculty

9:00 Introduction of Speakers and Overview
NY - *John B. Wood*
SF - *Michael E. Meyer*
CH - *Linda D. White*

9:10 Leasing 101-Fine Tuning the Basics
- Boilerplate and the lease as contract or conditional demising
- Commencement of: contract, term, possession or occupancy, rent and non-rent obligations
- Rentals, additional rentals and hidden profit centers – un-bundling the rent components work letter
- Macro Adjustments – "grossing up," percentage applications and "tax kickers" as finally determined
- The Area Fiction – rentable, carpetable, usable, allocable and fictional/impact on "proportionate shares"
- Repair and compliance responsibilities (the error of the "sketch attached"); back-door liabilities
- Redelivery conditions
- Services/the substandard specifications and resulting profits

NY, SF, CHI - John B. Wood

10:05 Break

10:20 Long Range Planning-Exit Strategy
- Assignment and subletting, corporate stock transactions, recapture, profit sharing and transfer of personal rights
- Recognition Agreements and Consents – unsuspected amendments
- Expansion rights, rights of first refusal/first offer
- Renewal and extension rights
- Early termination rights/puts
- Substitution of space
- Yield-up – costs to vacate

NY, SF, CHI - Linda D. White

11:15 Insurance
- No-fault, commercial insurability, liability and allocation of risk
- Waivers of direct liability and actions/insurer's subrogation rights
- Indemnities-back-door liability
- Landlord's underinsurance
- Fire, casualty
- Self-insurance

NY - Alan M. DiSciullo
SF - Jay L. Paxton
CHI - Jennifer A. Fox

12:05 p.m. - 1:30 p.m. Lunch

1:30 Operating Expenses and CAM/Audit Rights – Hidden Agents and Corporate Guerrilla Warfare Tactics
Tenant's Goals:
- Time periods – access to, use of and preservation of records
- Recovery of audit and legal costs, overcharges and interest
- Dealing with the landlord's requirement of indemnification
- Closure of exposure and survival of additional rental adjustments

Landlord's Goals:
- Closing books and ending exposure to claims – lender's certainty
- Confidentiality agreements and settlement undertakings
- Recovery of undercharges and survival of adjustments
- Exculpation and limitation of landlord's liability for repayment of overcharges
- Arbitration versus litigation
- Operating expenses – theory, operation and application

NY, SF, CHI - Michael E. Meyer

2:20 Lender's View of the Lease – Disappearing Ink or Hidden Asset
- Lease as loan security-preservation of the asset
- Estoppel – the back-door amendment
- Recognition agreements and non-disturbance almost
- Personal liability – guarantees/LLC & LLP/good-guy/burn-offs
- Lender's needs
- Lease superior of subordinate title/rights

NY - Andrew L. Herz
SF - Mary G. Murphy
CHI - Peter A. Sarasek

3:15 Break

3:30 Cutting Edge Development/Issues
- Tax issues and treatment of work and installation funds
- Proposed section 467 regulations
- Compliance audits and costs – stepped rent as alternative-fraud audit
- Full benefit of the deal letter/letter of intent
- Emerging fiduciary duties: *Maryland* case
- Partnership liability issues and the LLC and LLP (accidental liability) PC to LLP tax issues on "partner guarantees"
- Synthetic leases
- Foreign related entity investment reporting/income stripping
- Utilities-deregulation

Panel Discussion
NY - John B. Wood, Evelyn D. Giaccio, Arthur R. Klampert, Michael E. Meyer, James S. Saunders and Linda D. White
SF - Michael E. Meyer, Richard C. Mallory, Linda D. White and John B. Wood
CHI - Linda D. White, Alvin C. Katz, Michael E. Meyer and John B. Wood

4:30 Questions and Wrap-Up

FACULTY

NEW YORK CITY

CHAIRMAN:
JOHN B. WOOD
Sussman Sollis Ebin
  Tweedy & Wood LLP
New York City

Alan M. DiSciullo
First Vice President
Law Department
Dean Witter Reynolds Inc.
New York City

Evelyn D. Giaccio
Stroock & Stroock & Lavan LLP
New York City

Andrew L. Herz
Richards & O'Neil, LLP
New York City

Arthur R. Klampert
Goldstein Golub Kessler
  & Company, P.C.
New York City

Michael E. Meyer
Pillsbury Madison & Sutro LLP
Los Angeles

James S. Saunders
Principal Counsel
Friedman Realty Group
New York City

Linda D. White
Sonnenschein Nath
  & Rosenthal
Chicago

SAN FRANCISCO

CHAIRMAN:
MICHAEL E. MEYER
Pillsbury Madison & Sutro LLP
Los Angeles

Richard C. Mallory
Allen, Matkins, Leck,
  Gamble & Mallory LLP
San Francisco

Mary G. Murphy
Farella Braun & Martell
San Francisco

Jay L. Paxton
Ellman, Burke, Hoffman
  & Johnson
San Francisco

Linda D. White
Sonnenschein Nath
  & Rosenthal
Chicago

John B. Wood
Sussman Sollis Ebin
  Tweedy & Wood, LLP
New York City

CHICAGO

CHAIRPERSON:
LINDA D. WHITE
Sonnenschein Nath
  & Rosenthal
Chicago

Jennifer A. Fox
Assistant Vice President
National Accounts
Near North Insurance
  Brokerage, Inc.
Chicago

Alvin C. Katz
Mayer Brown & Platt
Chicago

Michael E. Meyer
Pillsbury Madison & Sutro LLP
Los Angeles

Peter A. Sarasek
Wilson & McIlvane
Chicago

John B. Wood
Sussman Sollis Ebin
  Tweedy & Wood, LLP
New York City

Program Attorney: Howard Maurer